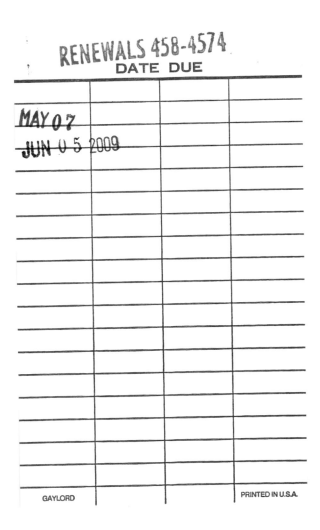

New Departures
>>>

New Departures

>>>

Rethinking Rail Passenger Policy in the Twenty-First Century

Anthony Perl

THE UNIVERSITY PRESS OF KENTUCKY

For Andrea

Publication of this volume was made possible in part
by a grant from the National Endowment for the Humanities.

Scholarly publisher for the Commonwealth,
serving Bellarmine University, Berea College, Centre
College of Kentucky, Eastern Kentucky University,
The Filson Historical Society, Georgetown College,
Kentucky Historical Society, Kentucky State University,
Morehead State University, Murray State University,
Northern Kentucky University, Transylvania University,
University of Kentucky, University of Louisville,
and Western Kentucky University.

Editorial and Sales Offices: The University Press of Kentucky
663 South Limestone Street, Lexington, Kentucky 40508–4008

06   05   04   03   02   5   4   3   2   1

Library of Congress Cataloging-in-Publication Data
Perl, Anthony, 1962–
    New departures : rethinking rail passenger policy in the twenty-first century /
Anthony Perl.
    p.   cm.
    Includes bibliographical references and index.
    ISBN 0-8131-2211-2 (cloth : alk. paper)
    1. Railroads—Passenger traffic—United States. 2. High speed trains—
Government policy—United States. 3. Transportation, Automotive—
United States. 4. Lobbying—United States. 5. Railroads—Passenger
traffic—Canada. 6. High speed trains—Government policy—Canada. 7.
Transporation, Automotive—Canada. 8. Lobbying—Canada. I. Title.
HE2583 .P47   2002
385'.22—dc21
2001004662

This book is printed on acid-free recycled paper meeting
the requirements of the American National Standard
for Permanence of Paper for Printed Library Materials.

∞ ♲

Manufactured in the United States of America

Contents

Acknowledgments

Like its subject, North American rail passenger renewal, this book has had a long gestation. I have been aided by many people during that time. In August of 1994, James Dunn Jr. and I sat down to lunch in a German Inter-City Express dining car and began discussing why such a transportation option was missing from the continent that we called home. Our conversation sparked a very productive research collaboration, yielding a series of articles that laid the intellectual foundation on which this book is built. I owe a great deal to Jim's encouragement over the years.

Much of my research has been supported by the Social Sciences and Humanities Research Council, most recently through Grant # 410-99-0800 which supported the data and information gathering needed to write this book. Thanks are also due to Calgary's Van Horne Institute for International Transportation and Regulatory Affairs, which awarded me a Resident Fellowship for the autumn of 2000 to work full-time on turning my research and ideas into a manuscript. Without that opportunity, this book would have arrived much later, and in a different form. I suspect that a study of passenger train options in Canada and the United States would have met with the approval of the Institute's namesake, William Cornelius Van Horne, himself a transplanted American railroader who helped build Canada's first transcontinental railway. I can only hope that the Institute's contemporary affiliates will be satisfied with the results of my enquiry. For those who seek even more Canadian content than is presented in the following pages, I will be publishing a special study of rail passenger policy options for Canada as a Van Horne Institute research report. More information about that report, and the Institute can be found at http://www.ucalgary.ca/UofC/departments/vanhorne/

Giving a professor several months of freedom to write a book can be a dangerous thing, especially for his research assistant. Donald White performed superbly in that capacity. No detail of legislation, historical documentation, statistical calculation, and graphical design proved beyond his ability to explore and master. When deadlines loomed, Don put aside plans for evenings and weekends and did whatever was needed to keep my work on track. And when there were not enough hours in the day to keep up with the schedule, John Roslinski and Reagan Petrie joined Don in assisting with research. Ms. Ella Wensel also deserves thanks for printing and re-printing many drafts of this manuscript, and keeping track of numerous shipments relating to this project.

Doing effective research requires a good library, and when the University of Calgary's collection proved lacking, our inter-library loan staff worked slowly but surely to obtain materials from across the continent. When these efforts occasionally came up short, I benefited immensely from the assistance of Ms. Danielle Hébert-Persaud at Transport Canada's Corporate Services Business Centre in Ottawa. I also made good use of the Library of Congress in Washington, D.C. Not all information is available in libraries, however, and several individuals deserve special thanks for contributing specialized data.

Françoise El Alaoui of the International Railway Union's High Speed Division provided access to ridership and usage information about the world's high-speed passenger trains. Pierre-Louis Rochet and Jean-Pierre Mathieu of SNCF International shared information about what the TGV had meant for SNCF's performance over the years. Professor Werner Rothengatter of the Institut für Wirtschaftspolitik und Wirtschaftsforschung at the University of Karlsruhe helped to obtain data on Germany's Inter-City Express since railroad restructuring in that country. And Dr. John Preston, Director of the Transport Studies Unit at Oxford University kindly shared his analysis of British rail passenger performance after privatization.

On this side of the Atlantic, Douglas Smith at Transport Canada, as well as John Udell and Paul-Émile Cloutier of VIA Rail provided me with valuable information about passenger trains in Canada. Neal Moyer and Arrigo Mongini at the Federal Railroad Administration pointed me to sources on railroad taxation in the United States. Thomas Till and Michael Mates of the Amtrak Reform Council also provided valuable input on Amtrak's performance. And Bernie Stankus at the Department of Transportation's Bureau of Transportation Statistics offered helpful guidance through the mountains of United States transportation data.

I also have to acknowledge the very detailed and valuable feedback on this manuscript that I received from Professor Tony Turrittin of York University (Toronto), Ross Capon of the National Association of Railroad Passengers, and from Brian Sullivan of Spatial Dynamics Ltd. Neither they, nor any of the others who have done so much to help, should be held accountable for any of the interpretations, errors, and omissions in this book. The responsibility for all the analysis that follows, and its faults, is mine alone.

When it came time to illustrate some of the issues and opportunities that I had written about, I put out a call for help to friends and colleagues who are more inclined toward photography and collecting memorabilia than I am. Many of them responded generously, yielding more materials than space allowed for publication and credit. Thanks are due to all who answered my request for assistance with visual aids.

Finally, I have to acknowledge a special debt to my wife, Andrea Banks. Her eagerness to share my passenger train preoccupations extends well beyond the scope of this book. For that reason, and so many others, I dedicate this book to her.

Chapter 1

Public Policy

The Key to Rail Passenger Renewal

The passenger train occupies a peculiar place among North America's transportation options. It has gone from being absolutely central to the economic and social life of this continent to being of marginal utility and relevance to most people. Trains were once integral to the emergence of modern life on this continent. Books like *Philosophy of Railroads* considered the meaning of this transport mode's fundamental transformation of life: much the way that today's gurus of the "new economy" now contemplate how changes in information technology are reshaping contemporary society.[1] But trains now play such a limited role in meeting mobility needs that they evoke more nostalgia than interest as a way to travel. Nowhere else in the industrial world was the passenger train's rise in importance so meteoric, and nowhere else in the postindustrial world was this followed by such a steep decline.

As on other continents, North America's trains came of age with, and in many ways enabled the spread of, the first wave of productivity, specialization, and diversification that is often referred to as the "industrial revolution." The mode of life that rail travel made possible looked entirely different than the world where horse drawn carriages and boats had provided the main means of mobility.[2] This essentially "modern" world would be much more recognizable to readers of this book than the way of life which preceded rail transportation. Mobility patterns introduced by railroads laid the foundation upon which North America's subsequent affluence, technological advancement, and even cultural accomplishments were built. The train's contribution to shaping the culture and economy of North America is arguably greater than in Europe, where "western" culture and commerce had flourished before rail transportation. Asia also experienced a more limited influence from the train's arrival, due to both its geography and the fact that much Asian industrialization occurred after the railroad's heyday.

Between roughly 1850 and 1950, depending on where on this continent one looked, passenger trains functioned as North America's nearly universal means of inland transportation. They moved the bulk of people going all but the shortest distances between cities, towns, and hamlets that were beyond the reach of ships and boats, and steadily displaced such competition even where waterways were navigable. Railroads brought settlement, industry, and commerce to places that had often seen only subsistence economic activity and indigenous native culture before their arrival. In no other place on earth did so much change so quickly once the passenger train came calling.

And yet despite this enormous influence, or perhaps because of it, North American passenger trains have experienced an exceptionally difficult adaptation to providing a less universal means of transportation—to changing from being *the* mode of transportation to serving as *a* mode of transportation. Perhaps the exuberant embrace that North American travelers appeared to have given to passenger trains at the turn of the last century tempted railroad executives to take their dominance for granted, blinding railroaders to the mass disaffection that began to emerge after the First World War and accelerated dramatically after the Second World War. Or maybe the exploitation perpetrated by an industry whose monopolistic excesses provided the word "railroad" with enduring meaning as a verb encouraged governments to over-regulate, on the one hand, and foster alternative means of mobility by road and air, on the other. Gregory Thompson documented both of these trends in his investigation of California's passenger train operations between 1910 and 1941. He also identified an important political constituency—real estate developers—who fought for "free" roads built by government to facilitate greater land development opportunities than profit-seeking railroads were willing to enable by expanding their passenger operations. Because of this "paradox of laissez-faire America, in which privately owned and operated railroads were incompatible with a society that highly valued the unconstrained exploitation of land," the rail mode's problems of industrial adaptation have been more acute in the United States (and Canada) than in most other developed nations.[3]

In Europe and Japan, where trains have also served as the predominant means of inland transportation, there is ample evidence that railroads have found a way to adjust their business practices and organization to accommodate the reality of new mobility alternatives. While the passenger train's adaptation to a world where people increasingly drive and fly is still very much a work in progress, with plenty of room for improvement, many of the world's affluent nations have seen railroads redesign their passenger service in ways that contribute to contemporary mobility needs. Those in North America have not. This book seeks to understand why the continent on which the world's greatest railroad revolution occurred, and which has led the world in other forms of transportation innovation, has experienced such great difficulty in making use of the passenger train in intercity mobility. Once North America's passenger train problem has been analyzed in some detail, the book goes on to consider what can be done about solving it.

1.1. Assessing the Passenger Train's Predicament: What Were They Thinking?

Some more historically minded readers might wish to begin analyzing the passenger train's decline in North America by looking to the train's apogee as a means of mobility. Such an investigation would certainly yield evidence of corporate arrogance and abuse on the part of railroads—towards their workers, their customers, and the communities they served. These acts likely contributed to a burden of ill will that railroads had to bear when they were no longer the only way to go. But that is not where this book will begin. Capable historians have already explored this theme on a larger scale, and this book will be long enough without performing a detailed search of the passenger train's glory days for seeds of its subsequent downfall.[4]

Rather, it makes most sense to start this search for solutions to North America's particular passenger train predicament at the time when the problem could no longer be ignored. It is important to know what was on the minds of industry leaders and government officials who eventually recognized that business as usual would not keep the passenger train viable. For it was the actions of those who first changed public policy in response to the passenger train's commercial shortcomings that ultimately failed to prevent these problems from mounting to the point of an industrial crisis. And it was that crisis which sent North America's passenger trains down a very different track than the one subsequently taken by the European and Japanese innovators who launched their respective passenger trains' successful renewal. What was it that the American and Canadian railroad experts missed?

Today's transportation problems are often the result of a previous mismatch between yesterday's ideas and what people then perceived that the future would bring. When those responsible for planning and managing transportation networks first recognize that important circumstances are changing, their actions can lead in two directions, depending upon how soon such change is identified and how it is reacted to. If change is anticipated, that means recognized *before* it actually occurs, and if the response can generate activity that capitalizes upon future opportunities, then the potential economic, social, or environmental deterioration that would have otherwise occurred under "business as usual" is prevented. Such a proactive approach to rail passenger redesign is exemplified by the Japanese Shinkansen project, which was initiated in the 1950s, well before Japan's rail system was displaced by air and road competitors as the primary mode of intercity travel. But when social, economic, and environmental cues are missed or misinterpreted, then change yields the challenge of curing problems *after* they have emerged. This is often done by first looking backward to diagnose what went wrong and then creating a solution to the problem out of this understanding. European initiatives to reinvent passenger train operations around high speed service, such as the French Train à Grande Vitesse (TGV) and German Inter-City Express (ICE) represent the success of such an approach to the rail passenger problem. Each of these success stories will be examined in detail below.

But, so far, *neither prevention nor cure* of this decline has been achieved by North American efforts to solve the passenger train problem. The long and costly initiatives to do something about the problem on this continent have not failed entirely, in that we still have intercity passenger trains operating over much (but not all) of North America. But they have also not yet succeeded in generating anything like the success of revitalization efforts found in Europe or Japan. In order to understand why North America has had so little success in solving, let alone preventing the severity of, its passenger trains' decline, we must identify the specific mismatch between what transportation experts had in mind about the train's future when it first started showing acute signs of economic dysfunction and what turned out to be the direction in which North American transportation subsequently headed.

It would be easy to criticize North America's postwar railroad executives who were first overwhelmed by the red ink of passenger train losses as clueless, or even conspiratorial, in their initial set of responses to the passenger train problem. In the 1950s, when the symptoms of serious trouble became incontrovertible, railroad leaders, their regulators, and a good part of North American society were seized by a new passion for mobility that greatly influenced judgements regarding future transportation priorities. As data on U.S. travel by air and auto presented at the start of chapter 2 illustrates, moving farther and faster became the core attributes of postwar American travel behavior. And since Americans were the first to begin shifting to air and auto travel *en masse*, there was no place else to turn for lessons about what to do when people stopped riding trains.

Being first turned out to be worst, when it came to puzzling over a new role for passenger trains in a world where driving and flying were on the rise. The idea of what would today be called an "intermodal" transportation system—and even the concept of transportation as an interdependent system of modes—would have been considered quite eccentric at the end of the Second World War. Instead, at the time when cars and planes were rapidly overtaking trains as America's preferred mobility means, transportation experts placed two attributes above all others in their assessment of issues and problems. These were speed and flexibility.

Furthermore, economic and political elites were convinced that physical mobility was closely correlated with both economic development and social mobility. In other words, the speed of aviation and the flexibility of motor vehicles were viewed as important drivers of economic growth and social progress. Railroads did not appear to have much more to offer in this equation, because the technology that generated faster and more flexible alternatives to the train was viewed as the single greatest determinant of individual travel behavior.

Railroads' lack of speed and flexibility was also seen as a strategic imperative in light of the Cold War. Trains had been eclipsed as a primary means of military transport following World War I, and rail technology was seen as offering little or no further military payoff, especially compared to aerospace and motor vehicles. Despite the occasional experiment in bridging rail and aerospace technology—such as the Union Pacific Railroad's introduction of a turbine powered locomotive, or the New York Central Railroad's experiment of welding an aircraft engine atop one of its passenger cars for a high speed test—rail technology was predominantly viewed as obsolescent and the service supported by that technology seen as en route to extinction. At the time, any limits to the growth of mobility such as congestion, energy availability, and environmental degradation, which are increasingly apparent today, either were not imagined or were viewed as being manageable by new technology.

The North American passenger train's problems were not helped by this mismatch between transportation decision-makers' views about the future and the potential contribution of passenger trains to that future. Preventing problems that would arise from the passenger train's decline, both within the rail industry and to the larger economy and society, was not on the minds of key decision makers when it could have done the most good. Chapter 3 chronicles the resulting strategies that American and Canadian rail regulators devised to ease the economic pain of what was perceived to be a terminal industrial malady. As a result, addressing the fundamental challenge of introducing new technology and new organizational solutions was deferred until the time of an industrial crisis, when the plight of the passenger train had reached a critical condition.

In taking stock of the passenger train's descent into crisis in North America, public policy emerges as the cause of significant missed opportunities for passenger rail redevelopment. As will be shown, public policy is not a panacea for renewing the passenger train. But it is an "enabler" that can be acted upon by managers who have the vision and know-how to make the most of new opportunities. Constraints on such innovation, beginning from the false premise that trains were technologically obsolete, proved to be so great in North America that only a crisis could yield change.

By the time that crisis had generated a significant initiative to preserve the last of the dying passenger train operations in North America, many decision makers in Europe and Japan had already sized up the costs of such a challenge in their countries and were experimenting with various renewal strategies that sought to prevent the train's decline from reaching such proportions. But other countries' efforts to facilitate the passenger train's transition into meeting one or more segments of their mobility needs began unfolding after North America's trains had taken a different policy track. Switching from the preservation policy that was enacted as an emergency brake on the precipitous decline of the train to one that enables renewal is essential to rebuilding North American passenger trains' capacity to provide meaningful mobility, but it is easier said than done.

1.2. A Primer on Public Policy, Policy Communities, and Policy Networks

Since policy can count for so much in shaping the future of passenger trains, it is important to clarify a few key concepts before delving into the details of how policy has influenced passenger trains. Let us begin with a basic definition. Most generally, public policy is the action, or inaction, of government in seeking to address or resolve problems that become part of the public agenda. Such public-sector action almost always combines with reaction and initiatives by private sector firms and nonmarket organizations that contribute to any country's "civil society." These reactions increasingly spill across traditional political boundaries and reverberate in a globalizing world. Not surprisingly, then, what governments seek to do in their policies and what they actually accomplish are usually two different things. But there is usually more than one opportunity to reconcile intent with effect, since policy regularly turns back on itself in cycles of initiative and (re)evaluation of consequences, followed by adjustment of the means and ends of subsequent action.

What makes the process of public problem solving described above different from the workings of any large organization is that, in the nations being considered in this book, it is done by democratically accountable governments. Although the form and degree of that accountability certainly differ, and can thus affect the results, public policy remains fundamentally distinct from the planning and problem solving of private companies, religious organizations, nonprofit institutions, families, and individuals. Unlike these private decision making processes, public policy is more or less open to input from citizens—including organized interests, the media, elites, and experts—and is sooner or later subject to feedback through the democratic process that underlies representative institutions. And public policy is, for the most part, compulsory.

What makes government's decisions about how to address a problem, or which issues to ignore, unique is that they are the only solutions in a society that are directly backed by the force of law. Only government can enforce its decisions upon all through laws, regulations, and financial measures. Public policy thus takes precedence over private plans, priorities, and projects. It can foreclose options that private organizations would otherwise pursue, such as producing cars without seatbelts, air bags, or pollution control devices. Such vehicles were commonplace until public policy mandated the incorporation of these specific features. And policy can launch new activities and products that would not otherwise have emerged, such as low-flow showerheads, childproof bottle caps, and "pooper-scoopers." As complex and chaotic as the contemporary world may appear, and as much as political leaders seek to minimize the role of "big government" these days, it would be a mistake to assume that public policy is any less important than it ever was. But, the way in which government and other policy participants interact over public policy is definitely changing.

Scholars have coined the term "policy community" to capture the sense of what lies behind the arrival, modification, or abandonment of contemporary public policies.[5] A policy community is the accumulation of individuals and organizations that join government's deliberations over the issues and options surrounding a domain like transportation. These participants are often referred to as "stakeholders" in the parlance of bureaucrats and media covering a policy issue.

Policy communities can originate ahead of government's embarking on a particular initiative, being drawn together because of economic and social trends that motivate demands for government action (or inaction) on certain problems or issues. Or they can coalesce once public decisions are made, at which point they provide a forum to assess, and influence, the streams of benefits and costs that arise from government's involvement in a given policy issue.[6]

When it comes to the policy community paying attention to passenger train issues and problems, participants include organizations representing industry (e.g., rail carriers, suppliers, designers, consultants, etc.); labor (e.g., unions); consumers (e.g., passenger associations); as well as the range of governments that are engaged in transportation planning, finance, and operations at the national, state, and local levels. They also include a more-or-less extensive range of competitors, environmentalists, NIMBY's, and other groups that may perceive a reason to have their say about a policy issue or area.[7]

Rail passenger policy in Japan, Europe, and the United States exhibits many differences arising from the way that political institutions shape the transportation sector and government's involvement in it. But there are also some important similarities among the participants who take part in deliberations and debate what to do about the passenger train's future. For one thing, the policy communities that consider passenger train issues and problems tend to be comprised of two distinct camps that fundamentally resemble each other, no matter which country's policy we are considering. Specifically, rail passenger policy communities are divided between participants who either express support for, or skepticism about, the passenger train's prospects—which leads them to embrace opposite conclusions about its future, and make different recommendations for its present.

The supporters within a policy community see passenger trains as a transport mode with much potential and plenty of opportunity for improvement, expansion, and revitalization. But they differ in their motivation for supporting such change. One subset views the success of passenger trains as an end in itself, and any policy that can achieve such an outcome as worth supporting. Some organizations, like labor unions, rail management (or rail passenger management, where it is separate), and rail suppliers, benefit directly and materially from current passenger train operations and are motivated to defend it, as well as press for expansion. Consumer associations also represent current users who depend upon existing train services. I label this subset of supporters as "advocates" of passenger rail. Advocates' support for policy options stems, first and foremost, from the perception of an existing benefit arising out of present-day passenger train operations. They seek to build future improvements upon current organizational and operational structures. Advocates are unlikely to support policy options that imply or involve a decisive break with present day practices and services.

Another subset of supporters sees passenger trains as a means to different ends and favors policies that can enable trains to help meet those outcomes. Such ends can include reducing the environmental impacts of intercity mobility, from local noise and pollution up through contributions to climate change. They can also address social equity concerns, by offering mobility options to those who are left behind by automobility and air travel. Or they can arise out of "new urbanist" visions of more compact and diverse land use that arise when living and work spaces cluster around train stations. And they can even include a variant of fiscal conservatism that views rail as less costly to the public purse than the auto and air modes, when all levels of public support are factored in.

I label this group of supporters "proponents" because their interest in passenger trains arises from, and incorporates the advancement of, other objectives. Not surprisingly, proponents are more heterogeneous than advocates. They are also more open to departing from the administrative and fiscal practices that comprise business as usual in current train operations, and may be quite critical of existing policies that do not generate commercial success or a growth in the number of travelers using rail.

Opposing both advocates and proponents during most rail policy community deliberations are the skeptics who see passenger trains as technologically outmoded, economically unpromising, and politically retrograde. About the only thing that skeptics have in common with supporters is that they each focus upon passenger train policy out of varied motivations. Some skeptics oppose the passenger train because of their association with, or participation in, alternative transport modes that could, or do, substitute for rail travel. Automotive and aviation interests, including the same categories of labor, management, and supply industry organizations that fill the ranks of advocates, regularly resist policy options intended to renew passenger train services. These skeptics can be identified as "contenders," and like advocates, they focus on rail travel as an, in this case unsatisfactory or problematic, end in itself.

Some of the opposition by contenders to rail is head-on, such as when regional airlines lobby against high-speed train projects, or bus companies criticize subsidies to passenger train preservation. But the majority of contenders influence passenger train policy indirectly, foreclosing potential tiatives by "crowding out" the fiscal space for rail within government's support for transportation infrastructure and operations.

Public spending on roads, airports, air traffic control, as well as aerospace and automotive research initiatives, is pursued with great zeal by contenders who may never directly engage the rail policy community. Such public spending is regularly designed to preclude resources from being allocated to other transportation alternatives or public spending priorities in general, of which passenger trains would be just one. This yields a zero sum sponsorship of competing mobility modes where government's investment in air and auto leaves the cupboard bare for rail options and initiatives.

A second subset of skeptics comes out against rail policy because its means are seen to clash with important economic or political principles. Such opponents can be considered "dissenters." Many transportation professionals with a background in economics or engineering would identify themselves as dissenters. Trained to regard rail as an antiquated, or even obsolete, technology for moving people, they view passenger rail policy options with development or revitalization objectives as doomed to failure. These professionals see efforts to revitalize rail travel as contradicting the "laws" of travel behavior whereby flexibility and speed govern consumer preferences. Dissenters can also be motivated by a more general political ideology. Opponents of big government envision any rail policy that includes public financial commitments as profligate public spending. Rail spending is seen as more problematic than investment in air or road infrastructure since the latter are well entrenched, usually in separate policy programs that leave no room for fiscal flexibility. Furthermore, aviation and road spending can, more or less, be justified as supported through the "user fees" of travelers who pay excise taxes on fuel or tickets.

The rail policy community described above has reacted to passenger train problems very differently in North America as compared to Europe and Japan. Their interaction on monitoring existing rail policy effects, evaluating the passenger train's recent performance, and debating prospective rail policy options has generated distinctive political dynamics that have been a part of very different outcomes. Policy researchers have developed categories to describe the ways in which policy communities influence outcomes by affecting government's authority to specify enforceable outcomes in one way or another. There are numerous typologies of the network dynamics that arise from policy communities' interaction over what options are to be pursued. Three principal variations of these policy networks are worth considering with respect to the passenger train.

When authority flows from the top down, policy networks are seen to be state directed. Here, government jealously guards its prerogative to make the decisions that count—those rules and laws that are binding for everyone. When government consistently shares some of its authority with stakeholders, policy networks can involve some degree of corporatism. Here, organized interests get to borrow some of the powers that would normally be exercised by government in the planning and implementation of policy. Some would see any degree of corporatism in a policy network as government's "selling out" the public interest to corporations or unions, while others see corporatism, up to a point, as a healthy sign of "public-private partnership" in cooperative problem solving. Pluralist policy networks are less consistent in the ways that government and organized interests relate to policy issues and problem solving. The degree to which public authority will be controlled by government, or be influenced by lobbying and other forms of pressure tactics, is up for grabs. As a result, policy solutions are likely to be pursued on an incremental basis, with piecemeal and fluid engagement of stakeholder coalitions that can back a particular policy option. Policy itself can also be up for grabs, offering competing interests the chance to shape government's action by being in the right place at the right time.

1.3. Fitting Railroads into Transportation Policy: A Starting Point for Rail Passenger Renewal

Transportation policy is the subset of public policy that supports, regulates, and otherwise influences the mobility of goods and people. It can range from the direct, explicit, and formal laws and regulations about transportation infrastructure, ownership, and operation to the laws and regulations influencing important inputs to transportation, such as energy, technology, taxation, and finance, or outputs from mobility, like environmental impacts. Transportation policy can also be shaped by fiscal and land use policies that influence where development occurs and what that development looks like.

Over the past fifty years, transportation policy almost always has had something different to say about the problems and opportunities facing railroads compared to what it did regarding the other modes of transportation. This is not surprising, given that railroads have a much longer policy history than their contemporary alternatives, aviation and motor vehicle transport. For better or worse, that history gave the railroads plenty of policy baggage, ranging from public ownership in some countries to rigid regulation in others. Automotive and aviation modes have certainly accumulated their own policy baggage over the years, but the key point is that it was qualitatively different than that of the rail industry.

Railroads entered the postwar decades with a "durable" institutional environment, one that entrenched longstanding administrative and financial arrangements in ways that constrained both the vision of rail policy community participants and their capacity to act.[8] This durability also limited interaction between participants in the rail policy community and the rest of the transportation policy community—further constraining policy development. The biggest difference between the rail, air, and road components of national transportation policy was found in the financial relationship between government and the respective carriers.

In the case of railroads, government was either an owner of railroad infrastructure, as in most European nations or through the Canadian National Railways, or a long-standing regulator of private enterprise. Because railroads arrived on the scene before other large-scale business enterprises, they often borrowed organizational attributes from the military. Uniforms, ranks, and a hierarchical command structure remain some of the more obvious evidence of this heritage. Such characteristics helped railroads mesh with government bureaucracy all the more easily, but they also distanced them from customers and communities in ways that other modes would avoid. The policy options concerning how the rail mode would deliver mobility thus came to be largely isolated from the new economic, social, and strategic priorities of the postwar decades. Rail policy was weighted down by precedents and obligations that extended back over a century.

Among the biggest pieces of railroads' baggage was their infrastructure. Building the tracks, signals, stations, and all associated facilities necessary to run rail operations had been a costly and complex affair. And whether public or private, all railroads viewed their infrastructure as an integral asset—even when its maintenance, taxation, and modernization imposed a substantial economic burden. When railroads lost their virtual monopoly over inland transportation in North America, their infrastructure represented a fixed cost that had to be met, regardless of the increasingly competitive market dynamics.

Automotive and aviation modes were part of a newer policy environment, characterized by less institutional durability. Institutional rules and roles remained flexible enough, in these modes, therefore, to incorporate changing priorities into new ways of relating to government. As a result, air and road modes benefitted by improving administrative and fiscal arrangements in their policy environment. Some of these improvements drew upon policy insights gained from the rail mode's increasingly burdensome relationship with government. Such modernization was exemplified by the way in which air and road infrastructure fit into these modes' development.

From airports to highways, automotive and air modes never sought to integrate infrastructure ownership into carrier operations. Infrastructure sponsorship was left directly to government—which could either delegate this to public, mixed, or occasionally private entities that were charged with developing and managing infrastructure on a, more or less, variable-cost recovery basis through the collection of some sort of user fee. This ranged from the link between gas taxes and interstate highway development in the United States to the private franchises awarded to French highway developers who then recovered all their costs, including the cost of capital, from toll revenues.

While infrastructure usually was supported through some form of tax expenditure, such as tax-exempt bonding for airport development in the United States and tax-free treatment of highway infrastructure assets, aviation and automotive operations benefited from other forms of sponsorship. These included military- and space-research funding that spilled over into supporting civilian aviation and automotive research and development. They also included postal contracts for airmail and parcel post, which had previously traveled by rail.

The tendency within the rail policy community has been to interpret the policy innovations that enabled such success among competitors as "unjust" or inherently suspect. This interpretation tended to view the rail mode's policy disadvantages as part of some grand conspiracy to enthrone the automobile and airplane as the predominant mobility modes. Evidence for such a grand conspiracy is lacking, compared to what has been assembled in support of more targeted conspiracies to replace rail transit with motor vehicles as the principal mode of urban transport in North America.[9] Instead, the rail policy community's paranoia regarding the air and road modes' reliance upon public support can be taken as evidence of insularity and inability to embrace the utility of new transportation policy instruments. Air and auto modes benefited from modern policy instruments and programs, as much as from modern technology, in their eclipse of traditional rail services.

As chapters 2 and 3 explore in full detail, this misalignment between the direction of a society's transportation policy priorities and how railroads were organized and managed could be addressed in two ways. Either railroads could respond to the signals of economic decline by cutting back within existing organizational and policy arrangements, or they could pursue a break with those policies and their established organizational structure. The former approach was pursued by North American railroads, with the passenger train at the vanguard of their effort to "do less with less." This exit from passenger transportation responsibilities eventually triggered a political mobilization of rail passenger advocates who succeeded in securing a range of protective policy measures—largely designed to preserve existing patterns of passenger train service.

Only after the passenger train had been switched onto the track of industrial preservation, and freight operations began to suffer from the same administrative and financial causes of commercial decline, did American and Canadian rail policy communities confront the need for more fundamental policy change and industrial reorganization. But by the time deregulation, subsidization, public enterprise, privatization, and other restructuring measures were finally applied to realigning the rail freight carriers' relationship to North American transportation policy, the passenger train had become embedded within a separate set of policy arrangements. In contrast, European and Japanese efforts to reinvent rail transportation were not complicated, and thus not constrained, by the additional organizational barriers arising from the preservation policy track that North American passenger trains got shunted onto in the response to industrial crisis.

Japanese and European transportation policies have enabled different kinds of breakthroughs that put passenger trains back into the mainstream of national transportation activities. This occurred not by emphasizing the preservation of the passenger train's past glories, but by coming up with a truly new mobility offering, one that could meet the needs of travelers *more effectively* than air and auto alternatives in particular circumstances. The remainder of this chapter focuses on these Japanese and European breakthroughs and seeks to identify what policy community attributes enabled railroads to: 1) look beyond their heritage and identify new technology and techniques for moving beyond business as usual to meet mobility needs, and; 2) grasp this opportunity to turn their business around in a declining market for traditional passenger rail services. Japanese experience sheds more light on the first of these points, while European experience illuminates the second, which is particularly relevant to North America's challenge of trying to reverse rail's declining share of the passenger travel market.

While North America's policy debates on what to do about passenger trains' plight generated preservation options, Japanese and European governments launched policy breakthroughs that led to rail passenger revitalization. In Japan, the achievement was to move beyond conventional technology operated in traditional ways to the Shinkansen model of high-speed, high-frequency, high-volume travel along new infrastructure that was purpose-built for meeting this specific segment of rail mobility. In Europe, the break-through came in adopting and adapting this new service package to a context of evident commercial decline.

A key distinction to keep in mind when considering the rail passenger innovations in both Japan and Europe is the one between the scientific re-search efforts seeking to create new rail technology, such as the magnetically levitated "trains" under development in Germany and Japan, and the engi-neering work to perfect new applications for existing technology that enables significant enhancement of the passenger train's performance. The biggest component of the technical breakthroughs that will be examined in both Ja-pan and Europe came from the latter form of innovation—creating new ap-plications for technology to enhance the passenger train's performance.

1.4. The Japanese Shinkansen: Proactive Modernization

After the Second World War, the Japanese pioneered an organizational and technical restructuring of passenger train operations that yielded a break-through in that mode's performance. Their Shinkansen model transformed passenger rail service, exhibiting several characteristics that exemplify a deci-sive break with rail travel's longstanding approach to moving people. These attributes, first brought together by the Shinkansen, can be found in subse-quent successful passenger train renewal efforts.

First, the railroad's role in transportation was no longer conceived of as being universal. Instead of being designed and operated around the premise that trains could, and would, move everything everywhere, the Shinkansen was designed to fulfill a particular segment of mobility needs by providing a service that was designed and organized specifically for that purpose. Unlike the railroad's industrial breakthrough in the nineteenth century, where the introduction and improvement of technology had preceded and shaped trans-port demand, the Shinkansen would follow the postwar, twentieth-century pattern of improving the performance of existing technology to meet new economic and social demands. This was the approach of the automotive and aerospace industries as they rolled out motor vehicles and aircraft in the 1950s.

Plans to build a rail line that would increase transport capacity between Japan's largest cities, Tokyo and Osaka, and continue on to the port city of Shimonoseki had been approved in 1939, with construction actually starting in 1941.[10] Had this traditional rail development initiative not been literally destroyed by the war in 1944, Japan's postwar passenger rail development might have looked quite different. For one thing, the prewar railroad had been run as part of the public bureaucracy, with little organizational change since the Meiji era. The Japanese National Railway (JNR) was launched in 1949 as one of the first organizations in a new system of public corporations. According to Yoshitake, creating such an enterprise was intended to curb the power of the very militant civil service trade union that appeared quite threatening to the American occupying government.[11] But this new organizational form also enabled a more commercial approach to rail management to take root than had been the case under public bureaucracy.

As well, the technological breakthroughs in rail vehicles, infrastructure, and propulsion systems that made the Shinkansen concept a reality were only achieved after the war, when Japan's "best and brightest" engineers were, at least for a time, less likely to be working for military suppliers and aerospace industries. In the early 1950s, some of Japan's top electrical, mechanical, and civil engineers were to be found working at the Railway Technical Research Institute (RTRI), the scientific arm of the rail bureaucracy that operated as a subsidiary of JNR. Their goal of increasing the speed of intercity passenger trains was something that had dropped off of the North American technology policy agenda, since aerospace and nuclear research were seen as top priorities during the height of the Cold War. Such work had also taken a back seat in Europe. But by May of 1957, RTRI's staff unveiled a breakthrough at a highly public conference marking the organization's fiftieth anniversary. There, RTRI engineers presented a paper entitled "High Speed Railway in the Future," which outlined the attributes of a combination of new infrastructure and rolling stock that could enable a passenger train to cover the 341.8 mile distance from Tokyo to Osaka in three hours. Strobel and Straszak identify this presentation as an "epoch-making event" in modern railroad development because it was the first time that a railroad organization had presented a vision running counter to the conventional postwar wisdom that trains' obsolete technology was propelling them into a state of terminal industrial decline.[12]

At the time that RTRI's technology breakthrough was made public, Japan's Diet had already approved a five year plan for incremental upgrading of the conventional, narrow gauge rail system. This existing policy had no potential for the kind of performance breakthrough which the Shinkansen's designers eventually achieved.[13] Not content with such a future, and doubtless aware of the progress that was being made with new technology at RTRI, JNR's president Shinji Sogo had already launched a special investigative commission in May 1956. Directed by JNR's vice president of engineering, this commission studied the need for an entirely new rail line between Tokyo and Osaka.[14]

The JNR commission's findings were released around the time of the RTRI report on how to transform the supply of passenger train service. Analysis of future travel demand suggested a perfect fit with this new potential to supply high speed trains because the demand for mobility was projected to grow so much that all modes would have to be expanded. The commission's most conservative forecast predicted that travel would more than double between 1957 and 1975, while freight shipments would increase 230 percent. Even with a proposed superhighway between Tokyo and Osaka in place, JNR's analysis projected that it could handle just 10 percent of this growth in passenger travel and only 5 percent of the increase in freight traffic.[15]

Within a week of the RTRI symposium, which had been calculated to highlight the railroad's ability to play a new role in meeting Japan's growing demand for mobility, JNR president Sogo applied to the Ministry of Transport for approval to begin "improving" the Tokaido line between Tokyo and Osaka. His request cleverly sought to gain approval in principle for rail development that went beyond the incremental upgrading that was called for in the five year plan.[16] Details and cost estimates that would arise from either building an entirely new high-speed line or pursuing more extensive upgrading of the existing narrow gauge line were left to further exploration once the government had given a green light to proceed.

Sogo's ability to gain such approval in principle gave JNR momentum in developing more detailed plans for deploying new rail technology. In August 1957, the JNR's trunk line investigation commission began work and quickly focused on adapting the new high-speed technology to rail's most promising market niche in Japan, moving large numbers of people quickly between its two largest cities. What would become the Shinkansen service concept was refined during this phase of analysis. The key organizational innovation was to separate the infrastructure of this new rail technology from the infrastructure that supported existing, traditional rail operations. The latter were designed, like that found on almost all other railroads, to integrate freight and passenger transport and to accommodate local, intercity, and very long-distance passenger services on the same infrastructure. But the Shinkansen would be significantly different.

The Shinkansen was not intended to serve all mobility needs at the same time. Therefore, it was not an extension of the "build it and they will come" philosophy that had characterized rail development schemes dating back to the mode's inception, as celebrated in Keefer's *Philosophy of Railroads*. Instead, the Shinkansen was the passenger train's first "new departure" of the postwar years. Autos and air travel had not yet overtaken trains in their share of the

Japanese intercity market, but Japanese rail planners remained sufficiently proactive and advanced the train's most competitive attributes before these other modes became dominant. Just as automotive and aviation planners and entrepreneurs were doing during the 1950s and 1960s, JNR's leadership proved quite capable of giving the traveling public something new and unique. Shinkansen was created to be faster than a car, while also more frequent and convenient than a plane. This design philosophy proved to be a winning concept, with its first victory being a formal approval from the Japanese cabinet for the project's launch on December 19, 1958.[17]

Gaining a policy commitment to turn the Shinkansen concept into reality was not as easy or straightforward as it might seem from the hindsight of the project's longstanding commercial and technical success. Japan's rail policy community did not champion the high-speed train concept as universally or enthusiastically as might be imagined today. Strobel and Straszak note that skeptics existed within the rail industry, both in Japan and abroad.[18] They viewed incremental upgrading of traditional train services as sufficient, based upon a conventional wisdom that saw rail technology as past its prime and of diminishing value to a society that was trying to catch up with, and even overtake, American and European economic development. A contemporary expression of this skepticism can be found in Kakumoto, who wrote that: "Unfortunately, motor vehicle and air transport capacity was 10 years too late to save the country from the expense of the Shinkansen. . . . Up until the mid-1950s, JNR did not have the funds to build the Tokaido Shinkansen and if it had waited until the end of the 1960s before deciding whether to launch the project, it would have questioned the need for constructing the new line. Instead, it probably would have added more double-tracked narrow-gauge sections to the high traffic-density areas."[19]

The policy network dynamic that emerged to deploy the first Shinkansen was a corporatist one, in which modernizers and visionaries in the rail policy community were able to make and sustain the case for this new departure by borrowing the powers of government for a time. JNR had been sufficiently distanced from the public bureaucracy to enable entrepreneurial leadership to advance the train's competitiveness, but it remained close enough to the government to appropriate the authority needed to realize the project.

The best barometer of that authority can be found in the Shinkansen's finances, which required further public infusions during the construction phase. When Japan's cabinet had authorized construction of the new line in 1958, a budget of ¥194.8 billion was approved.[20] The *New York Times* estimated the Shinkansen's projected cost at $540 million in 1959, equivalent to $3.2 billion in 2000.[21] Japan's fiscally constrained government approached the World Bank for a $140 million loan for the project. After performing an independent evaluation of the project, the Bank agreed to loan $80 million on April 24, 1961. To date, this was the third largest loan in the Bank's history and its largest transaction with Japan.[22] *Business Week* reported that the World Bank's support for JNR's Shinkansen "enrages many an American railroad man who would love to have access to similar sources of financing."[23] But unlike its American counterpart, Japan's rail policy community was in a position to engage the government in supporting its rail passenger development priorities.

The Japanese government proved willing to stake its international credit rating on JNR's promise of commercial success, exemplified by what one JNR executive told *U.S. News & World Report*: "We just can't lose money with so much business waiting for us."[24] By the time it was inaugurated, the Shinkansen's cost was almost double initial projections, with a budget coming in at over $1 billion. Rising land and construction costs were identified as the culprits at the time. But in retrospect, Hosokawa found evidence that the initial cost estimate produced by JNR's 1957 feasibility study had been "substantially higher" than the ¥194.8 billion budget that was presented to and adopted by government.[25] Nobody involved in the Shinkansen project ever offered a reason behind such an underestimate, but it certainly helped in obtaining government approval. When the budget overruns eventually started coming in, government made up the difference, in part because of its guarantee on the World Bank loan. But budget overruns also contributed to costing Sogo his job before the Shinkansen rolled out of the station, as he stepped down from JNR's helm in 1963. Sogo's determined leadership steered the corporatist policy network dynamic toward Japan's new departure in railroading.

Another aspect of the corporatist dynamic within Japan's rail policy community was the opposing interests that were not heard from when it came time to implement the Shinkansen. Environmentalists and adjacent landowners, who have come to have an important and often opposing role in high-speed rail development, were not heard from until after the Shinkansen entered service. Without a separate environmental impact assessment, of the sort that would send many attempts to launch high-speed rail in North America into a tailspin, there was no accounting for the cost of noise, vibration and community disruption that would arise. Strobel and Straszak point out that residents along the Tokyo to Osaka route were "not yet so sensitive about environmen-

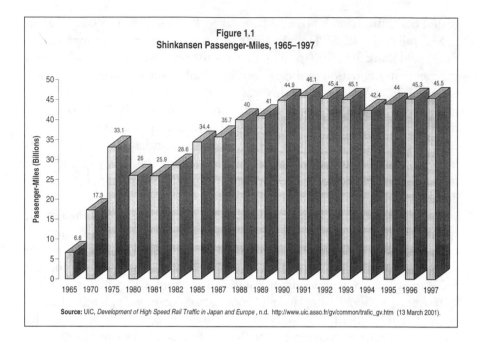

Figure 1.1
Shinkansen Passenger-Miles, 1965–1997

Source: UIC, *Development of High Speed Rail Traffic in Japan and Europe*, n.d. http://www.uic.asso.fr/gv/common/trafic_gv.htm (13 March 2001).

tal impacts" before the Shinkansen began operating.[26] Like those living along airport approach paths before jets entered service, the serious environmental impacts of new technology were not anticipated. But these proved to be acute and immediate. Yorino reports that soon after the train's debut, the "League Against Shinkansen Pollution" became active on behalf of local residents.[27] Between 1964 and 1975, 550 petitions and protest letters objecting to the Shinkansen's noise and vibrations had been submitted to government.

Another input that was not recorded was that of contenders, particularly those in the airline industry. The Shinkansen's impact on air travel between Tokyo and Osaka was immediate, with Japan Airlines' load factor dropping below 50 percent during the first year of Shinkansen operation.[28] All Nippon Airways, the other major carrier between Tokyo and Osaka, reported an 8 percent drop in passengers, in a market that was reported to be growing at 7 percent annually.[29] Air carriers were perhaps less strident in opposing rail competition because Japan's domestic aviation was tightly regulated in the 1960s.

The impressive results of the JNR's Shinkansen are presented in figures 1.1 and 1.2. Figure 1.1 illustrates the rapid growth in total travel by Shinkansen, measured by passenger-miles through the 1970s and 1980s. During the 1990s,

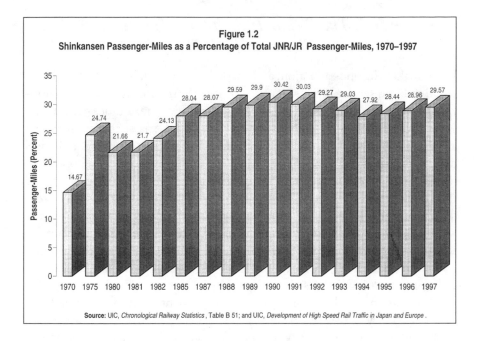

Figure 1.2
Shinkansen Passenger-Miles as a Percentage of Total JNR/JR Passenger-Miles, 1970–1997

Source: UIC, *Chronological Railway Statistics*, Table B 51; and UIC, *Development of High Speed Rail Traffic in Japan and Europe*.

Shinkansen travel began to show signs of maturity, with usage stabilizing around 45 billion passenger miles per year. This accounts for about 30 percent of the total rail travel, by distance, on Japan National Railways (later Japan Railways), as shown in figure 1.2. While ordinary trains still play a very important intercity transportation role, there is no question that the Shinkansen has become established as the core intercity passenger train service in Japan.

Japan's breakthrough in pushing ahead with passenger train performance during the 1950s offers a good example of how the rail policy community could generate a proactive linkage between new technology and innovative technique to create a new opportunity for this mode. Rather than being spurred by a loss of business or the prospect of industrial collapse, Japanese improvements in the passenger train represented the ongoing growth phase of a mode that was not yet "mature." And when the air and automotive competition did eventually increase to the point that rail began to lose market share, there existed a solid "core" passenger business that remains vital to this day. Japan's high-speed rail revolution disproved the hypothesis that passenger trains were inherently obsolete and that their technology had reached a dead end, like the stagecoach. It also set the stage for others to draw lessons about the passenger train's potential in the face of more daunting competition from other modes.

1.5. The French Train à Grande Vitesse: Reactive Renewal of a Rail Enterprise

What makes Europe's adoption, and adaptation, of Japan's approach to high-speed railroad service directly relevant to North America is that it was motivated by the imperative of reversing industrial decline. France's TGV has been the boldest of such attempts yet to transform the passenger train into an attractive mobility option. It has succeeded in doing just what technological determinists deemed impossible—providing an intercity rail travel option to which air and road users would voluntarily return after having experienced the competitive "advantages" of aviation's speed and the automobile's freedom to travel without a schedule or a reservation. In order to appreciate the whole lesson of French passenger train revitalization, we must first look at the accomplishment behind the achievement, the ability of railroad management, government officials, and the railroad supply sector to create and implement a new way of doing business.

Motivation for change came from government in the form of a "state directed" policy network. This was partly because French trains were relatively high on government's policy agenda compared to their perceived importance in North America. When government took over French railroads, which had become insolvent prior to the Second World War, it assumed responsibility for both past rail debts and future rail financing. Like Amtrak, the Société Nationale des Chemins de fer Français (SNCF), or French National Railways, was created as a "mixed enterprise," which would today be labeled a "public-private partnership." The private investors who had been bought out in 1939 remained as silent partners holding 49 percent of the new venture's equity. Profits from a consolidated and "modernized" SNCF were supposed to pay dividends to these investors until 1982, when their equity would be repurchased.[30] But as would later occur with Amtrak, the profits that were supposed to materialize did not, leaving government to make guaranteed dividend payments during the SNCF's first forty-three years.

SNCF's financing arrangements connected French government officials to the costs of the rail mode's economic performance much more directly than their American counterparts, who only received indirect signals through the regulatory process. The passenger train's incipient decline thus appeared as more of a public challenge to the rail policy community in France. Even in the 1960s, French intercity passenger trains earned money that, at least partly, offset losses on commuter and freight operations. Unlike the United States, France had an extensive public enterprise culture that linked a number of economic sectors under state "tutelage."[31] French trains were thus not in the institutional no-man's-land that American railroads occupied, being cut off from postwar transport policy initiatives by "virtue" of private ownership.

By the 1960s, French public enterprise was seen to be in need of administrative and economic renewal across the board. In 1967, a commission of experts was charged with exploring future options that could make public and mixed enterprises like the SNCF less dependent upon public finances. The resulting "Nora report," named after commission chair Simon Nora, had a significant influence over entities like the SNCF.[32] It presented a clear set of commercial principles for the operation of publicly owned enterprises, giving an "emphasis upon the need for them to operate as much like private enterprises as possible, putting commercial requirements before public service."[33] Following the fiscal crisis triggered by the oil shock of 1973, President Valery Giscard d'Estaing and Prime Minister Raymond Barre embraced economic liberalization to reduce public enterprise deficits.

The Nora report's guiding principle was to create transparency and differentiation between competitive market services and the social and public interest functions within state-supported business organizations. Where public enterprise was producing a good or providing a service below cost, then an explicit contract was recommended as the best policy instrument to specify the quantity, price, and subsidy level that government would support in the public interest. Rather than providing indirect subsidies through accumulating public enterprise deficits, debt write-offs, and other forms of creative accounting, the Nora report called for explicit valuation of what a public service was worth. Conversely, commercially competitive services were given a "green light" to be run like a business.

SNCF management saw the Nora report's recommendations as validating their intention to reinvent rail service from within.[34] SNCF had labored under an ambiguous mandate dating from its inception in 1938. Financial turmoil of the depression, the fall of the Third Republic, and the wartime Vichy regime had left SNCF in search of exactly the sort of commercial guidance that the Nora report was proposing. Government's application of the Nora report's principles to its relationship with the SNCF in 1971 led to creation of a five-year business-planning model, contracts for service, and other aids to give management more effective conditions for commercial development.

In the 1970s, SNCF's management sought to introduce a break from past railroad practices, as the Japanese had done a decade earlier. But SNCF would have to do even better in terms of revamping service characteristics, since the train was now competing to lure travelers back from the skies and the roads.

As in Japan, the point of departure was the most promising market niche. In France this meant the travel corridor between the two largest urban agglomerations, the "Ile de France" surrounding Paris, which had a population of just over 10 million in 1982[35] and the Rhone-Alpes region surrounding Lyon, with a population of slightly more than 5 million in 1982.[36] This was France's equivalent to the Tokyo–Osaka transport corridor, and like its Japanese counterpart, the existing rail infrastructure was reaching the point of overload. Building additional rail capacity was seen as inevitable, but the choice to create a new high-speed passenger railroad and concentrate the growing freight traffic on the existing, traditional, infrastructure was France's new departure.

In planning this new departure, speed was SNCF's goal, but cost was the challenge. French rail planners understood what Pavaux would confirm twenty years later, that travel time was related to transport ridership in a logarithmic fashion.[37] This is due to the fact that the business segment of air and high-speed rail travel was attracted by the ability to make a round-trip in a single day. Allowing for typical human rest and work behavior patterns, with eight hours of sleep and eight hours work, a total travel time of four to six hours proves attractive. More than six hours of total daily travel begins to discourage use of a mode, especially when a faster alternative is available.

Thus, the opportunity to make a journey by rail in three hours would begin to trigger modal shift from air in that market. Between two and three hours travel time, air and rail would be competitive, with modal choice becoming based on price and other service characteristics such as ease of access to the traveler's origin and destination. The question facing SNCF was what kind of technology could yield a two- to three-hour travel time at an affordable cost?

Part of the cost control solution was for the SNCF to keep authority over decisions on the technology that would be used to achieve the new passenger train's service objectives. Like JNR, SNCF became a leader in developing high-speed rail by keeping the design and engineering functions "in house." This provided SNCF executives with an ability to reconcile speed with cost, and to reject technological experimentation that would add unjustified expense.

An example of the alternative approach to technology development was the Aerotrain, a vehicle that would be suspended over its track by an air cushion created by turbofan engines while being pulled forward by a magnetic linear induction motor. Research support for this advanced technology was provided by the Regional and Economic Development Ministry, known as DATAR, not from the Transport Ministry. During the late 1960s and early 1970s, the SNCF's development of what would become known as the TGV and the independent Aerotrain project proceeded in parallel. This resembled

German efforts during the 1970s and 1980s to develop both the Inter-City Express (ICE), based upon fast train technology, and the superfast Transrapid, which relied upon magnetic-levitation technology.[38] But unlike the German Federal Railway, SNCF was able to make the case within government that deploying its TGV would meet both commercial and technical needs, and that proceeding with Aerotrain would squander resources. As a result, the TGV project went forward during the 1970s while the Aerotrain project was eventually cancelled.

French experience with the TGV and Aerotrain demonstrates that a key part of the challenge of revitalizing the rail mode is to make the case that it can be renewed with innovative techniques and improved technology, rather than replaced altogether with a more ambitious and costly technology for guided-ground transport. SNCF passed this significant challenge, which had not been faced by JNR, through retaining the confidence of government officials in the state-directed policy network. SNCF did this, in part, by encouraging rail suppliers to form a cartel that would spread the opportunities arising from producing the TGV and its associated infrastructure among major manufacturers. Within the rail policy community, this grouping created an organizational form that reflected the immediate industrial payoffs arising from rail renewal. When considering the inevitable trade-offs of industrial policy, public officials often tend to value the maintenance of existing jobs and profits in one sector more highly than developing a sector that will generate new jobs and profits in the future. This is especially true if the existing sector is under threat of industrial decline.

In this case, French rail manufacturing was sufficiently at risk from the potential costs of passenger trains' further decline—while also being in a position to benefit from the potential gains of rail revitalization—to weigh in favor of proceeding with the TGV. Investing in the less certain payoff from the Aerotrain's new technology also appeared likely to come at the expense of existing jobs and profits in the rail supply sector.

Public input into revitalization initiatives was virtually nil in the French rail policy community during the formative years when the TGV strategy was being developed. The state-directed policy network was run by elites, with very limited tolerance for protests from NIMBY's, delays from environmental impact analysis, and costs from mitigation of potential impacts. However, when French economic difficulties arising during the post-1973 "stagflation" created fiscal pressure to cut back public expenditure, skeptics within government who perceived rail transportation to be inherently obsolete did challenge the TGV project as an unaffordable boondoggle.

SNCF's response was to meet such dissenters part way, not by compromising the TGV's technology or cutting back on its objectives for competing in the market, but by extending the project's implementation schedule through a two phase deployment. Instead of building a new high-speed railroad all the way from Paris to Lyon, the SNCF opted to cover only two-thirds of that distance with new infrastructure and use existing tracks for the remainder of the trip. Such incrementalism would still permit the TGV to demonstrate its potential by reducing travel time from four and one-half hours on traditional trains to two hours and forty minutes, which fell within the "competitive zone" between air and rail options that Pavaux had documented. Mixing new and old infrastructure also guaranteed that travelers would experience the contrast between the TGV performing at its full technical potential along a good segment of their route, and the limitations of traditional operation. Such a contrast would provide a built-in opportunity to bolster support for extending the new infrastructure. The French contrast between modern and traditional rail operations, which are used sequentially by the TGV, yielded a much greater awareness of the passenger train's potential than the North American approach to incremental high-speed rail development. In both Canada and the United States, modern trains have been deployed over traditional infrastructure dating from the nineteenth century, where they predictably underperformed on a continuous basis.

The results of the TGV initiative provide the clearest evidence of passenger trains' potential for meeting a segment of modern mobility needs better than any alternative, and in so doing, generating profits in a competitive travel market. Figure 1.3 documents the steady growth of TGV ridership in France since the Paris–Lyon line opened in 1982. Patronage has climbed from 6.5 million in its first full year of service to over 73 million over a national network of high speed rail in 1998. Figure 1.4 reveals the growing role that the TGV plays in SNCF's operations, from carrying less than 1 percent of the SNCF's riders in 1982 to almost 10 percent in 1998. And in figure 1.5, which reveals that the distance traveled by TGV passengers is now approaching four-fifths of total rail travel in France, the fact that TGVs have become the mainstay of intercity rail travel becomes clear. Their importance to the SNCF's ongoing role in national, and even international, intercity transportation in addition to commuter travel in and around major cities cannot be underestimated.

The TGV has been a commercial success story along three dimensions. Each of these achievements has occurred after the new combination of technology and service significantly altered the behavior of intercity travelers in ways that contributed to the SNCF's bottom line, while often generating ad-

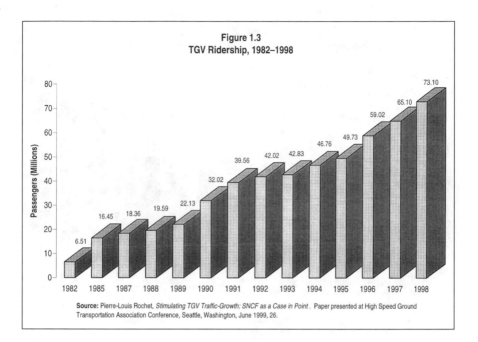

Figure 1.3
TGV Ridership, 1982–1998

Source: Pierre-Louis Rochet, *Stimulating TGV Traffic-Growth: SNCF as a Case in Point*. Paper presented at High Speed Ground Transportation Association Conference, Seattle, Washington, June 1999, 26.

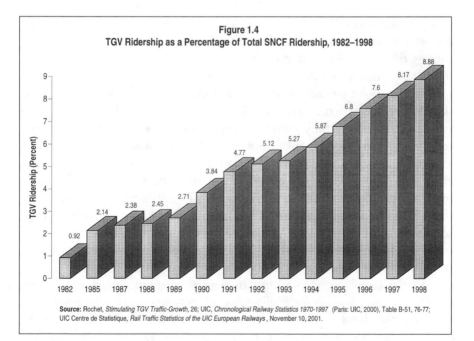

Figure 1.4
TGV Ridership as a Percentage of Total SNCF Ridership, 1982–1998

Source: Rochet, *Stimulating TGV Traffic-Growth*, 26; UIC, *Chronological Railway Statistics 1970-1997* (Paris: UIC, 2000), Table B-51, 76-77; UIC Centre de Statistique, *Rail Traffic Statistics of the UIC European Railways*, November 10, 2001.

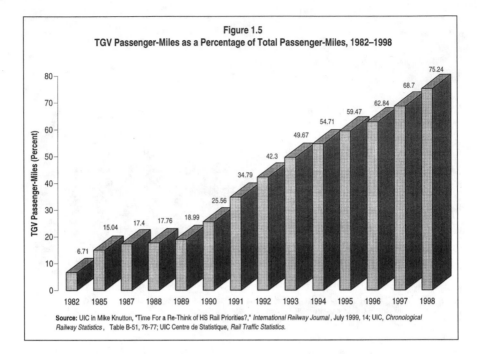

Figure 1.5
TGV Passenger-Miles as a Percentage of Total Passenger-Miles, 1982–1998

Source: UIC in Mike Knutton, "Time For a Re-Think of HS Rail Priorities?," *International Railway Journal*, July 1999, 14; UIC, *Chronological Railway Statistics*, Table B-51, 76-77; UIC Centre de Statistique, *Rail Traffic Statistics*.

ditional "social benefit" spin-offs. First, TGV operations have transformed the behavior of existing rail travelers. TGV's initial ridership triumph came in shifting the vast majority of train riders from traditional, preexisting services to the new, high-speed services.

Skeptics point out that these travelers were already riding by rail and thus should not be counted as evidence of the TGV's success. But such an interpretation misses both the commercial benefit to SNCF's bottom line and the external, societal benefits of shifting rail travel from a less commercially viable form of service to a more viable rail alternative. TGVs could, and did, charge a premium for the speed and frequency that made them more commercially viable than traditional trains. SNCF built upon this attribute by pioneering "yield management"–style pricing of European passenger train services.

Charging different prices for the same trip permitted better segmentation of the existing rail market into those riders who would pay a premium to travel at peak times—such as a 7:00 a.m. departure from Lyons reaching Paris at 9:00 a.m. and allowing for a full day's business—and those who would not. TGV off-peak fares were set to be comparable to traditional trains, thus leaving travelers who would not, or could not, pay a premium no worse off than

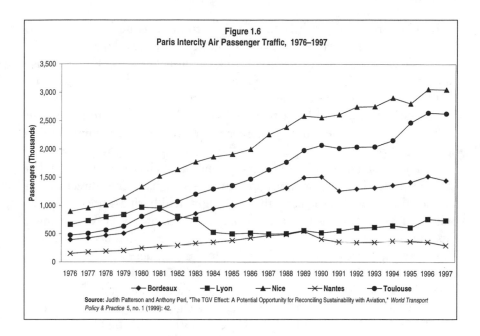

Figure 1.6
Paris Intercity Air Passenger Traffic, 1976–1997

Source: Judith Patterson and Anthony Perl, "The TGV Effect: A Potential Opportunity for Reconciling Sustainability with Aviation," *World Transport Policy & Practice* 5, no. 1 (1999): 42.

before. One important lesson of TGV's intramodal shift is that it is possible to tap into the reserve of commercial potential among existing rail travelers, some of whom will pay more for improved service, without such gains coming at the expense of those who perceive no alternative to preexisting, traditional train services. With the TGV's introduction, all rail travelers are able to share in the benefits of more modern operations.

Second, TGV service transformed the behavior of intercity travelers who had previously used air and road modes by drawing some segment of them back to the rails. Plassard found that 27 percent of TGV riders on the Paris–Lyon route had previously driven or flown.[39] Patterson and Perl have documented the "TGV effect" on air travel between French regional centers like Lyon, Nantes, Bordeaux, and Paris.[40] In each of these cases, airlines have scaled back on "shuttle" type air services by reducing the frequency of flights and/or the size of aircraft used on these routes. These trends are reflected in figure 1.6.

Each opening of a TGV line is reflected in a decrease in air travel to and from Paris, as seen in 1982 for traffic to and from Lyons, 1990 to and from Nantes, and 1991 to and from Bordeaux. Cities that lack high-speed TGV service, such as Nice and Toulouse, serve as the control cases, and they continue to exhibit increasing air travel to and from Paris.[41] The TGV effect has also extended beyond French borders through international high-speed trains derived from the TGV, such as the THALYS to Brussels and the Eurostar to London, which are creating their own successes in the travel market.

Evidence for the shift from road back to rail is less systematic, because data on the origin and destination of French intercity driving is hard to come by. On the TGV Atlantique line, which runs from Paris west to Nantes, and Southwest to Bordeaux, Plassard found that the auto's share of total travel in 1989 (pre-TGV) ranged from 48 percent to 22 percent, depending on distance, but dropped from 44 percent to 14 percent in 1993 (post-TGV).[42]

Gaining such market share from cars and planes has given the SNCF a strong commercial and economic boost. First, SNCF has gained directly from additional revenues, particularly those of high-yield business travelers. Second, the rail mode gains indirectly from the image of the TGV as being a superior means of mobility, a sought after way to travel that boosts the passenger train's market position and profile. In France, there are bumper stickers that boast "Mon autre voiture est un TGV" (My other car is a TGV). There is an undeniable, if hard to quantify, economic advantage for the rail carrier when its top trains are consciously recognized as part of a nation's mobility mainstream. Third, there is the opportunity to build intermodal partnerships with organizations that would have little interest in being associated with traditional train service, but that are eager to share in the TGV's success. These partnerships range from joint sales arrangements with car rental companies that set up their offices at train stations served by TGV, to "code sharing" arrangements with airlines that use TGVs as the equivalent of feeder aircraft for long haul flights to or from Charles de Gaulle airport in Paris, which now incorporates a TGV station.[43] These partnerships open new markets for rail service and demonstrate "win-win" opportunities for the rail mode to partner with other carriers and mobility providers. As a result, they can work to reduce the number of rail policy community participants who view themselves as contenders.

Third, the TGV has induced new travel demand. In so doing, it is the only type of train service in a half-century that has been effective enough to reshape travel behavior in ways analogous to autos and aviation. Plassard's travel surveys documented that 36 percent of riders on the Paris–Lyon line responded that they had not made the trip previous to the TGV. Among business travelers, Plassard found that the lower cost of same day travel between Paris and Lyon encouraged more frequent visits. Those who would have previously made a single trip, at a high air fare, now filled their agenda with multiple events and meetings and are making more frequent trips on the

TGV. This substitution of mobility for other costs, such as overnight hotel stays and more structured business activity, shifted spending onto the rails in ways that are similar to the effects seen with the rise of air and auto travel. More travel on fast trains is thus analogous to the trend toward more frequent, but shorter, vacations that involve more flying per year, or a household's obtaining a second or third motor vehicle and using it for more independent trips by family members who might have previously coordinated their travel in the same vehicle.

The TGV's commercial achievements went beyond reshaping the SNCF's economics. They also opened up new policy opportunities for the rail mode in France, in Europe, and across the globe. SNCF's experience boosted other European nations' efforts to introduce high-speed trains by demonstrating the economic opportunities of rail revitalization. The TGV also brought about the first "internationalization" of high-speed rail, by connecting this technology across borders (and rail-organization boundaries) to create high-speed links to Switzerland, Belgium, and the United Kingdom. Some of these expansions into Belgium and through the English Channel tunnel were supported by EU-level infrastructure investment for "trans-European networks." James Dunn and I have labeled this cross-border expansion a "second wave" of high-speed rail development.[44] The example of European high-speed rail renewal has even traveled intercontinentally, with Korea now implementing a TGV-derived high-speed train to serve the Seoul to Pusan route.

The TGV is the most straightforward example of postwar rail revitalization, just as the Shinkansen is the most clearcut example of proactive rail modernization. In both cases, the supportive segment of the rail policy community, dominated by advocates, was able to make a major breakthrough in rail passenger performance, which made an enormous difference to the train's position in a competitive transportation market. This accomplishment occurred ahead of the competitive onslaught of cars and planes in Japan and after that competition in France. Yet, in both cases it precluded the kind of preservation policy option that became the norm in North America.

These achievements occurred with a degree of insulation from both dissenters and contenders that would be unlikely in the North American political system. Whether through pluralism that gives open access to ideological dissenters or the privileged position of elite interests, the policy community environment for transforming rail looks much different, and more challenging, in North America than in it did in either Japan or France. Germany offers an example of rail passenger revitalization efforts occurring in a more complex, and contested, policy community environment. It is thus worth some attention before closing this chapter's initial overview of the difference that policy can make to the passenger train's prospects.

1.6. Germany's Inter-City Express Train and Transrapid Maglev: A Tale of How Policy Can Influence the Success and Failure of Renewal Attempts

Germany's rail passenger redevelopment efforts have differed from France's in a number of ways. They have occurred in a more complex policy environment, yielding both successful and unsuccessful examples of rail passenger renewal. Unlike both Japan and France, but with some parallel to North America, the German government never put all of its eggs in one basket when it came to supporting a renewal of traditional railroading. There has always been a strong level of support from within the German rail policy community for such renewal, but it has been balanced against the potential opportunity of a high-tech, and higher-speed, departure from traditional railroading, the magnetically levitated "Transrapid" vehicle.

In light of this ongoing tension between policy options based upon opposite premises—the renewal of a declining passenger carrier versus its more-or-less extensive substitution by a wholly different technology—Germany's achievements in rail passenger renewal appear as all the more impressive. Germany's success thus offers further evidence that innovation and change can be pursued under a less than fully supportive policy environment, where government's authority is decentralized and the contest among policy community participants over transportation priorities is more intense. This assessment of Germany's accomplishments begins by examining a traditional rail passenger carrier's success in launching a newly competitive service, the Deutsche Bundesbahn's inauguration of the high-speed Inter-City Express (ICE) train. It also considers the recently abandoned effort to launch magnetic-levitation technology between Berlin and Hamburg as a truly new departure in high-speed ground transportation. Both initiatives reveal important implications of how transportation policy influences the opportunities for innovation.

From a distance, Germany's rail policy community might appear similar to that of France, with perhaps even greater potential for a supportive coalition to get behind passenger train renewal. At its epicenter were the same two organizations that one would find in most other European nations, a publicly owned rail carrier, the Deutsche Bundesbahn (DB), or German Federal Railway, and a national transport ministry. The former was an obvious rail advocate, and was joined by politically influential labor unions and industry associations of rail suppliers in impressing the advantages and necessity of modernizing the rail mode upon the German Transport Ministry. Germany also possessed a larger subset of sustainable-transportation proponents within the rail policy community than did France, principally environmentalists who grew in power through the 1980s as the Green Party won seats in both the federal and Länder (state) parliaments.

But upon closer inspection, the DB turned out to be a more decentralized organization than the SNCF. This reflected the difference between France's traditional, unitary-government structure, with Paris sitting at the apex of an administrative and political hierarchy,[45] and Germany's federal-state structure, with a division of national and subnational governments comparable to that found in Canada and the United States. As a consequence, DB was accountable to a parliament where regional interests and issues played a much more important role during the years when the passenger train's decline was first being noted. For example, the Bundesrat, Germany's upper chamber, is organized around regional representation, with officials from the Länder serving as legislators. This meant that operations and budgets were open to greater influence by political representatives who were more interested in spreading resources and service regionally than concentrating them into a few commercially promising market opportunities. In administrative and operational terms, Germany's institutional structure made DB into much more of a regional railway—indisposed to focus its efforts on introducing new service for even the most promising corridor, if such development came at the expense of other operations.

As such, the renewal strategy that DB developed represented a less decisive break with past practices and services. Instead of proposing an entirely new high-speed line for the ICE train, DB planned to build two segments of new infrastructure that would run from Hannover to Würzburg in northern Germany and between Mannheim and Stuttgart in southern Germany. Even these new high-speed infrastructure investments needed to be regionally balanced. ICE trains would serve many other cities by traveling over upgraded and enhanced existing infrastructure. This allowed the ICE to cover much more of western Germany at the time of its inauguration than the TGV had done in France. While rail's new mobility benefits were thus distributed more widely in Germany, they were also spread more thinly there, since the ICE's top speed was limited to 174 miles per hour compared to the TGV's 186 miles per hour, and the typical ICE trip would include more travel at even lower speeds.

Geography and topography also made German high-speed rail more costly to implement than it had been in France. Travel was less concentrated around a single hub, with the Ile de France having no German counterpart. This required trains to serve more destinations, through either making additional stops or adding additional frequencies. Both options resulted in higher operating costs compared to the intense concentration of travel between the single city-pair of Paris and Lyon. As well, the terrain traversed between cities like Munich and Frankfurt was much more hilly, requiring more expensive infrastructure. The sustainability proponents within Germany's rail policy community also demanded, and won, costly measures to reduce the ICE's environmental impact. These included tunnels and sound barriers that had not been part of the original French or Japanese high-speed rail infrastructures.

Decentralization and diversity in the German rail policy community thus translated into higher costs for passenger train renewal. Resources had to be spread more widely in geographic terms, as well as shared more broadly with environmentalists who demanded mitigation measures as the price of their support. The resulting policy-network dynamic among rail supporters could be characterized as "constrained corporatism," where the government shared its power with rail managers to develop and implement a renewal strategy, but only to the extent that regional representatives and sustainability proponents could be satisfied. Germany's experience illustrates how a more diverse coalition of rail supporters could constrain the launch of a successful renewal initiative, compared to the more focused and exclusive policy community that worked to improve passenger rail's fortunes in Japan and France. That the German system required additional time and money was reflected in the ICE train's relatively late debut on May 29, 1991.[46]

The ICE project represented only a partial reinvention of the passenger train, compared to either Japanese and French high-speed services, because of its more limited infrastructure development and the trade-off between wider coverage and use of more conventional tracks at lower speeds. It was a product of greater political compromise, seeking to obtain widespread regional support in a federal parliament as well as accommodate environmental and NIMBY criticisms and demands for impact-mitigation measures (primarily against noise). It thus could not trigger a full-scale reorganization of Germany's venerable rail enterprise on its own, but the fall of the Berlin Wall and reunification led to such restructuring shortly after the ICE train's debut. What ICE did was to place a somewhat modest growth opportunity on the agenda

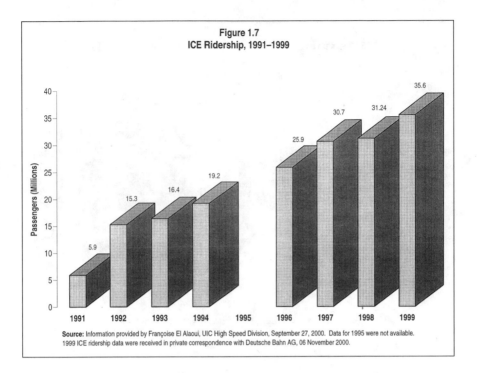

Figure 1.7
ICE Ridership, 1991–1999

Passengers (Millions)

| | 1991 | 1992 | 1993 | 1994 | 1995 | 1996 | 1997 | 1998 | 1999 |
| 5.9 | 15.3 | 16.4 | 19.2 | | 25.9 | 30.7 | 31.24 | 35.6 |

Source: Information provided by Françoise El Alaoui, UIC High Speed Division, September 27, 2000. Data for 1995 were not available. 1999 ICE ridership data were received in private correspondence with Deutsche Bahn AG, 06 November 2000.

of managers and policy makers who were deciding what to do about the future of a unified Germany's rail system. In so doing, the ICE provided evidence for the passenger train's future potential in Germany at a most opportune time.

It should come as no surprise to see that the ICE has produced some commercial success, but less than in France or Japan. Figure 1.7 illustrates the relatively steady growth of ICE patronage since its introduction, from 5.9 million in 1991 to 35.6 million in 1999.

Figure 1.8 shows that the ICE accounts for a relatively modest share of the German railway's passenger business, and that this share has leveled off at just above 2 percent in recent years. And in figure 1.9, the ICE's share of total rail travel by distance also appears to be holding steady at around 15 percent. This is much more modest than France, where close to four-fifths of the distance traveled by rail is aboard a TGV, or Japan, where that percentage is just below 30 percent.

The ICE's performance to date offers evidence that there is an alternative to the "all-or-nothing" debate about options for renewing the passenger train that participants in a rail policy community can get locked into, and which has yielded very little in the way of productive outcomes in North America. Ger-

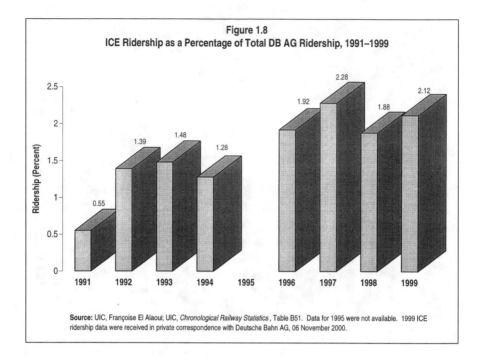

Figure 1.8
ICE Ridership as a Percentage of Total DB AG Ridership, 1991–1999

Source: UIC, Françoise El Alaoui; UIC, *Chronological Railway Statistics*, Table B51. Data for 1995 were not available. 1999 ICE ridership data were received in private correspondence with Deutsche Bahn AG, 06 November 2000.

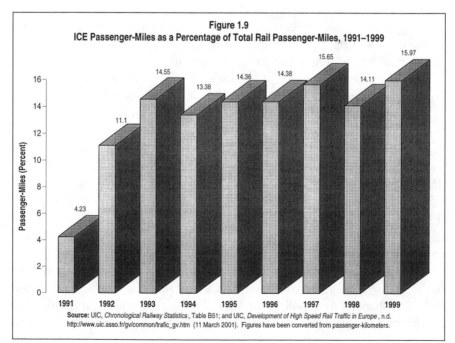

Figure 1.9
ICE Passenger-Miles as a Percentage of Total Rail Passenger-Miles, 1991–1999

Source: UIC, *Chronological Railway Statistics*, Table B51; and UIC, *Development of High Speed Rail Traffic in Europe*, n.d.
http://www.uic.asso.fr/gv/common/trafic_gv.htm (11 March 2001). Figures have been converted from passenger-kilometers.

many pursued the ICE option as part of an incremental approach to modernizing its traditional rail carrier. And while the ICE did not solve all of the DB's problems, it does complement further attempts at reorganization and refinancing that are discussed in chapter 2. It also enabled Germany to gain some mobility benefits from rail during the course of an even more ambitious, and ultimately unsuccessful, initiative to deploy magnetically levitated transportation domestically.

While the ICE was being created, a second policy community became engaged in considering what to do regarding Germany's intercity transportation options. It was comprised of participants who normally focused on science and technology issues and who were attracted to the passenger train's problem as providing an opportunity for a high-tech, higher-speed alternative to intercity rail—the magnetically levitated Transrapid vehicle. Within German government, the Federal Ministry of Research and Technology (BMFT) viewed magnetic-levitation technology as key to a "sunrise" industry—an opportunity for strategic economic development that could position Germany to be the leading exporter of maglev infrastructure and vehicles.

But to achieve export success, the maglev needed to become proven, as opposed to experimental, technology. That was where the link between this sunrise sector and the DB's potential "sunset" as an intercity passenger carrier came about. BMFT commissioned a study that identified the need for, and advantages of, introducing a high-speed rail network powered by magnetic levitation, that would operate independently of conventional passenger trains.[47] From this point on, Germany's maglev policy community focused on their technology as a solution to the rail mode's commercial problems. That solution would come not by renewing existing passenger trains from within, but by substituting new technology and infrastructure in their place.

Joining the BMFT in the maglev policy community were Messerchmitt Bolkow Blohm (MBB), Krauss-Maffei (KM), Thyssen-Henschel (TH), and the Technical University of Braunschweig, which had formed "Transrapid EMS" to develop and commercialize the technology into a working transport mode. In 1974, the Transrapid consortium was formed, and it began to receive BMFT funding in 1975. A long, protracted, and inconclusive process of both technical and policy development ensued, with periodic efforts to introduce maglev as a solution to changing German domestic transportation needs. These ranged from renewal of the DB to integration of the former East Germany, which suffered from poor transport links with the West.

Decisions made early on created a path-dependence that made the

Transrapid a tough sell at home. For example, opting for a lower-cost repulsive-magnet propulsion system precluded the integration of the maglev into existing rail infrastructure, in the way that the TGV or ICE could serve many markets by combining trips over new high-speed infrastructure with ordinary tracks. The maglev's need for entirely new infrastructure created a "zero sum" dynamic between Transrapid and conventional rail renewal. In some cases, rail skeptics were even more skeptical of the much higher cost of maglev, which was seen to be subsidizing the commercialization of future exports. In most cases, rail supporters pointed out how proven technology and existing products could meet German mobility needs at lower cost, and lower risk.

The dynamics of this maglev policy community can be described as clientele pluralism. The pluralist component refers to the much more fluid participation of organizations in this community. Potential supporters, as well as skeptics, both joined and left the ongoing deliberations regarding maglev depending on what route or market the technology was being considered for, and what terms of implementation and operation were proposed. At one time, for example, Lufthansa was involved as a prospective operator, while later on the DB came forward to fill this role. The clientelist component acknowledges the fact that the core participation in the community arose from BMFT's subsidization of research and development activities carried out by the Transrapid consortium.

While these organizations were certainly motivated by long-term rewards of commercialization and export, they were also focused on the short term grants for development and promotion of the maglev option. Atkinson and Coleman have pointed out that in a clientele pluralist policy network the state has no overarching goals "short of the prosperity of the sector itself."[48] Since clients interact with the state on maintaining their immediate benefits, such a network can go only so far in terms of industrial innovation.

The Transrapid consortium, plus its allies in the policy community, turned out to have the scientific skills and knowledge to advance research in this area, but they lacked the commercial savoir faire to succeed in its deployment. The former was within the purview of their policy community, but the latter required reaching a workable accommodation with the rail policy community, which proved impossible. Rail skeptics turned out largely to be maglev skeptics too. After some flirtation by Lufthansa, rail's contenders did not embrace maglev as an alternative to their current competition with the mode. Rail supporters, whether advocates or proponents, turned into skeptics on the maglev mode because it appeared to offer few benefits to them, and many costs. By the early 1990s, the maglev's technical readiness was no longer in doubt. It worked well enough on a test track, but its commercial potential remained unproven and awaiting deployment.

In the face of such an impasse, government reasserted its leadership by trying to reconcile the maglev and rail policy communites, in an effort to move the Transrapid off the drawing board. Policy scholars have termed such policy network dynamics "concertation." This required some restructuring of the state's participation in maglev and rail policy communities to harmonize support from advocates and proponents. This was accomplished by moving the BMFT minister, Mathias Wissman, to the transport portfolio where he was able to get that department "on side" for a proposed Transrapid line that would speed between Berlin and Hamburg in just fifty-eight minutes. Wissman touted the Transrapid as a key part of Germany's contribution to the "technology of the future" in March of 1996, when the Kohl government formally approved this deployment.[49]

This project was to be implemented through a public-private partnership between the Transrapid consortium, now known as Magnetschnellbahn-Planungsgesellschaft (MPG) and consisting of Deutsche Bahn; Adtranz, a joint venture of Daimler-Benz and ABB; Siemens; and Thyssen Industrie. The German government had committed DM 6.1 billion, with private investors to pick up any additional costs. At the time, consortium partners were expected to put in some equity, while commercial banks could also provide loans. But raising these additional funds from the private sector proved to be far more difficult than anticipated, and eventually became the project's undoing. Both economic and political problems added to the Transrapid's troubles.

On the economic side, MPG consortium members experienced changes in their business position that downgraded the Transrapid project's priority. In 1998, it was reported that "Thyssen's merger with Krupp relegated railway technology to a lower-priority division, Siemens railway section has been fighting losses for years and Adtranz's recent joint venture with Daimler and ABB has resulted in major losses."[50] The MPG's equity investment in the Berlin–Hamburg project thus never materialized. Then, after further analysis, the Deutsche Bahn revised ridership estimates for the new mode from 14 million per year down to between 9 million and 6.28 million per year, due to Berlin's slower than anticipated growth in employment.[51] And with no rush of private investors, it became clear that the government's DM 6.1 billion commitment had been underestimated. According to Franz Muentefering, Wissman's successor as transport minister: "[Transrapid c]osts were estimated to be at around 7.5 to 7.8 billion DM in 1995. Then it was said that one could somehow do it with 6.1 billion. But it was never realistically calculated."[52]

But if the risk tolerance of private partners, cost estimates, and calculations surrounding Transrapid's future traffic had all changed for the worse following the project's formal approval, then the level of political support to accommodate such challenges had deteriorated even more significantly. Germany's center-right Christian Democrats, who had been in government when the Transrapid project was approved in 1996, were defeated in 1998. They were replaced by a "Red-Green" coalition between the leftist Social Democrats and the ecologically dedicated Green Party. The Greens, in particular, had never accepted the need for the Transrapid project, claiming that the Berlin–Hamburg deployment would destroy thousands of homes in its path and then consume as much electricity as a city of 250,000.[53]

When the Greens and the Social Democrats hammered out their coalition agreement entitled "Departure and Renewal—Germany's Way into the 21st Century" in early October 1998, the Transrapid's departure was seriously affected. For the agreement specified that the federal government could not invest a pfennig more than the DM 6.1 billion that had been agreed to previously. Proposals to obtain additional public funds from the European Union[54] and loan guarantees from some Länder (state governments) where the MPG consortium had a large presence[55] were initiated in 1999 but led nowhere. This prompted Transport Minister Muentefering to call for scaling Transrapid's infrastructure back to a single track, which would reduce the line's capacity by up to 40 percent.[56]

Germany's environment minister, Jurgen Trittin, who belonged to the Green Party and was temporarily holding the transport portfolio during a cabinet shuffle, characterized his colleague's increasingly desperate attempts to keep the Transrapid on track by telling reporters that the project was a "long-running tragedy, which is now turning into a farce."[57] The MPG consortium began to crack under these combined economic and political pressures in October 1999, with the head of DaimlerChrysler's Adtranz unit, which was to build the Transrapid's vehicles, publicly announcing, "We are at the end, the project has no future under the circumstances at the moment and we should all admit it."[58] It took more than a year longer for the project to be formally scrapped, in part because both the government and its partners were intent on the penalties that could be claimed through the cancellation clauses in the original agreement. The MPG consortium announced that it was formally ending its development efforts on January 28, 2000, with Thyssen-Krupp intending to seek compensation of DM 160 million for the project's costs to date.[59]

Taken together, what do Germany's two tales of high speed ground transportation reveal about the role of policy in aligning ideas and interests with opportunities for the passenger train's future? Because Germany's two policy communities that focused on the passenger train adopted different, and not always compatible, approaches, policy options never came to include the kind of unqualified support for a dramatic reinvention of the rail mode from within, along the lines of either Japanese or French experience. Instead, policy communities and policy options tended toward either more- or less-ambitious approaches to innovation. The Transrapid option presented a clean break with the railroad's organizational and technological heritage, while the ICE train relied upon a high speed rail concept that was incremental to its core. Such dualism has yielded more intense debates about what to do regarding rail passenger redevelopment, more limited gains in the resulting performance, and more "equal" distribution of the advances that did occur. All of these attributes exist in North America's ongoing efforts to find a solution to its passenger train problem, yet none of them have shown even a fraction of the success of Germany's relatively limited achievements to date.

But before analyzing the causes of the policy stalemate that has constrained rail passenger renewal in North America, it is worth considering just how far ahead the policy options have moved elsewhere. Chapter 2 explores the more systematic reorganization of finance, management, and, in some cases, ownership that followed the initial accomplishments of the Shinkansen, TGV, and ICE. Once passenger rail had proven that it had a future in Europe, organizational and institutional changes have been put in place to maximize that potential. This stands in sharp contrast to the organizational changes introduced in North America before the passenger train had demonstrated much hope of commercial success, a contrast that is worth keeping in mind as one reviews the travails of Amtrak and VIA Rail in chapter 3. Chapter 4 examines the key attempts made to bypass the policy stalemate surrounding Amtrak and VIA by launching independent high-speed passenger train initiatives, none of which succeeded. Chapter 5 considers the recent attempt to "reinvent" Amtrak in pursuit of a legal mandate to attain commercial self-sufficiency by 2003. Once the policy gap that has hampered each of these initiatives has been fully explored, chapter 6 offers some suggestions on how to switch North American passenger rail policy onto a more productive track.

Chapter 2

Building on Achievement

A "New Model Railroad" for the Twenty-First Century

The rail passenger modernization achievements highlighted in chapter 1, dating from the mid 1960s in Japan, the early 1980s in France, and the early 1990s in Germany, have shown that technological determinists were wrong. In different geographic, economic, and social settings—with different policy communities and political dynamics—passenger trains could be either invented or reinvented to serve a useful purpose and in so doing attain commercial success. The accomplishments of projects like the Shinkansen, TGV, and ICE have raised the bar for all passenger railroads, including the ones pioneering these innovations.

Skeptics often argue that the geographic, economic, and even social and political circumstances must confine these rail renewal success stories to Europe and Japan. The litany of ostensibly unique attributes that make the Shinkansen's or TGV's performance exceptional is long and, at first, impressive. Some European and Japanese cities are more populous, more densely settled, and situated more closely together than many of their North American counterparts. Their gasoline costs double and triple the North American pump price, with a much larger share of that price claimed by various excise taxes. And governments across a range of political ideologies have been more open to active "industrial policy" initiatives entailing economic regulation, public enterprise, and public finance of economic activity. Among other consequences, these policies have led to extensive public investment in, and ownership of, rail and urban transit infrastructure. As much as these attributes may contribute to the sustainable prosperity of Europe and Japan, skeptics dismiss the policy options behind them as being "dead on arrival" in North America. But even accepting, for the moment, that some of these differences

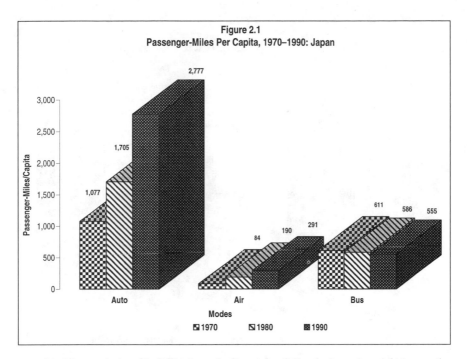

Figure 2.1
Passenger-Miles Per Capita, 1970–1990: Japan

are significant, it is still difficult to believe that North Americans have nothing to learn from rail passenger renewal successes abroad.

If that were the case, the gulf between characteristics that make the passenger train such an integral part of the economic and social fabric in Europe and Japan and those operating to marginalize the train's potential within North America would have to be so great that it would certainly affect other modes as well. The same conditions that supposedly privilege train travel in Europe and Japan would, presumably, show themselves in constraining these regions' demand for travel by road and air. Yet there is little evidence to support the claim that European and Japanese patterns of growth in road and air mobility are structurally different from those found in North America.[1]

Figure 2.1 shows the average per capita distance traveled by air, road, and bus in Japan in 1970, 1980, and 1990. Note the 158 percent increase in travel by autos as well as the 246 percent increase in air travel over these two decades. During the same period, figure 2.2 shows that travel by Japan's publicly supported railway organizations (JNR and its successors) dipped between 1970 and 1980, but then rebounded to post a 6 percent increase in passenger-miles traveled by 1990. Privately owned railroads, providing mostly regional and commuter services, recorded more consistent growth, with a 28 percent overall increase in passenger-miles over two decades. Only the bus mode experi-

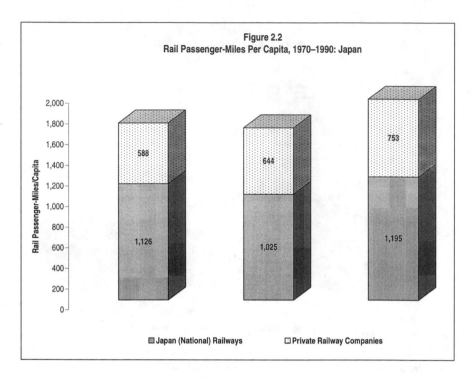

Figure 2.2
Rail Passenger-Miles Per Capita, 1970–1990: Japan

enced a decline in travel, dropping 9 percent over the two decades. In Europe, the pattern was similar.

Figure 2.3 illustrates a 90 percent growth in the average annual distance that Europeans traveled by auto between 1970 and 1990. Air travel increased even more sharply, by 344 percent, during this period. Yet as shown in figure 2.4, the distance traveled by rail grew by 18 percent. Although European data do not differentiate between intercity and regional or commuter rail travel, the nearly identical 17 percent increase in travel by tram and metro suggest that intercity and regional/commuter rail travel were growing at a very similar rate. As in Japan, the expansion of air and auto mobility did not equate with a "zero sum" decline in rail mobility.

The United States data illustrated in figure 2.5 reflect these same global trends of mobility, with the annual distance traveled growing 38 percent for auto and 150 percent for air. But the trend for intercity passenger trains shown in figure 2.6, showing a 17 percent decline in average distance traveled between 1970 and 1990, runs in the opposite direction. Even the distance Americans traveled by commuter rail saw a 234 percent jump between 1970 and 1980.

Taken together, these data suggest that the so-called fundamental differences in transportation demand between North America and the rest of the

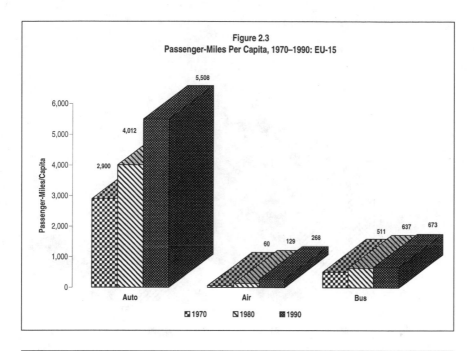

Figure 2.3
Passenger-Miles Per Capita, 1970–1990: EU-15

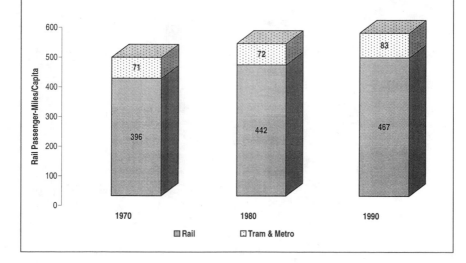

Figure 2.4
Rail Passenger-Miles Per Capita, 1970–1990: EU-15

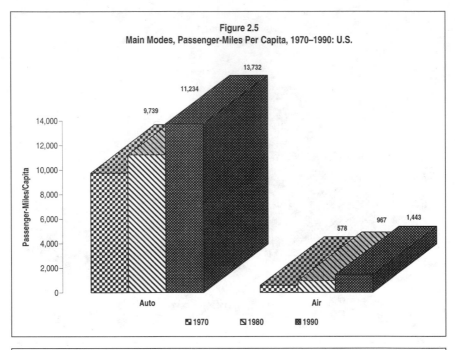

Figure 2.5
Main Modes, Passenger-Miles Per Capita, 1970–1990: U.S.

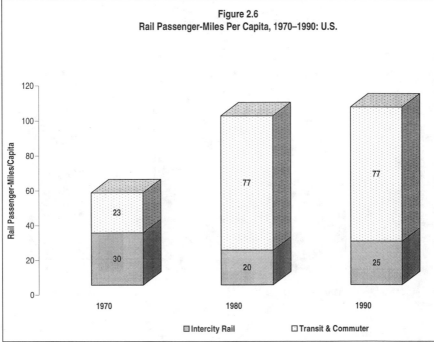

Figure 2.6
Rail Passenger-Miles Per Capita, 1970–1990: U.S.

world to which rail skeptics often point may not be so fundamental after all. What does appear to be occurring is an evolution of transportation systems in which the affluent, developed nations of the world are translating mobility options that were initially embraced in North America into "foreign" economic and geographic circumstances, but not the other way around. Data on personal travel reflect the results of European and Japanese efforts to adapt their passenger trains to complement the growing importance of air and auto mobility, while North America is confirmed as an outlier where the gap between rail travel and other modes has grown increasingly wider. This chapter explores the policy frameworks and perspectives behind rail passenger reinvention because they appear to be the most significant characteristics that do differentiate the twenty-first century's "new model railroads," found outside North America, from their counterparts that are struggling to survive on this continent.

2.1. Understanding the "New Model Railroad"

Ever since the New Tokaido Shinkansen's spectacular demonstration that modern passenger trains could attract large travel volumes and make money, some public officials, passengers, and even rail executives began to question why such success could not become the rule, rather than the exception. Such speculation usually led to questioning whether a railroad that combined the structure of a public monopoly with the function of a bureaucracy could effectively grasp the opportunities for commercial success. Not surprisingly, the answers that emerged reflected much about the political disposition of policy actors, as well as the criteria for commercial success in passenger railroading.

Some governments were ideologically disposed to see public enterprise as inherently problematic and thus became enthusiastic proponents of privatization. Beginning in Britain under Lady Thatcher during the 1980s, but spreading to less-extreme political leadership during the 1990s, governments around the world began to sell off utilities, airlines, and public infrastructure. Other governments were more reluctant privatizers, motivated by fiscal imperatives. They were simply strapped for cash. An economic downturn in the early 1990s and a growing consensus among global investors that public deficits were unacceptable left few governments in a position to pour subsidies into money-losing public enterprises. Government funding was reserved for core public services like health, education, and welfare. Governments thus sought to sell loss-making enterprises off outright, or pursued restructuring that would make them more "businesslike."

Because railways were often targeted for privatization after governments had some experience with selling off other public enterprises, the cumulative effect of this industrial transformation did not become apparent until well into the 1990s. But by the turn of the century, it became clear that a reform movement was sweeping the world's passenger rail operators, with significant changes in the way rail passenger carriers did business everywhere outside North America. In Japan, Europe, Africa, Latin America, and Australia, the railroads that ran passenger trains looked very different at the end of the 1990s than they did at the decade's beginning. Explaining, analyzing, and comparing these many corporate transformations would justify a book of its own, one that certainly deserves to be written. But given the costs of the ongoing stalemate over Amtrak's and VIA Rail's legitimacy during the 1990s, there is a more urgent need to understand the implications of this global change for North American rail passenger policy. Thus, before the definitive assessment of global rail passenger restructuring emerges, this chapter will offer an overview of how some key characteristics of these organizational transformations have affected passenger train performance, both for better and for worse.

James A. Dunn Jr. and I have identified a set of idealized characteristics from among the world's rail passenger commercialization and privatization initiatives and labeled them the "New Model Railroad" or NMR.[2] A good way to begin understanding what the NMR is all about is to identify the financial and organizational shortcomings of business as usual in public passenger railroading that it was designed to improve upon. The NMR was intended to replace the venerable Regulated Public Monopoly (RPM) model of rail passenger organization, which had become the late-twentieth-century norm in Europe and Japan. The RPM model appeared to have outlived its usefulness, as evidenced by a number of persistent and significant problems that contributed to the passenger train's failings as a transport mode.

RPMs were seen as too bureaucratic, possessing a rigid hierarchy of decision making that left little room for innovation and entrepreneurship in a transportation sector that was increasingly characterized by such attributes. With virtually all modes of transportation deregulated in Europe during the 1990s, and with even the tightly controlled Japanese domestic air sector opening up to new competition and carriers in the 1990s, passenger trains were seen to be increasingly disadvantaged by remaining under the control of bureaucrats rather than entrepreneurs.[3] But the traditional public passenger carrier suffered from more than indifferent, and perhaps mediocre, management.

RPM workforces also appeared unproductive in comparison with their counterparts at air and bus carriers. Rail labor unions had negotiated

longstanding work rules that were out of sync with both the productive pos-
sibilities of modern rail technology and the working arrangements of employees at competing carriers in other modes. Labor relations at RPMs tended
to be adversarial, with unions and management treating contract negotiations as a zero-sum bargaining exercise, rather than an opportunity to innovate and achieve mutual gains. Labor unrest was traditional, with strikes
and work actions leading to operational interruptions, service unreliability,
and lost revenues.

Partly because of their managerial and workforce constraints noted above,
and partly because of their industrial heritage as the first mode of motorized
mass transportation, RPMs had become mired in a "take-it-or-leave-it" marketing mentality that presumed their customers had no alternative. In fact,
nothing could be further from the case. Faced with real constraints on what
could be demanded of workers, rail management expected that passengers would
adapt themselves to make the most of service offerings rather than seeking
other mobility options that were organized around meeting the customer's immediate needs. This turned out to be an almost universally false hope.

RPMs were seen as dependent upon political patrons of one sort or another for protection from both commercial and democratic accountability.
When losses sent signals that customers were not satisfied with business as
usual, political patrons would allocate subsidies to the RPM. And when public protests at railroad inadequacies and failings emerged, RPMs would hide
behind their patrons and avoid dealing with the criticism. Conversely, whatever needs the patron identified as priorities would jump to the top of the
RPM's agenda—often at the expense of other services.

The overall legitimacy of RPMs was thus seen to be murky and suspect.
The cost of inefficiency and incompetence was often hidden behind byzantine
financial accounting. Even claims of commercial success like those made for
the TGV were tainted by the perception that public subsidies supporting one
part of an organization were somehow being funneled into other parts of the
enterprise. Lacking the market discipline of a private firm and the freedom of
information required of public bureaucracy, RPMs were viewed as suffering
from the worst organizational attributes of both the private and public sectors. The RPM was thus an organization with few defenders during the 1990s.

The NMR grew out of diverse efforts to break away from the RPM's
increasingly problematic tendencies by changing organizational focus in three
fundamental ways. First, rail management would change its approach and
build a new capacity to act, to take account of the market signals that customers and investors had been sending. Such efforts would seek to emulate the

agile corporate behavior found elsewhere in the transportation market. The test of this new capacity would be an ability to build a market presence in the way that Shinkansen, TGV, and ICE initiatives had demonstrated could be done.

In redefining their function from running a "political railroad" to managing a competitive transportation business, rail passenger executives would position themselves to "join the club" of private executives who forged corporate alliances, pursued acquisitions, and built partnerships. Passenger rail would thus be far better positioned to integrate into corporate alliances that increasingly shape the transportation sector—such as frequent-traveler reward schemes, computerized reservation systems, and co-branding—than if it was run along the bureaucratic lines of a RPM. This same commercial orientation, coupled with private ownership, would enable the development of ancillary assets, such as real estate adjoining stations and rights-of-way, which could generate revenues that remained untapped by the RPM.

Second, this transformation was intended to change the terms of employment in and around passenger trains. Following the initial trauma of losing the security and status that had come with RPM employment, rail labor was expected to view future job security and worker prosperity as dependent upon satisfying customers and adding value to society's mobility options. Workers would have to break the habit of seeing their future as being determined solely by contracts and legislation and look to their customers (and potential customers) as a source of opportunity. The test of this new outlook would be a convergence with the pay, productivity, and industrial relations stability found among competing transport enterprises in other modes.

Third, government would relate to passenger rail not as a "money pit" to be either avoided or exploited for political motives, but as an engine of growth akin to other transport modes. Under the NMR, public officials would be in a position to invest selectively and productively in rail passenger infrastructure that generated real social and economic benefits, rather than being tempted to continue the tradition of delivering patronage funding to "boondoggle" projects for favored constituents or influential interests. The test of the passenger train's new political credibility would be public investment in rail infrastructure on par with the scale and scope of fiscal support for air and road modes.

Paradoxically, public officials often find it easier to support private enterprises than they do to assist public enterprises—especially those with a commercial mandate. Tax breaks, public purchasing, and other forms of assistance are justified by the jobs that private firms like the NMR create, which are valued more highly than the public-sector positions in an RPM. In the transportation sector, governments usually make terminal facilities and, often, line haul infrastructure available to private carriers at cost. Airports and air traffic control facilities typify this form of infrastructure support for aviation, while the U.S. interstate highway system exemplifies the model for road transportation.

While the NMR's full range and variation of accomplishments in renewing passenger rail service will become more clear over time, there are already lessons to be learned from its adoption in various countries. Some of the most valuable of these concern what it takes to launch organizational transformation and the characteristics of new policy instruments that have been adopted to meet NMR goals and objectives. The choice of policy instruments adopted during this transformation has already made a difference in the distribution of costs and benefits arising from NMR operations. As in other transportation modes, and in industrial sectors more generally, it turns out that there is more than one way to woo customers and win revenues. Different trajectories of transformation from the RPM to the NMR appear to yield different tools for entrepreneurial rail managers to pursue success.

One key question to consider in the emergence of the NMR is who leads this exercise, and who follows that lead? Another question is whether the transformation retains a definition or vision of the "public interest" that orients the railroad's application of competitive techniques and technology, or whether commercial success is embraced as the end in itself. The following three sections offer evidence of different leadership modes, as well as different definitions of success.

By drawing from European experience, which most closely approximates the North American challenge of reversing declining market share and restoring commercial viability, one can identify three approaches to the reform of rail passenger management leading to the NMR. They are differentiated by the relationship between changes in rail technology and changes in administrative and organizational technique. Among European rail restructuring initiatives, those in France, Germany, and Britain provide clear examples of the three basic configurations of technology and technique that have guided transformation efforts. Each of these transformations will be examined in turn, in order to show how the differing leadership modes and policy instruments used to pursue NMR objectives originated in each railroad's distinctive mix of technology and technique.

2.2. French Rail Restructuring: Using New Technology to Set the Stage for Organizational Change

France exemplifies the technology-leading approach to rail passenger reorganization. Here, the SNCF transcended its business as usual RPM activities to launch a rail passenger renewal plan originating from in-house technical innovation. The TGV project's new application of technology to the mobility needs of a major French travel market succeeded in transforming the rail mode's competitive profile in a very public fashion. Given a "winning" set of technical attributes (e.g., two-hour travel time between Paris and Lyon), the TGV went on to establish a profitable set of organizational techniques—including a yield-management computerized reservations system, partnerships with airlines and auto rental companies, and co-branding that translated ridership gains into significant profits. Overall, the TGV project demonstrated that the right kinds of technical application could reverse rail's declining market share while simultaneously enhancing its commercial viability.

Without new managerial techniques at SNCF, the technology that made the TGV an effective competitor would not have been utilized to full effect. These techniques flowed out of a more entrepreneurial business model and more productive working arrangements that were grafted onto an existing RPM. Such commercial innovation was legitimated in a public-enterprise setting through two rationales.

First, organizational change was promoted as part of a proactive expansion of the RPM's public service mandate. Like the new TGV equipment and infrastructure, new roles for management and staff were presented as a means to modernize, and thus improve upon, the function of France's national railroad, not to undermine it. Second, this modernization initiative was not structured as a zero-sum transformation of existing arrangements. SNCF would continue to operate traditional intercity passenger trains wherever they were not replaced by TGVs. Without the threat of service abandonment, contract nullification, or workforce reduction, employees saw less to lose from implementing innovation. New techniques ranged from yield-management pricing, as discussed in chapter 1, to streamlined work rules that made staff associated with new train service more productive.

The TGV's undeniable success yielded benefits to all involved with the rail enterprise, creating a solid foundation for further transformation. Staff saw new and better jobs as being linked to growth in business. TGV passengers appreciated the higher quality of mobility that was created, often enabling new travel options, such as same-day trips between Paris and cities like

Lyon, Nantes, and Bordeaux that had been beyond the reach of many passengers. And local governments and businesses in regions served by the TGV saw economic development spin-offs from the train's improved performance. The TGV's success as a project positioned the SNCF to retain leadership of a much more ambitious program of rail renewal. Faced with widespread demand to distribute the benefits of TGV service throughout France, the SNCF built the TGV project into a transportation program of national significance, akin to autoroutes, urban transit, and airport development.

SNCF retained leadership of transforming the TGV from a project into a program by making the case that it possessed a unique technical capacity that had been validated by the TGV's success. It bolstered that case by demonstrating an ability to generate political credit for the TGV's achievements, which could benefit government while generating external economic benefits for industry and regions. The SNCF's ethos of commercial innovation thus remained the guiding paradigm for France's rail renewal program. New infrastructure and equipment were used as the keys to unlock the organizational constraints on rail passenger renewal. Policy instruments connected to infrastructure finance and industrial and trade policy for the manufacturing sector that produced the various components of the TGV system were thus all a part of the French NMR. Together, they were used to redefine the relationship between a public rail enterprise and the state.

As a public enterprise enjoying commercial success, SNCF was able to integrate "public interest" objectives into its renewal strategy, so that modernizing rail mobility could achieve more than just making money. These goals included environmental protection, energy autonomy, shaping urban and regional land use, and advancing social equity through targeted subsidies for travel by seniors, students, veterans and large families. New management techniques were viewed as means to these ends, and to supporting the successful deployment of TGV equipment and infrastructure. Organizational renewal thus flowed from technical renewal.

SNCF's TGV program further fueled public expectations, and hence pressure on French politicians, to both expand the scope of this service, and to upgrade the performance of other rail services to match the quality, if not the speed, of the TGV. The RPM business model looked increasingly threadbare to passengers and potential passengers who were left to make do with SNCF's conventional services. Public protests of a "two-speed" SNCF exemplify the way in which high-speed technology became identified with organizational reform and came to define the development of an NMR in France. These attributes marked the first stage of France's transition to an NMR.

They were domestically derived, but were then overlaid by a second, international dimension of rail reorganization that originated at the European level.

France's domestic political engagement in reinventing its passenger railroad preceded, and thus shaped, the implementation of another major policy instrument that was introduced to deal with European Union (EU) Directive 91/440, which ordered the separation of rail operations from infrastructure.[4] Such separation was viewed as a means to open railroad access to competitive carriers. More or less open access to tracks thus became an attribute of the European NMR that was imposed from above. Its application has differed widely—depending largely on the leadership and policy instruments that were brought together in national efforts to modernize the RPM.

France accommodated EU 91/440 by launching a second phase of rail reorganization, one that sought to channel the public enterprise component of renewal into an agency responsible for infrastructure, while enabling the SNCF to experiment with increasing degrees of commercial freedom. A new public corporation, Réseau Ferré de France (RFF), was created by the law of February 13, 1997.[5] Structured as an "Établissement Public Industriel et Commercial," RFF gained the mandate to own, manage, and finance the rail infrastructure that had been an integral part of SNCF. RFF works closely with France's national rail carrier, which is both RFF's biggest supplier of maintenance services and expertise and its biggest rail access customer. Most importantly, RFF services a debt of 134.2 billion francs (approximately US$18.4 billion) that was accumulated by the SNCF in prior years.

To date, RFF has obtained a "AAA" rating from three major credit bureaus: Moody's, Standard & Poor's, and Fitch/IBCA. This favorable credit rating rests largely on the strength of the French government's commitment to rail infrastructure as a public asset. Moody's characterized RFF's institutional framework as "an instrument for performing a public service mission" that "enjoys very strong support from the state." According to Moody's, "RFF is more like a financing vehicle bearing a public service debt than an operational entity," one that "is unlikely to ever lose its monopoly." Moody's assertion stems from their belief that institutional constraints would be unable to "challenge the state's ownership of the infrastructure."[6]

The French government's commitment of 37 billion francs to support RFF's infrastructure finance through 2001 bears out this assessment.[7] During 2001, RFF anticipates spending 9.5 billion francs on new infrastructure, of which 2.7 billion will come through negotiated subsidies from national and regional governments.[8]

The leading-edge technical capacity that SNCF had applied to renewing

French rail passenger prospects has thus been divided, but not diminished as a means of rail passenger renewal. RFF is applying this technical capacity to infrastructure modernization and development while SNCF is now focusing on perfecting its commercial and operational techniques. To conform to the EU directive, RFF is required to make its infrastructure available to alternative carriers, introducing the possibility of market competition within the rail mode. This potential contestability of the rail market would, in theory, provide SNCF with further incentives to implement the NMR's competitive business practices since other carriers could now enter the French rail market. Although such intramodal competition may yet blossom in freight or regional rail operations, the tight technical linkage between TGVs and their purpose-built infrastructure would certainly inhibit, and could easily preclude, having competition among high-speed trains, the most lucrative segment of the intercity rail market in France.

This second stage of transition to the NMR included public financial adjustments to facilitate both SNCF's and RFF's reorganization. For SNCF, public service contracts, a form of commercialization that predated the NMR initiative, have been decentralized to the regional governments which now act as collective "customers" in local rail mobility markets that are not self-supporting. This means that decision making about the scope and pricing of regional and commuter services is in the hands of officials who are regionally elected and accountable. Negotiations between SNCF and the regions are also improved by the potential for alternative carriers, such as urban transit operators or bus companies replacing SNCF as the operator and contracting for access with RFF at regional and local levels.

At the start of 2001, SNCF's president, Louis Gallois, told the financial reporters that he expected to turn a profit after years of losses. With such an accomplishment, France's NMR restructuring had come of age, enabling SNCF to link commercial success with public service in a business model where profit could become the norm. As Gallois put it, "I say we must make profits, it is the means of assuring our development and our future. . . . [W]e have such investment requirements ahead of us that we need to make profits to develop our capacity for self-financing. I also know there are business cycles, so we need a reserve. I try to tell SNCF that it is not shameful to make profits. On the contrary."[9]

While RFF will not be generating the kind of profits that SNCF has posted any time soon, economic productivity is also an integral part of the infrastructure provider's financial calculus. Where infrastructure investment is unlikely to be repaid from the access fees charged to SNCF, or other operators, both national and regional governments are expected to pay for the difference. According to RFF, the project share it funds "has to ensure sufficient return on investment so that its financial accounts will not suffer. Any variance between self-financing and the amount of the projects must be covered by external contributions (state subsidies, etc.)." However, RFF is not bound by a purely "financial rationale because investment choice continue [*sic*] to be public choices guided by economic and social efficiency criteria. It is the financing methods which are radically different, involving far more substantial public funds."[10]

France's rail reorganization has thus moved infrastructure financing much closer to the approach and public service criteria used for air and road investments. And while SNCF's recent profits have made headlines, it is RFF's new infrastructure policy that may well prove to be the most significant innovation in an already impressive string of accomplishments aimed at reinventing the train's place in French transportation.

2.3. German Rail Restructuring:
Balancing Technological and Organizational Change

German efforts to create an NMR have relied less on technical innovation and, in part as a consequence, placed a greater emphasis on new organizational and administrative initiatives. This balancing act has yielded significant organizational change, but has not yet demonstrated the extent of either successes or shortcomings found in France or the United Kingdom. One reason for these more equivocal results is that Germany's rail reorganization came to be led by government officials, with public enterprise executives taking on a supporting role. As a result, Germany's political tradition of accommodating geographically diffuse constituencies and disparate interests often tempered the commercial logic of emphasizing promising technology and profitable markets while exiting uneconomic operations. One recent report of the German NMR's mixed results to date linked commercial shortcomings to the political constraints on economic restructuring. Although many antiquated German industries had been refashioned or even abandoned during the 1990s, *The Financial Times* implied that old beliefs still lurked behind new organizations in the rail sector. Part of the problem facing Germany's NMR is that "Germans have unrealistic expectations for their railway system. They want it to be cheap, safe and punctual, and at no cost to the taxpayer."[11]

In the early 1990s, balancing high operational performance, commercial success, and public service appeared more realistic than it does after several years of reorganization efforts. Public officials embraced ambitious policy instruments that promised great results. The traditional understanding of a "public interest" could thus be reconciled with the dynamism of the market, at least in theory. These renewal efforts were also spurred by a particular event with a unique challenge, German reunification, and the need to come up with a policy for integrating an antiquated and commercially hopeless railway inherited from East Germany (the Deutsche Reichsbahn) into West Germany's railway, the Deutsche Bundesbahn (DB).

While technological innovation did set the stage for organizational reform in Germany, it was of a different kind than the French TGV breakthrough. As discussed in chapter 1, the ICE project grew out of an incremental strategy to renew German passenger trains. Its technical ambitions were bounded, on the one hand, by the prospective deployment of the higher-speed and higher-cost Transrapid magnetic-levitation "train," and by the political imperative to serve multiple regional travel markets within a federal political structure on the other. As a result, the ICE initiative relied on more limited innovations in both technology and technique, yielding a relatively modest departure from the existing RPM business model compared to France. This was evidenced by the smaller amount of new infrastructure that was built in Germany; by the fact that this new high-speed infrastructure was multipurpose, designed to be used by fast freight trains at night; and by the way in which the ICE was operated like other trains, both on and off its high-speed tracks.

This incremental approach did generate some commercial success, but not in the kind of dramatic commercial "triumph" that would have allowed DB's executives to take the lead away from politicians in the transition to a German NMR. Unlike the TGV, the ICE's development costs were much more visible than its commercial payoff. Expenses on ICE project development mounted during the late 1980s, at the same time that DB's operating losses were also climbing. Rather than waiting for this renewal initiative to turn the financial tide of red ink, the German government opted to create several external initiatives to review rail passenger policy.

A task force of ten "wise men" from industry, academia, and government was convened to study the railway's problems and recommend organizational and financial reforms to resolve the DB's long-term financial difficulties. Around the same time, an interministerial committee with representatives from the finance, economics, environment, land use and planning, and defense ministries looked into similar problems. In addition to these sector-specific committees on policy reform, a major report from the National

Deregulation Commission appeared in 1990 and called for far-reaching changes in the transport sector, including rail privatization and trucking deregulation.[12]

These initiatives expanded the, already broader, German rail policy community well beyond the French counterpart, where elites were the ones engaged with renewing passenger trains. Each of the three external reviews sought new ideas to address the financial dilemma facing DB. They thus brought in economists, planners, and public administrators to supplement the capacity of railway managers to design an industrial renewal strategy. Given this shift of expertise, from the specialized experience of railway staff to the broader—and more general—knowledge base that was created to address the rail problem, it is not surprising that questions of reorganization and new management techniques predominated in the search for solutions. During the early 1990s, the technical dimension of rail renewal was beyond both the competence and the confidence of many advisors working on Germany's railway problem.

The broad base of participation represented on these advisory bodies oriented their work toward revamping organization and techniques in rail passenger management. The scope for such change was vastly expanded by the chain of events that unfolded after the Berlin Wall fell and German unification became a reality. The need to modernize an even more antiquated RPM, the technologically obsolete and commercially bankrupt Deutsche Reichsbahn, changed the mode of rail renewal policy development from a corporatist network oriented toward incremental adjustment to a state-directed network that could compel fundamental structural transformation.

This particular break with past modes of policy development was part of a broader shift with traditional German policy making. Lehmbruch explains how the events of 1990 yielded a rupture of previous "semi-sovereign" West German policy network dynamics. He notes that the unification crisis brought about a "temporary breakdown of the quasi-'corporatist' linkage structure of the West German policy network . . . [as] the party system cut its communication channels to other corporate actors in the West German polity and assumed the position of an unconstrained sovereign decision-maker."[13] This change in the "rules of the game" in mid-game further undercut the corporatist alignment between DB and the transport ministry that had presided over an incremental renewal initiative like the ICE. When the DB and its supporters had accepted the creation of outside advisory groups, they were still operating under the old rules of policy making whereby the resulting findings would be addressed to, and by, the existing corporatist policy network. Rail policy community participants in general, and rail advocates in particular, did not get what they expected.

Instead, a state directed network left much room for skeptics and others to define "radical" restructuring as the solution to Germany's combined rail problems of unification and revitalization. An indication of how much would change in German rail policy development during the 1990s can be found in the degree of formal institutional transformation that became part of Germany's rail restructuring. In addition to amending Section Eighty-Seven of the German Constitution, over 30 federal laws and 150 federal regulations had to be enacted or modified.[14] In the first stage of this transformation, the law of December 27, 1993, the *Gesetz zur Neuordnung des Eisenbahnwesens*, merged the DB and DR into a single entity, the Federal Railway Authority (Bundeseisenbahn Vermögen), which would preside over radical restructuring.[15]

This organization was structured into two distinct divisions. Deutsche Bahn Aktiengesellschaft (DBAG) would combine all of the commercially viable (and potentially viable) activities of its predecessor RPMs, the Deutsche Bundesbahn and Deutsche Reichsbahn. These would include both freight and passenger operations, as well as their infrastructure. A second subsidiary, the Eisenbahn Bundesamt would assume responsibility for all of the noncommercial transition activities arising from rail integration. These would include the labor force transition mechanisms, liquidation of assets that were no longer needed, and payment of the past debts that had been accumulated by both DB and DR.

Once this first separation of the commercial from noncommercial rail restructuring activities was completed, a second stage of reorganization within the commercial side was begun. DBAG itself was turned into a holding company, under the same statutes that govern other private corporations in Germany. The DB holding company would preside over five subsidiaries. DB Reise & Touristik AG would be responsible for long distance intercity passenger trains, including ICE trains. DB Regio AG would handle short distance regional traffic, including commuter trains. DB Cargo AG would operate all freight trains and handle all freight traffic. DB Netz AG would be responsible for the ownership, construction, maintenance, and pricing for use of the track infrastructure. DB Station & Service AG would assume ownership, operation, and charging for the use of all railroad passenger stations. Both the subsidiaries and the parent company in this new DBAG family were supposed to begin acting as "market-conforming" companies immediately. In other words, they were supposed to focus on making money.

The rail reform laws creating these companies envisioned that any and each of them that had realized a profit for three years in a row could be opened up for private investment at some time after 2002. An exception was made for

DB Netz, the rail infrastructure company. Here, the government was precluded from selling any more than 49 percent of the equity in Germany's newly commercialized rail infrastructure.

As in France, responsibility for regional passenger services was passed from the national government down to local governments, in this case the sixteen Länder (or states) within the German federation. There were financial mechanisms built into this restructuring that enabled the German government to support the transition from RPM to NMR activities. Government would make payments to the holding company to compensate it for the lag in productivity created from the rapid integration of DR into a single operating entity. Capital funding would also be provided to upgrade the obsolete aspects of DR's infrastructure and equipment into conformity with the DBAG's current technical standards.

Germany's rail renewal is very much a work in progress. New technology embodied in the ICE has taken some steps toward demonstrating the passenger train's potential in a competitive transportation market, while new organizational techniques have been embraced to enable pursuit of new and expanding commercial opportunities. But the resulting organization also reflects the much broader socioeconomic restructuring that occurred following German reunification—the integration of two very different economic and administrative traditions, and two distinct sets of policy inheritances.

Reconciling the administration, finance, and operations of DBAG's predecessors was such a large mandate that it took several years before a clear picture of the new entity's performance began to emerge. Initially, DBAG appeared to be "on track" to meeting its financial targets and expectations. For example, government operating subsidies that had amounted to DM 7 billion at the start of restructuring in 1994 had fallen to DM 3 billion by 1999, and were slated for complete elimination in 2003.[16] This equivalent to what Amtrak's managers would label their company's "glide path to commercial self-sufficiency" would have positioned Germany's rail operators for privatization in 2004. But by 1999, the DBAG's shortcomings were becoming clearer, and these proved to be significant.

Balancing technological and organizational change turned out to be more difficult to accomplish in practice than in theory. This was evidenced by a two-year delay and DM 5 billion in cost overruns on the DBAG's two biggest modernization initiatives, a DM 8.8 billion high-speed rail line between Frankfurt airport and Cologne and a DM 4.5 billion rail tunnel beneath Berlin, which included a new central station for the nation's new capital. Mrs. Dagmar Haase, an executive of DB Netz, explained what went wrong when entrepreneurial management initiatives encountered traditional planning and policy practices. She noted that in the mid 1990s, enthusiastic executives "wanted to demonstrate that the [Frankfurt–Cologne] line could be built more quickly and more cheaply than had been possible up to then. As the goal was to open the line before 2000, new methods were sought. . . . The key points were to issue functional invitations to tender and award contracts before the completion of the planning process to encourage creativity and innovation in the construction industry. Unfortunately these things did not happen. In addition, conditions were imposed by the planning approval procedure, tunnels were extended, and new rescue concepts introduced, all factors over which we had no influence."[17]

DBAG's growing pains were not just confined to new development initiatives. Existing operations suffered a serious safety lapse, with a horrific derailment of the ICE at Eschede in June 1998 that left 101 people dead. Passenger rail's reliability also fell to a postwar low in 1999, with just 55 percent of trains arriving within a minute of their schedule.[18] DBAG's chief executive, Johannes Ludewig, described as a "close advisor to Helmut Kohl," Germany's former chancellor, was dismissed in 1999. By that time, it had become clear that DBAG's managerial problems had translated into major financial troubles.[19]

DBAG's new leader, Hartmut Mehdorn, quickly revealed the depth of the problems that had accumulated during the initial transition to an NMR. Financial and operational deficits had accumulated slowly at first, but when left unsolved they had derailed DBAG's effort to attain self-sufficiency. In 2000, the DBAG restated its financial forecasts to project a loss of DM 4.7 billion between 2000 and 2004, compared to 1999's profitable projections.[20] These sobering results were sufficient to lead (then) Transport Minister Reinhard Klimmt to declare that launching any privatization of DBAG in 2004 would no longer be possible.

Hartmut Mehdorn has expressed optimism in turning DBAG's fortunes around, as long as some of the difficult and controversial restructuring initiatives that had been sidestepped during DBAG's early years could be carried out. Proposed initiatives include a major cutback of DB Cargo's local freight facilities, with significant job losses that would be "highly sensitive politically."[21] DBAG's new chief has also stated that "about 20% of the 38,000 km network is uneconomic to operate" and that the corporation must do away with such money-losing operations.[22] German policy makers will either have to revisit these, and other, hard choices or give rail executives like Mehdorn greater autonomy to deal with such problems in the near future.

Moving Germany's rail system across the boundary between public sector and private enterprise has been identified as a policy objective. But it was initially left for the longer term, an echo of the incrementalism that typified the earlier era of West German industrial policy networks. The balancing act that arose from this tradition has already delayed the schedule for this privatization.

To date, the result of Germany's rail reforms cannot be labeled "privatization." Marketization would be a better term for the significant departure from past commercial and organizational models of both the DB and the DR. The various components of the new DBAG have each focused on managing business activities that correspond to commercial market segments. They have also been given a mandate to operate like a private enterprise, but within the limits of public ownership. Those limits are certainly not responsible for all of DBAG's initial shortcomings, but they will have to be overcome in order to realize the full potential of Germany's NMR.

What can now be said with confidence about the German approach to building an NMR is that it has produced both new institutions and new instruments for passenger rail renewal. Yet the success of those mechanisms will depend upon further innovation by either government or rail management. If government chooses to cut its costs and delegate further reform initiatives to DBAG's executives, then downsizing of uneconomic freight and passenger services could reduce the need for subsidies at the same time as rail's role in meeting German mobility needs is diminished. But if government remains engaged in trying to reconcile the costs of rail restructuring with the social benefits of moving freight and passengers by train, then greater public resources will be required to enable DBAG to live up to its potential.

Two recent policy initiatives suggest that the German government is not inclined to let DBAG's managers start swinging the budget axe found in their NMR tool kit just yet. In September 2000, Germany announced that it would invest up to DM 40 billion gained from the DM 100 billion-sale of new mobile phone licenses in rail infrastructure.[23] This move would give DBAG an infusion of technology, much needed after clear evidence that the balance between technical and organizational modernization had been lost in recent years, to the detriment of German technological capacity. Addressing this infrastructure deficit should enhance the competitiveness of both rail freight and passenger services, presumably reducing the scope of uneconomic activities. The German government has also announced plans to introduce highway tolls for trucks weighing more than twelve tons. The stated policy is to halt the growth of road freight and stimulate the expansion of rail freight, which

Transport Minister Klimmt had suggested should double by 2015.[24] Should these policy adjustments be implemented, DBAG's initial travails in the transition to an NMR may be remedied without scaling back the role of rail in German transportation.

2.4. United Kingdom: Transforming the Railroad's Organization Before Changing Its Technology

Great Britain's introduction of the NMR has attracted much attention on both sides of the Atlantic, partly because of its extensive and intricate organizational restructuring, and partly because of its embrace of privatization as an end in itself. Bold and sweeping rail restructuring like Britain's is bound to attract attention, and at first glance the approach appears to be a direct extension of the British "shock-treatment" model that was used to restructure other declining industrial sectors from coal mining to ship building. In that approach, private investors were invited in to restructure whatever the market deemed worthwhile and to liquidate the remainder. But the British mode of rail renewal is much more than an extension of generic and ideologically motivated privatization practices, as suggested by its complex structure and ongoing evolution. The British NMR variant represents an attempt to introduce quite innovative management techniques where technological initiatives had previously fallen far short of sparking a commercial comeback. This determination to renew rail passenger performance by reinventing its management and operational techniques in advance of applying new technology merits close attention on a continent where high-tech intercity passenger train experiments have regularly come up short.

The United Kingdom's Railways Act of 1993 represents the most extensive and elaborate privatization of a railroad yet undertaken. It is built upon a policy foundation that contains two distinct legacies from late-twentieth-century British industrial policy. One is generic, and originates from the neoconservative economic ideology that Lady Margaret Thatcher passed along to John Major, and which Tony Blair has subsequently tried to live with. Put simply, the idea that government has a leadership role in running the economy has been discredited to the point that even a Labor government must now formulate policy that can be implemented largely by private corporations. The second is particular, and grows out of a failed experiment in applying new technology to renew British passenger trains. Together, these policy legacies created a dynamic that enabled, indeed compelled, unprecedented organizational innovation. The resulting NMR was more ambitious in pioneering new techniques than any other restructuring to date, while at the same time being among the most modest in deploying new technology. These roots will be considered in turn.

The ideological impetus for replacing an RPM such as British Rail originated from the core of the Thatcherite neoconservative belief system. What may at first appear surprising is that a government in which "privatization" became virtually synonymous for "policy" in public sector restructuring left railways until last on its policy agenda. Airlines, airports, phone companies, waterworks, coal mines, electric utilities, urban transit, public housing, and dozens of other organizations all preceded British Rail in the transition from public to private enterprise.

This can be explained by recognizing that the Thatcher government, and its successor, applied an evolving strategy in the pursuit of privatization. Feigenbaum et al. write that "Conservative privatization policy has never had a single, overriding objective but has, instead, had a number of different and conflicting objectives, the balance of which has changed over time as policy evolved."[25] This evolving approach to privatization began by targeting public enterprises with either strong or weak commercial positions and only moving into the middle range of mediocre performers only later.

At the top end, commercially promising or successful public enterprises like British Telecom, British Airways, or the British Airports Authority could be quickly and profitably privatized since there was no shortage of investors ready to snap up their equity. Such successful privatizations would gain the government political credit in the short-term. Over the medium to long-term these privatizations were seen to advance the cause of "'popular capitalism' whereby shareholdings in privatized organizations would be widely dispersed amongst employees and the public at large." The anticipated result was "a reduction in 'them and us' sentiments and hence a decline in the appeal of trade unionism and perhaps also of opposition political parties."[26] Government naturally gave such hot prospects a fast track in order to cash in on these effects as soon as possible.

At the other economic extreme, the Conservative government displayed a resolute will to close the books on commercially unpromising or hopeless public enterprises like coal pits, steel mills, and shipyards that had lost out in global competition. Such "industrial euthanasia" was seen as essential to reducing public deficits and ending the state's support of uneconomic activity. Since pulling the plug in some sectors would likely generate a combination of political opposition and a need for transitional subsidies, government sought to deal with these controversies and costs earlier in its mandate rather than later.

The core transportation business of British Rail (BR) fell between these extremes and thus wound up low on the privatization priority agenda. Unlike the ancillary business units, such as hotels, trucking, ferry, and port operations, that were spun off during the 1980s, BR's train services did not perform well enough to attract the attention of investors anxious to snap up the top privatization prospects and thus generate an easy sale. Nor did they perform poorly enough to fall into the commercially hopeless category that should be dispatched well before the next election. Instead, BR's management took cues from the neoconservative market paradigm and implemented a commercial reorganization around core "business sectors" that was launched in 1982.[27] This model did a reasonably good job of boosting rail revenues and yield from its existing passenger base—which produced both improved commercial performance and a declining share of total travel by rail during the Thatcher government's tenure. British railway ridership dropped from 857 million passengers in 1985 to 702 million in 1994, while passenger-kilometers fell from 30.256 billion to 28.656 billion during the same period. Meanwhile, BR's revenues grew from £1.333 million in 1985 to £2.176 million in 1994.[28]

But eventually, after Lady Thatcher had passed the mantle of leadership to John Major, privatization policy reached the point at which the cabinet was prepared to deal with the middle range of public enterprises that were neither economic stars nor basket cases. Nearing the end of the Major government's mandate, British Rail appeared as the largest, and most visible, remaining RPM from the old economic order. Its time had come.

One ideological objective of this "late-in-the-game" privatization was to make the departure from the old RPM "election proof." Sensing a readiness among the British electorate for change, the Major government instructed bureaucrats in charge to create a privatization that could not be easily reversed by a possible Labor government that would bring contrary ideological orientations into power. *The Economist* quoted a top civil servant who claimed that elected officials simply directed her/him "to privatise the railways 'as soon as was practicable' and to make the process irreversible before the next election."[29]

The resulting policy opportunity to replace BR with an NMR gave the architects of privatization a clean slate in "deconstructing" the existing integrated model of commuter, intercity passenger, and freight operations combined with infrastructure provision. They opted for extensive industrial decentralization, separating BR into numerous private entities with independent control or outright ownership over tracks and stations, rolling stock, maintenance facilities, freight train operations, and twenty-five separate regional and intercity passenger train operating franchises.

One objective of this "Humpty Dumpty" rail restructuring model was to make it impossible to put BR back together again. But another was to multiply, and hopefully maximize, the chances that one or more organizations could apply the right combination of entrepreneurship and productivity gains to create a new market for, or enhance an existing market's capacity to support, commercially viable rail travel. This magic formula was seen to be elusive for even a privately owned integrated entity, which would have to deal with a range of market opportunities and constraints throughout British intercity travel. Faith in markets led to the assumption that there must be a formula for commercial success to be discovered, but the experience of BR suggested that the trade-offs facing an integrated rail enterprise would inhibit such discoveries.

There was also the sense that once the commercial breakthroughs were made, or at least embarked upon, the ability to successfully develop appropriate technology would also depend upon market-specific projects rather than systemic programs. This preference for market-specific technical initiatives that would be led by an organization dedicated to making profits arose from BR's failure to successfully deploy new passenger train technology along the lines of France or Germany.

British Rail's High Speed Train (HST) was the last (pre-privatization) commercial success that could be attributed to technical modernization. HSTs were lightweight, diesel-powered trains that could cruise at 125 miles per hour on main lines. Development of the HST began in 1969. In 1973, prototype testing began, achieving a record speed of 143 miles per hour on June 12.[30] The HST carried its first fare paying passengers on May 5, 1975, and entered widespread service in 1978 as the "InterCity 125." Britain's faster passenger train service proved a commercial success, with ridership growing on the lines that had these new trains. Like its counterparts in Japan, continental Europe, and the United States, the HST demonstrated that there were still market opportunities for fast and modern trains linking cities in three hours or less. This technical breakthrough had opened a window of opportunity for further passenger rail renewal in Britain.

But instead of using the HST's success to leverage greater government support for new "state-of-the-art" rail infrastructure, following the Japanese, French, and German examples, British rail executives concentrated technical innovation efforts on squeezing performance enhancements out of existing infrastructure. British Rail focused its in-house engineering resources on further advancing train technology, pinning the hopes for future technical breakthrough on the Advanced Passenger Train (APT). APT was an ambitious extension of HST technology that would combine turbine or electric propulsion with tilting-car body design to push operating speeds on existing tracks as high as 155 miles per hour. Such a strategy was expected to reduce the cost of high-speed rail renewal to fit within the British government's means.

A gas turbine–powered APT-E (E for experimental) tested the tilting technology between 1973 and 1975, achieving a top speed of 152 miles per hour.[31] The lessons of these tests were incorporated into an electric-powered APT-P (P for prototype), which reached a top speed of 162 miles per hour in 1979. APT-P was officially launched on December 7, 1981, and received mixed reviews from the journalists covering its debut.[32] Its tilting at high-speed was alleged to have left some passengers feeling queasy on its inaugural run, although the train's supporters claimed it was excess consumption of free drinks that was to blame. Following fine-tuning of its tilting mechanism, the APT-P operated in revenue service between London and Glasgow from 1982 to 1985.

After these few years of limited operation, the APT-P was withdrawn from service and BritRail Engineering Ltd., BR's research subsidiary, abruptly cancelled the APT development program. No definitive account of APT's abandonment has ever been published, but it is clear that the government and the rail management of the day preferred writing off over a decade's worth of research and development costs to taking the leap into financing a new fleet of high-speed tilting trains. Such costs would not have looked favorable at a time when BR's non-core assets were being sold off, as occurred with various components of British Rail Engineering Ltd. between 1987 and 1989.[33] What is clear is that the APT did not make the compelling commercial case for deployment that the TGV and ICE did. Like the Metroliner and other U.S. experiments of the time, APT was the product of a vehicle-focused technology strategy that sought to avoid the costly redesign and replacement of rail infrastructure.

Failure to deploy APT as part of a full-blown rail renewal strategy did not completely nullify these research and development efforts, however. Some of APT's technical advances were incorporated into non-tilting electric trains that British Rail subsequently produced. The tilting technology itself was sold to Italian rail manufacturers who perfected it in revenue service between Rome and Milan. These manufacturers are now selling new tilting trains to one of British Rail's private successors, Virgin Trains. That company's chief executive told an audience in 1999, "Had we held our nerve in the 1980s, tonight's [presentation would] have been all about how APT brought in the 'tilt effect' and my current concerns would be the mid life overhaul of the trains, upgrading their control system and the lack of progress on the infrastructure renewal negotiated with Railtrack as part of the West coast franchise."[34]

But the mixed results of previous technology policy left the architects of Britain's NMR quite skeptical of the power of rail technology to fix the passenger train's problems—and also leery of putting the fate of rail renewal in the hands of engineers and designers, as opposed to corporate entrepreneurs and managers. Picking and choosing from, largely imported, technology was seen as less risky, especially when a carrier had focused on the market needs of its particular operational environment. Small and focused organizational innovations were seen as the way to deploy a multitude of rail renewal strategies that would serve Britain's travelers best.

Six years after privatization, the British NMR has produced both celebrated successes and spectacular failures. As in Germany, the benefits of organizational change appeared earlier than its costs, leading analysts to offer positive initial assessments. On the positive side, privatization delivered more riders and revenue. Within two years, Britain's new rail owners began growing their business in just the ways that advocates of change had predicted. As illustrated in figure 2.7, Preston has calculated a 26 percent increase in passenger travel and 34 percent increase in passenger revenue between 1993 and 1994, British Rail's last year of operation, and 1999/2000.[35] This growth outpaced Britain's overall economic growth rate of 20 percent during the period.

With more riders and revenue, Britain's NMR should be reducing the cost of rail passenger operations to the public purse, as Gómez-Ibáñez suggested in 1999.[36] But others have pointed out that Britain's NMR actually receives more public funding than BR did, through operating subsidies built into franchise agreements, capital contributions to Railtrack, the private infrastructure owner, and regulatory and transaction costs incurred in creating and overseeing the NMR's complex organizational structure. Van de Velde describes Britain's NMR as "tightly regulated . . . perhaps even more than before."[37] Krause notes that Britain's NMR is receiving a total of £26 billion over 10 years, which is "more than British Rail got, and more than five times as much as the whole of BR was sold off for."[38] Some might consider such public spending more appropriate on private railroads, or at least more likely in a nation with a record of reluctance to invest in public enterprise. Whether by design or not, rail privatization thus aligns Britain's rail mode with the private air and road carriers who have benefited from government investments over the years.

Supporters of privatization initially claimed that public spending on Britain's NMR would decline over time, and perhaps disappear completely, once Britain's new rail owners had fully deployed their entrepreneurial energies and access to private capital. But this retreat of the state from passenger

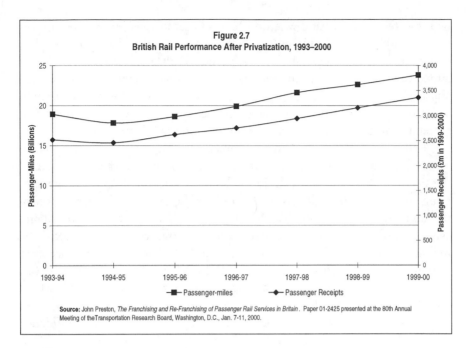

Figure 2.7
British Rail Performance After Privatization, 1993–2000

Source: John Preston, *The Franchising and Re-Franchising of Passenger Rail Services in Britain*. Paper 01-2425 presented at the 80th Annual Meeting of the Transportation Research Board, Washington, D.C., Jan. 7-11, 2000.

rail has not happened and shows no signs of occurring. A structural problem that became apparent following privatization was the conflicting economic assumptions and incentives between the infrastructure owner Railtrack, and the train operating companies (TOCs). Railtrack's tariff with the TOCs was initially structured so that "97% of its track-access income is fixed regardless of the number of trains [operated]."[39] This gave the infrastructure owner no financial incentive to meet the growth in capacity that would be essential to carrying the increased business that TOC franchises had presumed, and which private carriers were accomplishing. As a result, serious train delays grew in step with ridership, from 7.5 percent in 1997–98 to 8.8 percent in 1998–99. Passenger complaints also increased 154 percent between 1997 and 1999.[40]

Even more problematic was the diverging tolerance for risk related to infrastructure that emerged between Railtrack and the TOCs. Railtrack came to embrace a new maintenance philosophy that had been recommended by the McKinsey consulting firm in a report code-named "Project Destiny."[41] Rather than the traditional approach of maintaining infrastructure assets on a fixed timetable that presumed tracks, signals, etc., should be replaced or renewed before reaching an average age at which failure *might* occur, McKinsey recommended a new approach—maintenance on a flexible schedule that targeted infrastructure showing signs that it was *likely* to fail. Infrastructure would be inspected regularly and when problems became apparent, temporary repairs would be made. Replacement or renewal would then be performed, but only when signs of failure became apparent. Railtrack's new approach was aimed to squeeze more productivity out of its infrastructure assets, but this approach also shifted risk and potential cost onto the TOCs, which could suffer from reduced operational reliability as tracks, signals, and other infrastructure came closer to failing as part of routine rail operations.

Railtrack's new approach to risk management may have been responsible for an accident at Hatfield on October 17, 2000, in which a cracked rail caused the derailment of an express train traveling at over one hundred miles per hour, resulting in four deaths. But whatever the eventual determination of that accident's cause, it immediately triggered a crisis of confidence in Britain's NMR. The Hatfield wreck was actually less destructive than other accidents in recent years that have been caused by human error, such as a collision at Ladbroke Junction on October 5, 1999, that claimed thirty-one lives. But once it became known that Railtrack had known of the cracked rail at Hatfield months before the accident, and had planned to replace it on a date that fell two weeks following the accident,[42] the British public quickly lost confidence in the safety of Britain's NMR.

Ridership gains that had been built up over years quickly evaporated as Railtrack launched a massive slowdown of trains across its network, where emergency inspections revealed deteriorated track conditions. Emergency timetables changed so often in the months following Hatfield that Britain's trains were often running without an established schedule. Train drivers had to consult up to sixteen pages of special instructions on speed restrictions during the course of their trips, leading to concern that the risk of running through red signals would increase as a result.[43] The TOCs have been reported to have lost between 33 percent and 40 percent of their passengers under travel conditions that Prime Minister Tony Blair has described as "absolute hell."[44] *The London Times* editorialized that "no industry in Britain has gone from expansion to public ignominy in so short a time and with such disastrous results."[45] Hatfield and its aftermath could wind up costing Railtrack £300 million in penalty payments to the TOCs for late trains, reduced capacity, and lost business under existing operating agreements.[46] Even greater damages might emerge if the TOCs take Railtrack to court.

Before this crisis hit, the Blair government had proposed a new policy instrument, a Strategic Rail Authority that would develop a system-wide plan for rail's private providers to pursue, and then link it to further public investment in Britain's rail network. A "shadow" Strategic Rail Authority has been at work in advance of the legislation formally adding it to the NMR's architecture. Led by the veteran rail developer Sir Alisdair Morton, who served as cochair of the "Eurotunnel" consortium that built the Channel Tunnel, this new agency may be able to fill the vacuum of leadership and coordination that has emerged in the post-Hatfield crisis. Only time will tell whether Britain's recent rail passenger travails are a symptom of a fatal flaw in its NMR design or an unfortunate misstep on the road to privately led renewal of the passenger train's prospects.

2.5. Assessing the Dynamics of Creating NMRs

French, German, and British experience illustrates how the NMR is still far from being a wholly standardized enterprise. Unlike the global airlines, fast food chains, and running-shoe manufacturers that are differentiated primarily by their brand names, there has yet to emerge an archetypal formula for success in the passenger train business. Instead, there continue to be multiple strategies for reorienting rail organizations to maximize opportunities to move people productively and profitably in a new century. As has been shown in three European leaders' experience at reinventing railroads, these variations occur primarily along the dimension of how technological and organizational innovation are related.

The search for change can address the relationship between technology and technique in any of three ways. Changing technology can be given first priority, as in France. Once a successful adaptation of technology to market needs occurs, then new techniques of managing and marketing the new service can be introduced. A second approach seeks to change technology and managerial techniques in parallel, if not necessarily in sync, as occurred in Germany. The ICE introduced a means of enhancing market share and generating profits, while "marketization" was intended to instill the motive for such commercial success among the managers and workers of two traditional RPMs. Thirdly, changing managerial techniques can take on top priority, as in the British approach to privatization. Technological innovations are then left to the subsequent (and presumably) enhanced judgement and skills of market-savvy managers with a full stake in the commercial success or failure of such outcomes.

Leadership is a well recognized element of policy change, and the transition from RPM to NMR cannot occur without it. As shown in Europe, this leadership can be undertaken in very different ways. Leadership can be entrusted to technocratic elites within an RPM, who serve as core advocates in a rail policy community. When these individuals demonstrate a vision of future opportunities for the passenger train, a willingness to pursue such opportunities, and a capacity for achieving results, as occurred with the TGV triumph in France, then governments and other (perhaps more skeptical) policy community members generally defer to this in-house expertise. Followers continue largely as before in the rail policy community.

Leadership can also move away from managers of RPM rail organizations to other participants in the rail policy community, either by a power shift among existing supporters and skeptics or by the addition of new participants to the community. Germany's marketization effort demonstrates both such dynamics. The policy community was enlarged to include, among others, participants from the former East Germany, as well as both new proponents and skeptics brought into policy deliberations via advisory groups and panels. The corporatist consensus that gave the old DB a big say in policy options for its future (at the same time as requiring compromise with other interests) was superceded by a state-directed mode of organizational renewal that was triggered by reunification. This meant that the political leaders of the transition to an NMR gained much more authority than their predecessors in charge of the RPM had been able to exercise. Executives at DBAG are now following the new commercial paradigm that was introduced in Germany's marketization model to the point that they are pressing political leaders to either invest more in modernization or stop resisting the cutback of uneconomic services.

Alternatively, leadership can be divorced from the existing rail policy community—as the British privatization experience demonstrates. In this transition to an NMR, both the existing RPM and the rail policy community were taken apart and reconstituted into a completely unrecognizable form. Here, state actors (e.g., the Major government) took on the mantle of dissenters in the rail policy community that had long ago condemned the RPM. They presided over the sell-off of British Rail, with neither consultation nor compromise. In this state-directed transition, government's exclusive leadership created an organizational model that was distinct from both prior British privatization practices and other nations' rail restructuring. It has yielded a significantly different rail policy community containing many more supporters, each advocating a much narrower agenda. The numerous franchise holders and equipment, track, and station owners each pursue their own interests, both commercially and politically—leaving Britain's new rail policy community with a pluralist scramble to follow the dictates and opportunities of the market. This transformation of rail advocates from leaders into followers considerably limits subsequent opportunities for policy leadership, in the traditional sense of coordinated planning and systematic development, to advance the future of Britain's rail passenger mode. Such a departure from past policy leadership was exactly the intent of privatization architects.

Policy instruments, as distinct from the commercial and business tools used by NMRs, have also been adjusted and changed during this transition. Public financial support for both operating and capital needs was repackaged (and sometimes reduced) to reflect and indeed encourage new relationships between organizations and markets. In France and Germany, government's capital funding for rail was redirected to new publicly owned entities, RFF and DB-Netz, that were not controlled by a carrier. In the United Kingdom, public regulation of privately owned rail infrastructure was intended to produce track-access charges that would recover the cost of capital, including the cost of renewal and upgrading. And in all three nations, support for socially necessary or desired passenger trains (e.g., those routes or services that could not cover their costs from the farebox) was to be provided through explicit and specific commitments between regional governments and an outside source—a carrier in France and Germany and a franchise bidding scheme in the United Kingdom that provided for short-term (declining) subsidies to the TOCs.

The organization of public enterprise has been either formally abandoned, as in Germany and the United Kingdom, or significantly restructured, as in France, to enhance managerial autonomy and facilitate entrepreneurial activities. Another change was in the policy instrumentation that was to serve public interest objectives. In France, these objectives remained formal, consistent with earlier goals that had been the RPM's mission, and were incorporated in both national and regional service agreements with the SNCF. The enhanced commercial capacity of the NMR was seen as a means to better meeting these ongoing public interest objectives.

In Germany, formal public interest objectives also remained a part of the rail policy landscape. They justified ongoing public ownership of infrastructure and would certainly inform the mission of DB-Netz. Public interest goals were to be supplemented by commercial imperatives at the various operating subsidiaries of DBAG, presumably to the degree that private capital was introduced to these entities. The more that private investors had at stake in the DBAG's components, the more that commercial success would come to weigh as a policy objective. And in the United Kingdom, commercial success was elevated to the status of a primary public interest objective, an end in itself rather than a means to other ends.

2.6. Assessing the Strengths and Weaknesses of NMR Variants

The three variations of the NMR that have been considered in this chapter allow for an assessment of the strengths and weaknesses of different approaches to renewing the passenger train's potential. Those searching for a single, best formula from European rail renewal experience are likely to be disappointed by this concluding comparison because it does not declare a "winner." While it does suggest that there are options to choose from in building an NMR, it also suggests that not all combinations are possible. Objectives, instruments, and policy community participants can only be configured in certain ways. But precisely because the strengths of all approaches are not likely cumulative into a single "super-optimum policy solution,"[47] an explicit consideration of which strengths are most attractive, and which weaknesses least objectionable, is well worth undertaking.

The French style NMR demonstrates both the greatest degree of organizational continuity with the rail mode's past, coupled with the farthest advance in the application of new technology to infrastructure and operations. Its greatest strength is the success in modal shift back to rail. Its greatest weakness is the requirement for active government intervention to support the technocratic leadership of rail renewal over an extended time period. Both political and financial support for the rail mode remain obvious, and are made even more explicit by the new organizational arrangements that expose both government and public enterprises to criticism from policy skeptics. Such a policy is vulnerable to fiscal retrenchment, if government is not prepared to run a deficit in times when tax revenues fall short of planned spending.

Germany's NMR exhibits change on all fronts—the widest degree of reorganization and technical redesign among Europe's renewed railways. Its greatest strength has been the ability to accommodate a broad range of organized interests and different objectives into a genuinely innovative organizational redesign. Integration, regional balance, enhancement of productivity, and commercial development are all addressed simultaneously by the German NMR. Its greatest weakness is that it requires a schizophrenic alternation between state activism and societal accommodation that may have been unique to the timing and circumstances of German reunification. This weakness has become manifest in recent years when the constraints of consensus-based rail policy caused DBAG's commercial deficits to balloon while its performance deflated.

In the United Kingdom's NMR the word "new" takes on its most extreme, but also most focused, meaning. Here no attribute of the old RPM is left intact, except for its traditional technology. Looked at in terms of organization and technique, there is nothing about Britain's NMR that bears any resemblance to the prior RPM, or indeed to other railroads elsewhere in the world. But looked at in terms of technical attributes and the service characteristics that derive from them, there is not much difference between the RPM and the NMR. Even the most ambitious of the equipment upgrades and track improvements that TOCs implemented in selected markets, and that the Strategic Rail Authority is seeking to expand upon, still fall short of the breakthroughs exemplified by the Shinkansen and TGV. The greatest strength of this transition is the ability to unleash the full force (and fury) of market mechanisms to energize rail renewal. Commercial success has become the top priority of all engaged in the many aspects of Britain's NMR. The greatest weakness of this model is that it requires a high tolerance for transaction costs, and for uneven outcomes along the way. Winners may win big, but losers will also lose big in the successes and failures of British rail renewal.

Europe, and also Japan, went ahead with fundamental organizational and financial restructuring in their passenger railroads during the 1990s, at least in part because of the success of particular renewal projects like the Shinkansen, TGV, and ICE. These achievements had inspired hope among rail policy community members that such changes could be made for the better, in terms of the opportunities that would accrue to the passenger carrier and its workers (e.g., jobs, prestige, and profits). The same achievements also raised expectations on the part of citizens and their elected representatives that passenger trains no longer needed to be protected, preserved, or otherwise treated in a fashion that was unique to the mode.

Not all results from the subsequent efforts to create an NMR have matched the triumph of the high-speed rail projects that contributed to the larger movement toward renewal. But they have made progress in bringing the passenger train closer to the mobility needs of twenty-first-century travelers in many nations. Nothing like this has occurred in North America. In chapter 3, the very different roots of the policy stalemate that encircle Amtrak and VIA Rail are considered in detail. These events demonstrate why the public passenger railroads on this continent have not been in a position to take up the reinvention challenge that their European and Japanese counterparts moved on to following the success of specific high-speed renewal projects.

Sidetrack

How North American Rail Passenger Renewal Got Delayed by the Stalemate Over Public Enterprise Legitimacy

If one were to look at organizational and resource inputs as a guide to industrial renewal, then North American passenger trains' problems would appear to have been well on their way toward resolution in the 1970s. Even before French and German rail renewal efforts got serious, both American and Canadian governments had launched major fiscal and organizational changes in response to the passenger train's decline. The United States had reversed a thirteen-year period of regulated exit from the rail passenger business by launching a quasi-public enterprise called Amtrak in 1971. Canada initiated public subsidies for passenger train operations in 1967, and launched VIA Rail as an independent Crown Corporation, or publicly-owned enterprise, in 1977.

Both of these public enterprises were designed to focus exclusively on rail passenger renewal. They were organized around the principle that focusing new managerial resources exclusively upon passenger train marketing, service design, and operations would enable a reversal of fortunes for this mode. Unlike the other public enterprises around the world that engaged in rail transportation, including the European and Japanese national railroads and the Canadian National Railway, Amtrak and VIA would not have to contend with the, supposedly conflicting, demands of moving freight. Nor were they burdened with significant cost and responsibility for transporting commuters around major metropolitan areas. Their sole mission would be, in the frank language of one of Amtrak's first advertising slogans, "to make the trains worth traveling again."

Amtrak and VIA have expended substantial amounts of public resources since their inception. Between 1971 and 1999, Amtrak has received US$25.4

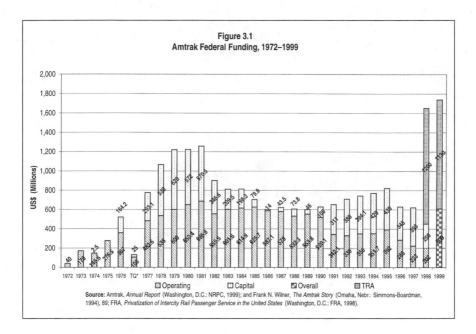

Figure 3.1
Amtrak Federal Funding, 1972–1999

Source: Amtrak, *Annual Report* (Washington, D.C.: NRPC, 1999); and Frank N. Wilner, *The Amtrak Story* (Omaha, Nebr.: Simmons-Boardman, 1994), 89; FRA, *Privatization of Intercity Rail Passenger Service in the United States* (Washington, D.C.: FRA, 1998).

billion in federal operating subsidies and capital grants.[1] These are detailed in figure 3.1.

VIA Rail has been granted $9.4 billion (Canadian) from 1979 through 1999 for operating and capital subsidies.[2] These are detailed in figure 3.2. While some would correctly point out that these sums pale in comparison to the public finance of aviation and road transport through direct public spending on infrastructure, traffic control, and policing related to these modes, the amounts that have been invested in North American passenger trains cannot be dismissed as negligible. Certainly in relation to the number of passengers carried, Amtrak and VIA have received quite generous levels of public funding.

At first glance, then, Amtrak and VIA would appear to have been well positioned to revive the passenger train in North America. They have had a quarter-century or more to come up with innovations that could turn the train's fortunes around. They did not have any distraction from this task by the freight and commuter responsibilities that burdened their predecessors and counterparts in Europe and Japan. And they could count on significant levels of subsidy and capital investment over a number of years. Why then has passenger train renewal made so little progress on the North American continent?

To answer that question, it is important to examine why so much time has elapsed and so much money has been spent, ostensibly on renewing North

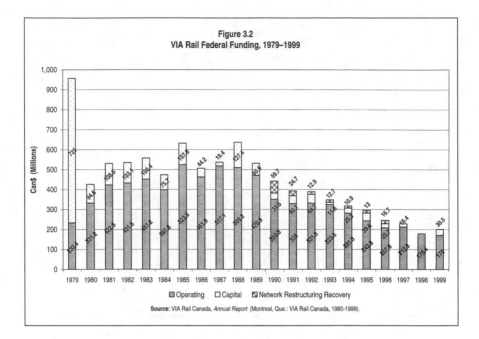

Figure 3.2
VIA Rail Federal Funding, 1979–1999

Source: VIA Rail Canada, *Annual Report* (Montreal, Que.: VIA Rail Canada, 1980-1999).

American passenger trains, while so little has been accomplished to date—compared to the real commercial achievements that European and Japanese railroads have demonstrated at various times over these same years. To explain why North America's reversal of fortune in intercity passenger railroading has been so long in coming, an examination of the causes and key attributes of the policy stalemate that currently constrains rail passenger opportunities on both sides of the Canada–U.S. border is in order.

Each nation's passenger trains operate under the very real and costly constraint of a policy stalemate regarding the rail mode's relationship to government and to other transportation modes. This constraint exhibits unique characteristics that arise from particular governmental structures and processes. These will be identified, with an eye toward understanding what these constraints have meant for Amtrak's and VIA Rail's tenuous legitimacy, and consequent enfeebled effectiveness, as public enterprises.

Amtrak's institutional isolation from the earmarked tax revenues and cooperative planning and management of infrastructure among national, state, and local governments is an oft-noted peculiarity of American transportation policy that constrains, and indeed forecloses, many of the options that could contribute to an effective rail renewal in the United States. VIA Rail is isolated both politically, due to its lack of any explicit authorizing legislation, and administratively, as a result of its separation from the private railways over which it operates, as well as the provincial bureaucracies that plan, regulate, and finance road infrastructure and the authorities responsible for airports and air navigation. VIA Rail was created by unilateral executive action, known as an Order-in-Council, and this sets it apart from all other transport modes and carriers in Canada. Airlines, freight railways, and marine operators each have been guided by specific legislation establishing their status (previously as Crown Corporations and more recently as privatized entities). VIA's lack of a legislative mandate leaves it open to considerable political uncertainty, since its favor can, and does, rise and fall with the government of the day.

North America's rail passenger policy stalemate also shares some common elements that will be considered. Specifically, the economic divorce between freight and passenger carriers in the rail mode, with freight carriers keeping the family estate (e.g., infrastructure), is a common characteristic that sets Amtrak and VIA apart from their competitors and constrains several options for enhancing commercial performance. Also, the rail mode's privately owned infrastructure places policy constraints for both passenger and freight operations by, among other things, creating different economic parameters compared to other modes. For instance, taxation and cost of capital burdens are greater for rail transport than for air and road carriers competing to move both freight and passengers.

3.1. The Regulatory Prologue

The roots of this North American rail passenger stalemate extend back to policies that were adopted by regulatory regimes that preceded, and in at least one important way precipitated, the choice of a specialized public enterprise as the principal policy instrument to address the passenger train's decline. Both Canada and the United States had longstanding regulatory regimes in place in the rail sector. Indeed, the Canadian Board of Railway Commissioners (and its successors) and the U.S. Interstate Commerce Commission (ICC) were among the oldest bureaucracies devoted to economic regulation in their respective countries. These entities had been created to limit the oligopolistic tendencies of the rail industry and to assert the public interest. But as other public agencies began sponsoring the development of air and road infrastructure and nurturing technology to provide alternative mobility modes, rail regulators were faced with the need to adjust to government's new and expanding role in transportation. The passenger train became the first policy challenge of this postwar transition to multimodal competition, presenting rail regulators with the problem of how to address industrial restructuring.

Industrial policy of almost any type involves an allocation of costs and benefits to both the participants in a policy community (e.g., firms, workers, customers, suppliers, and affected communities) as well as to the society at large. American and Canadian regulators responded to the challenge of restructuring the rail mode's passenger services by embracing different models of change, which in turn distributed the costs and benefits of uneconomic passenger train operations quite differently. By the time that these regulatory policies had lost legitimacy, on political grounds in the United States and on economic ones in Canada, their distinct distribution of benefits and costs had become a significant influence on the respective rail policy communities. The particular compromises upon policy options that have proven themselves to be fundamentally flawed would certainly have looked different had they followed from another form of regulatory regime. Both Amtrak and VIA Rail were created with considerable institutional handicaps that stand in the way of effective rail passenger renewal. Understanding these flaws, the first step toward correcting them, requires a careful appreciation of their origins, which will be considered in turn.

United States regulatory policy facilitated the decline and disengagement of the most traditional passenger advocacy group within the rail policy community—the carriers. It also encouraged the mobilization of an entirely different group of advocates—communities, users, and workers who refused to be left behind. In the first stage of this transformation, American railroads, which had been the previous advocates for passenger trains in the rail policy community, embraced a policy process designed to facilitate the exit from what had become an unprofitable line of business. Starting in 1958, U.S. regulators adopted the viewpoint advanced by both railroads and the ICC's staff that passenger train losses were an anomaly in an otherwise healthy transport mode, and that the solution to this policy problem was to enable railroads to leave the passenger business. The resulting passenger train abandonments concentrated both the benefits and costs of industrial adjustment on particular groups, as is evident in this policy's implementation.

During the 1950s, U.S. railroads pressed for, and won, the key regulatory policy change that would allow them to exit from passenger operations. The Transportation Act of 1958 shifted jurisdiction over most intercity passenger train services away from state regulatory boards, which had often proven more sympathetic to pleas for preserving passenger trains than they had to concerns about railroad profitability. Such authority was now delegated to the

ICC, which was instructed to weigh both the "public convenience and necessity" of a passenger train service and the possibility that ongoing losses from its continued operation would form an "undue burden on interstate commerce." In place of lengthy proceedings before one or more state regulatory tribunals, the 1958 act created a streamlined and uniform process that is well analyzed by Hilton.[3]

Under the new regime, railroads could give as little as thirty days public notice of their intent to discontinue a passenger train. From that time, the Interstate Commerce Commission had ten days to react. If the commission saw grounds for an investigation of the proposed train abandonment, it could order operations to be continued for up to four months. And if it found that the train service in question passed both the tests of being justified under public convenience and necessity grounds and not unduly burdening interstate commerce, the most that it could order was for the operation to be continued for one year. Then the process could, and usually did, begin over again. Hilton points out that intrastate train abandonments could be stayed on the sole finding that ongoing operation would not unduly burden interstate commerce. He attributes this less stringent standard to "greater political pressure for preservation of intrastate trains voiced by the state commissions to the House of Representatives."[4]

Hilton also finds evidence of political initiatives to preclude extensive passenger train abandonment in one fell swoop. When the Senate's initial version of the bill included a "net-loss" criterion which would have required the commission to uphold abandonment of any passenger service posting a net loss, the New York State Public Service Commission objected that this would put an end to most passenger train operations in the East. Senator Jacob Javits (R-NY) apparently succeeded in removing the net-loss criterion from the final version of the bill.[5] The stage was thus set for railroads to make their case for exit from the passenger business, not all at once, but train by train, beginning with the worst commercial performers.

Also in 1958, the ICC released a staff report on the passenger train's prospects that embraced the technological determinist thesis of this mode's inherent obsolescence. Simply entitled "Railroad Passenger Train Deficit," the report by examiner Howard Hosmer attributed declining ridership and revenues to an inexorable shift in consumer demand towards the better transportation technology offered by aviation and automobiles. The report noted that America's railroads had invested "about half a billion dollars" in new passenger train equipment between 1947 and 1956, while traffic declined precipitously.[6] Thus the problem did not appear to be one that could be solved by modernizing or improving upon the passenger train's characteristics. Rather, the train's competitive failings against the speed of air travel or the flexibility of driving were viewed as permanent. In Hosmer's judgement, "For more than a century the railroad passenger coach has occupied an interesting and useful place in American life, but at the present time the inescapable fact— and certainly to many people an unpleasant one—seems to be that in a decade or so this time-honored vehicle may take its place in the transportation museum along with the stagecoach, the sidewheeler, and the steam locomotive."[7]

The ICC's implementation of its new regulatory mandate on intercity passenger train services largely adopted the Hosmer report's premise regarding technological determinism. Protracted losses were viewed as evidence that the train service in question had entered a terminal phase of economic decline and should be abandoned. In deliberating over petitions to abandon routes and services, the commission placed the burden of proof on parties arguing against abandonment to show that a railroad's losses were either inaccurate or reversible. Without such evidence, the commission granted discontinuance.

Passenger train proponents were left to argue that losses had been overstated through, for example, an excessive allocation of "fixed" costs for track and corporate overhead that would remain whether the passenger service continued or not. After some initial challenges on such accounting questions, railroad lawyers and regulatory practitioners soon became adept at prevailing in these disputes. Sometimes, claims that losses were due to specific economic circumstances, such as a temporary downturn in a market's travel demand, rather than the passenger train's general decline, would yield a decision to continue operations. But this type of setback would usually precipitate a new application for abandonment within a year or two, during which time the railroad in question could hardly have been motivated to turn its passenger train performance around.

Between 1958 and 1971, the period when America's passenger train policy was largely in the hands of a national regulatory agency, railroads abandoned 75 percent of their passenger train mileage, compared to a base mileage operated in 1939.[8] This approach to restructuring transformed the rail policy community because it pointed toward only one logical conclusion: the abandonment of the remaining 25 percent of the passenger train mileage. This is because the same regulatory standards that proved up to the task of "rationalizing" (i.e., radically reducing) intercity rail passenger operations according to economic logic wound up creating major political tensions regarding the role of private railroads in meeting public interest responsibilities.

In interpreting the American railroads' "common carriage" responsibility to carry passengers as ceasing when that obligation imposed any economic burden, the ICC's passenger train policy concentrated the benefits of industrial restructuring on producers (i.e., rail carriers). Once such an easy opportunity for exit from uneconomic passenger service had been created, American railroads lost the incentive to create a passenger train renewal strategy, in the way that European railways eventually did. For American rail executives, such renewal appeared to be—and was—much riskier than simply cutting their losses and getting out of the business.

The ICC's application of rail passenger policy also worked to concentrate the costs of passenger train abandonment on communities, employees, and passengers that were left with reduced access, jobs, and mobility. By not identifying these costs as legitimate factors to be weighed, the 1958 Transportation Act presumed them to be less significant and worthwhile than the cost to interstate commerce of maintaining uneconomic intercity passenger train service. But while the recipients of these costs may not have realized the implication of the Transportation Act's economic priorities in 1958, regulatory practice worked to teach that lesson quickly.

Observers of public policy have long noted that feedback effects can work to reshape political dynamics over time.[9] This "policy creates politics" cycle is especially prevalent in economic regulation, which inevitably has an effect on the distribution of resources within a society. Observers of regulation have noted that the feedback effect from policies that work to concentrate the costs and benefits of economic activity are likely to engender adversarial political behavior.[10] In circumstances where one party's economic gains are seen to come at the expense of others, all participants in a policy community gain the incentive to organize and advocate their interests. This is just what occurred in American rail passenger restructuring.

By the mid-1960s, the ICC's implementation of regulatory policy had drawn the diverse losers in passenger train restructuring together into a new alliance. This alignment of workers, passengers, and local elected officials may have felt little in common before 1958, but once the new regulations took effect they shared the experience of having the costs of industrial decline consistently imposed upon them. The very public process, by which disputes over passenger train abandonment were adjudicated replete with public notification, open hearings, and administrative and legal appeals, created an ideal climate for drawing potential rail passenger advocates together into a coalition. As loss imposition resulting from the ICC's adjudication of discontinuance requests under the Transportation Act became clear, advocates were encouraged to look beyond the regulatory arena for policy options that would offer different, and more favorable, solutions to rail passenger restructuring. The American governmental structure, with its separation of powers, facilitated the pursuit of political activity to change existing policy arrangements. David Truman, one of the keener observers of American pluralism, noted that "the outstanding characteristic of American politics . . . is that it involves a multiplicity of co-ordinate or nearly co-ordinate points of access to governmental decisions" and that such "diversity assures a variety of modes for the participation of interest groups in the formation of policy."[11] Efforts to transform the ICC's regulatory regime demonstrated the effects of American pluralism in action.

The U.S. Congress, which had delegated regulatory authority to the ICC under the Transportation Act, became the focal point for protest and political action to change the terms of reference in rail passenger policy. Congress proved a receptive institutional setting for passenger train advocacy because senators and representatives operated to gain, and retain, political support on a regional- and issue-oriented basis. The legislative arena thus advantaged passenger train advocates in ways that regulatory proceedings had not.

Another key change in the terms of reference that emerged by the mid-1960s was increasing evidence of the fallacy that passenger trains' decline represented an economic anomaly for the rail industry as a whole. The same factors and forces that had stimulated people to travel by car and plane were also influencing a shift of freight to trucks, and to a lesser extent to air cargo. If the railroad's problem was more than a passenger train predicament—which the Hosmer report had darkly hinted at in pointing to "a disturbing overtone due to an implication that the passenger deficit may be a symptom of more deep-seated infirmities for which some remedy must be found if the railroads are to survive"[12]—simply facilitating exit from one segment of industrial activity would not, in itself, yield a successful restructuring and a sustainable economic future. New policy options appeared necessary to deal with the rail industry's economic troubles on a broader scale, opening the door to reconsidering where the passenger train might fit into such a future.

As various legislative proposals to subsidize, nationalize, or simply freeze the operation of remaining passenger trains worked their way through Congress, it became clear that passenger advocates within the rail policy community were on the verge of a political breakthrough. The ICC's regulatory framework, with its specific premise of passenger train obsolescence, had become delegitimated, partly due to the criticism of passenger train advocates, and partly because of mounting evidence that the rail industry's economic woes were much bigger, and more deeply rooted, than the passenger train problem. As a result, alternative premises—from preservation to renewal— were being taken seriously as the basis for a new industrial policy strategy.

The political risks of a major industrial collapse placed rail policy on the Nixon administration's agenda. At the same time, the economic risks of continuing passenger train losses, on the one hand, and the nationalization of rail assets on the other, motivated the rail industry to contemplate a legislated compromise between preserving passenger trains and abandoning them. The result was a narrow window of opportunity to create a public enterprise that could accommodate usually conflicting claims regarding rail passenger policy in particular, and rail industry restructuring more generally. Amtrak, America's unique policy instrument for satisfying these political demands, turned out to be the least offensive proposal to make it through an adversarial and divided policy community. However, it was not any one interest or organization's preferred option.

Amtrak satisfied rail industry demands for exit from the passenger business by superceding railroads' common carriage obligations in passenger transport. The new public corporation satisfied passenger train proponents and advocates by designating a national network of intercity passenger trains that would be maintained under quasi-public enterprise. And it satisfied the Nixon administration by adopting a "for-profit" mandate to limit the passenger train's future claims on the Treasury. As will be discussed more fully, Amtrak represented an entity that was fundamentally compromised by this need to compromise. The preceding regulatory regime had created intensely adversarial and competitive policy network dynamics that constrained the search for a more effective rail passenger policy, and burdened Amtrak with some heavy baggage from its inception.

Canadian regulatory policy approached the passenger train's economic decline from a very different starting point. Canadian railroads, dominated by the publicly owned Canadian National Railways, retained at least a measure of advocacy for passenger trains well after the initial signs of industrial decline had set in. These railroads and their regulators thus developed a policy that sought to maintain, rather than end, traditional passenger train operations, and to distribute the costs and benefits of that preservation widely.

To begin with, Canadian railroads were more accustomed to national government involvement and active engagement (accompanied by public investment) in guiding their industrial future. Canada's first transcontinental railway had not been completed until 1887, almost a generation later than its American counterpart. And government aid for ongoing development efforts of the Canadian Pacific Railway (CPR) had persisted up to 1897. Canadian

National Railways (CNR), the larger passenger carrier, had been nationalized beginning in 1917 and had been used as an instrument of active industrial policy since its inception.[13] It took almost a decade to sort out CNR's organizational arrangements following the government's plunge into large-scale rail reorganization. Following CNR's establishment, rail regulation had emphasized stability over competition by accepting, if not entrenching, a rail transport duopoly in Canada.

Over the ensuing decades, the two national carriers, publicly owned CNR and privately owned CPR, had become accustomed to coordination in place of competition for many aspects of their business, including a "pool" of passenger train operations between major cities in central Canada that lasted from the late 1930s to the mid 1960s. CNR and CPR also became accustomed to negotiating with government over rail policy matters. In place of the political conflict that regularly broke into the open in the United States, Canada's rail policy network contained many of the corporatist elements found in Europe. Furthermore, the railroad's position as the dominant national transportation mode persisted much later in Canada than in the United States and had consequences for enabling regulators to sanction a broader distribution of costs incurred in preserving passenger train services.

Part of the rail mode's economic vitality in Canada stemmed from the fact that Canada's federal constitution assigns responsibility for road transportation almost exclusively to the provinces. This absence of a national mandate for highway development, coupled with Canada's vast geography and great distance between population centers, thus oriented road transport to develop as a means of meeting local and regional mobility needs long before it became a major mode of long-haul intercity transportation.[14]

Air travel was under federal jurisdiction, but was also tightly regulated and structured in a parallel form of duopoly, with Air Canada being a public enterprise and Canadian Pacific Airlines being privately owned. Thus, despite the long distances between major population centers, Canadian air travel took longer to gain the market share found south of the border. Another aspect of this dominance was the railroad's solid position in freight transportation. In the 1950s and early 1960s, both CNR and CPR could cross-subsidize passenger losses from freight revenues because air and truck competition had not yet reached the point where rate increases would simply drive business away.

As a result of the Canadian transport sector's economic and political characteristics, the rail policy community that faced the passenger train problem looked, and acted, much differently than its United States counterpart. The rail industry as a whole did not abandon its advocacy for passenger services, primarily because the publicly owned CNR interpreted its mandate more broadly than did the CPR. For CNR, meeting shareholder expectations meant maximizing more than the direct revenues that could be accumulated in moving both people and freight. Rail mobility was seen as creating larger benefits for the society than the simple sums on a balance sheet. This contrasted with CPR's more orthodox approach to profit maximization and preference for exit from the passenger business over either preservation or renewal. The difference in these positions can be seen in the two railroads' testimony to the House of Commons' Standing Committee on Transport.

In 1966, the CPR identified "effective demand" as the market test that it applied in considering the future of its passenger services: "Effective demand is the demand for a service at prices which meet the cost of providing that service. . . . Throughout its history, the policy of the Company has been to meet fully the effective demand for passenger service and it intends to do so in the future. . . . The Company has always been reluctant to discontinue a service, and has never done so until after its studies established that the effective demand had gone and could not be recovered."[15]

This approach would have been little different from many U.S. railroads' approach to passenger management. But the CNR reflected a more proactive approach. Its testimony noted that "Effective demand . . . will come about only with an effective effort and effective service."[16] CNR went on to report that it had taken "a positive stand on the need for expanding the passenger business and benefit to be derived by the public from its use, and [that] intensive efforts have been made to attract the public to rail service as a modern, efficient, and pleasant mode of travel."[17]

There are various explanations for the different ways in which CNR and CPR approached the passenger train problem. Some scholars of bureaucracy have claimed that the inability to appropriate any earned surplus disposes leaders of public sector organizations to maximize total budget size rather than seek profits.[18] Others suggest that political constraints on allocating the factors of production and in revising goals encourage public enterprise executives to focus on improving their "top line" (i.e., performance capabilities) much more than their "bottom line" (i.e., profit).[19]

Without public enterprise playing a major role in Canada's national rail duopoly, rail passenger policy would have looked much more similar to that of the United States. But because CNR sought to balance public service and commercial return more evenly than did CPR, Canada's rail policy community retained industry advocacy for passenger trains through the early 1970s, at least a decade longer than south of the border. Advocacy for operating passenger services within the rail industry, however, did not translate into a level of government support for renewing passenger trains in parallel with Canada's development of road and air modes.

If Canada would have possessed the "critical mass" of industrial design and engineering skills for passenger railroading found in Japan, France, or Germany, then its rail policy community (led by CNR) might have been better positioned to pursue policy options that went beyond preservation. But given the rail sector's more limited industrial capacity, efforts to combat the passenger train's decline were confined largely to marketing, pricing, and service innovations such as CNR's "Red, White, and Blue Fares," a pricing scheme that foreshadowed the airline industry's yield management by at least a decade.

Canadian railroads and their regulators thus embarked upon an industrial strategy that sought to spread the cost of passenger service deficits broadly. More limited competition from planes and road transport meant that the actual cost of those deficits would be less than in the United States, at least through the 1960s. Evidence of this approach can be found in the Board of Transport Commissioners' ultimate formulation of its regulatory policy for adjudicating proposals to abandon passenger trains. In the year before it gave way to the new Canadian Transport Commission, the Board noted that it had exercised its responsibilities for adjudicating proposals to discontinue passenger trains by taking into account "all relevant factors, including the need of the public for train service and the kind of service given, the volume of patronage by the public and the prospects for patronage in future, alternative transportation services, revenues and expenses of the service, and the burden to the railway company of continuance of service and the effect on it of discontinuance."[20]

Initially, Canadian railroads' market dominance in freight transportation enabled the cross-subsidy option that emerged from such a redistributive regulatory approach to cover the passenger deficit. Passenger operations could be factored into the railways' cost base by regulators, leading to slightly higher freight rates. When shippers paid those higher rates, consumers eventually paid an indirect and invisible "tax" for passenger train preservation.

But by 1967, when the National Transportation Act (NTA) was proclaimed, the level of competition for freight transport had reached a point where passenger train losses could no longer be quietly cross-subsidized. And the gap between passenger train costs and revenues was too large for the railways to absorb without damage to their bottom line. It was this damage that brought the passenger train's economic problems onto Canada's public policy agenda more directly. As in the United States, the passenger train's predicament became part of a larger sectoral realignment in Canadian transportation.

The NTA sought to realign policy in light of the increasing competition among modes. It was inspired by the findings from the MacPherson Royal Commission on Transportation, which had concluded that the Canadian transportation industry, and the rail sector in particular, had passed beyond the "infant industry" stage where government support and protection were justified. Under these circumstances, the commission embraced regulatory liberalization declaring that "the railways' role as an instrument of national policy promoting settlement and production of traffic by the incentive of cross-subsidization . . . is obsolete."[21]

Enacting a new regulatory regime during Canada's centennial year, amid renewed attention to the symbolism of railways in general, and passenger trains in particular, as an instrument of nation building, made for a gulf between the cold economic logic of the Royal Commission's recommendations and the "hot" political passions that were stirred up in centenary celebrations. Given these circumstances, no government would have chosen to cut back passenger trains if public funds were available. And at this point in history, Canada's fiscal policy was not constrained. As a result, government moved to formalize the prior policy of preservation and back it with direct subsidy.

The NTA left room for the new Canadian Transport Commission (CTC) to support the continuation of passenger trains under guidelines that were far broader than the MacPherson Commission's recommendation that such services were justified only when "essential" (i.e., providing service to communities with no other means of public access) or "economic" (i.e., covering their costs through commercial receipts).[22] In a 1970 decision on CPR's petition to discontinue passenger service between Victoria and Courtnay, British Columbia, (a train that remains in operation to this day), the Rail Transport Committee (RTC) set out its rationale for looking beyond immediate commercial performance. The basis for this more expansive regulatory view was found in the NTA's distinction between the terms "unprofitable" and "uneconomic." The Committee noted: "To the extent that there are any differences in shades of meaning between these two words, the Act intends that such differences should be reflected in the Committee's considerations. The principal difference in meaning lies in the emphasis which the word 'uneconomic' lays on the intrinsic or fundamental nature of unprofitability, as opposed to temporary unprofitability or unprofitability which could be eliminated through operating changes within the present capability of the railway system."[23]

This distinction left room for the RTC to introduce public service (e.g., service quality) and nonmarket criteria (e.g., future changes in demand) that had inspired CNR's earlier cross-subsidy of passenger deficits. In this and other cases, even though the train's operation was found to be unprofitable, the service was not judged uneconomic.

To enable preservation, the NTA authorized the CTC-RTC to order public funding for 80 percent of the deficit from a particular passenger service's continued operation. Instead of associating the public interest with efficiency gains that the rail industry would achieve by exiting from unprofitable activity, the RTC weighed such benefits against the costs of reduced community access, rail employment, and passenger mobility. As a result of this balancing effort, the CTC opted for service abandonment in only eleven of the seventy passenger service petitions that were brought before it between 1967 and 1973. The remaining fifty-nine train services, representing the bulk of Canada's national rail passenger network, were approved for public subsidy.[24]

Canada's regulated cross-subsidy and subsidy schemes did more than just preserve passenger train operations. They also supported continuity and cohesion in the structure and function of the rail policy community through the initial decline of passenger trains, by enabling the preservation policy option through distributing both the costs and benefits of such preservation. For a time, government Ministers, rail executives, and regulatory leaders found common cause in subsidizing passenger losses at the expense of freight shippers (20 percent) and taxpayers (80 percent). As long as freight competition was limited and tax revenues were plentiful, neither shippers nor the public would delve into the passenger train's circumstances closely enough to challenge this cost distribution.

By picking up the tab before individuals and organizations bearing the cost noticed this price, Canada's government precluded mobilization around the costs of rail passenger restructuring. And by enacting this arrangement into the National Transportation Act, Parliament took up its role as the arbiter of policy disputes over how, and when, to restructure passenger operations. But unlike in the United States, government was not being pressured to change its regulatory policy framework by industry interests. Advocates for a new approach to addressing the passenger train problem and proponents of renewal were not mobilized in the way that radical change and extensive abandonment had done in the United States.

3.2. Incrementalism Without a Cause: the Transition to Public Enterprise

Public enterprise was adopted as the least objectionable policy instrument for rail passenger restructuring in both the United States and in Canada after regulatory policies had experimented at either extreme of the range of industrial restructuring options that could be applied to resolving the passenger train problem. In the United States, the ICC's regulation of rail passenger service drew from the laissez-faire end of economic doctrine, embracing policy instruments that would facilitate economic euthanasia for a declining industrial sector. U.S. regulators had rejected both the premise that the passenger train's decline was anything other than a terminal malady and most claims that sought to share the costs of retrenchment. The ICC presided over this downsizing until the rail mode retained just a skeletal network of intercity passenger transport. Moving to bury what remained of the rail passenger network's corpse proved politically untenable as cutbacks had mobilized a new coalition of policy advocates. Their activity tipped the balance of activity within the rail policy community, thereby influencing government to recognize multiple policy objectives from exit to renewal, and seek to pursue them by shifting instruments from regulation to quasi-public enterprise.

In Canada, regulators had chosen instruments from the interventionist end of economic doctrine that complemented government's leadership in the rail industry. This rationale interpreted the passenger train problem as arising from a market failure in which the full value of the train's employment, access, and mobility benefits were not recovered from the fares that were being paid. Public enterprise, a longstanding instrument of the Canadian government's initiative in transportation policy, took the lead in implementing cross-subsidy as a fiscal instrument that could correct for market deficiency. When the passenger train's losses mounted, such cross subsidy was complemented by direct public subsidy, an even more interventionist fiscal instrument. But while this subsidy scheme stabilized the supply of passenger train service, it did relatively little to change its declining position in relation to rapidly growing air and road alternatives. Keeping the passenger train on economic "life support" was not a policy without pitfalls, as costs mounted and usage stagnated. Eventually, preservation began to appear pointless as an end in itself, and the rail policy community accepted the need for a new enterprise to pursue a more commercially promising mission of rail passenger restructuring and revitalization.

In moving beyond the "all-or-nothing" approach of regulatory intervention to address the passenger train problem and choosing a new combination of policy goals and instruments for rail passenger renewal, both the United States and Canada were influenced by their respective rail policy communities. Neither of these policy communities proved adept at generating a coherent set of policy goals that could effectively be matched to a cluster of policy instruments enabling dramatic improvements along the lines of Japanese or European initiatives. Instead, the corporate entities and economic instruments that emerged from American and Canadian efforts at redesigning rail passenger policy have proven themselves ill-suited to the task of industrial renewal.

Amtrak and VIA Rail each exhibit significant and, some would argue fatal, flaws that constrain progress in renewing the passenger train. Instead, both of these entities have become trapped in a particular type of policy stalemate that inhibits the kinds of change needed to move beyond stagnant, or declining, commercial performance. Examining the specific nature of Amtrak's and VIA's policy goals and their fit, or lack thereof, with instruments will demonstrate why both companies have been trapped in this extended policy stalemate that, in itself, has become a significant obstacle to renewing the passenger train.

Amtrak's structure and its function represent a problematic muddle of both strategies and tactics regarding how to deal with uneconomic passenger trains. From a distance, Amtrak's ambiguous objectives and haphazard instrumentation might look similar to many other U.S. policy domains where creative "fudging" around disputed goals and contested instruments allows for subsequent compromise and fine tuning, in the celebrated tradition of American incrementalism. Charles Lindblom, one of America's most articulate proponents of incrementalism in policy analysis and implementation, would likely have argued that the passenger train's transition from private to public enterprise should not be expected to pursue a neat formula for success.

Lindblom once wrote that the choice facing policymakers is not between options based upon partial knowledge and limited analysis, on the one hand, and complete information underpinning comprehensive planning, on the other. In the real world, policy actors face a choice between the deliberate and designed incompleteness of incremental policy solutions and the ill-considered and accidental incompleteness behind purportedly comprehensive solutions.[25] Unfortunately, though Amtrak's organizational deficiencies were indeed deliberate, they could not be described as intentional. Larger economic and political forces had made the regulatory status quo untenable, thus demanding a policy "solution" in which efficacy took a distant second place to immediacy. Exploring how, under the force of circumstances, the rail policy community's conflicting priorities for passenger restructuring simply got translated into incompatible goals will demonstrate how this pathological variant of incrementalism institutionalized a policy stalemate into Amtrak's organizational structure.

For the railroads, Amtrak's immediate goal was to rid their industry of further economic responsibility for the passenger train, and its ultimate goal was to preside over a definitive end to this mode of transport. As a means of ending passenger service, Amtrak represented a second-best solution to the straightforward abandonment process that the ICC had sanctioned up through the 1960s. But the difficulty in making a clean exit from the last of their passenger service obligations convinced rail executives that an organizational intermediary had become necessary. Amtrak would assume managerial responsibility and financial liability for the remaining intercity passenger trains, leaving railroads free to pursue profit through their freight operations. Many railroads expected Amtrak to bring down the curtain on the "grand finale" in the American passenger train's long-running drama. Amtrak thus represented a policy "ceiling" in terms of tolerable government intervention for the railroads. To the rail industry, along with many skeptics from other modes and ideological dissenters, Amtrak's greatest accomplishment would be to prove that passenger trains had no future by failing commercially, then going out of business, thus wiping the rail passenger policy slate clean. For these skeptics, Amtrak was to be a self-effacing policy initiative.

Railroads' normally reflexive opposition to any form of government intervention was finally overcome by the urgency of both economic and political threats from alternative policy options. Economically, decline was now reaching a point of crisis for the industry's core freight business. Railroads' share of intercity freight transport had declined from 68 percent in 1944 to 44 percent in 1960.[26] High revenue producing shipments (e.g., food products, less-than-carload freight, and "express" traffic) had suffered the greatest diversion to road and air competition. As a whole, the industry's economic performance was worrisome, with 1971 seeing the lowest corporate earnings since 1932.[27] With just a 3 percent industry-wide rate of return, some analysts questioned whether "the industry as a whole has underlying weakness propelling it toward nationalization."[28]

In the Northeast, where competitive dynamics most favored this shift to trucks, the drain of passenger losses hit railroads especially hard. During January and February of 1970, the Penn Central Railroad was losing $375,000 a day on its passenger train operations.[29] When the Penn Central entered bankruptcy protection, it was the largest corporate failure, to date, in American history. The drain of passenger losses had contributed to this company's downfall, and rapid relief from future losses appeared essential to sparing more carriers from the same fate. News coverage from these dark days quoted the Senate Commerce Committee's Surface Transportation Subcommittee chair as raising the specter of much more sweeping public intervention in the rail sector: "Senator Vance Hartke [D-Ind.] warned today that nationalization of American railroads was a distinct threat if there was a financial collapse of the industry. The Indiana Democrat said that, because of 'frustration' with the railroads' recurring complex problems and prolonged crises, 'nationalization is no longer a nasty word' on Capitol Hill."[30]

While America's rail industry as a whole avoided this extreme of government intervention, it is almost certain that a "free enterprise" solution to the crisis would not have occurred without a public enterprise being created to run passenger trains. A Federal Railroad Administration report[31] characterized the Rail Passenger Service Act of 1970 as the first of four legislative initiatives that laid the foundation for the rail industry's economic renewal.

Politically, the mounting evidence of decline in freight transport, combined with growing advocacy for passenger train preservation, legitimated the possibility of government intervention. Labor unions, the National Association of Railroad Passengers, and an assortment of other passenger train proponents that had coalesced through the ICC hearing process were stalking the halls of Congress and getting a positive reception to their pleas for government intervention. Proposals for publicly initiated reorganization of passenger train service had been floated in Congress as early as 1961, when Senator Winston Prouty (R-Vt.) had requested Commerce Committee staff to study alternatives to operation by existing carriers. This report raised three policy options: a new private carrier that could amalgamate passenger services (akin to the Pullman Company's pool of sleeping and dining cars); a new publicly owned carrier; and "a new joint public-private corporation with controlling interest in private hands and Federal interest in the form of a loan or purchase of preferred stock, or other senior and marketable instrument."[32] The latter policy option appears to have been the earliest conception of a renewal strategy that would mix public and private enterprise in a new organization dedicated to revitalizing passenger trains.

In 1969, a year before the Penn Central bankruptcy, the Department of Transportation presented three policy options for rail passenger reorganization to the Senate Commerce Committee.[33] The first option was a federal matching grant program that would be administered by state or local organizations ready to make investments in rail passenger infrastructure or equipment, which private carriers would continue to operate. The second was a private corporation (initially called "Railpax") that would be jointly owned by the railroads and the government and would focus on developing profitable operations in promising markets. And the third option was to provide federal capital grants for equipment and infrastructure used by services that were either profitable or would be supported by operating subsidies from state and local government.

When states did not come forward to embrace any of the "cooperative" policy options, and Congress appeared poised to pass a more costly and interventionist public enterprise, the Nixon administration announced that it would support a mixed enterprise option. Speaking for the rail industry, Stuart Saunders, chairman of Penn Central, had testified that the financial balance in a mixed enterprise would be entirely one-sided, stating, "you wouldn't get a penny of private money put into this thing."[34] But while railroads insisted that a for-profit, mixed-ownership passenger carrier would never succeed, they reluctantly, but literally, bought into the concept. The way in which Railpax was structured offers evidence for the claim that railroads viewed it as a prelude to the passenger train's demise.

The Rail Passenger Service Act of 1970 left railroads free to choose whether to join in the new quasi-public passenger initiative or not. Those that opted out of joining the new mixed enterprise were not eligible to go before the ICC with any further petitions to discontinue passenger trains until 1975. The twenty carriers that did choose to participate were required to invest a sum in the new venture. Such payments would constitute the rail industry's dowry to marry off their equivalent of an old maid, their aging and unattractive passenger trains. This amount was to be "computed by one of three formulas, whichever was most favorable to the railroad: (1) 50 percent of the fully allocated passenger deficits of the railroad for 1969; (2) 100 percent of the avoidable loss for all intercity rail passenger service operated by the railroad during 1969; (3) 200 percent of the avoidable loss for the intercity rail passenger service operated in 1969 by the railroad over routes between points chosen for the basic system, as determined by the corporation's planning."[35] The railroads' dowry approached $200 million, which was to be augmented by a $40 million federal grant and access to $100 million in loan guarantees.

In return for their initial investment, which could be paid either in cash, in kind through the transfer of passenger cars and locomotives, or by a credit against the fees that the new enterprise would pay to run passenger trains over these carriers' tracks, railroads obtained permanent relief from their passenger service obligations. They also received the choice of taking common stock in Amtrak, or obtaining a one-time tax deduction for this expense. The Penn Central, Milwaukee Road, and Grand Trunk Western railroads each took the stock because they had no taxes against which they could write off their investment.[36] Of the sixteen railroads that were still paying federal taxes, only one, the Burlington Northern, elected to take stock in the new entity. This demonstrates that most railroads did not ever expect Amtrak to make a profit, and saw no value in holding a stake in this new carrier. For these carriers, the greatest return on their investment in what became Amtrak was the long awaited opportunity for a complete exit from the passenger business.

Media coverage of Amtrak's inauguration lends further credence to the hypothesis that the skeptics in America's business community viewed the new initiative as a chance to pursue the path of industrial exit to its logical conclusion, while supporters among labor and consumer organizations saw this as the opening act of a much more ambitious renewal drama. The *Wall Street Journal* highlighted the apparent contradiction of creating a quasi-public enterprise to accomplish what the railroad industry had been denied by the Interstate Commerce Commission, the green light to abandon hopelessly unprofitable passenger trains: "The Rail Passenger Service Act, which established Railpax, makes it clear that the government, in sustaining rail passenger service, intends to take the very methods that the railroads themselves have been denied by the Interstate Commerce Commission [i.e., reducing train operations drastically]." Citing the fact that the number of trains would be cut from 366 to 185, the paper asks: "Why couldn't the railroads have been given the power Railpax was given? Why was a new corporation needed to do what the railroads themselves have wanted to do?"[37]

A *New York Times* columnist wrote, "The problem is that the whole operation, so far, appears defensive—as if operating passenger trains were an unpleasant duty, like keeping an old and feeble person alive, that everyone will someday be glad to shed."[38] Anthony Haswell, the chairman of the National Association of Railroad Passengers suggested that the political compromises leading to Amtrak had yielded a compromised policy: "Amtrak's directors have chosen not to build their own organization but, rather, have made their corporation simply a contract with the individual railroads that will continue to operate the trains. . . . Amtrak is operated by people who don't want it to succeed. . . . I have to regard this day as discouraging though of course we are going to continue our fight."[39]

Secretary of Transportation John Volpe was perhaps the only public official who expressed unreserved enthusiasm upon Amtrak's inauguration, stating "It lays the foundation . . . for what in my opinion is destined to become the all-time comeback in the history of American transportation."[40] Elsewhere in the rail policy community, it soon became clear that nobody had gotten what they wanted out of the exercise. Why was there so little satisfaction with policy following so much political initiative?

For skeptics, Amtrak was like the guest who would not leave a party. Railroads, in particular, were not slow in relating to Amtrak as a contender. For just as passenger trains continued to compete with air and bus alternatives, they also occupied the railroads' privately owned infrastructure that otherwise could have been used exclusively for profitable freight transport. The Rail Passenger Service Act granted Amtrak the right to access railroad infrastructure on an "avoidable cost" basis, while receiving priority (at least in principle) over freight operations. This was the closest that government had come to exercising public authority over private infrastructure since 1920, when the Director General of Railroads and head of the United States Railroad Administration, William G. McAdoo, ended emergency control over the nation's rail network, instituted during World War I. In exiting the passenger business, railroads were required to open their infrastructure up to passenger operations, basically at cost, for a period of twenty-five years. During that time, Amtrak was to be at times aggressive and at times reluctant in exercising this authority. At its most active, Amtrak has used this "extraordinary power it had been granted by Congress to seize track from the Boston & Maine and reconvey it to [the] Central Vermont" Railroad,[41] imposing an expropriation equivalent to the eminent domain proceedings usually pursued by states and cities to build roads and airports. This was not exactly the clean break with passenger operations that American railroads had envisioned in 1971.

But for passenger train advocates, there was nothing temporary or tentative about Amtrak's mission. Their goal was nothing less than renewing the passenger train. The $140 million in federal support, which was exhausted in less than a year, was viewed as just the down payment on much more ambitious public leadership of, and investment in, rail renewal. With Washington pouring billions into highway construction, airport expansion, and air traffic control, advocates viewed public spending on new and better trains as wholly appropriate. Contrary to the rail industry's vehement denials, supporters viewed the passenger train's economic decline as entirely reversible once government began treating this mode akin to others and investing large sums of money in Amtrak. From the advocacy perspective, Amtrak was expected to spend public resources in order to fill America's tracks with new passenger trains and these trains with new passengers.

Advocates expected Amtrak to accomplish this turnaround in the course of meeting their specific needs. For organized labor, Amtrak was both a guarantor of job security and an entity that could enhance workers' standard of living. Security meant running passenger trains with the same workforce that private railroads had previously used. It also meant maintaining the same work rules and seniority provisions that had prevailed. And job security also meant compensating any workers who might be displaced by the transition to new operating arrangements (including any downsizing of future train services), with up to six years' wages as a severance package. These terms were written into the Rail Passenger Service Act.

For many smaller- and mid-sized communities, Amtrak's goal was to maintain, if not improve, access to locations that were increasingly left behind by airlines and bus companies. Even if the number of passengers was few, and the immediate market prospects dim, Amtrak was expected to find a way to thrive by serving the many hundreds of communities that other carriers were passing up. For railroad passengers, and in particular the approximately 10,000 members of the National Association of Railroad Passengers, Amtrak's national scope was also quite important. In addition to wide coverage, Amtrak was expected to refurbish the passenger train's unique and prized amenities. Sleeping cars, dining cars, and observation cars made train riding a pleasurable experience for railroad aficionados, even though such services also boosted costs quite considerably. The new Amtrak was expected to succeed by providing the frills and flourishes that private carriers had trimmed back in their efforts to contain costs. The passenger train's traditional amenities were thus expected to be maintained at the same time as new investments in technology and market development were made.

For its supporters as much as its skeptics, Amtrak was a second best solution to more extensive or ambitious forms of intervention—ranging from more generous subsidies to private railroads to outright nationalization. Kent Weaver characterized the tenor of the times in noting that when it came to railroad restructuring, "Innovation in policy instruments served as a substitute for innovation in policy."[42] It represented a policy "floor" for government intervention in rail passenger restructuring. Just like the railroads that viewed Amtrak as a transitional initiative, many advocates also saw this quasipublic enterprise as a stopgap measure. But unlike the railroads, they expected any shortcomings to trigger further moves away from the passenger train's demise, with increasing government intervention.

And for the Nixon administration, Amtrak was just one of numerous expressions of political cynicism being applied to the exigencies of governance. Rather than confronting, or even seriously considering, the disputed issues surrounding the passenger train's decline—or undertaking the arduous work of developing a new federal partnership with states and localities that were justifiably reluctant to enter the morass of rail passenger renewal with so little policy support—the administration put Amtrak forward as a means of avoiding the problem. The goal that mattered most to the executive branch at the time that Amtrak was created (perhaps as a result of its other and more sinister political activities), was deniability. Such denial came in three variants with respect to Amtrak.

First, Amtrak was intended to create the appearance that rail passenger renewal could be accomplished without tremendous adjustment costs. To subdue the political mobilization that concentrated adjustment costs had precipitated during the railroads' regulated exit, Amtrak would deny the need for further sacrifice by workers, communities, and users. This would hopefully curtail further pressures on Congress. To meet this goal, the administration accepted fantastic predictions of profitability that were forecast by the Department of Transportation and discounted the sober warnings about Amtrak's economic failings put forward by the Office of Management and Budget. By the time the Rail Passenger Service Act was signed, even analysts within the Department of Transportation viewed their forecasts as being fictional. Weaver quotes a DOT official admitting that favorable rail passenger analysis had "got to be a flat-assed lie. It had really blown the whole analytic effort, but by that time we were so committed to the program that we wouldn't let them [OMB] win."[43]

Second, Amtrak was supposed to deny the legislative proponents of more "radical" approaches to economic intervention in the rail sector an opportunity to control the policy agenda. Amtrak would thus serve as a kind of "policy blocker"—occupying the institutional and administrative space that a more ambitious and costly program would have otherwise fit into. Like the drugs that prevent various physiological signals from triggering receptors in the body, a policy blocker is intended to prevent the stimulation of specific receptors in the body politic (e.g., organized interests, a particular branch of government, or a particular level of government) from springing into action.

The Rail Passenger Service Act of 1970 sidetracked a more ambitious proposal for rail passenger renewal that had been reported out of the Senate's Commerce Committee in April 1970. Responding to calls for subsidy by the Association of American Railroads and for some new policy guidance by the Interstate Commerce Commission,[44] this bill would have designated a "basic national system" of passenger trains, authorized operating subsidies for those trains, provided financial assistance for modernizing and replacing passenger train equipment, introduced federal supervision of service standards, and tightened the ICC's control over train discontinuance.[45]

Amtrak also took over responsibility for ongoing implementation of the High-Speed Ground Transportation Act of 1965, which had funded fast train demonstration projects between Boston, New York, and Washington. In the six years between 1965 and Amtrak's creation in 1971, the jet powered "Turbo-Train" was introduced between Boston and New York, making the trip in four hours, and the electric "Metroliner" cut train schedules between Washington and New York to under three hours. During the following twenty-nine years, Amtrak scrapped the Turbo-Train and slowed down the Metroliner. Only in 2000, when electrification was extended to Boston and the next generation Acela Express train went into limited service, has Amtrak realized any significant improvement upon the operating performance that existed when it took over the initiative to bring high-speed train travel to America's Northeast.

And third, Amtrak was meant to deny future policy-makers the opportunity to blame government for the possible collapse and termination of America's passenger trains. Such blame, if it were to arise, could then be focused on Amtrak's leadership rather than the government's transportation policy deficiencies or alleged connivance with railroad companies, as had been the case in recent years. Amtrak has exhibited an enduring, and exceptional, ability to attract blame for the passenger train's ongoing shortcomings over the years. This unenviable quality would have satisfied at least some of its architects' desire to pass the "hot potato" of passenger train problems along quickly. Indeed, some of its architects have gone on to become perennial critics.

The ongoing intervention to preserve uneconomic trains has become a favored whipping boy for opponents of big government. President Reagan, in particular, would periodically remind the American public that they were being "railroaded" and "taken for a ride" by subsidies to Amtrak. But Amtrak has not (yet) had to take the blame for the end of intercity passenger train service, because it remains in business—an outcome that probably would have surprised many of its architects in the Nixon administration.

Given these disparate and conflicting policy goals, it is hardly surprising that Amtrak has been locked into a policy stalemate that cannot overcome the original sin of its poor institutional design. On October 18, 1971, less than six months after Amtrak had begun doing business on May 1, 1971, Secretary of Transportation John Volpe returned to Congress requesting an additional $170 million subsidy just to enable America's new passenger railroad to survive through the government's fiscal year (i.e., through March 31, 1972). This marked the start of an ongoing subsidy program that has now passed the $25 billion mark.

Whatever "honeymoon" that there was, or might have been, between supporters and skeptics came to an abrupt end. Instead of the miraculous transformation in passenger train performance that would have been required in order to satisfy all of the demands and expectations surrounding its creation, Amtrak revealed itself to be a worse commercial loser than almost anyone had been willing to publicly admit during its inception. What this launched was an, as yet, unending and unforgiving series of congressional appropriation deliberations—often generating fierce budget battles to keep America's intercity passenger trains running. Supporters and skeptics have since engaged in often intense political conflict over the public funds devoted to the passenger train's future, with the key difference being that this future was now contested through the fate of an enterprise (Amtrak) that had been created as a non-solution to the policy problem!

Amtrak's thirty-year history has seen much lobbying, political negotiation within Congress, and conflict between Congress and the executive branch, with very modest change in the passenger train's place at the bottom of American intercity passenger options. For all the sound and fury attending these debates, there have been only limited and sporadic efforts made to revisit the tough choices and disputed visions that would need to be addressed, if not reconciled, in order to significantly improve the passenger train's prospects in America. Instead, supporters and skeptics have largely debated past one another, each basing their arguments for or against the passenger train from the very real contradictions that are embodied within Amtrak as an enterprise. In this sense, most of the debate and political conflict surrounding Amtrak has reinforced and entrenched its organizational deficiencies.

Rail passenger skeptics from George W. Hilton[46] to the Cato Institute[47] and the Reason Foundation[48] criticize Amtrak for failing to live up to its "for-profit" mandate. In so doing they exaggerate the significance of the direct subsidies the corporation receives and ignore the fact that these are in lieu of the indirect subsidies that are part of other transport modes' finances. For example, figure 3.3 charts Amtrak's cost-recovery ratio, which has shown considerable improvement, from 0.48 (i.e., obtaining only forty-eight cents of revenue for every dollar in expense) since 1980 to 0.78 in 1999.[49] While debates rage over how to measure revenues and expenses in assessing Amtrak's commercial performance, to be discussed below, the fact remains that Amtrak's corporate "bottom line" has been well above the much admired French, German, and Japanese railways for many years of its recent history.

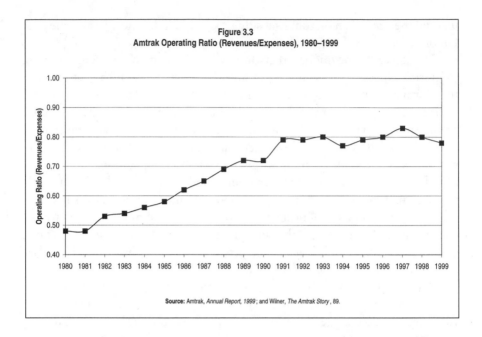

Figure 3.3
Amtrak Operating Ratio (Revenues/Expenses), 1980–1999

Source: Amtrak, *Annual Report, 1999*; and Wilner, *The Amtrak Story*, 89.

This performance also beats most American public transit operators, who go about their "money-losing" business with far less political opposition than Amtrak. In 1999, for example, New York City recovered 71 percent of its transit agency's costs from the farebox. Washington obtained a recovery of 66 percent. Chicago got just 50 percent of its transit costs out of the farebox. And Philadelphia recovered just 44 percent of its costs from users. These losses attract far less in the way of criticism.[50]

Skeptics also take issue with supporters' enthusiastic claims for Amtrak's external benefits in terms of energy savings, congestion relief, and reduced pollution. Love, Cox, and Moore claim that "even a doubling of train ridership would reduce energy consumption and traffic congestion by less than 0.1 percent."[51] In so doing, they rely on average measures from aggregate data that depict Amtrak as a "drop in the bucket" of America's intercity mobility. This approach ignores the very real marginal contributions to congestion, energy, and pollution relief that Amtrak makes in specific, and quite major, travel markets (e.g., New York–Washington). The marginal effect of dumping a peak-hour trainload of passengers into already overcrowded airports (such as La Guardia and Reagan-National) and onto gridlocked highways is quite different from the unrealistic assumption that they will travel evenly throughout the day and around the nation. Such a failure to distinguish between average and marginal cost estimation leads to questionable claims like the following: "The *average* subsidy to a New York–Los Angeles rider exceeds $1,000. The estimated round trip subsidy per passenger for a Denver-Chicago trip is $650. It would be cheaper for taxpayers to shut down routes like these and purchase discount round-trip airfare for all Amtrak riders."[52]

While the individual price of a few off-peak plane tickets between Chicago and Denver might be cheaper than a rail passenger's average subsidy, the cost of buying many tickets a day, numbering into the hundreds at peak travel times such as Fridays, Sundays, and holidays, would not be such a bargain. Airlines have long ago embraced the marginal cost pricing concept which seems to escape Amtrak's skeptics when they decry the "waste" of high subsidies.

When it comes to frames of reference by which to judge passenger trains' potential, skeptics continue to insist that the technological determinism underlying the ICC's regulated exit policy was more legitimate than the market failure created by government's fiscal favoritism of road and air infrastructure. In a world where speed and flexibility are seen to count for almost everything in terms of intercity travel behavior, the traditional passenger train's prospects against aircraft and automobiles continue to appear unpromising. And when high-speed rail's potential can no longer be ignored, it is dismissed as being an appropriate responsibility for private sector leadership. Modern trains are presented as very costly, as long as one overlooks the public expenditures on aviation and highways. Robert W. Poole's testimony to Congress on behalf of the Reason Foundation exemplifies this perspective. He stated, "To the extent that viable market opportunities for [high-speed rail] services exist, they are best pursued as individual private or public-private ventures, each tailored to the market it seeks to serve and competing mostly with air service in that market. . . . Since airlines are by-and-large not subsidized by American taxpayers, neither should high-tech rail systems be subsidized by our taxpayers."[53]

The techno-economic obsolescence paradigm, which informed the regulated exit strategy that had set the stage for Amtrak, has subsequently been discredited by the freight railroads' effective and profitable restructuring to compete against trucking and even air freight carriers. No other transport mode (even including ocean shipping) exhibits the schizophrenic combination of obsolete passenger technology and competitive freight technology that skeptics would attribute to railroads in America. Clearly, then, part of the problem must extend into the realm of organization and technique. Skeptics thus overlook the major policy opportunity for redeploying financial and human resources in American passenger rail operations in ways that could attract new riders and hence boost both the train's commercial revenues and positive externalities.

Rail passenger supporters are similarly trapped in this unproductive policy stalemate when they defend Amtrak as the last bastion of American intercity passenger train service. In so doing, they are also prone to exaggerate the value of the benefits that it provides and to look the other way regarding some of its costs. With less than 4 percent of the market for intercity travel by common carrier, dropping to 0.5 percent if travel by automobile is included, Amtrak as we know it can hardly be viewed as the centerpiece of a successful and sustainable American transportation policy that its supporters claim. Amtrak's equity, energy, and environmental contributions often fall short of what its supporters claim either do exist or could exist. And in most cases, these claims fall short of what is possible due to the organizational deficiencies that beset Amtrak.

In place of technological determinism, the American rail policy community's passenger advocates and proponents are drawn to another dogmatic frame of reference. They embrace a long-term historical perspective that highlights the past policy injustices perpetrated against railroads relative to air and road development, as well as by the railroads themselves against passenger trains. The title of *Getting There: The Epic Struggle between Road and Rail in the American Century* captures the spirit of this historical perspective, encapsulated in author Stephen Goddard's claim that: "Road and rail, had they competed on a level playing field, might each have thrived without substantial public subsidies. But when a country needs both modes and decides to feed one and starve the other, it ends up shouldering the loser's dying carcass as well. Congress's decision to invest in forty-one thousand miles of broad 'freeways' doomed any chance the railroads had to recapture a solid share of passenger traffic."[54]

Peter Lyon's book *To Hell in a Day Coach* depicted railroad management as eager accomplices in this industrial decline: "For at least a generation all of [the rail industry's executives] have, for sundry reasons, persistently sought to scuttle most of their passenger service, and some of them have contrived to slaughter their passenger business entirely. There has been nothing sly or underhanded about this policy; on the contrary, it has been diligently plugged by the presidents of the biggest and most influential railroad companies."[55]

In addition to emphasizing past wrongdoings, American passenger train advocacy also looks forward to a time when energy and environmental needs will again make passenger trains a necessity. Joseph Vranich's book *Supertrains* epitomizes this forward-looking optimism regarding passenger trains' ability to save America from gridlock and pollution. He catalogues the litany of economic, energy, and environmental drawbacks from relying almost exclusively on cars and planes for intercity travel in the United States and expresses confidence that "when environmentalists, business interests, and beleaguered travelers all start speaking positively about Supertrains, then it's only a matter of time before they'll all be riding them together."[56]

This perspective is echoed in the public statements of rail passenger advocates. Speaking on behalf of the U.S. Conference of Mayors, Thomas Kaine claimed that "high-speed rail will boost our economy's productivity, increase safety, create jobs, and enable our highways and airports to fulfil their potential."[57] The president of the High Speed Ground Transportation Association stated, "Until high-speed ground transport is developed as a 'missing link' in an efficient transportation system, our nation will continue to suffer the consequences of lower productivity, increasing traffic fatalities, decreased air quality, and reduced energy efficiency."[58] Even the passenger train's inability to keep pace with other modes' growth can be presented as a future advantage, as when the National Association of Railroad Passengers declared that "the significant unused capacity in existing and potential short-distance corridors represents a great opportunity for federal and state investment, because as transportation demand grows, so will rail's cost-effectiveness advantage compared to other modes.'"[59]

By looking backward to past policy errors, excepting those related specifically to Amtrak, and forward to future policy opportunities, supporters avoid the more difficult confrontation of Amtrak's current shortcomings. Instead, they remain in a more-or-less-permanent defensive mode that has led to many missed opportunities to redeploy Amtrak's resources more effectively. Among rail passenger supporters, Amtrak's advocates have also exploited the corporation's dependence on public subsidy in order to secure specific and concentrated benefits.

Organized labor has sought to preserve traditional working arrangements that put Amtrak at a competitive disadvantage with discount airlines and bus companies. Statutory prohibitions on contracting out work and mandates to pay displaced workers up to six years' wages in "labor protection" were the price of union support for the Rail Passenger Service Act, and both provisions have been defended vigorously by organized labor and its supporters.[60] Speaking on behalf of such interests, Gregory Lawler depicted Amtrak's labor protection mandate as having virtually no cost: "You continually hear it is as if labor protection is somehow hurting Amtrak's financial performance. Last year, they paid approximately $500,000 to employees who lost their jobs. Those are insignificant labor protection costs, $500,000 with expenditures in the billions."[61] In addition to their support of labor protection mandates with the railroads, labor unions are alleged to have been instrumental in the ouster of at least one Amtrak president, Thomas Downs, whose abrupt departure is examined more closely in chapter 5.

Regional constituencies have, at various times, obtained passenger routes and services that were among Amtrak's most uneconomic because their member of Congress had influence over Amtrak funding. At its inception, Amtrak added a train across southern Montana to its national network (in addition to a train route across northern Montana) when Senator Mansfield (D-Mont.) was majority leader. During the 1970s, Amtrak ran up to three trains a day across West Virginia when Senator Robert Byrd (D-W.Va.) was majority leader and Representative Harley Staggers (D-W.Va.) chaired the House Committee on Interstate and Foreign Commerce. In the 1980s, Amtrak upgraded the track between Philadelphia and Atlantic City and ran several trains a day on that route when Representative James Florio (D-N.J.) chaired the House Commerce Committee's Transportation Subcommittee. A passenger train through Idaho and eastern Oregon that had been engineered by Senator Frank Church (D-Idaho) kept running through the tenure of Senator Bob Packwood (R-Oreg.) as chairman of the Senate Committee on Commerce, Science, and Transportation. Following the retirement of these elected representatives, Amtrak dropped these trains. Such routes were abandoned sooner or later after the member of Congress ceased to have a direct role in Amtrak's legislative affairs.

Not only have Amtrak's troubled origins clouded the distinction between a problematic public enterprise, in particular, and the passenger train's potential more generally, they have also blocked the passenger train's incorporation into the policy framework governing the relatively successful performance of all other transport modes in America. Amtrak's organizational deficiencies are not wholly internal, although its structure has posed many problems for managers of a public-enterprise, for-profit passenger carrier. Some of the most problematic constraints on renewing the passenger train in America have arisen from Amtrak's institutional isolation within the American transportation policy framework.[62] With conflicting policy goals, a contradictory mandate and a contested mission, Amtrak was simply "not ready for prime time" in its ability to orchestrate the passenger train's comeback as a productive member of the larger American transportation policy community. Amtrak fell short of the institutionalized norms by which other modes, and even the freight railroads, did business in a number of ways.

The contentious relationship between Amtrak and America's freight rail-roads is just the beginning of the passenger train's anomalous position. No other American transport mode operates with the degree of organizational separation between freight and passenger carriage that is found on the rail-roads. When both sides of the rail transport mode were confronting decline, this separation appeared to be a necessary evil—a way of isolating the acute contagion of passenger decline from the weak commercial immunity of rail freight transportation.

But after the passenger train had been quarantined, and freight railroads achieved considerable success in commercial renewal, Amtrak stood out as the "poor relation" in economic terms (i.e., assets, trackage, employees, and balance sheets) as well as in political terms (i.e., lobbyists, campaign contributions, and media advertising).[63] More than any other transportation mode, America's freight railroads pride themselves in "paying their own way" through privately owned, taxed, and unsubsidized infrastructure. This environment, over which more than 95 percent of Amtrak's route-miles are operated, is not a welcoming one in either economic or political terms.

Rail infrastructure capacity was downsized during the 1980s following the industry's deregulation. With economic and traffic growth in the 1990s, there are now real bottlenecks and peak-time capacity shortages in American rail infrastructure. As a result, the opportunity cost of accommodating current passenger operations, let alone expanded service, is perceived to be high by Amtrak's infrastructure landlords. In practice, Amtrak trains take second place to freight much of the time.

Upgrading freight railroads' infrastructure in key markets to meet passenger needs has been a slow and costly process. Some states (e.g., California, New York, Michigan, and Illinois) have invested in such efforts. But state investments in rail infrastructure have been relatively small-scale upgrades to segments of a passenger train's route, not the full-scale refurbishment of an entire route's tracks. Amtrak has also invested much more heavily in an entire route, its flagship "Northeast Corridor" between Boston, New York, and Washington, where it owns most of the tracks. Rail passenger infrastructure investment has translated into ridership and revenue gains primarily where entities other than freight railroads (e.g., states, regional transportation districts, or Amtrak) have assumed ownership. To date, adding or upgrading infrastructure for high-speed passenger operations on freight railroads' rights-of-way has been a anathema to rail executives. Until recently, freight railroads have made it clear that they do not welcome more passenger trains, especially the types of high-speed, high-frequency services that have succeeded in bringing travelers back to the rails abroad. Some railroad executives have just begun to express an interest in public infrastructure investments that could mutually benefit both passenger and freight operations. These tentative signals of détente between the freight railroads and government are discussed in chapter 6.

The passenger train's infrastructure needs have also been sidetracked by Amtrak's isolation from the institutionally "durable" trust funds that were created first by states, and then by Washington to support highway development.[64] These funds have been broadened and replicated at the national level to support airport and air traffic control infrastructure, waterways, and urban public transportation. Revenues are generated by dedicated excise taxes ("user fees") on fuel, tickets, and other consumption related to a particular mobility mode. Trust funds now represent the gold standard in terms of America's fiscal policy in transportation, and only Amtrak and the intercity passenger train remain outside the loop where the vast majority of these funds are raised and appropriated.

Initially, no trust fund was proposed for Amtrak because the corporation was designed to be for-profit and thus fully self-supporting, in the tradition of modern American railroads. Skeptics assumed that passenger trains would not be around long enough to require extended public support. As figure 3.1 details above, during the decade after 1971, Congress dispensed both capital and operating assistance with a relatively generous hand. Amtrak's appropriations climbed from $40 million in 1971 to $907.3 million in 1981. But the Reagan administration viewed deficit spending on programs like Amtrak as intolerable, and sought reductions, and sometimes elimination, of public funding to the corporation. It was only following the threat of being "zeroed out" of the federal budget that Amtrak began to seek a permanent and stable funding source. This search for fiscal stability marked the start of "reinvention" efforts that are detailed in chapter 5.

But after 1981, once Amtrak began to focus on restructuring for a fiscally sustainable future, it was too late to claim that the corporation could only survive with a dedicated funding source. A decade of ad hoc subsidies had established a pattern of congressional bargaining over Amtrak's routes and services that suited a majority of federal legislators who could either take credit for "saving" Amtrak from its foes each year, or heap blame on Amtrak and its allies as exemplars of wasteful big government. Amtrak's ongoing political stalemate also made it too early to reinterpret the "original intent" of Amtrak's architects as allowing room for harmonization with the rest of American transportation funding.

Other modes, including public transit, saw Amtrak as a budgetary rival and did not want to admit one more player with a huge potential appetite for infrastructure spending to the federal transportation financing mechanism. Congressional jurisdictions meant that Amtrak would have to move either all or part of its legislative supervision from the House Commerce Committee to Public Works, a transfer that both committees resisted.

Amtrak's stalemate has also switched the rail passenger policy community off the main-line intergovernmental policy network that operates for other transportation modes. With very limited exceptions (e.g., California, New York, North Carolina, and Washington state), passenger train policy has been an "inside the beltway" deliberation since Amtrak's creation. Unlike other modes, which have sunk deep roots in state transportation departments—roots that are well fertilized by 80 percent and 90 percent matching grants from federal trust funds—Amtrak is viewed as a money pit rather than a gravy train when it enters into state transportation policy consciousness at all.

Congress has staked out whatever political credit there is to claim for maintaining or improving Amtrak services. U.S. senators and representatives are typically in much greater evidence whenever Amtrak has a new train to show off or new service announcement than are governors, state legislators, or mayors. Just the opposite is the case when a new road is opened or an improvement is announced. To the extent that states have an economic connection to Amtrak, it is as often-dissatisfied customers forking over half or more of the losses on short-distance trains that are not part of Amtrak's core system. Instead of getting much credit for these trains, states more often face blame from skeptics for wasting money on some of Amtrak's slower and less attractive train services, or from supporters whenever the state balks at paying the bill. And since these funds usually subsidize operating losses, there are no new highways, airports, or subways to point to. There are also no local jobs, contracts, or appointments to make as a result of most state supported Amtrak trains.

Even most of the states that pay for local service lack a sense of ownership in the passenger train in the way that their elected officials and transportation bureaucrats for virtually every other mode have. As a result, states have not generally supported Amtrak's efforts to obtain a guaranteed funding source, especially when this could come at the expense of the fiscal formulas found in existing trust funds and matching grants. An organization that embodies this intergovernmental policy network, the American Association of State Highway and Transportation Officials (AASHTO) has fiercely defended federal transportation trust funds and matching formulas against all comers, including Amtrak.

In 1996, Amtrak sought a half-penny allocation from the 2.5 cents of gas taxes that had been diverted to paying down the general treasury's deficit in the 1990 Omnibus Budget Reconciliation Act. But even this half-cent reduction in a 2.5 cent trust fund increase was hotly opposed by the highway supporters in the intergovernmental policy network, who easily carried the day. Amtrak had no better luck with seeking its half-cent from the public transit account in the federal gasoline tax trust fund. There again, modal opposition tapped into the deep intergovernmental roots led the states to easily fend off a "tax grab" from Washington.

The "for-profit" mandate insisted upon by the Nixon administration endures to this day as a test that Amtrak must pass before serious transportation policy options involving the passenger train will be entertained beyond the ranks of Amtrak advocates and proponents. The Amtrak Improvement Act of 1978 came closest to discarding this market test by modifying the corporate mandate to read that Amtrak was to be "operated and managed as" a for-profit company. This hinted that actual profits need not occur in order to judge the enterprise a success, as long as Amtrak was run in a businesslike manner, and made a positive contribution to intercity mobility in the larger sense of net social benefits.

But the current governing statute, the Amtrak Reform and Accountability Act of 1997, returns to operating profit as a litmus test for Amtrak's future. An Amtrak Reform Council (ARC) was created to monitor the corporation's progress toward commercial "self-sufficiency" by 2002. Should Amtrak require further operating subsidies after 2002, ARC is charged with submitting a plan for rationalization, while Amtrak would prepare a liquidation plan. Congress must act upon these plans within ninety days. If Congress were not to endorse the rationalization plan, the act requires the Senate to introduce a liquidation resolution that would wind down the company, and with it America's intercity passenger trains. Until 2003, at least, the question of how (and if) Amtrak can achieve commercial self-sufficiency appears likely to dominate rail passenger policy deliberations in the United States. Amtrak is sparing no effort to meet this target. Amtrak's "reinvention" initiatives and the debate surrounding them are explored fully in chapter 5.

If Amtrak's mission and mandate were compromised from the outset due to an unwillingness, or inability, to resolve fundamental disputes regarding the role of the state and the market in rail passenger renewal, then VIA Rail suffered from an at least equally problematic inception. VIA was created through an Order-in-Council (the Canadian equivalent of an Executive Order) and has operated since 1977 without any explicit legislative framework.

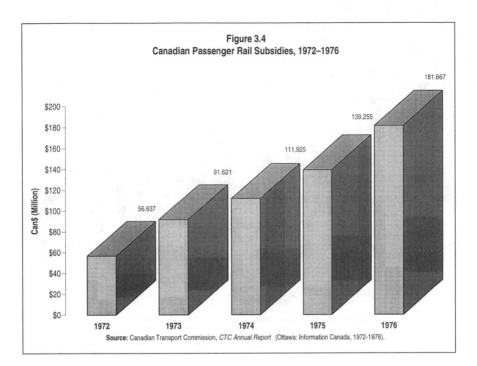

Figure 3.4
Canadian Passenger Rail Subsidies, 1972–1976

Source: Canadian Transport Commission, *CTC Annual Report* (Ottawa: Information Canada, 1972-1976).

Neither goals for public enterprise passenger railroading, nor how VIA fits into transportation policy are established in Canadian law. Lacking this framework, VIA has lived under several "official" mission statements that have been made public, as well as numerous political directives regarding what it should or should not be doing that have never seen the light of day. These are discussed below. Exploring this "incredible lightness of being VIA" demonstrates how politically demobilizing subsidies and closed door deliberations among elites have combined to place Canada's rail policy community in a parallel, but no less intractable, stalemate over passenger train renewal. Like the American experience preceding it, Canada's creation of a public enterprise to renew passenger railroading was compromised by leaping into policy instrumentation before more fundamental decisions about the relationship between passenger trains and transportation policy goals had been made.

Subsidized preservation of passenger trains operated by Canada's two principal rail carriers lasted less than a decade. The principal economic effect of this instrument, beyond maintaining train services, was a fiscal redistribution of the federal government's transport expenditures. Passenger train subsidies accounted for 68 percent of the total funds granted to the rail sector

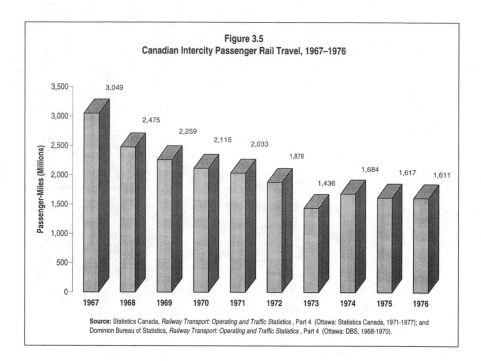

Figure 3.5
Canadian Intercity Passenger Rail Travel, 1967–1976

Source: Statistics Canada, *Railway Transport: Operating and Traffic Statistics*, Part 4 (Ottawa: Statistics Canada, 1971-1977); and Dominion Bureau of Statistics, *Railway Transport: Operating and Traffic Statistics*, Part 4 (Ottawa: DBS, 1968-1970).

under various provisions of the National Transportation Act.[65] While the amount of total rail subsidies initially dropped, from Can$110 million in 1967 to Can$78 million in 1970, they began to rise again in the 1970s, reaching Can$139 million in 1972. The specific passenger train subsidies received by CNR and CPR are illustrated in figure 3.4. They show a steady increase through the 1970s, from Can$56.6 million in 1972 to Can$181.7 million in 1976.

The CTC's own staff exhibited skepticism regarding the fiscal implications of passenger train preservation through regulated subsidy, writing: "A policy that got started as a result of regional complaints about the level of freight rates has been converted largely into one to maintain lightly patronized rail services. . . . Few would doubt that a large part of those funds could more effectively be used to upgrade the railway properties where capacity is becoming inadequate for the foreseeable growth of traffic, but transportation policy, despite the cathartic effect of the MacPherson Commission, remains largely influenced by a nostalgia that persistently confuses the present with the past."[66]

The decline in Canadian passenger train ridership is presented in figure 3.5 above.

Skeptics later claimed that if the CTC would have followed the MacPherson Royal Commission's guidance and used subsidies to facilitate exit from uneconomic passenger train operations, the fiscal crisis that precipitated an ill-considered rush into public enterprise could have been avoided. Writing in *Canadian Public Policy*, Julius Lukasiewicz stated: "The government's passenger rail policies have been limited to passive regulation and protection of past practices, in spite of mounting evidence . . . of the basic soundness of the MacPherson [Commission's] 1961 plan. Contrary to MacPherson's recommendations, the passenger rail abandonment and subsidy provisions of the 1967 NTA have been used to maintain rather than to discontinue obsolete passenger trains, at a high cost to the public."[67]

Politically speaking, these subsidies had served as an anesthetic that diminished the intensity of policy debate over what to do about passenger trains, compared to the very heated deliberations that had occurred in the United States. During the critical years leading up to VIA Rail's creation, the rail policy community remained a relatively closed circle of elites within government (both the cabinet and the Canadian Transport Commission), public enterprise (Canadian National Railways), and private enterprise (Canadian Pacific Railway). Communities, workers, and passengers faced little or no exigency that would mobilize their organization and subsequent engagement within the rail policy community.

As a result of this insular orientation by government officials and agencies, Canada's rail policy community was essentially a state directed network during the transition from subsidized regulation to public enterprise. But unlike the state directed network that would launch the TGV project in France, Canada's rail policy community lacked a critical mass of engineering expertise with the capacity to integrate new technology into new ways of doing business. Attaining the passenger train's potential in Canada's most promising travel markets would thus have to be pursued with limited technological innovation.

One reason that market-focused technological innovation did not occur was that the actors who were focused on rail policy, in both government and public enterprise, viewed their mandates in national terms. In the world's second largest country, a national transportation policy perspective did not lend itself to concentrating on promising travel markets of several hundred miles and then emphasizing high-speed rail renewal initiatives that could not be developed on a national scale. Provincial governments occupied the jurisdictional position that would have facilitated a policy focus on rail's most promising competitive characteristics, but Canada's intergovernmental policy relationships were even more constrained in transport than was the case in the United States.

Canadian provinces hold nearly exclusive jurisdiction over road transport, to the extent that the national highway network consists of a single road, the Trans-Canada Highway, which was started in 1949 and not completed until 1965. Except for Ontario and British Columbia, where governments owned the intraprovincial railroads, the Ontario Northland Railway and the British Columbia Railway, provinces had no direct responsibility for rail policy during the years leading up to creation of VIA Rail.[68] No province perceived the kind of stake in rail passenger restructuring that was associated with road and urban transit policy issues. As a result, train renewal initiatives that focused on Canada's most promising market segment(s) were never given the top priority that they received in Japan, France, or Germany. The jurisdiction with responsibility for rail was simply not capable of placing such a revitalization strategy high enough on its transportation policy agenda to yield action.

Cubukgil and Soberman capture the challenge of parsing Canada's more closely guarded policy deliberations for an answer as to what the architects of VIA Rail had in mind. In trying to explain why VIA Rail was created they find that the railway's origins are not clear: "Some viewed the decision as nothing more than an attempt to mimic the establishment of Amtrak. . . . Others believed that the architects of VIA (all housed within the upper echelons of the Ministry of Transport) genuinely felt that the railways had been unresponsive to the principles of the National Transportation Act and that as a result, change could only be achieved through the creation of a new organizational structure. Yet others considered the creation of VIA as a mindless attempt to relieve the railways of all responsibility for passenger services and burden the government with the extra costs of superimposing additional overhead on an already uneconomic system."[69]

There is enough evidence for each of these conflicting rationales to support the conclusion that, as in Amtrak's case, VIA Rail represented an incoherent amalgamation of policy objectives that members of the rail policy community could only agree to disagree over.

But where VIA differed from Amtrak was that its creation lacked both the overt public debate over contending rationales for rail passenger restructuring and the decisive break with past institutional arrangements. One longtime observer of Canadian passenger railroading saw VIA as more of an extension of previous policy than a break with past shortcomings. Mark Bunting wrote, "Since the late 1960s, when railway passenger subsidies were introduced, the direction and management of the railway passenger system has suffered from a hodgepodge of political interests, and a lack of strategic direction."[70] Within that hodgepodge of political interests were some who saw VIA as the beginning of the end of Canada's intercity passenger service and others who viewed it as the launch of a rail passenger renaissance. The only certainty was that not everyone could be satisfied in their expectations of VIA. But it turned out to be possible to create a policy stalemate that satisfied no one.

Evidence in the public record strongly supports the claim that the Transport Ministry pursued public enterprise in an effort to shift control over policy away from the Canadian Transport Commission and launch a more exit-oriented rail passenger restructuring strategy. On January 29, 1976, the Transport Minister tabled a document entitled "Directive for the Guidance of the Canadian Transport Commission on Rail Passenger Services" in Parliament. This document expressed considerable skepticism in the commission's tendency to preserve passenger train operations stating, "Substantial evidence exists of unnecessary costs, duplication of effort and services, and misuse of rail passenger service characteristics in the current network of rail passenger operations in Canada." The directive went on to call for a new rail passenger system plan for Canada, which would be based upon principles that were aligned with the MacPherson Commission's economic paradigm. The directive's first four principles illustrate the ministry's identification of operational consolidation, service "rationalization," and subsidy reduction as key elements of a new rail passenger strategy:

> (a) a substantial reduction in present levels of subsidy to rail passengers and a much greater degree of economic self-sufficiency in operation should be achieved.
>
> (b) the basic network should include a main rail framework and connecting services by rail or other modes and avoid unnecessary duplication of services.
>
> (c) common use of facilities and common provision of service support wherever feasible between both CN and CP.
>
> (d) capacity offered should be more closely related to traffic actually carried on a continuing basis and less costly service or equipment alternatives should be considered.[71]

The background paper accompanying this directive noted that when the National Transportation Act was proclaimed in 1967, "it was felt that only some trains would be uneconomic but instead all passenger trains in Canada became so."[72] The document went on to propose that:

"the most suitable roles for passenger trains in Canada are in the provision of:

 • high speed service in areas of high population density over short to medium distances, where there are large volumes of travelers

 • basic surface transportation over long distances, where service levels somewhat above those on a bus are required

 • high capacity commuter services in large urban communities.[73]

The government stated a commitment to improve the attractiveness, efficiency, and economy of Canada's passenger train operations where "passenger trains are well suited and well patronized." But it also pledged that "where passenger trains are poorly suited or patronized, other more appropriate modes will be encouraged to replace them."[74] In pursuing this transformation, the government claimed that "care will be taken to determine the types of improved rail services Canadians are willing to use and pay for before major expenditures are made."[75] In the short term, the bulk of the government's effort to assess what type of rail service Canadians would use and pay for was focused inward within the rail policy community, taking the form of closely guarded negotiations with Canada's two major rail carriers.

The biggest addition to the rail policy community came in the form of Transport 2000 Canada, a nonprofit association that was organized in 1976, in the wake of the government's announcement of its new rail passenger policy. Transport 2000 (T-2000) can be viewed as Canada's "brain trust" of consumers interested in public transportation. One of the organization's founders described its inception and early action as follows:

> Transport 2000 Canada, formed in Ottawa in April 1976 as the Canadian offshoot of a citizens' coalition for public transport in Britain and France (created respectively in 1972 and 1975); and the Saskatchewan Rail Committee, which [was] founded in February 1976 as the Regina Committee for Rail Passenger Service. Both organizations came into being as a direct result of concern about federal government rail policy and of the need to provide a voice for pro-rail public opinion in the hearing process. . . . In June 1976, the Saskatchewan Rail Committee affiliated with Transport 2000 (joining groups from British Columbia, Ontario, and Quebec), and the two organizations presented a joint brief at the final series of transcontinental hearings in Ottawa. . . . Just as in the United States the National Association [of] Railroad Passengers (N.A.R.P.) had helped muster public opinion for the creation and support of Amtrak, so Transport 2000 and its affiliate groups set out to crystallize and encourage pro-rail attitudes in Canada.[76]

Transport 2000 differed from America's National Association of Railroad

Passengers in three important ways that reflect its different place in the policy community. First, T-2000 was not, and never has been, a mass-membership organization. Lacking the highly mobilized and adversarial politics generated by the American approach to regulated exit, T-2000 never had the opportunity to recruit thousands of members for passenger train advocacy. Second, T-2000 has been a fairly decentralized organization, reflecting Canada's much looser political confederation compared to the United States. Thirdly, and partly as a result of these first two characteristics, T-2000 was always dependent upon government grants and research contracts to maintain a paid staff and office in Ottawa. When these grants were scaled back in the 1980s, and then canceled in the 1990s, the organization's capacity to act as an advocate for passenger train policy was correspondingly constrained. But in the transition to VIA Rail, and through its struggles during the 1980s, T-2000 provided a visible and vocal source of advocacy. But the key attributes of, and constraints upon, VIA's organization were the product of closed door negotiations between the government and the railroads.

Publicly, CNR and CPR appeared to be in accord on changing government's role in renewing passenger railroading. Their policy statements reflected a new consensus on government responsibility for this travel mode. In lieu of their prior differences in evaluating the merits of passenger service, CNR and CPR moved toward a "middle ground" on policy. CNR's 1976 annual report made its move toward a market-oriented corporate philosophy clear by stating: "There may be a feeling that a Crown Corporation like CN should be concerned with social responsibilities rather than profits. It would, however, be socially irresponsible for CN to provide services without any concern for their economic viability. It should not be up to the management of CN to decide on subsidy programs to assist certain regions, commodities, or loss-making services; such decisions should be in the hands of Parliament. CN should be able to concentrate on operating its services efficiently, receiving full compensation for any function performed as a public service and with incentives towards efficient and economical operation built into the system."[77]

As CNR moved away from its longstanding emphasis on public service, CPR also signaled its openness to greater government involvement in passenger railroading. Speaking at a conference that T-2000 organized in October 1976 on the future of Canada's passenger trains, CPR's director of passenger operations stated, "CP Rail is not only vitally interested in rail passenger services and its role in providing them, but is, in view of recently-stated government policy, considerably more amenable to the continuation and upgrading of those services which the government feels are required in the national interest."[78]

To the extent that Amtrak's creation influenced the Canadian rail passenger policy, it did so by drawing attention to the very different opportunities that a break with past patterns of organization and operation was seen to offer. Government was likely tempted by the link between consolidation and "rationalization." Bringing disparate passenger train operations together under Amtrak appeared to have enabled a massive reduction in service. If Canadian passenger services could be cut by 50 percent, in the way that Amtrak's launch had cleared away many of America's hopelessly uneconomic passenger trains, then the Canadian government would be well along on its way to rationalizing the rail passenger network. Labor and consumer organizations appraised Amtrak's creation quite differently. For these organizations, public enterprise had been a first step toward greater government involvement and investment in a mode that had been shortchanged under previous arrangements. As in the United States, about the only thing that both supporters and skeptics of passenger rail could agree upon was that change from the status quo was desirable.

While CNR and CPR could agree that government should pay them in full for any uneconomic services that it would not let them abandon, they were far from the state of economic desperation that had led their American counterparts to accept the government's dictates regarding the terms of public enterprise. Behind closed doors, CNR and CPR quite strenuously opposed both one another and government on the way in which passenger train operations should be reorganized. CNR's preferred approach was to create a subsidiary Crown Corporation that would run passenger trains as a "cost center" in the same way that its other unprofitable operations were being spun off into subsidized entities. A number of such entities emerged following CNR's embrace of the market model.

Terra Transport was created in 1977, the same year as VIA, to handle rail and road transport of both freight and passengers in the province of Newfoundland, which had joined Confederation in 1948 with a narrow gauge railway that had never earned a profit. CN Marine was launched in 1978 to operate subsidized ferry services in Atlantic Canada. A then-confidential government memorandum on rail passenger policy charted the ups and downs of deliberations about how to organize a public rail passenger enterprise: "By January, 1977 Transport Canada, CN and CP had agreed that unification would be best achieved by placing all marketing responsibilities in one corporate organization. The parties accepted the incorporation of a non-compromised CNR subsidiary as an expeditious means to establish a marketing corporation, subject to there being adequate protection of CPR interests."[79]

But once reorganization was launched, agreement on the new structure for passenger train management proved to be elusive:

> CNR legal officers incorporated VIA Rail Canada Inc. on January 12, 1977 under the Canada Business Corporations Act (CBCA). Cabinet Decision 37–77RD approved the use of a non-compromised CNR subsidiary in February, 1977 with the provisos that CP was to have a representative on VIA's Board of Directors and that steps were to be taken to establish an arms-length relationship between CNR and VIA. The Governor-in-Council authorized CNR by order to acquire shares in VIA.
>
> A unanimous shareholder's agreement was drafted to limit CNR's powers over VIA. CN felt that the agreement was too complex and did not clearly indicate what CN's responsibilities would be in regard to VIA. CP refused to place a representative on VIA's Board of Directors unless there was a shareholder's agreement which limited CN's powers over VIA. Finally, it was decided to establish VIA as a Crown Corporation under Schedule D of the Financial Administration Act (FAA) and to transfer control of VIA to the Minister of Transport.[80]

While the specific points of contention that precluded launching VIA as a subsidiary of CNR remain shrouded in secrecy, the government's own summary of events suggests that CNR wanted more from this new organization than either CPR or the government were prepared to accept. CPR refused to enter into a joint operation that would give its principal competitor access to proprietary information, such as operating costs, as well as any responsibility for operations over its own infrastructure. And government was apparently not prepared to provide this new entity with the autonomy and clearly defined objectives that CNR thought necessary for the new entity to remain as one of its subsidiaries.

The result was a compromise that deferred these, and other, contentious organizational considerations. VIA Rail was launched with neither an explicit mandate, nor a clearly defined mission. Standing apart from both CNR and CPR, VIA Rail would initiate a limited consolidation of management along with a complete transfer of financial responsibility for Canada's existing intercity passenger trains. When VIA went into business, the only real difference it made to passenger railroading was that 100 percent of the losses were now being paid out of Canada's federal treasury. Testifying before the Canadian Transport Commission shortly after VIA's establishment, CPR's manager of passenger services suggested how little had changed: "VIA Rail Canada has been incorporated to market and administer rail passenger services in Canada for both CN and CP Rail. However, the responsibility for operational planning and the actual running of trains remains with the railway over whose lines the service is provided."[81] Put more bluntly by a rail passenger skeptic, "All of the current attempts to improve the situation of passenger rail in Canada amount to no more than superficial manipulation of the existing system; new logos and bright colors on old equipment are the most visible, and about the only result."[82]

Another form of continuity accompanying VIA Rail's creation that has largely been obscured by the debate among and between the federal government and Canada's railroads was the degree to which rail labor was insulated from the costs and risks of passenger train restructuring. At the outset of deliberations over a new rail passenger policy, cabinet directed the Transport Minister to "develop a policy to assist railway employees adversely affected by service rationalization."[83] These measures turned out to be even more generous than those incorporated into the Rail Passenger Service Act in the United States. There, railroad employees who transferred to Amtrak got to maintain their wage scales and work rules, and became eligible for up to six years of "labor protection" payments (at 100 percent of salary) in the event that they were subsequently laid off work. In Canada, rail workers employed by VIA eventually became eligible for lifetime labor protection payments in the event that their jobs were subsequently eliminated and they remained otherwise unemployed. This level of insulation from the costs and risks of industrial adjustment has made a difference to organized labor's participation in the rail policy community. While labor unions certainly supported the creation of public enterprise, their mobilization and advocacy did not approach the intensity found in the United States, at least in part because the threat of an industrial collapse with huge job losses was less severe.

VIA Rail's creation resolved none of the structural challenges to operating modern and effective passenger trains that would have involved revisiting transportation policy. VIA, like Amtrak, served as a policy blocker to avoid making disputed decisions. The opportunity to initiate fundamental change—in both the technology and techniques of passenger railroading—was thus missed. The reasons for this policy shortfall differed from those that had been at work upon Amtrak, but the effect was similar.

As in the United States, Canada's political executive found it easier to create new policy instruments that deferred a day of reckoning with the passenger train's predicament than it did to create explicit policy goals for such industrial renewal. The Order-in-Council that established VIA Rail was sufficient to create a new Crown Corporation, but it did not give VIA the legal status of a rail operator under Canada's Railway Act. That required inserting a clause into the 1977 budget legislation, with a Can$1 appropriation for VIA. This clause, recorded as Transport Vote 52nd, was approved in Parliament, without debate, on March 29, 1977. By the government's own appraisal, this backdoor entry into public enterprise "was expeditious and avoided the uncertainty which accompanies either a CTC application for a certificate of public convenience and necessity or the introduction into Parliament of a constituent act for VIA."[84]

This "uncertainty" that might accompany a wider ranging political debate over passenger rail's future place in the Canadian transportation system was not welcomed by government officials. Instead, the Canadian Transport Commission was viewed as "the logical body to identify the public interest concerning the various services" through public consultation over what a restructured national network should look like.[85] But unlike the United States, these consultations went on in parallel with, and in isolation from, the negotiations over how VIA Rail should be structured.

At the time of its launch, VIA's mandate remained implicit and its means of attaining these objectives were incomplete. All that was clear was that VIA would operate Canada's intercity passenger trains subject to *both* the fiscal resources provided by government and the regulatory decisions made by the Canadian Transport Commission. Rather than placing contradictory, but explicit, objectives into law as had occurred in the Rail Passenger Service Act, Canadian rail passenger policy left implicit contradictions in place through dividing the jurisdiction over passenger train policy between Transport Canada and the CTC.

Societal input on VIA's goals and the bulk of advocacy for passenger trains were focused on the Canadian Transport Commission while the demands of industry and intergovernmental policy participants were directed to the Transport Ministry. All participants in Canada's rail policy community were to pay a price for this compartmentalized deliberation. Canadian passenger train advocates were unable to make their case for renewal as effectively, being directed away from the political arena where key debates were ongoing about VIA's structure and role. But Transport Canada officials also felt themselves to be constrained in rationalizing rail services by sharing policy jurisdiction with the CTC, whereby: "the Minister only exercises marginal control over key factors such as route selections, service quality and safety standards. . . . The practical conclusion which flows from this situation is that Transport Canada is in a poor position to either control or predict future subsidy levels unless it has a very good working relationship with the CTC."[86]

Such arrangements left VIA reliant upon ad hoc policy cues from various origins in government, passed along through annual subsidy allocations, regulatory orders, a politically appointed Board of Directors, and periodic executive staffing decisions.

Lacking a formal mandate, a critical mass of mobilized advocates within the rail policy community, and a powerful "champion" among Canadian elites to take an interest in its success, VIA's formative years as a public enterprise were characterized by painstaking and costly efforts to establish the basic policy framework that had been left incomplete at its inception.

Under these circumstances, VIA was left to make the most of a very weak organizational foundation. Its first business plan presented goals that no government agency had been prepared to commit to paper. That plan made clear that the objective of VIA was "to develop improved, attractive, efficient rail passenger services and, at the same time, reduce the financial burden of the Government resulting from the provision of those services."[87] VIA Rail's initial managers understood the difficulty of their task. Their business plan noted that VIA would be operating in an environment in which "a complex relationship between the Corporation, the operating railways, the Canadian Transport Commission and Transport Canada will evolve." Because of this, the plan noted the importance of VIA's ensuring "that its managerial capabilities are protected while at the same time ensuring that it lives within the statutes of the country. Should VIA find that this becomes difficult or impossible, it will make recommendations for changes to the appropriate authority."[88]

Between 1978 and 1981, VIA struggled to accommodate the conflicting signals for subsidy reduction being sent by Transport Canada (and through it from the Ministry of Finance and Treasury Board) and for service preservation by the Canadian Transport Commission. The results proved disappointing because "the creation of VIA Rail gave responsibility to an organization for providing rail passenger service without corresponding *authority* to control the largest components of both costs and revenues."[89] Most of VIA's costs were dictated by charges from CNR and CPR for almost all operational aspects. Track access, train crew, station use, and equipment maintenance were all charged on a "cost-plus" formula that had been approved by the CTC, and was not subject to public disclosure or audit by VIA. Although never made public, the terms of these contracts appeared to extend the same cost base that had been used to calculate the 80 percent operating subsidy to the new fee structure.

As shown in figure 3.2, subsidies to the new Crown Corporation grew rapidly during its early years. Aside from the Can$725 million capital expenditure in 1979 to acquire rail passenger assets from CNR and CPR, the most

notable attribute of VIA's early finances was the 81 percent growth in its operating subsidy over three years from Can$232.4 million in 1979 to Can$422.3
million in 1981. The enterprise that was supposed to have applied the brake
to rail passenger subsidies appeared to be fiscally out of control.

On July 27, 1981, Transport Minister Jean-Luc Pepin announced that
the cabinet had exercised its prerogative power, bypassing the Canadian Transport Commission's regulatory framework for evaluating rail passenger service needs, and issued an order-in-council directing VIA to cut 19 percent of
its services. This action brought an end to the initial phase of shared jurisdiction over passenger rail policy between the CTC and Transport Ministry.
And while it stopped the escalation of passenger rail subsidies, the Pepin
downsizing also triggered an intensification of political debate over rail passenger policy.

The official opposition—the Conservative party—seized upon these cutbacks and launched a "Task Force on Rail Passenger Service" that held fifteen
days of hearings across Canada during the late summer of 1981. These hearings resulted in a report on intercity rail passenger services that was subtitled
"The Last Straw." This report highlighted the support for passenger trains
that was still searching for effective expression within the rail policy community. It embraced the substantive arguments brought forward by passenger
rail advocates, concluding that "the government's current policy of increasing
the level of subsidization for other modes of transportation while decreasing
the support for rail passenger service is extremely short-sighted and totally
out of tune with Canadian transportation needs and concerns regarding energy conservation, urban sprawl, pollution and safety."[90]

The task force report also criticized the government's exercise of prerogative powers emphasizing that "the decision to cut rail services made by
Order-in-Council has seriously impaired the role of the Canadian Transport
Commission as protector of the public interest in transportation services."[91]
Moreover, the report argued that "the arbitrary manner of affecting the cutbacks in this circumstance, constitutes a serious abuse of executive power by
the Government of Canada."[92] With Canadian political debate about the passenger train's future more overt and animated than at any time in postwar
years, the 1980s could have been a time of substantial policy reform and renewal. But this was not to be the case.

Instead of reforming policy, a fiscal "stop—go" cycle of increased expenditures followed by cutbacks ensued as successive governments sought to pursue
varied objectives without restructuring VIA's organizational constraints. The
key variable in determining Canada's rail passenger policy during the 1980s

turned out to be the government of the day's fiscal tolerance for subsidizing passenger trains. Policy was expressed as a greater or lesser willingness to preserve passenger trains through subsidy. And in these ups and downs, no policy objective or instruments for an industrial restructuring that might enhance the productivity or competitivity of VIA's services were ever institutionalized.

Soberman characterized this period as a time when "government schizophrenia on rail passenger policy has certainly muddied the waters."[93] Whether funds were being added or cut from passenger rail budgets during the 1980s, there was no "game plan" behind rail passenger policy, other than the balance of power between cabinet ministers who accepted public enterprise as legitimate in passenger railroading and those who did not. VIA's revised corporate mission statement of 1983 illustrates the organization's lack of capacity to lead rail passenger renewal. In place of the substantive focus on "improved," "attractive," and "efficient" train services that had been noted in VIA's original (1978) corporate plan cited above, VIA's Board of Directors approved a new mission statement on November 8, 1983, committing "to serve the people of Canada by providing safe and efficient services to meet the needs of the travelling public in accordance with federal government policy."[94] In place of introducing improved and more attractive services, the focus had shifted to following government's lead.

In the early 1980s, that political leadership directed VIA to participate in technological development that was expected to reverse the passenger train's decline in Canada at a fraction of the cost of Japanese, French, or German renewal efforts. The innovation that was supposed to deliver such a leap in performance was the Light Rapid Comfortable (LRC) train. This "made-in-Canada" approach to solving the passenger train's predicament was to be delivered through a policy partnership between Transport Canada, VIA Rail, and the Bombardier Corporation. In the 1970s, research staff at Transport Canada's Transport Development Centre had identified a type of new passenger train technology that promised the benefits of high speed at a bargain-basement price. Such a payoff would come from producing a lightweight, diesel powered, tilt-body train that could operate on existing rail infrastructure at 120 miles per hour. Bombardier Corporation, a Canadian transportation manufacturer that had recently entered rail equipment production by acquiring the Montreal Locomotive Works, was chosen to produce the LRC.

Forging an industrial partnership between government, public enterprise, and a private manufacturer to develop new and innovative technology is no easy task. To succeed in rail passenger renewal, a critical mass of know-how is required.[95] Not only must these skills be in place, but they must also be shared among the partners—including government transport agencies that bankroll the initial research and development, the manufacturer(s) that produce new equipment, and the rail carrier(s) that will introduce these trains into commercial service. Canada did not possess this configuration of rail technology capacity during the LRC's development. An internal report from VIA Rail painted a damning picture of the formative phase of the LRC project. The report noted that since the beginning of the contract with Bombardier Inc. (formerly Bombardier-MLW), the company "has been in arrears in all phases of the work. In our view this condition was due in part to a shortage of skilled mid-management personnel and engineering resources, especially during the first twelve months of the contract, plus inexperience at all levels in the management of contracts entailing time, cost and performance constraints."[96]

The report alleged many shortcomings on the part of Bombardier including:

> Attempts to ignore its own tendered technical data, especially in the early contract stages.
> . . . Continuous delay and procrastination in development of Specification LRC-2–78. Attempts to oversimplify specification data in critical areas.
> . . . Refusal to publish agreed sections of specification stating it would not do so unless company was granted cost relief.
> . . . Negative contract administrative effort and the obscuring of facts to prevent Project Office from ascertaining true picture of program status.
> . . . Constant state of re-organization, inadequate project management, lack of co-ordination.
> . . . Lack of adequate engineering resources at outset of contract.[97]

These and other symptoms of a problematic partnership were borne out in the LRC's performance, which fell far short of what had appeared to be a sure bet on the drawing board. In reality, the LRC arrived much later than expected, cost more than predicted, and delivered less than had been promised in improving the passenger train's attractiveness to travelers. Unlike Amtrak's Metroliner project, which had included just enough infrastructure improvements to enable significant reductions in travel time, the LRC equipment did not attain the technical breakthrough of tilting technology that could have achieved a significant speedup of VIA's schedules in the 1980s.

A study on passenger rail's potential conducted for the Science Council of Canada characterized the Canadian rail manufacturing sector's technical capacity to pioneer new intercity passenger technology as "limited," noting: "the LRC train, although designed for existing tracks in terms of its pendular suspension (i.e. tilt body feature) for passenger comfort and higher speeds on curves, is controversial and expensive. The existing design of the locomotive (used for LRC trains) has heavy axle-weight and is expected to result in high track maintenance costs for operating speeds in excess of 90–95 mph (144–152 km/hr). Therefore, the LRC's cruising speed capability of 120 mph (192 km/hr) cannot be gainfully utilized."[98]

Testifying before the Senate Standing Committee on Transport and Communications in 1984, VIA's president Pierre Franche was more diplomatic, but still clear that Canada's rail supply sector was short on the skills needed to generate a technical breakthrough that could renew intercity passenger trains: "We see vehicles of new Canadian design coming into use, but with the inevitable breaking-in problems which almost always accompany innovation—particularly since the Canadian industry has built hardly any new trains, other than commuter coaches, since the 1950s. Innovation is, therefore, largely new to this generation of passenger railway people."[99]

In fairness to those who struggled to make the LRC succeed, it must be pointed out that the Can$91 million allocated to this entire project[100] was less than the US$81 million that had been spent more than a decade earlier by government and industry on the U.S. high-speed ground transportation initiative that yielded the Metroliner.[101] Canada's budget for developing new rail passenger technology was just a small fraction of the capital investment that Japanese, French, and German governments had devoted to launching their high-speed rail renewal. Pierre Franche acknowledged that the true cost of LRC deployment had simply been deferred by spending so little at the outset. Franche explained that the LRC "did not attract the level of research and development investment which many countries have put into their new fast trains. . . . One could easily argue that our teething troubles today are somewhat the price of innovating in Canada and providing employment in Canada without large research and development costs."[102]

The Liberal government's strategy of redeploying subsidies from operating expenses to capital spending on new equipment may have set the stage for a long-term industrial renewal of Bombardier's rail passenger technology capacity, one that has recently been put to use in producing high-speed electric trains for Amtrak's Acela service. But it offered little, if any, boost to VIA's efforts to renew Canadian passenger trains in the early 1980s.

When the Conservative party defeated the Liberals in 1984, a new set of rail policy priorities was brought into government with them. Their first order of business was to fulfill a campaign promise dating from the party's 1981 task force that had produced "The Last Straw" report. Six routes, including both CNR's western transcontinental line and CPR's Montreal–St. John, New Brunswick, train, which had been abandoned in 1981, were relaunched in June 1985. In the meantime, a Rail Passenger Action Force was launched to set new goals for VIA Rail and recommend the appropriate institutional framework for achieving them. Transport Minister Don Mazankowski launched this task force with some very ambitious rhetoric insisting that it would produce tangible results: "I don't want a report. I want decisions and action to help move the system into the 21st century. . . . We've poured billions of dollars into the system. Now it's time for Canadians to get their money's worth."[103]

He implied that the Action Force's recommendations would provide the blueprint for significant new policies. But this was not to be the case. The Action Force's report was never released. While the government later claimed that Action Force analysis and recommendations were taken into account in drafting Bill C-97, the subsequently aborted attempt to give VIA Rail a legislative foundation and policy framework, the truth is that skeptics in the transportation policy community joined forces to derail the ambitious proposals for both organizational change and significant capital reinvestment that the Action Force was preparing. Since these conflicts went on behind closed doors, there is little evidence of the "trench warfare" that first undermined the Action Force and then swung government toward a more skeptical passenger rail policy. Most of this reversal in the Conservatives' initial support for passenger rail renewal must be inferred from what did not happen.

Besides the Action Force's non-report on rail passenger renewal, there was a failed attempt at establishing a legislative framework for passenger rail policy during 1986. The Conservatives had endorsed calls for rail passenger legislation during their years in opposition and received virtually unanimous support for such action from researchers and independent investigators who had explored VIA's problematic performance during the 1980s. This unanimity is evidenced by the convergence of input regarding the passenger train problem from both the Science Council of Canada and the Economic Council of Canada. These nonpartisan advisory bodies to the federal government, before being closed down themselves, called for rail passenger legislation in the 1980s. The Science Council published a report in 1980 which raised the need for a legislative framework, concluding that "one option worthy of consideration would involve definition of institutional, jurisdictional, and legislative changes that would grant to VIA, (among other powers and responsibilities), control over rolling stock maintenance facilities, ownership of stations, and complete control or ownership of those tracks with potential for exclusive or almost exclusive passenger train use."[104] By 1985, the Economic Council was even more insistent that "establishing a clear set of objectives is the first institutional issue that must be resolved so that VIA Rail can adopt appropriate strategies to promote service quality. Again, the appropriate level of service quality will depend on specific objectives defined for Canadian rail passenger service. Clearly defined objectives are also necessary to determine the degree and nature of subsidization."[105]

On February 24, 1986, the government introduced a Rail Passenger Transportation Act in the House of Commons. Bill C-97, as it became known, sought to fill the long-standing legal vacuum that had ensued after VIA's creation by Order-in-Council. But the legislation never made it through the parliamentary stages (i.e., hearings and passage by the House of Commons and the Senate, royal assent by the Governor General, and final proclamation) required to become law. In fact, Bill C-97 never made it past a first reading before Parliament was prorogued (dissolved) for an election in November 1988. At a hearing of the House of Commons Standing Committee on Transport on May 21, 1987, the fact that rail passenger legislation appeared to be going nowhere led the New Democratic Party's transport critic, Hon. Les Benjamin, to question then Transport Minister, Hon. John Crosbie, on the government's commitment to legislating an explicit rail passenger policy for Canada. Their exchange went as follows:

MR. BENJAMIN: Mr. Minister, I have been on this committee every year since VIA Rail was formed, in 1976. . . . Every year every Minister, every government since then has said that we are going to get a VIA Rail Canada Act. One was put on the Order Paper and then disappeared. Can you tell us when there will be a national rail passenger act? Are you going to bring one in or not? Has the government decided to proceed or has it decided not to bother, just to leave VIA Rail hanging out there?

MR. CROSBIE: . . . With respect to the question of VIA Rail legislation, I intend to review that in the fall with the Cabinet and we will make a decision then as to when we are going to go forward with the legislation. We are not proposing to go forward at the present session because of the very, very full legislative agenda that already exists.

MR. BENJAMIN: . . . When I speak of leaving VIA Rail out to dry, to hang out there by itself, I am talking about an enterprise that, unlike Air Canada or Canadian National, does not have a legislative framework under which to operate. . . . Is it your policy and is it your intention to bring in a national rail passenger act?

MR. CROSBIE: That is my intention, yes.

MR. BENJAMIN: Good. You are the sixth [Transport] Minister to say that to me.

MR. CROSBIE: At least we are consistent.[106]

While it is not worth overanalyzing an initial version of legislation that never saw the light of day, there are some points in Bill C-97 that merit attention since they reveal a growing tension between skepticism and support for rail renewal coming to the fore in this attempt to create a new policy framework. Chief among these were Bill C-97's explicit commercial performance criteria for Canada's public enterprise passenger railroad, and its creation of an automatic mechanism to shed services that could not meet these standards. More than one commercial target was identified, given the wide range of services provided by VIA:

> The financial performance objective of the Corporation shall be to recover from its operations:
>
> (a) at least 100% of the specific costs of each corridor service;
>
> (b) at least 60% of the specific costs of each transcontinental service; and
>
> (c) at least 40% of the specific costs of each regional service.[107]

Train services that failed to meet these targets for two consecutive years were to be discontinued unless an agreement was signed with a third party (e.g., provincial government or other organization) to cover the loss.

Bill C-97 also proposed to enhance VIA Rail's status as a tenant on rail infrastructure owned by CNR and CPR, by giving VIA full access to their billing information and specifying that railroad charges were to be renegotiated based on the principle of "direct costs" of providing various services. VIA's business plan for 1996 included a planning assumption that such legislation would reduce VIA's payments to CNR and CPR by at least 10 percent.[108] VIA went on to describe the new legislation as being of "fundamental importance" to its future, stating that: "It changes several aspects of VIA's role in providing a safe, modern, efficient, and reliable national rail passenger service. The legislation will provide the corporation with a constituent Act clearly enunciating its mandate. VIA will have more flexibility in the delivery of services; the relationship with CN and CP will be more clearly defined and the system of compensation to them will be made fairer."[109]

When no legislation materialized, VIA tried to put as positive a face on this missed policy opportunity as possible. Its 1998 business plan noted that the reelected Conservative government might reintroduce rail passenger legislation "at a later date" and in the meantime "VIA and the other railway companies have been instructed to comply with the spirit of the proposed legislation. Accordingly, new agreements are under negotiation."[110]

In place of the explicit commercial criteria and necessary administrative reforms to attain them that had appeared within reach in 1985, VIA was again left in legal limbo, and subject to short-term political agendas in cabinet. Like much of Canadian economic policy following the government's embrace of the U.S. Free Trade Agreement, soon followed by the North American Free Trade Agreement, political choices were ostensibly now delegated to the marketplace. So, too, with rail passenger policy, as reflected in VIA's third official mission statement in just one decade. In 1988, VIA's Board committed "To serve travelers in Canada by providing an efficient rail passenger service responsive to market needs."[111] Government directives would now amplify those market signals, with an orientation that was fairly obvious for uneconomic services provided by obsolete technology.

In 1989, VIA was thrust into yet another restructuring, one that prioritized a rapid reduction of its operating losses above all else. This restructuring was announced shortly *before* VIA's own internal study on future development options was to have been released and also before Transport Canada and the National Transportation Agency were scheduled to release findings of their own investigations into rail passenger performance.[112] The VIA Rail study had identified a Can$3 billion high-speed train development in the Quebec–Windsor corridor as the most promising option to boost both VIA's commercial performance and rail's role in Canadian passenger transportation over the long term.

VIA President Dennis DeBelleval, a former Transport Minister in the province of Quebec, had adopted a much more public and entrepreneurial role than his predecessors, and was publicly promoting the opportunities that would arise from a high-speed rail development strategy in Ontario and Quebec.[113] He sought new investment from both the government and private partners to finance this high-speed train service, claiming that it would ultimately generate the revenue required to preserve other VIA services while lessening the need for operating subidies. But the politics of being too ambitious about VIA's long term renewal proved fatal when the government wanted immediate cutbacks. DeBelleval was fired by Transport Minister Benoit Bouchard on May 3, 1989.

DeBelleval's principal miscalculation was political. He did not expect the Conservative government's renewed emphasis on the market to translate into such drastic and immediate subsidy reductions. Writing to the transport minister on the day of his dismissal, DeBelleval protested that he could have accomplished the goal of commercial renewal through much less disruptive means if he had been given "more commercial elbow room" to modernize VIA's Quebec–Windsor corridor.[114] At a press conference immediately following his dismissal, DeBelleval claimed that the government was "insisting too much on financial matters and not on what should be the role of the train in 10 or 20 years."[115] For the next ten years, government policy would dictate that VIA reduce its role as a passenger carrier considerably, while improving the efficiency of its remaining operations.

VIA Rail's bottom-line commercial performance during the 1980s and 1990s is presented in figure 3.6.[116] The turbulent results of the 1980s reflect the cost of the political impasse regarding what to do about passenger trains. VIA was only able to cover a third, or less, of its costs from passenger revenues during the 1980s. But commercial performance improved steadily during the 1990s, reaching an all-time-high operating ratio of 0.57 in 1999. Once government dropped the boom on a growth-oriented corporate strategy and emphasized cost control with service reduction, VIA demonstrated an ability to improve its efficiency as a carrier quite considerably.

Pressed by a Conservative government determined to reduce its deficit, yielding a Can$100 million subsidy cut in 1992, VIA became a leader in squeezing greater efficiency out of traditional public passenger rail operations during the 1990s. This occurred through significant restructuring in the way the

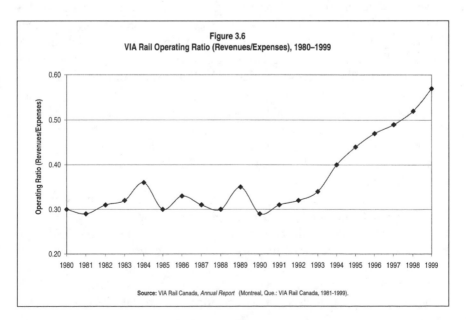

Figure 3.6
VIA Rail Operating Ratio (Revenues/Expenses), 1980–1999

Operating Ratio (Revenues/Expenses)

Source: VIA Rail Canada, *Annual Report* (Montreal, Que.: VIA Rail Canada, 1981-1999).

corporation did business. Everything except the number of trains being operated was subjected to cutback. Two of VIA's five maintenance centers were
closed and eight hundred management positions were eliminated. This was
followed by a new collective agreement in 1998 that abolished the venerable
position of "conductor," eliminating 252 operating positions. Today, customer
service agents who perform the "hotel" service functions during a train's journey (e.g., preparing and serving meals, making beds, or assisting travelers on
and off the train) also collect tickets. VIA was able to increase the number of
these positions by ninety, and still save Can$15 million annually.[117] Thus, the
expenses that are counted in assessing VIA's performance after 1989 do not
include the restructuring costs arising from both extensive route and service
cuts of 1989 and the subsequent "re-engineering" of corporate structure, since
these did generate significant labor protection and other transitional payments.

The current Liberal government, which came to power in 1993, did little
to change many of the market-led economic policies put in place by the Conservatives, and no policy departure from VIA's cost-cutting efforts was initially entertained. By the late 1990s, VIA's ability to pull further cost reductions
out of a hat was drawing to an end. And its ability to maintain passenger
revenues, let alone increase them, was being threatened by a lack of capital for
maintaining its existing services. At a time when much of the rest of the world
was assembling new model railroads, various government investigations were
made into policy alternatives that might yield a sustainable future for Canada's
passenger trains. Transport Canada commissioned two studies into passenger
rail franchising, although their findings were never made public. And the
House of Commons' Standing Committee on Transport held public hearings in 1998, yielding a report entitled "The Renaissance of Passenger Trains
in Canada." That document favored "public-private partnerships" as a means
to resolve VIA's equipment and infrastructure challenges, and depicted franchising as a "win-win" solution to such partnerships. The Committee's report
also estimated that if VIA's organizational status was left unchanged (e.g., as a
non-commercial Crown Corporation) Can$800 million in capital would be
needed "over the next few years" to maintain services.[118]

Only in April 2000, when VIA was "running on empty" in terms of its
need for capital renewal, did the Liberal government announce a $401.9 mil-
lion capital injection over the coming five years.[119] The operating subsidy cap,
now $170 million, remained in place, and nothing was said regarding any
legislation or larger policy framework. VIA was thus pointed toward a chance
to further improve its performance, but left with much less in the way of both
resources and explicit goals that have accompanied Amtrak's recent organiza-

tional reform. No mandate to reach commercial self-sufficiency, as found in the Amtrak Reform and Accountability Act, exists in Canada. For better and for worse, VIA's set of economic and political circumstances during the 1990s allowed it to improve efficiency by shedding many routes and restructuring from within. But these changes did not provide for the development of a policy framework in which VIA could become a new model railroad with the legal status to make the most of Canada's passenger train opportunities.

Through a different set of circumstances than Amtrak experienced, VIA Rail has also found itself institutionally isolated and constrained by a stalemate regarding its goals and objectives. Executives, like DeBelleval, who got too far ahead of government's ambiguous position on passenger trains found themselves undercut by opposition to too much entrepreneurship from other constituencies in the rail policy community.

With the paths to serious and substantive policy reform blocked by the institutionalized stalemates surrounding Amtrak and VIA Rail, and the management of public enterprise filled with executives who (correctly) saw more risk than reward in pushing beyond this political impasse, some policy entrepreneurs have sought to bypass or leapfrog what appeared to be dead ends in rail passenger policy. Chapter 4 considers the varied efforts and initiatives that have been pursued largely within state and provincial governments' jurisdictions to launch commercially competitive passenger trains.

> *Chapter 4*

False Starts with High Speed

State and Provincial Efforts to Leapfrog Amtrak's and VIA's Perennial Problems

Policy, like nature, abhors a vacuum. Until Amtrak's arrival on the scene, the United States could credibly claim to have been developing a passenger train renewal strategy that would utilize high-speed technology like the Japanese or Europeans to build a new market for intercity travel by rail. Canada was also experimenting with passenger train renewal prior to VIA Rail. But by 1980, these renewal efforts had slowed to a crawl, with rail policy community participants focusing their attention on the political version of trench warfare that beset Amtrak and VIA in light of their murky mandates and contested legitimacy.

Amtrak's and VIA's struggles to simply survive during the 1980s and 1990s yielded a growing gap between European and Japanese accomplishments in passenger train renewal, and North America's focus on preserving trains that showed little sign of recovering the ground that had been lost to automobiles and aviation. This difference between what some trains were proving themselves capable of, and what Amtrak and VIA were actually delivering, left a void, which entrepreneurs would try to fill. What ensued was twenty years of false starts and failed attempts to bypass or leapfrog national transportation policy constraints on passenger rail revitalization. These unfolded through varied project-specific initiatives led by policy entrepreneurs who sought to innovate from the bottom up, and often from outside the national transportation policy process.

North America's sole intercity rail renewal success story, the Metroliner, and the transition to its recent successor, Acela, provide a stark contrast to several combinations of unattained policy objectives and unsuccessful policy instruments that were created by rail passenger advocates working in, or with, the state and provincial governments. The cumulative aftermath of these failed attempts has positioned "outside the beltway" rail policy initiatives on either of two distinct paths.

In some cases, such as the projects that were put forward in Ohio and Texas, rail passenger renewal initiatives were predicated upon bold leadership by either government or private enterprise. This leadership was expressed through proposed commitments to finance new trains and infrastructure solely from the public treasury, or through private capital markets, respectively. Such initiatives were decisively rejected by the followers who would have been essential to move these projects forward. The electorate in Ohio and the investors behind a Texas rail development consortium were both presented with the choice of buying into passenger train renewal. Both voters and investors turned thumbs down and stopped these projects in their tracks, putting a halt to such efforts in these states and elsewhere. Such decisive rejections undermined the legitimacy of rail passenger renewal proposals that depended upon either enacting new taxes or accepting new levels of financial risk. In other words, defeats of proposals also became defeats of the principle that new approaches to rail passenger transport should become either a fiscal priority of state government, or a commercial priority of venture capitalists. They thus represented "dead ends" in rail passenger policy development. But not all state level initiatives led to such dead ends.

In other cases, exemplified by the policy initiatives pursued in California and Florida, the approach taken to organizing renewal was both more nuanced, and at times less transparent, in the leadership and funding options being developed. In these efforts, government and private industry sought mechanisms to share the burden of organizing and funding passenger train renewal. This working relationship between states and industry was more complex than the efforts by either side to lead the renewal elsewhere had been. Seeking to form a partnership that could adjust responsibilities and risks depending upon the phases of the project, and the political and economic surprises that would inevitably arise, appeared more attractive once the magnitude of the rail renewal challenge became apparent. For this very reason, when governments and/or industry walked away from these projects, the failure did not undermine the concept of rail passenger renewal in its entirety. States like California and Florida have seen very ambitious passenger train renewal proposals come and go, without discrediting the rail mode as a passenger transportation option. In such cases, whether through compromise or co-optation, incremental improvements in conventional intercity services, usually in conjunction with Amtrak's operations, became the "second best solution" that supporters and skeptics could settle upon following their battles over more ambitious renewal initiatives.

Analyzing the lessons of state-level rail passenger renewal builds upon Dunn and Perl's assessment of the types of "political infrastructure" that enabled the Metroliner to get off to a successful start, highlighting the gaps in that infrastructure that subsequent state-level initiatives fell through.[1] In so doing, this analysis also modifies the hypothesis put forward by Aggarwala that state-level initiatives will be the most important source of a rail passenger renewal breakthrough, given the pattern of other modes' development over the course of history.[2]

Looking back over the achievements and shortfalls of American transportation development, Aggarwala posits that new surface infrastructure-based initiatives (e.g., canals, railroads, and roads) are first brought to the policy agenda by private entrepreneurs seeking an opportunity to pioneer potentially lucrative mobility innovations. These efforts almost inevitably fall short, due to the extensive up-front costs and high risks faced by truly innovative infrastructure. If the failure of private initiative is big enough, that is, if it raises public awareness or policy community engagement of the issue or infrastructure option, then the federal government will usually support a "one time only" demonstration project to address the anticipation that was raised by private entrepreneurs.

Should the results of such a demonstration project be successful or impressive, then other subnational jurisdictions will seek to launch their own initiatives with this infrastructure to avoid being left behind. As such subnational initiatives expand and bear fruit, those states that are left behind because they lack the geographic or demographic attributes to make a go of this new type of infrastructure on their own will clamor for federal involvement to help them close the gap. Eventually, a critical political mass will be reached. States that are still searching for ways to initiate new infrastructure development will strike a bargain over engaging the federal government's support with those states that are already in the lead.

Such a deal usually yields a funding formula that permits states already developing the new form of infrastructure to continue their efforts while also allowing other states to launch their infrastructure development. That formula, in turn, attracts the support of a nationwide policy community devoted to enshrining the new mode's development support scheme in a legislated framework. Sabatier has used the term "advocacy coalition" to identify specific attributes of the policy communities engaged in American national governance along the lines of the process described above.[3] Mode-based advocacy coalitions are one of the products of the transportation policy cycles that both Aggarwala and Dunn have depicted.[4]

But any historical development cycle of transportation policy must be modified to take account of at least two particularities of the rail passenger mode. First, as much of a departure from past technology as European and Japanese high-speed trains can offer, they still represent a difference of degree within, rather than a difference in kind from, a long established mode. At least so far, the high-speed variant of passenger trains remains at least partly tied into the rail mode's existing infrastructure, and thus linked to the advocacy coalition associated with that mode. For example, the French TGV runs over a purpose-built right-of-way during its very high speed operations, yet continues to use traditional rail infrastructure at either end of the line to access urban centers as well as less populated destinations via branching onto conventional rail lines. The reinvention of passenger railroading associated with high-speed technology is thus closer to the very significant transformation that accompanied the introduction of jet powered aircraft in civil aviation than it is to the arrival of an entirely new mobility mode. Only magnetic-levitation technology presents a yet to be implemented infrastructure option that could claim status as a truly new mode.

Second, there is likely to be policy feedback at work in this cycle of transportation infrastructure development in which the institutional arrangements of past modes' policy sponsorship influence the dynamics of subsequent modes' development. The terms by which governments supported railroad development were influenced by what had occurred in aiding the construction of canals, and the terms of national highway infrastructure development were influenced by the rail mode's sponsorship. In each case, policy community members drew lessons from past experience and sought to "build a better mousetrap" as they secured national government support. For example, the advocacy coalition for road infrastructure moved beyond the front-loaded support mechanisms of cash or land grants and pioneered the concept of "user fees," also known as dedicated taxation. This expanded government's support from that of initial donor to ongoing banker and financial broker, a lesson that was adopted by the subsequent advocacy coalition forming around aviation infrastructure, but one that proved quite difficult for the rail mode to retrofit into its infrastructure organization and financing. Thus, the policy dynamics confronting high-speed rail development would be doubly influenced both by the feedback from other modes as well as by its specific inheritance from the rail mode, as proponents of projects in several states and provinces have discovered. The only rail renewal initiative that can be considered extremely successful drew upon the rail mode's policy inheritance rather than relying upon new policy community participants and relationships.

4.1. Origins of the Metroliner: America's Most Successful Rail Renewal Initiative

Before delving into the details of North America's many unsuccessful attempts to create rail renewal alternatives to Amtrak and VIA Rail, it is worth recognizing the achievement and lessons of the one rail revitalization project that has yielded an unmitigated (e.g., commercially justified) success—the Metroliner. The Metroliner deserves attention both because it actually worked and because it demonstrates how a particular configuration of interests and organizations within the rail policy community could generate the kind of innovations that were comparable in kind, if not in degree, to European and Japanese successes. The short lived partnership between government; a private railroad owning the infrastructure between Boston, New York, and Washington; and the rail supply industry yielded a considerable degree of success that put the Metroliner in the same commercial ambit, if not necessarily the same technological league, as the Shinkansen, the TGV, and the ICE.

While the Metroliner did not keep up with the speed of Japan's and Europe's fastest trains, it did keep pace with their commercial performance by covering its costs and generating an operating profit. Unlike Amtrak, which represented a policy stopgap prepared by an administration anxious to forestall greater intervention in the rail sector by Congress, the Metroliner experiment arose from a much more proactive partnership between government and industry that sought mutual benefits for all parties. Although there are some important similarities between the Metroliner experiment and rail revitalization initiatives abroad, there is also one key difference. Whereas the European and Japanese efforts began at the core of the rail policy community, initiated from within publicly owned railroads working closely with senior officials in transportation ministries, the Metroliner experiment was launched through a much more disparate and transitory partnership between a privately owned railroad, train manufacturers, legislative policy entrepreneurs, and the belated engagement of executive branch bureaucrats implementing a customized rail renewal effort.

The 1960s were an ambitious time for policy making in the United States. At the apogee of activist government, epitomized by the Johnson administration's Great Society, public officials were uninhibited in advancing national government leadership to solve challenging problems in health, education, welfare, and other social policy domains. In more specialized areas, such as surface transportation policy, complementary activist initiatives tended to emerge within Congress, with one or more legislators acting as their political champion. Such was the case with this particular experiment in passenger train renewal.

U.S. federal government activism in surface transportation on a comparably grand scale had actually been launched ahead of the Great Society, starting in 1956 with the Eisenhower administration's Interstate Highway Program. This program did much for opening up many regions of the nation, by offering excellent road-based accessibility to rural areas and undeveloped land between cities that would be transformed into the suburban landscape that is now ubiquitous. But it did relatively less for the most developed and densely populated region of the country—the Northeast metropolitan region from Boston to Washington. At a time when the momentum of economic development was just beginning to swing away from the Northeast and Midwest, and areas in the South and Southwest were experiencing the first wave of the Sunbelt boom, Rhode Island's junior Senator, Claiborne Pell (D), offered an ambitious vision for the economic development of his own region.

In a book entitled *Megalopolis Unbound*, Pell sketched out a socioeconomic vision of the Northeast that identified its own unique mobility needs as both a defining characteristic and a central policy challenge, writing: "We are developing in America a new kind of urban society of vast proportions—a society unique in its sheer size and scope and concentration of energies and activities. . . . [This] 'new order' calls for a new dimension in public outlook and public-policy planning: if we do not match the scale of Megalopolis with our solutions of Megalopolitan problems, we may find ourselves unable to carry forward into the new order some of the basic values of our civilization. Particularly is this true of all facets of the problem of human mobility."[5]

At a time when America's sprawl (both on a national scale to the south and west and on a regional scale to the suburbs and exurbs) was just beginning, the population density of this Northeast megalopolis was presented as a competitive advantage that could yield a critical mass of skills and talent unique to the United States. Instead of competing with one another, as had been the economic pattern in the nineteenth century, Boston, New York, Philadelphia, Baltimore, and Washington could now complement each other by linking their business activities and pooling their human capital.

But this strategy could only succeed if the transportation and communication links throughout the region were robust enough to facilitate the much heavier interchange of people, goods, services, and information that would

arise from such a regional economic integration. The economic space between Boston and Washington required "some new kind of intermediate transportation that will be much faster and more efficient than individualized transit
but that will be fully compatible with it" to make Pell's vision a success.[6]

Unlike other regions of the nation, where the physical space existed to
introduce vast new infrastructures (e.g., twelve-lane superhighways and mega-
airports like DFW, which boasted that it occupied a land mass larger than
Manhattan Island), the Northeast Corridor between Boston and New York
lacked the room for the new air and road infrastructure that the federal government was sponsoring to meet America's mobility needs elsewhere around
the country. The Northeast thus faced a physical development context similar to Europe and Japan, with limited and costly options for new infrastructure encouraging a search for existing infrastructure assets that could be
upgraded and enhanced. The Boston–New York–Washington rail infrastructure was a perfect candidate for such upgrading. Pell asserted that in the Northeast "the public interest would be well served by rail transportation if only that
service could be revamped and tailored to meet the needs of the market."[7]

Between Boston and New York, the New Haven Railroad linked major
city centers (e.g., Providence, New Haven, and Stamford) while between New
York and Washington, the Pennsylvania Railroad's line linked Philadelphia,
Wilmington, and Baltimore. Both railroads were under-performing, losing
business on both their freight and passenger operations. Pell characterized
the railroads' situation as one of "technological retardation" explaining he
chose to "use the term 'retardation' instead of 'obsolescence' to emphasize
that railroads are not obsolete but have simply lagged behind other modes of
transportation and failed to exploit their natural technological advantages."[8]
The opportunity to introduce new technology and techniques to overcome
that retardation and meet the region's expanding mobility needs was a key
part of Pell's policy vision. He was well placed to do something about it.

The vehicle that Pell designed to launch the Northeast rail renewal
opportunity was a policy based upon what would today be labeled a "public-
private partnership." The senator recognized that in the midst of profound
industrial decline among Northeastern railroads, government would have
to "prime the pump" to move such a partnership along. Pell sought to lay
the foundation for such a new model railroad[9] in the Northeast by drafting
the High-Speed Ground Transportation Act of 1965 (HSGTA) and
shepherding it to enactment. The law authorized $90 million, equivalent to
just over $489 million in 2000 dollars,[10] to establish and fund a new Office
of High-Speed Ground Transportation (OHSGT). This agency would plan,

organize, fund, and evaluate high-speed demonstration projects. Their implementation would be left largely in the hands of private sector partners, the railroads that owned the infrastructure and manufacturers that would build new trains to run over them.

Originally administered by the Department of Commerce, the Office of High-Speed Ground Transportation moved to the newly created U.S. Department of Transportation (DOT) in 1967. By that time, planning had reached the point where DOT was ready to sign contracts with its rail passenger renewal partners. The most ambitious of these contracts was executed with the Pennsylvania Railroad (PRR), America's largest rail passenger carrier and the principal train operator between New York and Washington. OHSGT committed to invest $6.7 million, later raised to $11 million, to support the PRR's acquisition of a new generation of electric-powered, self-propelled passenger cars that could run at 160 miles per hour and make the trip from midtown Manhattan to Capitol Hill in under three hours.[11] This particular route had three specific advantages that raised its promise as a test bed for rail passenger revival.

First, the New York to Washington travel market, including intermediate destinations of Philadelphia, Wilmington, and Baltimore, was the nation's busiest and was still growing. The new Metroliner could thus succeed by either capturing the growth in travel (i.e., new trips) between these markets, or by recapturing some of the business that had been lost to car travel and the airlines. The Northeast travel market had previously spawned commercial success in transport innovation. In 1961, Eastern Airlines pioneered the "air shuttle" service concept of hourly "mass transit" style flights between Boston, New York, and Washington that has since spread to other markets.[12]

A second advantage for this route was that it had the most developed and, arguably, most modern rail infrastructure in North America. The Pennsylvania Railroad had spent $126 million during the height of the Depression to electrify 1,405 miles of trackage, including those between New York and Washington, using government loan guarantees provided by the Reconstruction Finance Corporation.[13] In 1935, the PRR's new electric passenger express cut the schedule from four hours fifteen minutes to three hours forty-five minutes. Electric power on this route would enable the Metroliner to test out advanced propulsion technology and lightweight equipment design, which formed the technical core of Japanese and European breakthroughs in rail passenger renewal. Unlike Europe and Japan, which had extensive electric rail infrastructure, the North American rail network relies largely on diesel powered locomotives that are efficient for the low-speed transport of freight, but are not well suited to speeds over one hundred miles per hour. This placed a considerable constraint on rail passenger initiatives outside the Northeast.

A third, and quite particular, advantage for renewing the passenger train between New York and Washington was the willingness of the Pennsylvania Railroad's executives to work with government on this initiative. Itzkoff noted that "Pennsylvania Railroad Chairman Stuart Saunders placed his road's corporate prestige on the line, promising two and a half hour service between New York and Washington by the fall of 1967."[14] In an industry that had largely soured on passenger trains' potential—and where CEO's took pride in remaining aloof from government sponsorship, which was boosting their air and road based competitors each year—the Pennsylvania Railroad stood apart. First, it needed something important from government: approval of its merger with the New York Central Railroad.[15] Second, its leaders knew that the OHSGT and its supporters in Congress wanted something from railroads in the Northeast, namely, cooperation in experimenting with passenger train renewal. This coincidence of needs made the Pennsylvania Railroad uncharacteristically accommodating to government's partnership proposal on a passenger train renewal demonstration.

Terms for the ensuing partnership between the OHSGT and the PRR reflected the railroad's desire to retain economic control over the project, while also earning political goodwill that would hopefully pay off in its merger request. At the outset, government committed just $11 million into launching the Metroliner project, compared to the Pennsylvania Railroad's $44.5 million initial investment. When the cost overruns relating to delay and debugging these trains, detailed below, were totaled in 1970, the PRR, General Electric, Westinghouse, and the Budd Company had spent over $60 million of private funds on the project, while the OHSGT had put in $12.9 million of public money.[16] Thus, unlike Amtrak, the Metroliner project passed a key market test from the outset in that the government's private partners were willing to put significant sums into making the demonstration a reality.

Another important difference between the Metroliner and subsequent North American rail renewal initiatives was that an "indigenous" U.S. rail manufacturing sector still had an interest in developing new passenger train products. Three major manufacturers emerged as bidders for the Metroliner project. General Electric, Westinghouse, and the Budd Company each sought the Pennsylvania Railroad's $21 million rolling-stock contract. An indication of government's preference to boost technological capacity across the rail sector can be seen in the somewhat unusual decision to split the order among all three bidders, and in particular between GE and Westinghouse, which both specialized in electric propulsion technology. The political dynamic of this partnership pointed toward distributing the benefits of rail passenger research and development more widely than a fully private procurement process for new rolling stock might have yielded.

The Budd Company would build the passenger car bodies and integrate the propulsion systems into them. General Electric and Westinghouse would design and manufacture different types of electric motors, braking systems, and communications and signal equipment. The Metroliner's specifications included a cruising speed of 120 mph and a top speed of 160 mph. Its performance criteria were similar to the Shinkansen. But unlike the Shinkansen, and the future TGV and ICE, the Metroliner project included no new infrastructure. This helps to explain why this train holds one, and only one, speed record among the world's fast trains: The Metroliner was implemented in just four years. This sprint from being a proposal, through project development, to a service launch could occur because no new right-of-way had to be acquired, and no track and electric power infrastructure had to be constructed. The Metroliner project also predated any federal environmental impact assessment requirements, and the lack of new infrastructure meant that opposition from local NIMBYs that would stymie future high-speed rail initiatives did not materialize. As a result, the Metroliner's four-year project-development speed record is unlikely to be beaten, either in the United States or abroad.

But the Metroliner's speedy development and modest budget came at a price. The short-term cost was a, perhaps inevitable, period of debugging equipment that had been rushed into production without either a prototype or the "design and test phase" that would have enabled refinement of new technical concepts and applications.[17] At General Electric and Westinghouse, a lack of experience in high-speed rail passenger technology led designers to seriously underestimate the challenge of incorporating state of the art electronics into a passenger train that would have to operate over infrastructure designed in the 1930s. *Business Week* quoted a source stating, "No one connected with the design . . . realized what a big step they were taking."[18]

Instead of the custom tailored fit between new electric trains and purpose-built tracks and power distribution systems that turned the Shinkansen and TGV into immediate success stories, the Metroliner's high-tech features fared poorly on an infrastructure that was designed long before the transistor had been invented. For example, the height of the electric transmission wire that fed power to the Metroliner varied from 18.5 feet to 26 feet above the rails. As the Metroliner's rooftop current collector, known as a pantograph, bounced along the wire at high speeds it regularly lost contact with the power supply. The resulting electrical fluctuation, ranging from full power to none at all, wreaked havoc with the Metroliner's solid state circuitry, much the way that plugging and unplugging today's desktop computer every minute would take quite a toll on the hardware. The results, summed up in an evocative phrase that the Metroliner suffered from "bugs inside the bugs," meant that a fleet of forty-eight cars could only yield twenty-four working units for an operating schedule.[19]

But while these bugs could eventually be ironed out, the longer-term cost of the Metroliner project's lack of new infrastructure yielded a permanent performance constraint. The Penn Central Railroad (successor to the PRR) invested heavily in upgrading tracks between New York and Washington. Its assistant vice president, James W. Diffenderfer, noted that "over 400 miles of track have been laid with continuous welded rail at a cost of over $19 million, providing the high-speed inside tracks and, in many cases, all four main tracks with new 140 pound rail."[20]

But Diffenderfer also made it clear that the Penn Central was either unprepared or unable to transform its New York–Washington infrastructure into a "world class" high-speed railroad: "The heavy use which this track receives under both high-speed freight and passenger operations necessitates continuing expenditures for track surfacing and alignment over and above the $32 million which has been invested" to date. "Specifications forced upon us by the Department of Transportation in our contract agreement and written by consultants who were aiming at the ideal rather than the practical have been extremely difficult, if not impossible, to meet on a continuing basis. We believe they should be interpreted as the ideal at which we should aim rather than the minimum standard to which the track must be constantly maintained."[21]

As a result of the Penn Central's financial limitations, underscored by the corporation's bankruptcy, discussed below, less than half of the route between New York and Washington could ever accommodate 120 mph operations. And the Metroliner's 160 mile per hour sprints remained an engineer's dream that was never realized.

Given the performance limitations of operating on modestly refurbished traditional infrastructure, shared with freight traffic, commuter trains, and conventional intercity trains, the Metroliner could only cut the travel time between New York and Washington to three hours. When city-center travel times are factored in, the Metroliner came close to the speed of the hourly air shuttle, which had a flying time of forty-five minutes. But it was not a decisive advantage, akin to the TGV's two hour travel time between Paris and Lyon. This constrained the Metroliner's market penetration, which has never captured more than 50 percent of travelers between New York and Washington, and thus did not renew rail's status as the dominant carrier in the way that the TGV would later do for major French travel markets.

Despite these constraints, the Metroliner proved to be a success with the traveling public. Enough of them were willing to try the new train, and pay a premium fare, to make the service commercially viable. Soon after its debut, the Metroliner was covering its operating costs, and bringing in a modest profit, quite significant at a time when passenger train losses were mounting in all other services.[22] For thirty-one years, the Metroliner has retained this place of pride in North American passenger trains' commercial performance. It has been the only regularly scheduled passenger train on this continent to post consistent profits.

4.2. From Demonstration to Distraction: How the Metroliner's Results Got Crowded Out of the Rail Policy Agenda During the 1980s

The Metroliner and the High-Speed Ground Transportation Act that gave rise to it arrived on the U.S. railroad scene more than a decade before the French inaugurated their TGV and more than two decades before the German ICE entered service. The most important results of this experiment turned out not to be technical but organizational, as the Metroliner and the even more "bug"-infested TurboTrain from New York to Boston never came close to their performance specifications in revenue operations. The Metroliner demonstrated that a configuration of government, a rail carrier and infrastructure owner, and equipment manufacturers could redesign rail service and come up with a passenger train that attracted new riders and revenues. This alignment of rail policy community participants had functional similarities to the French and German alliances that would push ahead with rail passenger renewal. The principal difference was that the U.S. rail carrier was privately owned and that it put in the largest share of investment, thus making government a junior partner in the renewal venture.

The partnership that gave rise to the Metroliner was permanently fractured when the merged Penn Central Railroad filed for protection from its creditors in 1970. This railroad collapse was the largest corporate bankruptcy in American history at the time. The domino effect of Northeast and Midwest railroad bankruptcies turned the executive branch's attention to freight industry restructuring, with the Federal Railroad Administration and Department of Transportation devoting considerable administrative and bud-

getary resources to reorganization of the rail freight sector.[23] Congress similarly gave reorganization and regulatory reform of freight railroads a higher
priority than renewing passenger trains. As well, Amtrak's political stalemate
complicated any follow-up to the Metroliner's commercial success by linking
the Northeast's rail renewal to debates over passenger train prospects across
the country.

When the Northeast's bankrupt railroads were restructured into Conrail,
a public enterprise freight carrier, title to most of the tracks between Washington and Boston got transferred to Amtrak, with parts that had been bought
by Connecticut and Massachusetts remaining under state ownership. During
the 1980s, improvements under the Northeast Corridor Improvement Project
(NECIP) repaired deferred maintenance that had accumulated during the
Penn Central bankruptcy, as well as introduced new signaling and electrical
power distribution technology that filled in some of the gap between new
equipment and old infrastructure. NECIP made train operations more efficient, reliable, and safe, but these improvements did not translate into competitive advantages for the passenger train, measured either by travel time or
frequency.

Between New York and Washington, hourly Metroliner service has remained the norm since 1970, despite the fact that air shuttle service doubled
its frequency from hourly to half-hourly when New York Air launched a competing hourly service between Boston, New York, and Washington in 1980,
which was sold to Pan American Airways and upgraded to full "shuttle" operations in 1986. Continental Airlines added its own shuttle between Washington and Newark airport, just across the Hudson River from Manhattan, in
1988. Between New York and Boston, where electrification ended at New
Haven, Connecticut, trains offered an incredibly slow trip time of over five
hours and were uncompetitive with both driving and air travel.

4.3. Moving Beyond the Metroliner: Extending High-Speed Trains to Boston and Launching Acela

By 1990, it had become clear that Amtrak's embattled stewardship of America's
intercity passenger trains was not, in itself, going to produce the kind of renewal initiative that could equal, let alone surpass, what the Metroliner project
had done for rail travel between Washington and New York. But while the
ongoing development of modern, marketable, and competitive passenger train
service in the Northeast could be sidetracked by the bankruptcy of freight
railroads and then delayed by the political standoff between Amtrak's sup-

porters and its skeptics, it simply presented too much of an opportunity to be neglected indefinitely.

The same economic and geographic attributes that had made a rail passenger revival appear attractive to Claiborne Pell in the 1960s were no less promising thirty years later. Indeed, another favorable characteristic could now clearly be added to the list of rail's advantages—the mode's relatively modest environmental impact. In a region where air- and water-quality problems abounded, the rail mode's energy efficiency and potential to be powered by electricity gave passenger trains a further advantage in meeting mobility needs.

The political momentum for doing more to renew passenger trains in the Northeast closely followed Senator Pell's original prescription for policy development. In *Megalopolis Unbound*, the senator had identified the need for state governments to take an active part in the passenger train's future. He wrote that the "most appropriate form of agency [to renew passenger trains] would be a public authority. . . . [S]uch an authority could be formed by a compact agreement among the eight states of Megalopolis—Massachusetts, Rhode Island, Connecticut, New York, New Jersey, Pennsylvania, Delaware, and Maryland—plus the District of Columbia, for the express purpose of owning, operating, and maintaining railroad passenger service."[24] While Amtrak's quasi-public structure had taken on certain attributes of a public authority, these were quite distant from state governments' engagement. States played little role in the organization, management, and funding of passenger trains, unlike the active intergovernmental dynamic in other areas of American transportation policy.

But in the 1990s, Northeastern states opted to take a more active role in developing the passenger train's potential. This advocacy came from the Coalition of Northeastern Governors (CONEG), a quasi-governmental research and advocacy organization created in 1976 by the governors of Maine, New Hampshire, Vermont, Massachusetts, Rhode Island, Connecticut, and New York. Among its priorities were "transportation and the economy, environment and energy."[25] Rail passenger renewal explicitly entered CONEG's policy agenda in July 1986 when it directed the CONEG Policy Research Center, Inc. "to form a High Speed Rail Task Force." Concerned with NECIP's failure "to accomplish fully its goals of rapid, reliable, and economically sound intercity rail passenger service, the Governors charged the Task Force to study the feasibility, applicability and benefits to the Region of enhanced high speed rail passenger service."[26] The CONEG Policy Research Center produced a series of reports on Northeast rail passenger options essentially validating both the mobility challenges that *Megalopolis Unbound* had foreseen in the

1960s, as well as the opportunities that more effective passenger train services could open up. Regarding the former, CONEG's analysts found that "continued economic growth of the Region has resulted in increasing congestion. The adverse affect on the movement of people and goods caused by increasing congestion at the Region's airports and on its highways is a threat to the Region's economic and social vitality. The very nature of a service-oriented economy has placed increased demands on an aging transportation infrastructure with a limited ability to expand capacity."[27]

While CONEG's researchers considered incremental steps that could be taken to improve existing service, and intermediate technology that could improve performance without the high cost of electrification, achieving parity with the Metroliner's performance was endorsed as a policy goal. The task force recommended that "a trip time as close as possible to 3 hours from Boston to New York by train would provide a safe, efficient alternative to the air and related ground congestion which is prevalent throughout the Region."[28]

Again harking back to the 1960s, CONEG's analysis highlighted the power of partnership in improving the passenger train's potential. But in the intervening decades since the OHSGT, the potential partners had changed. In the massive reorganization that transformed the bankrupt Penn Central Railroad into the publicly owned, and subsequently privatized, Consolidated Rail Corporation, title to much of the track between Washington and Boston had passed over to Amtrak. The remainder was owned by the states of New York, Connecticut, and Massachusetts. With commuter trains and freight operators now provided with statutory access to this publicly owned rail corridor, the challenge of optimizing new technology and upgrading infrastructure would require a much more intricately designed set of cooperative arrangements among state governments and Washington—in addition to coordination between Amtrak and the freight and commuter carriers. CONEG concluded that "the problem involved in reconciling the interests of these parties are substantial, but more tractable than the problem of securing real estate that is virtually unavailable and where available prohibitably [sic] priced."[29]

When it came to paying for this round of renewal, CONEG's staff proposed a solution somewhere between the private sector leadership of the original Metroliner demonstration and the full federal funding that had supported NECIP during the 1980s. Private investment in new equipment and infrastructure was viewed as most effective in the context of government remaining the senior partner in Northeast rail passenger renewal because "for a true public/private partnership to be successful, government must share some of the risks inherent in such a scenario and show the financial community its commitment. These commitments may be in the form of outright upfront grants for particular elements, loan guarantees or annual grants to cover debt service."[30] Governors were encouraged to consider investing in intercity rail passenger renewal to spur modernization forward. As with roads and transit, state matching funds would imply shifting some authority for rail passenger policy "outside the beltway." CONEG's staff insisted that "if Amtrak is to assume an active state financial role, it must be willing to accept state involvement in prioritizing allocation of funds and acceptance of operating alternatives."[31]

Creating a new intergovernmental fiscal instrument that would meet the needs of Northeastern states was an idea that never materialized. Washington's rail passenger policymakers, particularly those in Congress, were reluctant to share authority over renewing Amtrak's prime asset with states, even if the latter were considering putting up some money. The Northeast's governors found that advocating federal spending on rail renewal was more workable than negotiating a major new fiscal partnership, as reaffirmed in their 1997 Policy Statement entitled "The Growth of Intercity Passenger Rail Reflects." In this document, "the Governors direct the staff of the CONEG Policy Research Center, Inc. to develop a legislative strategy to provide a federal role in the development of a corridor funding strategy."[32] After identifying the need for rail passenger renewal, CONEG had thus focused its political efforts on mobilizing the Northeast's congressional delegation.

This effort to catch up, both with the high-speed rail renaissance in Europe, and with the Northeast's own travel needs which were increasingly ill-served by congested highways and airports while the rail corridor remained under-developed, was championed by Senator Frank Lautenberg (D-N.J.). Lautenberg was quite outspoken in his support for federal involvement in this rail passenger renewal initiative, asking, "Does it make sense to talk about spending billions of dollars for another Boston-area airport when for less we could have in place by 1997 a high speed rail system that could better serve the region? . . . It's absurd that the United States has sat by and watched other countries develop high speed rail systems while the last two Administrations fought to kill off our own."[33]

Lautenberg was soon joined by Senator Daniel Patrick Moynihan (D-N.Y.) in finding the funds for further Northeast rail passenger imporvements They were well placed on the Senate's Transportation and Appropriations Committees, respectively, to secure money for extending electrification from New Haven to Boston. Unlike the Metroliner demonstration or the Northeast Corridor Project, this initiative was not linked to a new program, or even a special project name. Electrification and associated upgrading of tracks between New Haven and Boston proceeded as part of Amtrak's regular appropriations legislation. The Amtrak Authorization and Development Act of 1992 allocated $470 million specifically for upgrading the Northeast Corridor to permit a three-hour travel time between New York and Boston.[34] This funding was subsequently increased to $600 million.[35] Following an Environmental Impact Assessment approval process, electrification and track reconstruction commenced in 1996.[36]

Also in 1996, eighteen high-speed train sets were ordered for $754 million through innovative international financing from Canadian manufacturer Bombardier, which had acquired a license from the French TGV builder Alstom to adapt the design to North American specifications.[37] While the tracks and trains were being (re)built, Amtrak launched a search for a new brand name that would differentiate America's first 150 mile per hour train service from its predecessors. In March of 1999, the Acela brand made its media debut, with Amtrak committing $20 million to market the new train's identity.[38] Acela would replace the now venerable Metroliner in Northeastern travel vocabulary. Construction and testing delays pushed the gala inaugural of Acela Express to November 16, 2000, with revenue service of one Washington–New York–Boston round-trip commencing on December 11, 2000. Acela Express is the most significant passenger train renewal initiative to make it off the drawing board—in both policy and technical terms—since the Office of High-Speed Ground Transportation had set the stage for the Metroliner.

In many ways, Acela Express is the progeny of the Metroliner. This new service is, literally, taking over from the Metroliner in providing premium train service between New York and Washington. It will also extend the original service concept of the Metroliner to the full range of travel markets between Boston and Washington. Acela came into being because state governments in the Northeast noted the contrast between the Metroliner's success south of New York and the ineffectiveness of traditional trains between Boston and New York, and set the stage for a champion in the Senate to take up their call for action in building upon one of the very few strengths in America's passenger rail network.

Whether the Acela program will spur further rail passenger renewal initiatives in other regions of the United States and Canada depends upon both its own commercial performance (i.e., its capacity to generate new ridership and turn a profit), and the lessons that policy community participants draw from the much larger number of failed attempts to introduce passenger train renewal in states outside the Northeast.

4.4. The First False Start: American High Speed Rail Corporation's Failure to Bring Bullet Trains to Southern California

The first significant rail passenger renewal initiative that sought to bypass the policy stalemate in national government was a literal departure from Washington-based efforts on the part of some Amtrak executives. They left the corporation to pursue rail renewal efforts that seemed beyond Amtrak's grasp in the early 1980s. In April 1981, Amtrak president Alan Boyd had commercial renewal development in mind when he announced plans to "diversify and thus strengthen the company's weak financial position" by "studying four potential routes to host profitable Japanese bullet trains as well as a plan to expand [Amtrak's] package express service."[39] These efforts sought to build upon the "Emerging Corridors" analysis that had been conducted jointly by Amtrak and the Federal Railroad Administration at the end of the Carter administration.[40] Testifying to Congress about the proposed Rail Passenger Systems Act of 1981 that would have designated up to twenty high-speed corridors and allocated $2 billion in federal funds to match state and private investments in their development, Boyd stated that Amtrak's "preliminary conclusion is that bullet trains can also be profitable in this country."[41]

But when the Reagan administration declared war on Amtrak subsidies, among other attributes of big government, rail passenger renewal was promptly crowded off of the federal policy agenda by the more immediate political debate over Amtrak's survival. In the meantime, Amtrak's vice-president of government affairs, Lawrence Gilson, left the corporation to become full-time president of the new American High Speed Rail Corporation (AHSRC), in which Boyd would serve as part-time chairman. The *Los Angeles Times* reported that Gilson had been "shepherding Amtrak's own bullet-train studies for more than two years."[42] During the course of these studies, the Japanese National Railways, the Japanese Shipbuilding Foundation (which included rail car builders), and Ishi Shibi Corporation of Tokyo gained sufficient enthusiasm for entering the prospective North American bullet-train market to propose investing a total of $8 million to fund preliminary planning and business development efforts.[43] These funds, matched by $2 million from U.S. sources, formed the working capital for AHSRC's launch.

The AHSRC, which was created as a spin-off from Amtrak, was both exceptional and precedent-setting for future high-speed rail policy initiatives in the United States. Two exceptional characteristics of the AHSRC project were its relatively short distance and its up-front commitment to Japanese bullet-train technology. Because it would run only 131.5 miles between the Los Angeles International Airport, Amtrak's Union Station in downtown Los Angeles, and San Diego, the Japanese bullet train's slightly lower top speed, compared to the French TGV, was not a limitation on performance. The proposed travel time of fifty-nine minutes (downtown to downtown) was seen as quite competitive with the automobile, which would be the principal travel alternative in this market. The AHSRC project has been the only proposed North American intercity rail passenger renewal initiative to embrace Japanese technology publicly. All other initiatives have looked to European rail technology, or its derivatives.

Ties between Amtrak and AHSRC went beyond the personnel who moved from developing rail passenger renewal inside one organization to pursuing it at the other. Amtrak loaned AHSRC $750,000 in seed money, which was eventually repaid with $100,000 in interest.[44] AHSRC would operate the new train service under license from Amtrak, which had a legal monopoly on intercity rail passenger service at the time.[45] Although the terms of this license were never disclosed, some form of profit sharing likely would have been included. Had it worked, this approach of spinning off a market-focused subsidiary from Amtrak that would develop profitable high-speed passenger trains in a promising travel corridor could have been replicated across the country. But instead, AHSRC's failure set two important precedents that subsequent high-speed rail entrepreneurs would have to live with.

First, AHSRC's business plan entrenched the proposition that, unlike for-profit air and road based carriers, the federal government's transportation spending should be off limits to commercial renewal efforts in passenger rail. Partly to counter accusations of conflict of interest and the existence of a "sweetheart deal" between Amtrak and its spin-off, AHSRC went out of its way to insist that no federal involvement would be required to launch high-speed rail in Southern California. In lieu of the massive contribution to highway and airport infrastructure budgets that came from federal grants, the AHSRC's initial projected cost of $2.9 billion was proposed to be funded by up to $1.3 billion in tax exempt (but not government guaranteed) revenue bonds issued by the State of California, $700 million in Japanese investment, $500 million in equity, and $400 million from commercial banks.[46]

The project was immediately endorsed by California's governor, while the state legislature rapidly enacted the California Passenger Rail Financing Commission Act, which authorized the issue of tax-exempt revenue bonds for rail passenger projects that would run services at 120 miles per hour or faster. These moves suggested that a high-speed rail renewal could indeed be launched without recourse to the national government's treasure trove of transportation investment. Speaking during the height of attention and controversy surrounding this project, California's treasurer, Jesse Unruh, reminded his audience of a joke that made the rounds in Sacramento in 1982 to the effect that "if the train is half as fast as the legislation passed for it, it would be a huge success."[47]

But skepticism was not long in taking its toll on AHSRC's efforts. Critics of the project claimed that the ridership study which had been prepared by Arthur D. Little (ADL), and upon which the company's business plan had been built, was virtually fraudulent. An outside "expert" hired by opponents of AHSRC, discussed below, "accused American High Speed Rail of deceitfully manipulating figures to support the bullet train proposal" because ADL had forecast large numbers of travelers using the line for short distance commuting.[48] AHSRC's credibility on projected ridership and revenues was not helped by its refusal to release the full version of ADL's market study.

AHSRC Vice-President John Lagomarcino told one reporter that "while we are not seeking to keep competitors out of the market, we don't want to give them data that would help them to determine markets and financial opportunities without their paying for it."[49] But this rationale never dispelled the suspicions surrounding AHSRC's commercial forecast, and the doubt regarding what would happen to the government-issued revenue bonds should the new train fail to generate projected revenues. The transportation director of California's Public Utilities Commission reflected this skepticism in an interview with *Business Week*, stating that "if [AHSRC] can show they can build it and operate it from fares, it's the best thing since sliced bread" but "I fear they may get halfway through, run out of money, and come running to government to finish it."[50]

Concern that AHSRC might stick California with a big bill for bullet-train development dogged the project throughout its existence. Even potential allies of renewing intercity passenger rail, such as regional public transit operators, viewed the AHSRC as a threat, because it might subsequently compete for state financing. The president of the Southern California Rapid Transit District publicly warned AHSRC that "the minute any particular piece of [your financing] puzzle cannot be filled completely by funding from the private sector and it becomes dependent upon public funds, then you've crossed into an area where the competition is fierce and the likelihood of being successful in getting any of those dollars is probably nil."[51] The acid test of AHSRC's business plan was its reception among prospective investors, for whom the absence of government guarantees or federal participation were decisively negative.

In November 1984, AHSRC announced cancellation of the project after failing to raise just $50 million of private equity. AHSRC's investment banker, Steven Greenwald of First Boston Corporation, revealed that private financing efforts had stalled just above $25 million because investors were unwilling to put their money into a transportation project being developed entirely in the private sector. He stated that $50 million was "an extraordinary amount of risk capital to raise for one venture, when it was going just for further studies."[52] In his own postmortem on the project, AHSRC president Gilson noted that "to banks, projects with government guarantees are presumptively safe, and those without are presumptively risky."[53]

A second major policy precedent that was set by the AHSRC initiative concerned environmental impact assessment and mitigation. No matter how limited government's support of this project might have been, the public's outcry against a major new infrastructure meant that AHSRC would have to comply with the same environmental and planning regulations that applied to major public works projects such as airport or expressway construction. This precedent would create a significant hurdle for subsequent high-speed development proposals. At first, AHSRC had sought a different environmental review process than that being applied to publicly sponsored projects based upon the premise that a private rail passenger developer should not have to meet the full range of demands placed upon public agencies. Legislation establishing the California Passenger Rail Financing Commission included amendments to the California Environmental Quality Act, which "caused confusion by appearing to exempt [high-speed rail] projects from the Environmental Quality Act, or at least to preclude . . . candidates such as the California Public Utilities Commission and the Department of Transportation from being the state environmental lead agency."[54]

Despite the AHSRC's initial position that "theoretically the California Environmental Quality Act applies only to public corporations," it soon became clear that anything less than a full environmental impact review would not survive the political pressure generated by organized opponents.[55] The United Citizens Coastal Protective League was organized from a "tiny group of oceanfront homeowners living next to the planned route in Cardiff," a wealthy community in San Diego County. The group's leader, Robert Bonde, professed a complete "lack of faith" in AHSRC's intentions, stating that "the [California Passenger Rail Financing Commission] law was written originally to try and get around the requirements, so we have no certainty or confidence that [American High Speed] will do anything it promises, especially now in terms of mitigating [environmental damage]." He was equally candid in describing what motivated his opposition to the project, telling one reporter that "the thought of high-speed trains every 10 minutes past his dream home was almost too awful to fathom."[56]

AHSRC took an adversarial stance toward its critics, seeking to portray them as selfish NIMBYs who were standing in the way of the greater good, including environmental quality, in Southern California. In one public address, AHSRC President Gilson stated, "Let the critics yell from the street corners that the sky is falling. Those who will look at the transportation needs of Southern California, weigh the alternatives, and study the logic of American High Speed Rail's plan, will conclude with us that there is an imperative pointing to the earliest possible completion of this project. It is a project that will work. The alternatives for transportation in the region are too horrible to contemplate."[57]

But Southern California was not Japan, where the millions of people already riding conventional trains vastly outnumbered those living alongside the route of a proposed high-speed train, and where government had close ties to a public rail passenger carrier. In California, Mr. Bonde's nightmare of bullet trains spoiling the ambience of an exclusive oceanside neighborhood proved to be more compelling than Mr. Gilson's vision of the congestion and pollution that would be created by sticking with "business as usual" in transportation planning.

Requiring private investors to pay for a full scale environmental impact assessment was sufficient to kill the project's financing potential, as indicated by AHSRC's failure to raise the $50 million required to fund those studies. Even after AHSRC's demise, Gilson insisted that the project would have been environmentally sound, if not superior to intercity travel alternatives, while lamenting that "public and government reactions were a series of 'what ifs' and 'why nots' that threatened to sink the project in a tidal wave of studies and alternative analyses, all with a seeming indifference to the cost and time delays."[58]

Although AHSRC raced to failure quite quickly, California's rejection of this particular project did not equate with opposition to all forms of passenger train renewal. On the contrary, AHSRC's demise actually stimulated demand for more "reasonable" public sector initiatives to enhance the passenger train's role in California. This more moderate approach was exemplified by the vice chairman of the Oceanside Transportation Commission, who had been active among bullet-train opponents, when he commented, "Oceanside and the other cities along the Southwest Coast Corridor are not opposed to rail, but are determined that disruptions to the community of the magnitude suggested by AHSRC will not be accepted. What will be accepted, and what we are now directing our efforts toward, is an improved level of Amtrak service including . . . more frequent schedules. We can easily live with 90 mph" speeds.[59]

Following the AHSRC's demise, proponents of rail passenger renewal in California, including many who had been skeptical of bullet trains, embraced an alternative policy approach of incrementally upgrading existing train service. Such measures proved popular with the electorate, which voted in favor of several bond measures to invest in incremental improvements. In the 1990 general election, Californians passed two referenda that raised large sums for rail investment. Proposition 108 provided for $1 billion in general obligation bonds to fund specified rail projects, and Proposition 116 authorized borrowing another $1.99 billion for intercity, commuter, and urban rail projects statewide.[60]

Other proponents sought to continue studying future high-speed options which have been presided over by both a state high-speed rail commission and now a California High Speed Rail Authority (CHRSA). In 2000, CHSRA received $25 million in state funding to develop an environmental impact report on a high-speed rail link between Sacramento and San Diego via the Bay Area and Los Angeles. Ironically, this was the exact amount that would have enabled AHSRC to stay in business and develop an environmental impact statement on high speed rail sixteen years earlier.

The CHSRA's vice-chair described funding for the environmental review as a "major milestone" and stated, "The funds in the 2000–2001 budget that Governor Davis signed provide the Authority the means to begin the process that will lead to a high-speed train system for all of California."[61] Yet despite this three year funding commitment, the *Wall Street Journal* had listed the CHSRA among its "losers" for 1999, because the authority's much more ambitious plan to put a referendum for high speed rail bonds on the 2000 ballot got sidetracked.[62] California's latest funding for contemplating high-speed rail thus appears as another form of consolation prize.

4.5. The AHSRC's Aftermath: A Policy Inheritance of High Hurdles in Project Planning

Following the AHSRC's demise, subsequent rail renewal efforts would each have to deal with the substantial constraints of its "policy inheritance." This term was coined by Hugh Heclo to characterize the accumulation of rules, precedents, and expectations that accumulate from government's action, or inaction, regarding a given problem. He wrote that "policy invariably builds on policy, either in moving forward with what has been inherited, or amending it, or repudiating it."[63] As America's history of high-speed rail setbacks illustrates, this inheritance can also constrain subsequent policy instead of facilitating its implementation.

Proponents of launching passenger rail renewal outside Washington now faced the twin precedents of being denied access to public funding for aspects of project development that were commonplace in other transportation modes, yet also being held to the same high environmental and planning standards of public agencies. Such a policy inheritance from the AHSRC's efforts required entrepreneurs to muster the organizational and financial resources for a long and demanding political campaign. No sprint toward new service along the lines of the Metroliner, or even the original Shinkansen or TGV lines, would be possible because demanding environmental and planning requirements would have to be met. And both the formal and informal analysis of alternatives that would occur in evaluating any proposed leap into rail passenger renewal would contrast the cost of any "big bang" approach with the option of incrementally upgrading traditional trains.

In transportation system development, particularly that involving infrastructure, time spent scoping out environmental impacts and their mitigation strategies equals money. The direct cost of that planning process would be only the first obstacle. Environmental impact assessment would almost certainly be followed by even more expensive mitigation measures (e.g., tunnels, noise barriers, detours around sensitive areas, etc.). But the first obstacle was significant in that it put the price of planning serious rail renewal beyond the scope of discretionary funds that a state department of transportation or a state legislature's transportation committee might be able to allocate to stimulating development. Small scale support from such sources could, at best, set the stage for a rail renewal initiative by hiring consultants to scope out economic and technical options. Moving further into serious project development would require a greater organizational commitment and a more ambitious financial objective.

Serious attempts to launch rail passenger renewal at the state level were certainly impacted by the need to meet the post-AHSRC requirements for project planning. A state-level organizational entity has to be created with a focused mandate on rail passenger development. This can range from an authority to a commission to a bureau within the state's transportation department. A key part of such organizations' work to date has focused on trying to implement a funding formula that could then bring the project to fruition. The three examples that follow each illustrate a particular approach to meeting this challenge. To date, none of them have succeeded.

4.6. Ohio's Rail Passenger Plan: How Selling a "Cadillac" During Hard Times Closed the Door on State Financing for Rail Passenger Renewal

The first alternative to California's quick sprint toward high-speed rail came out of the state of Ohio, which charged an independent agency, the Ohio Rail Transportation Authority (ORTA) with creating a plan for a "made in Ohio" intrastate passenger train system that would be brought before voters in a referendum. According to Joseph Vranich, Ohio's foray into rail passenger renewal was the brainchild of Arthur Wilkowski, a "determined state legislator from Toledo" who was as much impressed with European and Japanese breakthroughs as he was skeptical of Amtrak's ability to renew passenger trains. Vranich wrote that Wilkowski "declared that Amtrak would never provide the short-distance corridor services needed in states like Ohio, and was bitter in his denunciation: 'The Amtrak system would not work in Ohio. We will build this system on the ashes of Amtrak.'"[64] ORTA became the administrative vehicle for transforming the vision of an intrastate rail passenger network supported by Wilkowski and others into a concrete plan that would be brought before voters in the form of a referendum on a sales tax increase to pay for the costs of system development. Operations would become self-supporting, with surplus profits used to pay for infrastructure upkeep and renewal.

ORTA was unique among the many public organizations that have presided over rail passenger renewal efforts at the state level. Unlike the other entities' single policy focus on planning and administering high-speed train development, ORTA had two disparate mandates that led to quite varied missions, as summarized in a report to the state legislature: "First, ORTA is the Ohio state agency specifically designated by the Federal Government to assist in the promotion of a sound and efficient rail freight transportation system, in part through implementation of the branchline assistance programs initiated by Congress in the Regional Rail Reorganization Act of 1973 (3R Act), the Railroad Revitalization and Regulatory Reform Act of 1976 (4R Act), the Local Rail Service Assistance Act of 1978, the Staggers Rail Act of 1980, and the Northeast Rail Service Act of 1981. Secondly, ORTA has the responsibility of developing a safe, modern, effective intercity rail passenger system for the citizens of Ohio."[65]

On the one hand, this duality gave ORTA an institutional raison d'etre that extended beyond the life of any specific rail passenger development proposal. Defeat at the polls in 1982 of the sales tax proposed for high-speed rail would not mean the collapse of ORTA's planning and administrative capacities, as was often the case when a single purpose agency or a specialized department of state government suffered a political defeat in its rail passenger development efforts. But on the other hand, ORTA's economic planning and management activities were oriented in exactly opposite directions. Assessing the final disposition of branch lines that were proposed for abandonment in the rail freight reorganization following the Penn Central's bankruptcy involved picking up the pieces from the last act of a long running saga of economic decline. Developing a plan for statewide high-speed rail passenger service was more akin to writing the opening chapter of a drama set well into the future.

Ohio, with its image as a "rust belt" state, reflected in ORTA's other policy responsibility of dealing with abandoned railroad branch lines, would at first appear to be an unlikely setting in which to champion publicly-supported rail passenger renewal. The primary in-state travel markets, the busiest of which being the "3 C Corridor" from Cleveland through Columbus to Cincinnati, were not suffering from anything like the congestion and pollution that had featured in the AHSRC's case for bullet trains in Southern California. Nor were Ohio's growth predictions pointing to the kind of future gridlock that would trigger a crisis—a typical route to policy innovation in the United States.

The most significant policy "problem" that high-speed passenger trains were proposed to solve was centered neither on mobility, nor the environment, but on industrial decline. As ORTA's other policy responsibility for subsidizing or abandoning rail branch lines demonstrated, Ohio's heavy industries had fallen on hard times by the early 1980s. During the 1970s, "manufacturing employment dropped 6 percent overall resulting in a loss to the state of 91,000 manufacturing jobs."[66] With the decline or relocation of many manufacturers, both Ohio's railroads and its industrial sector were seen to be in need of some policy initiatives.

This classically Keynesian premise behind rail passenger policy influenced ORTA's planning priorities away from the more incrementalist approach that was exhibited in its early study of policy options. In 1979, ORTA was recommending "the use of the conventional diesel or diesel electric engine in the initial implementation of the Ohio system. Conventional technology was chosen because it can operate effectively at all the speed alternatives studied (60 MPH, 80 MPH, 110 MPH, and 150 MPH) and because it provides a system that can be implemented by the target date of 1985."[67] The capital cost for a 110 mile per hour passenger service was estimated at between $505 and $972 million.[68]

But by 1980, planning had shifted to a 150 mile per hour electrified, state-of-the-art high-speed railroad. Instead of being a problem, the huge pricetag of such a system was now portrayed as a benefit: "It is projected that ORTA's system would generate procurement of materials and equipment in the range of $300–500 million a year during the peak years of construction. Construction industry payrolls would range from $300–500 million in peak construction years. Total spending generated in the Ohio economy from the construction of the rail system could amount to approximately $20 billion . . . [because] $1 of construction spending would generate $3–4 in total spending, based on economic analysis for this study."[69] Construction of the elaborate new infrastructure would stimulate the economy by demanding many inputs from in-state manufacturers of steel, concrete, and other building materials. There would also be an employment boost in the hard hit construction and manufacturing jobs. Such effects would help cushion the blow of economic restructuring in Ohio.

This leap from incremental development into top-of-the-line high-speed technology was also justified by the advantage of introducing an alternative energy source in intercity transportation, with ORTA proclaiming in 1980 that "the era of cheap, plentiful petroleum is over!"[70] ORTA's planning horizon was increasingly focused on the long term, where Ohio's leadership in North American high-speed rail could open up new opportunities for high-tech manufacturing of fast trains and related technology. The agency claimed that "through the ORTA project, Ohio can become the center for high-speed rail passenger technology in the United States. As interest grows in other states for similar service (as it undoubtedly will) Ohio companies could sell the expertise, equipment, and techniques they developed. Ohio already possesses an outstanding industrial base with the necessary infrastructure and skills to meet the requirements of the high-speed rail technology. Whether it be steel, vehicle construction, or sophisticated electronic controls, it is, or can be, made in Ohio."[71]

Although such a strategy of short term economic stimulus and long term industrial development looked pretty promising to ORTA and its supporters, spending such big sums during tough times proved anathema to fiscal conservatives and bullet train skeptics.

Ohio's budget went into deficit in 1980, as a result of lower tax revenues from a declining economy and increasing payments for various forms of social assistance. Dealing with the deficit brought about a noticeable change in Ohio's policy and politics. As Paul noted, "Prior to the pending financial crunch, the high speed project had enjoyed bipartisan legislative support. As the crisis deepened, that changed. . . . In the last general election the state senate changed from a Democratic to Republican majority, and ORTA's most vocal detractor became president pro tempore of the Ohio Senate."[72] In its session prior to the November 1982 election, the Ohio legislature enacted a temporary 1 percent sales surtax to meet the state's budget deficit. This tax hike was viewed by some as a part of the reason that Ohio voters turned down ORTA's plan and its 1 percent additional sales tax by such a wide margin of 2.4 million to 710,000.[73] One reporter looked back on this defeat and blamed planners and politicians who "were trying to sell a 'Cadillac' system to a recession-plagued electorate, to people more concerned with getting a job than with getting a ride on a high-speed train."[74] Since Ohioans voted down high-speed rail (HSR), no other HSR project has sought to renew passenger trains based on a new tax, or even a preponderance of public funding from a state government.

The Ohio project's decisive defeat at the polls turned out to be a delegitimating event for proponents of government-led (and publicly financed) rail renewal initiatives at the state level. Elections are the final court of appeal in democratic politics, and the policy judgment rendered on high-speed rail was a complete condemnation. Following this repudiation by voters, state governments have been reluctant to take the lead in funding bold initiatives in rail passenger renewal. Instead, states with grand plans for rail passenger renewal have sought to pursue them in partnership with private investors. The fiscal retrenchment at both the national and subnational levels in North America, which is only recently becoming less acute, effectively closed the door on a publicly-led funding formula for the kind of dramatic, yet costly, rail passenger renewal that was promised by ORTA's high-speed rail initiative.

4.7. The Failure of Private Sector Financing to Bring TGVs to Texas

With the path to public finance at the state level blocked by deficit burdens, not to mention the ever vigilant guardianship of air, road, and transit transportation trust fund beneficiaries, high-speed rail entrepreneurs sought to develop a model where state governments could nurture a project by providing political rather than economic support. This approach to rail passenger development would place government in the role of franchise broker and regulator of development efforts, but leave project financing in private hands.

The Texas High-Speed Rail Act, which became law in May 1989, embodied these principles.

This act created an independent state agency, the Texas High-Speed Rail Authority (THSRA), and authorized it to solicit and evaluate proposals to build and operate a high-speed rail system in the state. THSRA was empowered to "award a franchise to the private sector to construct, operate, and maintain a high-speed rail facility, if the authority determines that the award of a franchise is for the public convenience and necessity." The act also stipulated that "legislative appropriations or other state funds may be used only for planning but not for financing, acquisition, construction, maintenance, or operation of the high-speed rail facility."[75]

Assessing the project's failure in hindsight, the THSRA's former executive director, Mark Burns, suggested that the national stalemate over rail passenger policy was echoed in the terms of the Texas High-Speed Rail Act and the subsequent controversy that flowed from what the law did, and did not, say. He wrote: "Both the genesis and the content of the Act reflect the strong and counterproductive sway held by both proponents and opponents of a high-speed rail project. Proponents successfully passed legislation without the benefit of any significant grass root-based support in the populace. Instead of being based on a perceived and articulated need, coupled with significant public involvement, [the decision to proceed to the assessment and possible award of a franchise was] presumably justified by the unusually high level of responsibility and risk to be assumed by private enterprise. . . . [Yet] although the project evaded some procedural hurdles, the Act was stretched and burdened by its opponents to include aspects calculated to lead to its demise."[76]

One such burden that would subsequently be seized upon by project opponents was the determination of whether high-speed rail was in the public interest. Rather than making such a determination in legislation, as would be the norm for other state supported transportation projects and programs, the Texas legislature delegated that responsibility, and the debate surrounding such a finding, to THSRA. The legislature specified that THSRA apply the traditional regulatory standard of "public convenience and necessity" in making this determination. Thus the controversy over such a finding was both deferred and distanced from the legislative arena.

Organized opponents would later claim that the case for proceeding with passenger rail had not been made, pointing to a finding in an advisory report for THSRA stating that "neither applicant has shown that award of a franchise would be a public necessity."[77] By contrast, the utility of infrastructure development was simply presumed in the work of Texas agencies that were developing highways and airports. Former Federal Railroad Administrator Gil Carmichael underscored the shortcoming that arose from creating a separate set of administrative procedures and policy norms for a Texas rail passenger renewal initiative. After the project had failed, he stated, "All of us involved in the Texas TGV made the same error. The Texas High Speed Rail Authority should not be a stand-alone agency, but part of the Department of Transportation. If the Texas DOT adopted the Authority, the project could be under way in this decade."[78] Joseph Vranich added that the Texas franchise process turned a policy initiative that was initially intended to nurture rail passenger development into an adversarial and litigious policy trap because it "permitted objections, counterclaims, and requests that are guaranteed as part of due process in a courtroom, but are ridiculous in trying create [sic] a business enterprise."[79] But these obstacles did not appear particularly problematic at the time the THSRA was launching the franchise process.

In 1990, following the failure of the mixing of public and private financing arrangements in Southern California, and Ohio voters' rejection of a publicly planned and financed high-speed rail project, the Texas call for private leadership appeared tempting to European train manufacturers. Flush with the success of its TGV, French manufacturer GEC-Alsthom had already exported high-speed train technology to Spain and was in the process of producing trains for the Channel Tunnel crossing into England. The Texas franchise appeared well suited to creating a North American beachhead for the TGV. GEC-Alsthom partnered with Bombardier Corporation of Canada, which held a North American manufacturing license for the TGV, and Morrison-Knudsen Corporation of Boise, Idaho, a diversified rail engineering and construction firm, to form the Texas TGV Consortium.

Germany's Siemens, builder of the ICE train, was anxious not to be left farther behind in the export market for high-speed rail. It and German partners ABB Verkehrstechnik GmbH and AEG Westinghouse Transport-Systeme GmbH allied with Texas-based Brown & Root of Houston, HCB Contractors of Dallas, and the H.B. Zachary Co., of San Antonio to form the Texas FasTrac consortium. Both bidders paid a $400,000 fee to the THSRA along with their franchise applications. This "user fee" approach to supporting the Texas High-Speed Rail Authority would subsequently draw fire from skeptics who claimed that it undermined the agency's independence.

But for prospective franchisees, this complete lack of public funding was initially seen to bring with it fewer constraints on project development. In particular, environmental and planning requirements initially appeared to be less formidable in a business-friendly state like Texas. What ensued was a spirited bidding by two consortia with ties to each manufacturer, and corresponding HSR technology. In 1991, the authority awarded a fifty-year franchise to a group that came to be known as the "Texas TGV."

The Texas TGV's proposal envisioned an inverted "Y"-shaped network that would connect Dallas–Fort Worth in the north of Texas to Houston on one branch and Austin/San Antonio on another. As part of the ensuing franchise agreement, Texas TGV effectively agreed to pay for the authority's ongoing budget, and other expenses relating to public sector activity in high-speed rail. The THSRA had received a $1 million start-up loan from the state treasury, against which Texas TGV paid $100,000 in 1992 and agreed to pay $100,000 per year thereafter to retire the debt. The agency's annual report also indicated that the "Texas TGV Corporation agreed to pay $555,829 to the Texas Turnpike Authority for the costs of a high-speed rail project study conducted in 1986."[80] These funds were in addition to payments from Texas TGV to cover the remainder of THSRA's operating budget for 1992. A subsequent performance review of the authority criticized this method of direct financing from the private sector, without funds flowing through the Texas legislature: "The current system, in which THSRA's budget is approved and its operating expenses paid by the *franchisee*, results in a system that gives a regulated entity significant control over its oversight agency's operations. For instance, the franchisee has little incentive to move funds from agency administration to regulatory functions, or to ensure that sufficient funding is allocated to regulation. . . . [T]he overall relationship can easily give the appearance that the agency is controlled by the regulated entity. The current system does *not* provide adequate assurances that the agency receives the funds needed to protect the public's interests by regulating the franchisees appropriately."[81]

Paying for the authority's operations turned out to be among the least challenging of Texas TGV's franchise obligations. Two other requirements turned out to be particularly problematic. First, since the project would require new safety regulations from the U.S. Federal Railroad Administration, constituting a form of government "action" under the National Environmental Policy Act, a complete environmental impact statement would have to be prepared at Texas TGV's full expense.[82] Public hearings would be required to obtain input from en route communities about the project's full range of impacts. These public concerns, plus detailed engineering and scientific assessments about the Texas TGV, were required to be assembled into a complete environmental impact statement that would be reviewed by state and federal environmental regulators. Second, the consortium was also required to come up with $170 million in equity financing by the end of 1992.

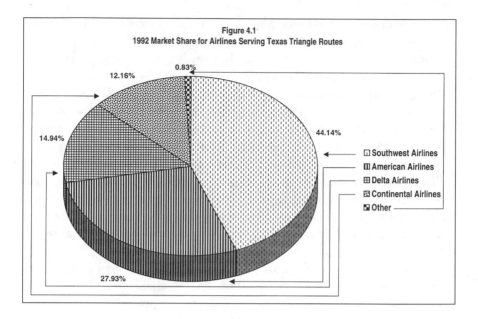

Figure 4.1
1992 Market Share for Airlines Serving Texas Triangle Routes

Another form of scrutiny facing the Texas TGV would come from the courts, where Texas-based Southwest Airlines launched three lawsuits against the project and the Texas High-Speed Rail Authority. This unprecedented level of opposition from a potential competitor in a public forum, as opposed to the behind-the-scenes political conflicts that have dogged many state-level rail passenger initiatives, merits closer attention because it reveals the position of passenger rail's adversaries in an unusually clear light. Southwest Airlines, which since deregulation has consistently performed as America's most profitable air carrier, correctly perceived a lot to be at stake in another travel mode's arrival in its home state.

Figure 4.1 illustrates the distribution of air traffic among carriers serving the Texas Triangle in 1992.[83] At over forty-four percent of the total, Southwest Airlines had the most to lose, by far, from competition with high-speed trains. Feldman reported that at the time, 6.6 percent of Southwest's total traffic was either originating in or destined to the cities that Texas TGV would serve and that 26.7 percent of Southwest's passengers flew to or from Texas, where 180 out of the carrier's 1,400 daily flights originated. Little wonder, then, that Southwest viewed Texas TGV as "enemy No. 1" and fought the project "down and dirty."[84]

Southwest's outspoken chairman, Herb Kelleher, did not mince words, or threats, regarding his opposition to the Texas TGV. Calling high-speed rail supporters "economic illiterates," he went on to challenge Texas TGV's claims head on: "They are saying that the roads and the airways will be so congested that the train will be the best alternative. . . . So I have no ambition, no imagination, no ingenuity. What the hell, bring on the goddamn trains, right? Horses—t! If that's the case, I'll just buy some 757s and double the number of seats between Houston and Dallas. The whole thing is just so ludicrous!"[85] When San Antonio mayor Nelson Wolff floated the idea of us-ing improvement fees to provide rail access into his city-owned airport, Kelleher publicly threatened to pull all of Southwest's flights out of San Anto-nio. These accounted for 30 percent of San Antonio's scheduled air service. Kelleher told a meeting of his own employees that if the Texas TGV obtained any assistance from the municipality, "San Antonio could become a train town instead of a plane town."[86]

Kelleher's combativeness took perhaps its greatest toll on Texas TGV in the courtroom, where the airline filed three lawsuits challenging the THSRA's administrative procedures. Southwest objected, on procedural grounds, to not having been granted standing in "discovery" to fully explore and cross-examine the claims of the franchise bidders. It also objected to the authority's finding that the Texas TGV franchise would meet the "public convenience and necessity" test, claiming that "the proceedings were fundamentally un-fair, the [authority's] Board had been illegally constituted, and the rules were invalid."[87] Southwest's legal claims were rejected before both trial and appeal judges, but these lawsuits had a chilling effect upon Texas TGV's financing efforts.

In 1992, Texas TGV's chairman, Glenn Biggs, wrote to THSRA Chair-man Herschel Payne "describing litigation initiated by Southwest Airlines, and stating that the Corporation considered resolution and/or completion of these matters essential before a successful equity investment offering could be advanced."[88] Even without winning in court, Southwest's legal actions had put Texas TGV's required fundraising behind schedule. And when Texas TGV was desperately seeking some form of federal support to give confidence to potential investors, Southwest worked with even larger and more powerful allies to block policy action. Helen Ng reported that "Congressional pressure helped to kill a federal subsidy for Texas TGV, because it was allegedly dam-aging to Boeing's friend and customer, Southwest Airlines."[89]

Texas TGV's "investment grade" ridership forecast by Charles River As-sociates helps explain why Southwest Airlines and its colorful chairman de-voted so much effort to battling a mode which was publicly disparaged as an unworthy competitor. This study predicted that Texas TGV's lines would carry 14 million people and generate $618 million in annual revenues by 2010. Diversion of traffic from other modes ranged from 21 percent to 31 percent, among five different scenarios, leading Charles River Associates to note, "This is a very significant travel impact for a single new transportation facility serving a large existing market; it will have important impacts on the amounts of air pollution and energy consumption involved in transporting intercity travelers in Texas, and it will have potentially significant impacts on the congestion levels at airports and on interstate highways in future years."[90]

Although Powell noted that "most commentators give Southwest the lion's share of the 'credit' for killing this opportunity for high-speed rail in Texas,"[91] the Texas TGV's demise cannot be blamed entirely on Southwest Airlines' machinations. While besieged by its principal air competitor on the economic and legal front, Texas TGV faced a wider and growing grassroots political opposition as its environmental impact study (EIS) process unfolded. Thirty-nine public hearings were organized—one in each county that the Texas TGV would pass through—events which THSRA characterized as "among the largest number of scoping meetings ever held in connection with the preparation of an EIS for a single project."[92] Over 4,000 public participants provided a total of 15,000 separate comments.

Burns noted that these meetings served an unintended purpose in that "opponents of the project used these scoping meetings, organized by the Authority and paid for by the Franchisee, as opportunities to spread their own message."[93] Almost 50 percent of the speakers at scoping meetings were from outside the county in which the scoping meeting was held. Robey attended some of these meetings and provides a flavor of the largely negative reaction outside the major metropolitan centers. A resident of Zorn, Texas, testified at one hearing that in his community "there is not one person for it. We don't understand it, we don't want it."[94] But this response was relatively calm compared to "the Lockhart meeting [where] feelings were so impassioned that threats of violence were made and the executive director of the THSRA told me he was glad the police were present." A group calling itself DERAIL (Demanding Ethics, Responsibility, and Accountability in Legislation) began lobbying against the Texas TGV project, publishing a pamphlet entitled "A Ticket to Nowhere" that attacked the Texas TGV as a $6.8 billion boondoggle.[95]

Some of the skeptics who were so vocal at environmental scoping sessions, or who contributed to DERAIL's efforts, were classical NIMBYs who would bear the costs of noise and infrastructure intrusion on their lands, or through their communities, without receiving any mobility benefit, since the

TGV would only stop in major population centers. Others were ideological dissenters, who still saw privately funded HSR as an extension of big government, which had awarded the franchise and was going to sell out small towns and local interests for the benefit of foreign companies.

But another source of skepticism emerged from inside the Texas government, when the comptroller of public accounts issued a highly critical report on THSRA's administrative practices. This watchdog of the public purse had been invited to conduct a performance review by THSRA chair Lena Guerrero in May 1992.[96] But instead of calming public concerns about this project's fiscal risks, the report only served to fan the flames of opposition to any public role in rail passenger development. The report depicted a classic case of bureaucratic "capture" by industrial interests, and linked these to small, but relatively damning, accounts of waste and mismanagement. To begin with, the performance review challenged THSRA's role as a facilitator of private enterprise in transportation, claiming this was an illegitimate policy that had been advanced by staff against the wishes of the agency's board. The report identified "an apparent conflict between the philosophy of the board and that of management," concluding that "as a result, THSRA lacks unity of command. Transcripts, agency correspondence, internal memoranda and interviews support [the Texas Performance Review's] conclusion that agency management favors the loosely structured role of partner, facilitator and supporter of the high-speed rail effort and the franchisee. In contrast, the board desires cautious oversight and monitoring, with a fiscally conservative approach to staff spending."[97]

The evidence of management's excess appears relatively modest when viewed from afar. Twenty-five thousand dollars was spent on buying new furniture, $1,550 in leasing plants, and $440 on the purchase of bottled water for staff. Findings that lambast the agency for paying "$500 to rent a hotel room for hearings when the state's General Services Commission *might have been able* to locate a state-owned building for the purpose, at no cost to the agency" suggest a "zero tolerance" standard for agency expenditure on anything different from other government agencies' purchasing.[98] Burns noted that "although the Authority was effectively spending Texas TGV's money, not the taxpayers' money, [this] report painted a picture of a 'rogue' agency out of control."[99]

One reason for such critical findings may have been the point of comparison. THSRA's functions remained outside, and somewhat at odds with, the long-standing mandate of the Texas Railroad Commission, a quite traditional elected regulatory body that was charged with overseeing the business environment of freight rail carriers, as well as pipelines. There was some overlap between the boards of the Railroad Commission and the THSRA, which may have explained some of the tension between the board and staff. THSRA Board member Bob Krueger also sat on the Texas Railroad Commission, and pronounced himself an early skeptic of high-speed rail. Once Texas TGV began lobbying for federal tax-exemption for bonds that it sought to issue, Krueger declared that Texas TGV had violated its pledge to build the project with private money, and lost his confidence as a result. He stated that "if you have one set of statements in courtship and another after marriage, it's likely to guarantee either divorce or conflict."[100] Another dimension of this inter-agency rivalry came to a head when THSRA Chair Lena Guerrero ran for a seat on the Texas Railroad Commission. During that campaign, Robey reports that "it was revealed that she had not told the truth on her résumé when she claimed to have graduated from the University of Texas."[101] Guererro's subsequent resignation from the THSRA only added to the cloud hanging over the agency.

Skeptics on THSRA's Board came within one vote of shutting down the Texas TGV project on November 13, 1992, when a five to four vote extended the franchise deadline for raising $170 million in equity by one year.[102] Texas TGV claimed that the lawsuits from Southwest and bad publicity arising from the environmental scoping process had generated a chilling effect on the capital markets. That chill did not abate in 1993, however. Running down to the wire, an unorthodox convertible-debenture scheme was prepared which would raise $170 million in an issue on December 11. These notes would have been converted into stock at the (unspecified) time of Texas TGV's initial public offering. In the meantime, these notes were to have been backed by a $225 million letter of credit from the Canadian Imperial Bank of Commerce and were counter-guaranteed by $75 million of "drawings" provided by the Morrisson-Knudson (M-K) Company.[103] On December 10, M-K chairman William Agee withdrew his company's guarantee on $75 million of these notes.[104] Bombardier and GEC-Alsthom had refused to join M-K in making such a guarantee, leaving M-K no alternative according to their vice-president, Gil Carmichael, who said, "We had to withdraw because we simply could not ask our shareholders to bear this exposure alone."[105]

Following this failure to meet the franchise terms, behind-the-scenes negotiations on terminating the franchise ensued. Burns reports that on August 19, 1994, an agreement was presented to the THSRA Board that terminated the franchise and provided for Texas TGV to pay for the authority's operating costs through the 1995 fiscal year and repay the state treasury all revenues that remained outstanding from previous general revenue advances.[106] In return for these payments, plus the transfer of all nonproprietary information about the project to the state, the authority forfeited the right to collect on Texas TGV's $2.5 million abandonment bond. Robey estimates that Texas TGV's private partners lost a total of $40 million that had been put into franchise acquisition and initial planning and assessment work.[107]

The Texas TGV's failure was a delegitimating event for the proponents of market-led rail passenger renewal. Ambitious claims had been made about high-speed rail's profitability abroad and commercial potential at home, but when it came time to ante up, investors had been leery. The inability to attract investors at a time when "junk bonds" for very tenuous ventures could find willing buyers seemed to confirm the claim of Amtrak's supporters and others who insisted that rail passenger policy could not be market-led or even market-based. The problem was that following Ohio's rejection of a public finance option, few state governments (and certainly not Texas) were going to go out on the fiscal limb for rail passenger renewal initiatives. As in Ohio, the considerable resources that had gone into designing a "custom-tailored" rail passenger renewal policy were wasted once the garment was rejected. The organizational efforts that had been devoted to rail renewal in Texas were effectively discarded along with Texas TGV's franchise.

4.8. Florida's Public-Private Partnership in Rail Passenger Renewal

Florida initially approached high speed rail development during the 1980s in much the same way that Texas had. The Florida High Speed Rail Transportation Commission Act, which became law in 1984, established a body to receive and evaluate franchise proposals for privately financed high-speed rail development.[108] Two such applications were received in 1988, but "after two years of review, it became apparent that further pursuit of a franchise under the conditions established was futile."[109] The franchising process was abandoned in 1990, but, unlike Texas, the goal of rail passenger development did not die with the franchising approach.

Following this false start, Florida sought to create a new policy option that fell somewhere between the governmental leadership that had been repudiated in Ohio and the private entrepreneurship that had reached a dead end in Texas. What appeared necessary was a public-private partnership that could juggle the many and varied leadership roles and financial responsibilities that were apparently needed to launch state-level passenger rail renewal.

Unlike California's earlier, and fickle, courtship between industry and government, Florida's partnership would be cemented by an initial commitment of public money for the kinds of preliminary project planning and assessment activities that had defeated both the AHSRC and the Texas TGV initiatives.

In addition to sharing in the planning and environmental impact assessment costs, Florida's legislature indicated a willingness to invest $70 million per year, plus a 4 percent inflation adjustment, for a minimum of thirty years and a maximum of forty years, to support high-speed rail infrastructure. These funds would service infrastructure bonds using a portion of Florida's gasoline tax. Many American states have legal, and in some cases constitutional, prohibitions on expending gasoline tax revenues on anything other than road related projects.[110] Free from such a prohibition, Florida had explicitly earmarked 14.7 percent of its gas tax for non-highway expenditures.[111]

Such a dowry, while small in relation to the level of government support routinely extended to air or road infrastructure, made Florida's planned high-speed rail development far more attractive to private industry than prospects in other states. During most of the 1990s, aside from Amtrak's renewal of the Northeast Corridor, Florida was where rail passenger entrepreneurs focused their energies. The result was, without question, the most serious and sophisticated state-level effort to invent a commercially successful rail passenger service to date in North America.

In 1995, the Florida Department of Transportation received five proposals from consortia offering quite a wide range of organizational and technological options for a public-private partnership designed to deliver a commercially competitive train service between Miami, Orlando, and Tampa. Two of these proposals sought to pioneer ultrafast magnetic-levitation technology at costs estimated to fall between $3.8 billion and $5 billion. Three other consortia offered various conventional rail technologies ranging from a tilting electric passenger train that would share existing railroad infrastructure, costing just $740 million, to super-fast bullet trains on brand new infrastructure costing $20 billion.[112] Following evaluation of these proposals, the Florida DOT selected the Florida Overland eXpress (FOX) consortium as its preferred partner.

FOX was composed of both seasoned participants as well as some newcomers in the struggle to launch North American passenger renewal at the state level.[113] Equipment builders GEC-Alsthom (now Alstom) of France and Bombardier of Canada had been part of the Texas TGV consortium and were supplying the Acela train for Amtrak's upgrading of the Northeast Corridor. They each would contribute 15 percent of the $349 million in equity to capitalize FOX. Fluor Daniel Corporation, which had been retained by AHSRC to do the engineering for Southern California's putative bullet train in the early 1980s, got on board the FOX project with a 30 percent equity stake. And Odebrecht–Campanhia Brasileira de Projectos e Obras, a multinational construction firm specializing in major public works, was a newcomer to high-speed rail development, joining the FOX consortium with a 30 percent equity stake.[114]

Numerous consulting organizations and two financial advisors, Bear Stearns and Banque Nationale de Paris, filled out the FOX consortium. The only gap that turned out to be significant in this private sector alliance was a carrier that would eventually operate the trains. FOX had proposed selecting such an operator further along in the project, but this turned out to cost rail passenger supporters both technical credibility on ridership estimates and political influence when opponents moved in to kill the initiative.

The FOX consortium's $349 million equity commitment was certainly significant to the private partners in Florida's high-speed rail development, yet it would account for just 4 percent of the project's projected costs. Taking the full cost of capital into account, the U.S. General Accounting Office estimated that FOX would require up to $9.3 billion. Figure 4.2 illustrates the range of investment sources and mechanisms that had been proposed to meet these costs.[115]

The $70 million in annual appropriations from Florida's gas tax would have serviced tax exempt state infrastructure bonds worth $2.146 billion, representing 23 percent of the FOX project's costs. These bonds would be effectively guaranteed by gasoline tax revenue. Another $3.346 billion in so-called system infrastructure bonds would be serviced from FOX's operating revenues, making up 36 percent of project costs. While not publicly guaranteed, these system infrastructure bonds would have been tax-exempt and secured by a senior lien on the FOX project's infrastructure. Another $2 billion in debt was anticipated to have come from the federal government's Transportation Infrastructure Finance and Innovation Act (TIFIA), which had been enacted in 1998.[116]

TIFIA represented an important policy breakthrough for rail passenger renewal efforts because it linked federal financial support to state-level projects for the first time. TIFIA had been expanded to include rail passenger investments following the assiduous teamwork of state bureaucrats in the Florida Department of Transportation (FDOT) and key members of Florida's congressional delegation. For the first time, these advocates built a coalition of support among federal legislators from regions that could benefit from fed-

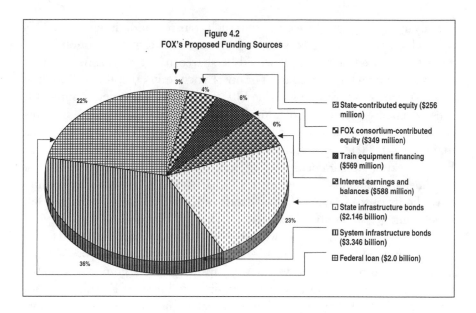

Figure 4.2
FOX's Proposed Funding Sources

eral rail passenger investment in state projects. FOX was specifically mentioned in the legislative conference report accompanying TIFIA, which identified the project as one of national importance and directed the U.S. Department of Transportation to favorably review FOX's forthcoming request for TIFIA funding.[117] FOX had thus staked its claim at the front of the line among state-supported rail passenger projects seeking federal assistance. According to FDOT's rail director, the state's leadership in putting its own money on the table first led to a serious project that was more credible than previous high-speed rail schemes: "We knew we couldn't wait for the federal government to initiate . . . a [high-speed rail finance] program. Instead, we decided to approach Washington with a feasible project that would have a reasonable chance of getting funded."[118]

Compared to airport and road infrastructure investments, the share of federal support in this successful rail passenger development mechanism was relatively small, and the terms were far less generous. But the principle that Washington would share the costs of rail passenger development with states and private partners had been established in TIFIA. This precedent has turned out to be the FOX project's greatest policy legacy.

In addition to the ridership and engineering analyses that had been de riguer in preceding high-speed rail initiatives, the FOX consortium sponsored some sophisticated econometric and environmental modeling to depict the advantages that would accrue from such transportation innovation. This research explored the project's "external benefits" in terms of economic and environmental advantages that would be shared by all Floridians, whether they set foot on a high-speed train or not. Lynch found that the 6.13 million annual passengers forecasted to ride FOX in 2010 would generate some impressive effects on the rest of Florida's transportation system.[119] These included: 1.4 million fewer auto trips, or 261 million less vehicle-miles on Florida highways; 60,000 fewer aircraft flights, or 559 million less passenger-miles in Florida's skies; annual energy savings equivalent to 16.2 million gallons of gasoline; annual emission savings of 130,171 tons of pollutants; 1.6 million fewer hours of roadway congestion each year; and five fewer deaths and 380 fewer injuries in intercity travel between Miami, Orlando, and Tampa.

These beneficial outcomes were intended to help justify the varied forms of direct and indirect public investments called for by the FOX consortium's plan. Project director David Gedney encapsulated the argument for public commitment to this innovative partnership as follows: "If Florida does not invest in a high speed rail system, it is clear that it must invest massive amounts of money in other forms of transport if it is to prevent gridlock and sustain a competitive economic position for its citizens. Virtually every other option has a much higher cost, little or no private participation and little or no revenue streams associated with them. . . . The Florida high speed rail program makes too much sense not to be taken as a serious transport solution."[120] But while the FOX project gained important momentum from the federal policy breakthrough in TIFIA, environmental and economic opposition had also been building at the state and local political levels.

Skeptics and opponents had intensified their criticism of the FOX initiative during 1998. A group called Derail the Bullet Train, headquartered in Boca Raton, campaigned against FOX in both the state capitol and through the environmental review process. Its executive director told the media, "We won't see [FOX] as dead until the last nail is put in the coffin."[121] Critics attacked six state legislators who had participated in a French-government-sponsored rail study tour as having "sold out" to rail promoters. A FOX spokeswoman defended this activity by stating: "If we didn't have any airports and we were talking about building one, I think everyone over a period of time would go somewhere to look at one. I think their constituents would want [state legislators] to do that."[122]

James Thrasher, the new Speaker of Florida's House of Representatives, exhibited a high degree of skepticism regarding FOX and the rail study tour, telling the *Wall Street Journal:* "I don't think I need to go over there [to France] to understand what a train looks like, a fast train. And I think perceptions do mean a lot. Even if it's an ethical thing to do, in my position particularly, I'm better off not doing that."[123]

Rail passenger skeptics gained ammunition against FOX from official reports that emphasized the project's risk and minimized its prospective rewards. A 1998 report by the Florida Transportation Commission recommended that legislators "use utmost caution" in relying on FOX's ridership projections and consequent estimate of social benefits.[124] The commission engaged the consulting firm of Wilbur Smith to review ridership forecasts that had been prepared for FOX by KPMG Consulting and Systra, an arm of the French National Railways. North America's lack of experience with high-speed passenger trains led Wilbur Smith to question whether FOX would attain the level of passenger diversion from both auto and air travel, as well as the level of "induced" (or new) demand for trips that KPMG and Systra had forecast. Wilbur Smith's vice president, who had done the review, was quoted as saying that a forecast of 5.2 million passengers in 2010 was more realistic than the 6.13 million and 8.25 million estimates that FOX's consultants had projected.[125]

Commenting on the Florida Transportation Commission's recommendation to proceed cautiously, the chair-designate of Florida's House Appropriations Committee was quite negative. Representative Jim King told the *Wall Street Journal:* "It's really more than the ridership. . . . The real question is whether the total state commitment over two decades, which would be about $2 billion, could have more economic impact if spent on such transportation projects as more and better roads."[126]

At the request of U.S. House Budget Committee Chair John Kasich (R-Ohio), the U.S. General Accounting Office (GAO) reviewed FOX's financial prospects in light of possible federal support through TIFIA and issued an equally gloomy assessment. That GAO report echoed concerns over ridership forecasts raised by the Florida Transportation Commission, suggesting that an estimate of 5.59 million riders was justified and that such a patronage level would be unlikely to service all of the project's debt.[127] It also rejected FOX's 2.6 year timetable for completing environmental review, stating that such a process takes "on average over 5 years to complete."[128] The report went on to warn that the magnitude and risk of the FOX project could constrain subsequent allocations of federal support under TIFIA because FOX would consume the bulk of a $530 self-insurance fund that had been allocated to cover potential defaults. The GAO concluded that "providing the Florida project with a $2 billion federal loan would constrain the [DOT's] ability to fund other projects that are potential candidates for credit assistance."[129]

Many major transportation projects in America have been built in spite of skeptical assessments by government regulators and watchdogs that raise, often justified, warnings. The Denver International Airport (DIA) is just one relatively recent example of such a megaproject that prevailed over the skeptics and NIMBYs that emerged to oppose it. This airport's opening was delayed by over two years and its construction cost ballooned from $1.5 billion to $5 billion. Designed to serve as a hub for three major airlines at the same time, and built to handle 56 million passengers, DIA is now home to just one airline hub and saw only 30 million passengers in 1995.[130] Built twenty-four miles from Denver's center in order to mitigate noise pollution—making it the city with America's most remote single airport—the facility began generating noise complaints from its opening, and these have grown since 1995.[131] Such infrastructure megaprojects avoid being wrecked on the shoals of skepticism, in part, because of the advocacy of the transportation carriers that will benefit from them. Carriers were either disengaged, or on the opposite side of Florida's transportation policy community, when this moment of truth arrived for the FOX project.

Florida's 1998 gubernatorial election yielded both a change of administration and party in power, and with them, a change in numerous state policies. Republican "Jeb" Bush had won on a moderately conservative platform. The FOX project had not featured prominently in his campaign, but it was one of the first significant policy reversals that he implemented. Just nine days after inauguration, Governor Bush announced that his administration would withhold all funding for the FOX project from its forthcoming 1999–2000 budget, in addition to blocking the release of already appropriated funds that had not yet been spent. Citing the U.S. General Accounting Office's report, the governor portrayed FOX as the kind of big government boondoggle he had been elected to prevent.

Governor Bush issued a press release in which he stated, "It's the job of a Governor to make difficult decisions, and this one has not come without lengthy, careful consideration."[132] The governor went on to state that "while I am not opposed to the general concept of high speed rail, there are other transportation needs where we can have an immediate and significant impact on our business climate." Among the investment priorities Bush identified for state funds that would have been spent on FOX were "expanding major road arteries to relieve road congestion in our urban centers, such as the I-4 project between Tampa and Orlando," and "improvements for aviation projects to support additional freight and passenger service." These reallocations suggest the governor's transportation policy priorities. Undoubtedly, they were appreciated by Florida's air and road carriers who had found a solution to improving their own business climate. Local public transit agencies also received a windfall from FOX's demise, with additional funds directed to develop light-rail transit in the Orlando area and to expand transit services that would bring riders from "welfare to work."

At the start of 1999, it was the public sector that walked away from an apparently well developed and smoothly functioning partnership, providing the FOX consortium with a final payment of $5.9 million, on top of the $22.4 million that had been expended previously, to defray development and planning costs.[133] FDOT's rail office was restructured, with director Charles Smith leaving the civil service. Under the Bush administration, Florida did not withdraw from passenger rail renewal initiatives entirely. Offering a "consolation prize" to rail supporters in his first budget, the governor proposed appropriating $5 million to reroute some of Amtrak's existing trains over freight railroad trackage to serve communities along the Atlantic Coast between Jacksonville and West Palm Beach.[134] At the time of this writing in 2001, even this incremental enhancement of passenger rail service in Florida has yet to be implemented. Despite showing so much promise relative to preceding state initiatives, the Florida formula for public-private partnership could not dodge the bullet fired by a governor who was both skeptical about rail passenger renewal and inclined toward FOX hunting.

4.9. Canadian Provincial and Corporate Rail Passenger Renewal Initiatives

Canada has seen far less than the United States in the way of rail passenger renewal efforts that were initiated by entities outside the federal government. Since VIA Rail was downsized in 1989, two proposals for introducing commercially competitive, high-speed passenger trains have originated beyond Ottawa. Both focused on all or part of the largest existing rail travel market, currently served by VIA Rail's conventional trains in the 767-mile-long corridor between Quebec City, Montreal, Ottawa, Toronto, and Windsor. The fate of these initiatives illustrates the even greater challenges faced by those seeking to bypass the policy stalemate found at the federal government and reflected in VIA Rail's lack of a legislative mandate.

The first of these initiatives was presided over by the Ontario-Quebec Rapid Train Task Force, hereafter referred to as the Task Force. This Task Force was announced by the Premiers of Ontario and Quebec in June 1989.

Media coverage offered several reasons as to why Ontario and Quebec should take the lead in inter-provincial rail transportation, a policy domain that fell under the federal government's jurisdiction. Some speculated that the transportation priorities of provincial leaders had changed, as when a reporter for *The Globe and Mail* claimed that high-speed rail had become "a pet project of [then] Ontario Premier David Peterson, who was captivated by the TGV when he took a trip between Lyon and Paris."[135] Following Ottawa's drastic cutback of VIA Rail that year, provincial leaders could be seen to be scoping out their own role in this policy domain. Quebec's political leadership had exhibited a long history of support for its "provincial champion" in the transportation industry, the giant Bombardier Corporation. McCarthy wrote that "Quebec, under both Liberal and Parti Quebecois governments, has been an enthusiastic booster of the high-speed rail system, given that much of the design work and construction of the rail cars would take place in the province."[136]

Another impetus behind this study was seen to arise from the delicate state of relations between English and French Canada. The Task Force was, at times, presented as an exercise in rebuilding Quebec's trust and confidence in the aftermath of the failed Meech Lake Accord, which had promised Quebec an honorable place in confederation by, among other things, recognizing its status as a "distinct society" in Canada's Constitution. Ontario's co-chair on the Task Force, Robert Carman, suggested that jointly studying a physical link that would connect Quebec with the rest of Canada would bode well for national unity, since the Task Force's work would demonstrate that "there are things that the two provinces are working together on."[137]

Another explanation of the Task Force's origin suggested that it was created to deflect criticism and controversy over another study released by the quasi-governmental Road and Transportation Association of Canada which had recommended $17 billion in new highway investments nationwide.[138] In the ensuing battle between railroads, truckers, and automotive interests, the high-speed rail option could offer a possible compromise in limiting the need for expanding highways in Ontario and Quebec, by shifting car traffic to the rails.

The Task Force was lean and worked quickly, compared to similar efforts being carried out south of the border. Eight appointed members were supported by a staff of nine civil servants, seconded from the Ontario and Quebec governments. In addition to these staff resources, the Task Force had a budget of just Can$2 million and released its final report in May 1991, less than two years after its inception.

The Task Force evaluated rail policy options through a typical range of analytical and outreach activities. In terms of analysis, the Task Force hired consultants to perform seven work tasks ranging from reviewing previous studies to generating environmental and socioeconomic projections of fast trains' impact. Consultants' activities centered around modeling the costs and commercial performance of three rail renewal scenarios, featuring 200- , 300- , and 400-kilometer-per-hour train service relying upon different rail technology. The Task Force also held six public hearings in major cities between Quebec City and Windsor, as well as six "municipal meetings" with selected officials from smaller en route communities. Written submissions were also accepted and consultations were held with manufacturers, banks, railroads, and consulting organizations specializing in high-speed rail. Task Force members also went on field trips to experience rail passenger operations in Italy, France, Germany, Japan, Sweden, and the United States. The result of these many, and varied, activities carried out quickly and cheaply was a report that raised more questions than it answered.

In brief, the Task Force concluded that a high-speed train service in the Quebec–Windsor Corridor was technically feasible and could generate an operating profit, but that any such initiative would require government to finance most of the needed infrastructure. In terms of socioeconomic impacts, the Task Force found that high-speed rail could reduce congestion at "key" airports and along major highways between Quebec and Windsor. The report did not anticipate that high-speed rail would help to ease urban traffic congestion, nor did it offer an estimate of the environmental impacts of high-speed rail. When it came to transportation policy, the report observed that the "success of high speed rail systems elsewhere has been related to the willingness of governments to shape consumer choice by policy interventions in the market-place or by direct financial support."[139] Canadian transportation policies that raised the cost of automobility to levels found in Europe or Japan were judged remote since "increased fuel taxes, the introduction of toll roads or increased license fees would be met by taxpayer dissatisfaction."[140]

The Task Force recognized the limits of its analysis. For example, data on travel demand in the Quebec–Windsor Corridor had been drawn from a 1987 study conducted by VIA Rail, since time and funding did not permit the Task Force to collect new data.[141] As a result, high-speed train patronage may have been depressed by extrapolation from existing rail passenger ridership. As well, little or no induced demand was taken into account given the lack of experience with such a phenomenon for rail travel in modern Canada.

The Task Force supported rail passenger renewal in general, stating "the potential of the rail mode to provide intercity transportation at a cost which is less than that for a significant increase in freeway or airport capacity argues for an investment in high speed rail at an appropriate time in the future."[142] But it also recommended proceeding slowly, saying "before there can be any financial commitment by governments to an investment in high speed rail, [the existing knowledge] base needs to be supplemented by intergovernmental discussion, by additional private sector business information, plus more detailed review of work already initiated by the Task Force."[143] Canada's first provincially led attempt to renew passenger railroading had thus stopped well short of the contemporaneous initiatives among American states. Instead of debating policy options that could actually launch a commercially competitive passenger train service, Canadians were left with an analytical debate on how to better study such policy options.

Media reports suggested that Ontario and Quebec were considering an additional $4 to $6 million worth of rail passenger analysis to fulfil the Task Force's analytical recommendations.[144] Even before the Task Force's final report was released, Bombardier Corporation, North American licensee for the TGV technology, proposed a more ambitious venture. Anticipating that the Task Force's budget and timetable would produce a policy review that was suggestive, rather than conclusive, Bombardier sought government's commitment to a "detailed feasibility study" project that would cost between $30 and $50 million.[145] To sweeten the offer, Bombardier had assembled a consortium of six banks in Canada and France that were prepared to contribute one-quarter of the costs. Bombardier would ante up another quarter, providing government with a "half-price" offer on the kind of analysis that could launch high-speed rail renewal.

Ontario and Quebec continued their engagement with the study of rail passenger renewal, but rather than accepting Bombardier's politically charged offer of an *ex ante* analytical partnership, they joined formally with Ottawa in supporting a $6 million, three-year, tripartite government effort. The resulting Quebec-Ontario High Speed Train Project Report was issued in August 1995. With the federal government now joining the high-speed rail policy analysis effort, the degree of skepticism regarding passenger rail was noticeably greater than when the provinces had taken the analytical lead.

On the one hand, the tripartite report elaborated upon the Task Force's demand modeling to come up with more optimistic forecasts. Eighteen percent of the new train's riders were predicted to shift from air travel, yielding a 44 percent drop in air travel and a net reduction of $99 million in airline revenues.[146] And whereas the Task Force had predicted 7.79 million riders for a 184.6 mph train in 2010, the tripartite study predicted 12 million riders in 2005 growing to 19 million by 2025.[147] The analysis ranked a 186.4-mile-per-hour system linking Montreal and Toronto via Dorval with a station adjacent, but not connected, to the airport there as the most favorable of several route and technology scenarios. Such a design was projected to generate internal rates of return of 8.27 percent for government and 12 percent for private investors.[148] Private financing of 28.6 percent of such a project's $10.7 billion cost was judged to be "quite possible."[149]

But despite these positive findings, the report was more negative on the socioeconomic outcomes than the provinces' analysis had been. Despite the 44 percent drop in corridor air travel, as well as a reduction of 4.8 to 7.6 million annual intercity auto trips between 2005 and 2025, the need for airport and road expansion was not predicted to change, generating no net savings to government on infrastructure investment.[150] The benefits from a projected 20 percent reduction in energy consumed by corridor transportation and accompanying reduction in air pollutants[151] were judged to be "marginal."[152] There was seen to be "little export opportunity" from implementing high-speed rail, even though Canada was judged to have a "strong, fully integrated, internationally competitive rail supply industry" and research and development were considered necessary to adapt the European high-speed train design to a North American operating environment.[153]

Based upon these discordant analytical results, the report recommended that government proceed with more detailed engineering, environmental, and financial analysis only if the private sector would pay for half of future planning efforts and also commit to assuming all risks of project construction and management. Furthermore, government would have to resolve whether it was prepared to fund at least two-thirds of costs that could run as high as $18.3 billion, depending upon the route and technology, before proceeding further. While the tripartite study recommended that these huge challenges be resolved before proceeding any further with high-speed rail development, it also recommended that the "governments revisit these issues in three to five years" if these hurdles had not been overcome.[154]

Such recommendations called for the policy equivalent of leaping tall buildings in a single bound. Unless a rail development partnership happened to include Superman, the tripartite report would send their initiative right back into the political stalemate surrounding VIA Rail. Such findings prompted an anguished denunciation from Professor Julius Lukasiewicz, a long-time skeptic of Ottawa's preservationist policies and an equally strong advocate of rail passenger modernization based upon high-speed technology. Lambasting the perennial indecision of federal rail passenger policy and noting that the tripartite report was the tenth study of commercially feasible rail renewal in the Quebec—Windsor Corridor to be conducted since 1970, Lukasiewicz wrote: "It is truly amazing that North American society, generally at the forefront of technological progress, has been unable to modernize its passenger train, the oldest mode of mechanical land transport. Today a 300 km-h train is still seen in Canada as a creature belonging to some foreign species, which could not survive in North America and, if imported, could not live unless protected by huge public subsidies."[155] He urged government to abandon efforts to preserve VIA Rail and take the plunge into high-speed rail development, but such calls for action went unheeded in Ottawa's seemingly perpetual policy impasse over what to do about passenger trains.

Skeptics countered that government studies represented a weak foundation upon which to build any partnership with private investors in a commercially promising transportation venture. Richard Soberman reminded readers of the market-focused Fraser Institute's guidebook to Canadian transportation policy that government consultants and bureaucrats had a poor track record of prognostication regarding commerce, technology, and transport.[156] Among the more serious gaffes were studies that had:

"justified the need for Mirabel Airport on the basis of tremendous growth in airline traffic and the inability of Dorval to accommodate such growth, leading to a $600 million investment in an airport that no one wants to use."[157]

"constructed Terminal 2 at [Toronto's] Pearson International Airport for international carriers, eventually occupied by Canada's largest domestic carrier, on the premise that Terminal 1 could not handle the new generation of jumbo jets."[158]

"concluded in 1972, that a 56 mile network of magnetic levitation vehicles could be constructed in Toronto (as well as in Ottawa and Hamilton) in 5 years, using readily available "off the shelf" technology (yet to be placed in commercial operation anywhere in the world, 20 years later) at about 30 percent of the cost of conventional rapid transit."[159]

Soberman went on to ask, "Based on this record, are private investors going to line up to invest in a high speed rail system because consultants to government conclude that such service will be profitable?"[160] Soberman concluded that "if private firms considering investment measured in terms of billions have to ask government to underwrite studies costing a few millions, how seriously should they be taken?"[161]

Both Ontario and Quebec heeded such cautionary advice and retreated from rail passenger renewal following their exploration of policy options with Ottawa. Facing hard choices in health- and social-program cutbacks that accompanied their respective budget deficits, Canada's two largest provinces pulled back from seeking involvement in federal policy responsibilities that carried price tags as large as rail passenger renewal. Other provinces have been even more circumspect in considering such initiatives. And unlike American states, provinces have also been leery of contributing to upgrading VIA's existing services. Canada's constitutional division of powers has given provinces full funding responsibilities for their road networks, without the lavish matching grants that come from gasoline tax trust funds in the United States. The result is a very limited appetite for rail passenger innovation among Canadian provinces.

When the tripartite report opened the door to private-sector leadership in renewing Canada's passenger trains, there was a pause before industry took up that challenge. Almost three years elapsed before Canada's second proposal for rail renewal to be initiated outside of the federal government emerged. A private consortium modeled on the FOX project, known as LYNX, came forward with a plan in 1998. Under the LYNX proposal, the private sector would build, and partially finance, a turnkey project for a 198.8 mph passenger train between Quebec City, Montreal, Ottawa, and Toronto. A two hour twenty-one-minute schedule between Montreal and Toronto was proposed, via Ottawa, which would have been one hour and forty minutes from Toronto. The Quebec City–Montreal travel time would have been one hour and eleven minutes.[162]

Among the industrial team that had been assembled, Bombardier and GEC-Alsthom would manufacture TGV-type trains, SNC-Lavalin and AGRA Monenco would construct the rail infrastructure, and AXOR and Ellis-Don would build the bridges, buildings, and structures. Projected to cost $11.1 billion in total, LYNX was forecast to be in full operation by 2008 and carry 15.9 million annual riders by 2025. The consortium also predicted a $9.281 billion boost to Canada's GDP and the creation of 175,158 jobs through the construction and development of LYNX.[163] Environmental, trade, and tourism benefits were also claimed, but not forecast with the precision of financial and economic impact estimates.

When it came to financing, the LYNX consortium proposed raising $3.6 billion to pay for the rolling stock and associated high-speed rail technology.[164] Government was left to pay for the $7.5 billion in infrastructure investment, which LYNX claimed would generate a 12.4 percent internal rate of return, with $1.179 in net cash outflows between 1998 and 2022, followed by steadily increasing cash inflows through 2067. The LYNX prospectus recommended a forty-one-month-long Project Development and Financial Close Phase during which "governments and private partners would share equally in owning and financing this $102 million mandatory second phase of the project."[165] This apparently innocuous language, invoking the spirit of partnership that was much in vogue at the time, would later come to be seen in a very negative light.

This plan made headlines in 1998, but just as quickly sank to the bottom of Canada's transportation policy agenda as no government, either federal or provincial, came forward to embrace it. Transport Minister David Collenette, who had endorsed both high-speed rail development and public-private partnerships for renewing passenger trains, appeared more comfortable dreaming about the LYNX than treating the consortium's proposal as realistic. He was quoted as saying: "In my wildest dreams, if you asked me whether there should be a high-speed train in the corridor, I would say yes. . . . The question is whether government can afford to be part of it."[166]

Behind this cautious reaction from an avowedly pro-rail transport minister lay skepticism that the LYNX's claim of fully repaying public finance in its infrastructure was too good to be true. The House of Commons Standing Committee on Transport (SCOT), which reviewed a much more detailed project proposal than the one made available to this author, found a number of troubling issues. Its analysis emphasized some fairly large risks to government that could not have been coincidental in the LYNX project's financial design.

To begin with, in assigning the order of priority for applying operating revenues to expenses, the LYNX proposal had placed infrastructure lease payments to the government last, thus assigning the highest financial risk to the public sector. SCOT's report noted that "the private sector achieves a return of investment of 10 percent before any funds are distributed to governments."[167] As a result, any shortfall in projected ridership would have the greatest impact on public return on investment. For example, a 5 percent shortfall in ridership would reduce the public's return from 12.39 percent to 10.25 percent, and a 25 percent ridership shortfall would further cut that return to 6.81 percent. SCOT also noted that the LYNX forecast of 11.1 million annual passengers in 2008 was significantly above the tripartite study's estimate of 8.8 million.[168]

Another problematic financial projection was the $110 million that LYNX presumed government would save on subsidy payments to VIA Rail. Once LYNX entered service, VIA was assumed to exit the Quebec City–Toronto portion of the corridor. Yet such a retrenchment might generate more costs than savings. SCOT questioned whether VIA Rail could even continue to exist in its present form if it were deprived of the revenues generated from this core market segment, which went into cross-subsidizing the highly un-profitable services in other parts of Canada. Should VIA implode completely, labor protection payments of up to $135 million per year could ensue. And even if just the jobs in the Quebec City–Toronto Corridor were lost, there would be labor protection payments that had not been factored into the LYNX projections. SCOT's report noted that if VIA's subsidy savings got removed, the government's rate of return dropped from 12.39 percent to 9.05 percent.[169]

SCOT also warned that the proposed joint feasibility study between gov-ernments and the consortium was effectively a point of no return. The "man-datory second phase" that had been suggested in the prospectus meant much more than "an invitation to participate in new studies." At this phase, the consortium asked for a commitment by the governments: "Under the terms of the agreement proposed by the consortium, if the projections of the con-sortium are confirmed by the additional studies but the governments never-theless decide not to make the investment, the governments would be responsible for the private share of the next phase as well as their own part. In other words, the consortium is asking for a commitment now, at least to the extent of $118 million, to the project, subject only to what can be described as a due diligence process."[170]

Such analysis served to convince the federal government that LYNX was, indeed, too good to be true. Minister Collenette answered his earlier ques-tion about the affordability of high-speed rail by stating, "I've been saying [for] the last year that what we want to do with passenger rail is get the private sector involved to refinance the equipment needs of Via Rail so the govern-ment doesn't have to put up money. This is a proposition which involves some government money."[171]

The partnership terms proposed by LYNX proved to be well beyond the government's tolerance for risk and predilection for investment in rail pas-senger renewal. But once this became clear, no subsequent meeting of minds has generated a compromise, or synthesis, of the various financial and admin-istrative options that had been weighed by provinces and the private sector over the preceding decade. With Ottawa returning to deal with VIA Rail's needs to maintain a skeletal, but national, rail passenger network, a decade's worth of deliberation over renewing the most commercially promising mar-ket for rail travel that currently exists in Canada has effectively been set aside. In the words of one reporter, "the future of rail travel remains a murky mess on Canada's high-density business travel corridor."[172]

4.10. Lessons from North America's
Subnational Efforts to Renew Passenger Trains

The long litany of failed initiatives outlined above does not make for inspiring reading. This discussion would be utterly disheartening, except for the fact that it enables one to extract something of value out of the repeated failure to transplant the passenger train's commercial success from Europe and Japan to North America. The projects noted above, and several others too, have served as the equivalent of laboratory rats in a series of, as yet unsuccessful, policy experiments. What, then, are the lessons to be learned from these false starts in passenger train renewal?

First, trying to leapfrog the limitations of Amtrak and VIA Rail has not proven to be an effective starting point. Whether rail passenger renewal entrepreneurs wish to work with these public carriers or not, they cannot avoid the policy impasse that accounts for the anomalous position of these two organizations. Amtrak and VIA Rail have been relegated to the sidelines in the past, in part because proponents are reluctant to bring in the "baggage" of the policy stalemate that surrounded these organizations. However, that baggage does not belong only to these two organizations, but actually to the issue of where the passenger train fits into North American transportation.

Starting from a "clean slate" may appear possible in theory, but in practice there has been no magic formula that has produced a successful match between the train's commercial potential and the economic and political needs existing in a single state or province. Numerous customized political and economic configurations have been experimented with, yet none has proven resilient enough to create a niche among the well entrenched and vigorously defended fiscal, regulatory, and commercial positions of automotive, aviation, and even urban transit providers in Canada and the United States.

Both public and private leadership for the kinds of change needed to create economic and political space for modern passenger trains have been rejected at various times by voters and investors. Furthermore, public-private partnerships have proven to be unstable, and not up to the challenges and opposition that arise and persist during the long march to actually launching a project, let alone completing it. Bad luck, bad timing, and bad tactics are not sufficient to explain the steady stream of defeats and rejections of so many project formulas over so much time.

Second, among all but one of the fiscal variations and organizational configurations to launch rail passenger modernization that have been mooted since the Metroliner, one key attribute has been consistently missing. What made the Metroliner and Acela succeed while "FOXes" were hunted by hostile politicians and "LYNXes" got caught in analytical traps was the existence of a *carrier*, an organization that would manage the interface between technology, infrastructure, and the travelers who would eventually make any transportation service succeed commercially. Putting the technology and the infrastructure ahead of the carrier, and through it the user, has led to repeated dead ends in trying to introduce high-speed rail into North American transportation policy. One can hardly imagine airports being developed ahead of airlines or highways ahead of trucking companies and auto manufacturers, who play an analogous role to common carriers in linking drivers to transportation infrastructure. But that is exactly what decades of rail passenger initiatives have sought to do, in vain. Some carrier component—either a reformed Amtrak or VIA, or a full-blown alternative (an airline, or freight railroad, or even a nontraditional, multimodal transport operator like the British Virgin Group) is certainly one of the "missing links" that could cement together the critical mass of a North American rail passenger development initiative.

Finally, while the participation of an established or new carrier in passenger train renewal policy development appears necessary, it may not be sufficient to get the project off the drawing board. Some way to reconcile national transportation policy with the particular opportunities available in promising regional travel markets will have to be found. Whether this would require "negative innovation," through exemption from some of the regulations, taxes, or inelligibility from revenue streams currently available to other transportation ventures (e.g., tax-free bonds for airports or highway and transit trust funds in the United States), or "positive innovation," through the invention of new fiscal, regulatory, or taxation support mechanisms, remains to be seen.

Some way to revisit and resolve the policy impasse that impedes changing the economic "rules of the game" for passenger railroading will have to be found before one or more subnational renewal initiatives can begin to approach the potential for meeting, or even exceeding, the unique results of the Metroliner and Acela initiatives in the Northeast. With Acela's entry into service, attention has turned back to the efforts of Amtrak to resolve the rail passenger policy impasse by reinventing itself from within. That initiative is explored in chapter 5.

Reinventing Amtrak

The Drive for Commercial
Self-Sufficiency by 2003

By the mid 1990s, the time was ripe, some would say overripe, for a major overhaul of the policy stalemate that surrounded, and constrained, North America's passenger train operations. More and more evidence was piling up to suggest that the results of "business as usual" in public enterprise passenger railroading could not be sustained indefinitely. The United States experienced these effects first, with Amtrak's commercial performance suffering from the combined effects of deferred maintenance and economic slowdown, accentuated by management's miscalculation of the degree to which intercity rail passengers would continue to travel in the face of fare increases and service frequency reductions. After achieving a 9 percent growth in passengers from 20.3 million in 1986 to 22.2 million in 1990, Amtrak's ridership gains melted away during the next six years, reaching 19.7 million riders in 1996, a low that had not been seen since 1983. This high-water mark is evident in figure 5.1, which details Amtrak's ridership from 1980 to 1999. The steady progress made in improving commercial performance during the 1980s had also leveled off, with Amtrak's cost recovery ratio hovering around 80 percent during the 1990s, as shown in figure 3.3 of chapter 3. Both rail passenger supporters and skeptics were thus moved to question the status quo.

Supporters saw mounting evidence that passenger trains' decline could be reversed when fundamental policy supported such revitalization. European success stories with passenger train renewal were being reported by various governments reflecting a full range of ideologies. France's TGV had been launched by a Socialist-Communist coalition government whose transport minister, Charles Fiterman, was barred from entering the United States dur-

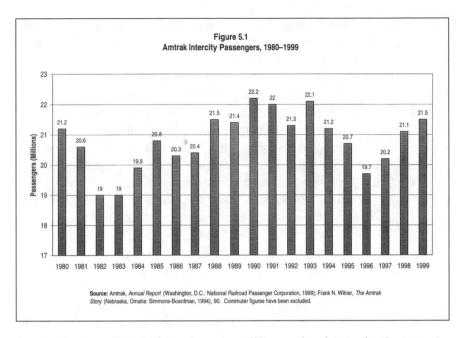

Figure 5.1
Amtrak Intercity Passengers, 1980–1999

Source: Amtrak, *Annual Report* (Washington, D.C.: National Railroad Passenger Corporation, 1999); Frank N. Wilner, *The Amtrak Story* (Nebraska, Omaha: Simmons-Boardman, 1994), 90. Commuter figures have been excluded.

ing the Reagan administration because of his membership in the Communist Party of France. In Germany, the ICE had been inaugurated under a centrist government led by Christian Democrats. And at the extreme right of mainstream politics, the British Conservatives' privatization of public transport, which was about to be extended to intercity rail, had also drawn attention. All of these efforts had appeared to yield more promising results than Amtrak's policy stalemate. The only common policy attribute shared by these initiatives was the decision to move beyond a regulated public monopoly's acknowledged limitations in delivering public transportation.

At the same time, homegrown initiatives to turn the tide of rail passenger decline appeared to be making little headway. The now-established pattern of false starts with subnational high-speed rail initiatives in California, Texas, and in the Ontario-Quebec Corridor underscored the deficiencies of trying to develop passenger renewal initiatives that ignored the 800-pound gorilla in the room, a national transportation policy that had no place for intercity passenger trains except as an object of (limited) public charity. Making real progress in revitalizing North American passenger trains would require confronting the problematic, and perhaps dysfunctional, relationship between private railroads, public passenger carriers, and national government. Amtrak's best efforts to meet its conflicting policy mandates appeared to be falling short, both of the commercial benchmarks that supporters had embraced during the 1980s and of the enhanced commercial performance that air and bus carriers were demonstrating by contrast.

On its own, this evidence might not have yielded the kind of policy transformation that was initiated. But when political realignment in the U.S. Congress was added into the mix, America's rail passenger policy community came to embrace a significant, high-stakes rail passenger renewal initiative. As is typical of postwar U.S. policy development, this break with past practices occurred in stages and has been influenced by conflicting premises regarding the rail mode's potential as a passenger carrier. Whatever the outcome of these changes, the 1990s will be remembered as the decade when running Amtrak like a traditional railroad was no longer judged to be an acceptable end in itself.

5.1. Amtrak's First Foray into Reinvention: The "Claytor Commitment"

The first act in this drama of breaking away from previous rail passenger policy was played out within Amtrak, when the leadership of its most influential and talented CEO came to an end. W. Graham Claytor Jr. had assumed Amtrak's presidency in 1982 at the age of seventy and remained at the corporation's helm for eleven years, the longest tenure of anyone to hold that job. Claytor combined the talents of a respected railroad executive and a consummate Washington insider. He presided over, and prevailed in, some of the corporation's most contentious budget battles with the Reagan and Bush administrations, both of which had sought to end federal funding for intercity passenger railroading.

Claytor brought enormous credibility to Amtrak, at a time when it was politically essential for the corporation's survival. He had been a widely admired railroad executive, leading the Southern Railway when it was chosen by Dun's Review as one of America's five best-managed companies.[1] He had also occupied several top positions in the executive branch—serving as secretary of the Navy, acting secretary of transportation, and deputy secretary of defense during the Carter administration. Corporate America, especially the rail sector, and the senior levels of the executive branch were home to some of Amtrak's greatest skeptics, making Claytor's prestige in such circles all the more valuable.

Claytor's track record in running both a railroad and large parts of the U.S. military also positioned him well to refute attacks by skeptics, who worked hard to do away with Amtrak during the Reagan and Bush administrations. When challenged by opponents in the administration and Congress claiming that Amtrak remained illegitimate because it could never pass the market test that had been laid out in its for-profit mandate, Claytor fought fire with fire.

He redefined the market test that had been used to challenge Amtrak since its creation, and then wielded it as a weapon against political opponents. The "Claytor commitment" that bought Amtrak close to a decade of congressional support was elegantly simple. If Amtrak was provided with adequate and assured capital investment (funding for new equipment and infrastructure analogous to the funds poured into air and road modes) and relieved of productivity constraints imposed by many of the administrative and legal anomalies arising from its quasi-public status, it would be able to attain commercial self-sufficiency by 2000.

Claytor's bold move went far beyond his previous position on Amtrak's commercial prospects. When interviewed in 1985 about what it would take for Amtrak to turn a profit, he claimed that all indirect (i.e., capital) subsidies to airlines would have to be terminated—yielding a 50 percent increase in ticket prices, and that the price of gasoline would have to reach $3 per gallon.[2] But between 1989 and 1990, when Amtrak was approaching an 80 percent cost recovery ratio, yet also confronting the costs of under-investment (e.g., a growing amount of deferred maintenance and deterioration in physical plant) during the Bush administration, the strategy of adapting Amtrak's finances to fit into the pattern of public support for all other modes began to evolve. Rather than passively awaiting the (distant) day when air and road users would start paying the full price for use of these infrastructures, Amtrak acted to reposition its financial reference points in order to put some distance between an operating budget that could show numbers in black ink and a capital budget where public funding that enabled such profits would be directed.

Amtrak and its supporters sought to narrow the definition of subsidy to focus on federal grants that covered operating losses. Claytor's first public pronouncement of this new approach came in testimony to the House Energy and Commerce Committee's Transportation and Hazardous Materials Subcommittee on May 17, 1989. Responding to a query from Congressman Bob Whittaker (R-Kans.) on how Amtrak's high per capita subsidies could continue to be justified, Claytor responded that his objective was "to move toward self-sufficiency. That is to say, to break even on an operating cost basis. . . . I'm quite certain that we can continue to move toward that at a pretty good clip and we may very well be able to make it shortly after the turn of the century, which is only 10 years away."[3]

When Amtrak published its 1989 Annual Report, early in 1990, this commitment had become formalized in the president's letter. There, Claytor wrote:

"Amtrak is committed to continuing its efforts to enhance service while decreasing its need for federal financial support. Indeed, with adequate capital support and several critical changes in the law to reduce our operating costs, it is now Amtrak's specific objective to cover 100 percent of its operating costs by the year 2000. This is an ambitious goal, one thought impossible several years ago, but we believe that it is achievable and we are committed to it."[4]

The Claytor commitment was politically astute, in that it gave centrist legislators (conservative Democrats and moderate Republicans) a justification for rejecting demands from the executive branch and other skeptics to do away with Amtrak's funding. Claytor's prior service as secretary of the Navy and deputy secretary of defense gave him both access to, and respect from, the legislators who decided Amtrak's fate. This political capital proved a catalyst to create the most significant elaboration, and modification, of Amtrak's commercial mandate since the ill-fitting combination of a for-profit mandate and public subsidization had been cobbled together in 1971. Under Claytor's leadership, Amtrak made both commercial and political progress. It gained credibility for being run "like a railroad," especially when this translated into higher revenues and lower costs.

But as effective as the Claytor commitment proved in defending the corporation from skeptics intent on zeroing out its federal support, it was not powerful enough to unlock the vault in which the bulk of America's transportation spending was securely guarded—the federal trust funds supporting air, road, and public transit capital spending. In 1990, Claytor reminded a Senate subcommittee that: "For several years, Amtrak has advocated creation of a unified surface transportation trust fund, supported by federal gasoline 'user fees,' that would provide in a consistent and coordinated manner the federal investment in surface transportation. Both Amtrak's depreciation and its expanding capital needs for the next decade could be met by allocating just a penny—one cent—of federal gasoline user fee revenues to Amtrak. With this relatively modest financial support, Amtrak would be able to provide enhanced conventional and high-speed rail passenger service that would alleviate growing air and highway congestion in many areas of the nation at far less cost and with less adverse environmental impact than the enormously expensive construction of new airports and highways."[5]

But the opposition to "sharing the wealth" that was generated by these lucrative transportation trust funds was much more intense than the level of resistance mounted during Amtrak's previous legislative struggles. Organized interests seeking to keep their subsidies well insulated from larger budget battles allied with fiscal conservatives in both Congress and the administration (e.g., the Office of Management and Budget and the Treasury Department) opposing any expansion of trust fund spending programs. In his final round of congressional testimony, Claytor proposed that Amtrak be allocated one cent of a 2.5-cent temporary addition to the gas tax that had been enacted to reduce the deficit. He suggested that such an investment would be in keeping with the spirit of the original tax because it would constitute "taking away the penny and putting it in another place where it will . . . also result in deficit reduction, because it's going to replace money [for Amtrak's operating losses] that's otherwise going to have be appropriated out of general funds."[6] Claytor went on to claim that such dedicated capital funding "would result in an Amtrak almost unrecognizable by today's standards, with an expanded national route system, numerous high-speed corridor services, state-of-the-art passenger trains and maintenance facilities, and the ability to fund all of its own operating costs."[7] This vision of Amtrak's potential was not sufficient to bring about the desired funding arrangements.

But when Claytor stepped down from leading Amtrak at the age of 81, just five months prior to his death, the limits of existing organizational and financial arrangements were about to be reached. Amtrak's commercial performance was again beginning to flag. Part of this was due to stiffer competition from other modes, while part came out of the inability to shed all of the constraints on productivity that Claytor's commitment had been premised upon. The result was a corporation that came to be judged on its progress toward eliminating operating subsidies, yet lacked the key policy instrument (dedicated capital funding) that management had been counting on when it made the commitment to break even on operations.

While Amtrak maneuvered through political debates concerning its approach to satisfying the new profitability mandate, its commercial competitors focused on a much clearer economic target. Deregulation of air and bus carriers, restructuring within the auto industry, and a declining real price for energy created the conditions for extremely strong competition to train travel. Among common carriers, both airlines and bus companies had survived the 1980s by boosting their productivity and honing their ability to maximize market opportunities. These enhancements were not intended to outperform Amtrak, but they had that effect, with the passenger train's market position (and Amtrak's revenues) becoming collateral damage from post-deregulation airline competition. Figure 5.2 shows the distribution of travel by common carrier in the United States from 1985 through 1997. While the share of travel by air grows slightly, both bus's and rail's "modal split" decline during these years. Only rail's modal split declines continuously, albeit in very small amounts.

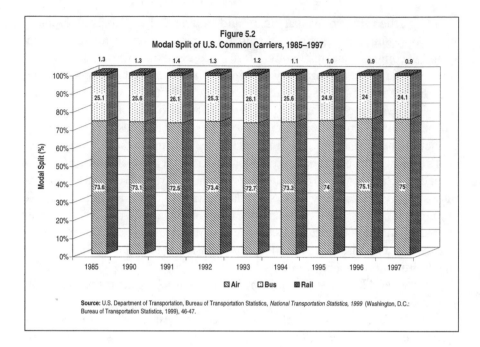

Figure 5.2
Modal Split of U.S. Common Carriers, 1985–1997

Source: U.S. Department of Transportation, Bureau of Transportation Statistics, *National Transportation Statistics, 1999* (Washington, D.C.: Bureau of Transportation Statistics, 1999), 46-47.

The auto industry was similarly riding high from an even longer period of restructuring that yielded higher-quality, better-engineered, and lower-priced vehicles. This combined with energy prices that fell below 1980 levels kept automobility going strong, accounting for 90.2 percent of American intercity travel, as shown in figure 5.3. Despite Amtrak's best efforts, intercity rail's share of total travel fell from 0.3 percent in 1970 to 0.2 percent in 1990. The operational enhancements and productivity gains that Claytor had delivered by making Amtrak a leader among railroads had run their course in terms of bottom-line results.[8] Operating passenger trains using best practices from the railroad tradition was not proving sufficient to close the gap between costs and revenues.

5.2. Repositioning Amtrak to Attain the Claytor Commitment

Following what *Railway Age* characterized as a "long and often delayed search," Claytor's successor, Tom Downs, was appointed on December 7, 1993.[9] He had little choice but to accept the challenge of the Claytor commitment, while recognizing that further organizational innovations within Amtrak would be a critical component of the renewal needed to achieve the promised improvement in commercial performance. On the perennial problem of under-funded

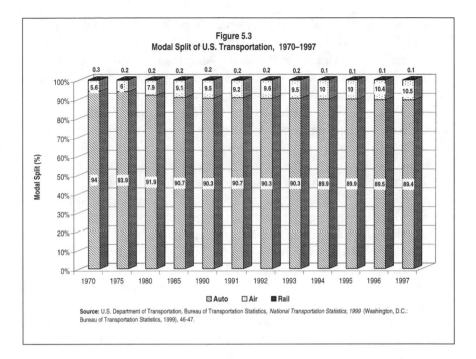

Figure 5.3
Modal Split of U.S. Transportation, 1970–1997

Source: U.S. Department of Transportation, Bureau of Transportation Statistics, *National Transportation Statistics, 1999* (Washington, D.C.: Bureau of Transportation Statistics, 1999), 46-47.

capital, Downs did his best to remind the rail policy community of a key component of the Claytor commitment that remained outstanding: Amtrak's need for a dedicated source of capital funding. But Downs also recognized the difficulty of making this case.

As he put it in one interview: "Part of the original deal was a capitalized company. Graham [Claytor] said it consistently, and what everybody heard was, 'Yeah, we know you need the capital, but we really appreciate you getting economically self-sufficient in the year 2000. We don't have enough to do the capital this year; talk to us next year.'"[10]

Recognizing that Claytor's "Am-penny" proposal for gas tax funding had been decisively defeated in Congress, Downs began his advocacy by scaling back the amount of tax redistribution that would fuel a rail passenger trust fund. He sought a half-cent commitment from the gas tax, the smallest amount that could justify the effort of creating a separate funding stream for passenger rail. He also requested that Congress add intercity rail to the eligible options on which states could spend their federal gas tax revenues, joining a long list of alternatives to new highway building that had been authorized under Section 1006 of the Intermodal Surface Transportation Efficiency Act of 1991.[11]

As a former state transportation official who had worked in both New Jersey and New York, Downs recognized the power of fiscal partnerships in transportation programs to both support Amtrak's immediate capital needs and to build the political foundation that would anchor the putative intercity rail passenger trust fund as firmly as its road and transit counterparts. Amtrak's isolation from ostensibly flexible federal funding appeared to be a promising point of access for gaining entry into the mainstream of American transportation policy. As Downs put it: "Governors can now spend their federal transportation dollars on highways, transit, safety, bike trails, scenic easements, even historic preservation. But they cannot spend a dime of it for any intercity rail passenger use. We know that states want to invest in rail. Amtrak has negotiated partnership agreements with eight governors for continued rail service. More flexibility in the use of federal transportation funds at the state level would help us develop more partnerships with communities that are demanding innovative transportation solutions."[12]

Along with this more incremental and decentralized approach to meeting Amtrak's capital needs, Downs also recognized that meeting the Claytor commitment depended upon organizational change from within that would enable Amtrak to build ridership and revenue in a more competitive commercial environment. Managing a variety of large organizations gave Downs a different organizational perspective from those held by preceding Amtrak CEOs. Rather than identifying Amtrak's success with best practices in the railroad sector, Downs looked to innovations in both "new public management" and in transportation firms beyond railroads as examples for organizational redesign. These perspectives led him away from the traditional hierarchy and centralization that imbued Claytor from both the railroad and military traditions.

Downs sought to run Amtrak less like a railroad in the classic sense, and more like a business where market strengths were cultivated through customer focused entrepreneurial initiatives. This meant doing away with the organizational hierarchy that centralized decisions in a Washington, D.C., headquarters, one that appeared "top heavy" to a CEO who found that "on the mechanical side, there were 11 layers between me and the person working on the tracks, and on the service side, there were 10 layers between me and the person working on the train."[13]

Downs launched the most significant organizational change in Amtrak's existence by creating Strategic Business Units that would decentralize decision making about operations and service planning from headquarters to three focused entities. Soon after their creation, Resor assessed these new organizational entities.[14] Amtrak's Northeast Corridor business unit would take on operational responsibility for routes between New England and Virginia, carrying about half of current passengers. It would also take the lead in developing the most ambitious, and most promising, dimension of Amtrak's renewal, the launch of new Acela high-speed service train between Boston, New York, and Washington. The Intercity business unit would take responsibility for the long-haul and regional trains that formed the core of Amtrak's traditional passenger operations, carrying about 40 percent of total passengers. And "Amtrak West" would be the unit to focus on the 10 percent of rail passengers traveling within and between California, Oregon, and Washington. It would also manage the ridership growth and service expansion that was already under way in this region by focusing on the needs of state governments that were already supporting intercity rail service and seeking to develop opportunities for further incremental upgrading.

The considerable organizational change that went into Amtrak's restructuring was certainly traumatic for many traditional railroaders within its ranks. Decentralization, combined with a 21 percent[15] cut in train operations, yielded a reduction of 5,600 employees and $435 million worth of expenditures.[16] The objective of this painful exercise was to position the corporation to take advantage of both commercial and policy opportunities that could be more effectively seized at a local or regional level beyond the Capital Beltway. But the entrepreneurship that such a clean sweep of internal management now enabled would still depend upon the financial and policy framework that Congress and the administration provided to Amtrak. And once again, the political stalemate over what to do about intercity passenger trains became a constraint on change.

5.3. Legislating Amtrak's "Reform"

While Tom Downs was launching organizational change within Amtrak, the 1994 midterm elections changed the role of Congress in reinventing Amtrak. With the Democrats losing control of the House of Representatives for the first time in forty-two years, the political relationships that Amtrak and rail passenger advocates had cultivated with legislators chairing committees and subcommittees were suddenly ruptured. For the first time in Amtrak's existence, Republican legislators in both houses of Congress would take the lead in deliberating over the corporation's budgeting, appropriations, and oversight.

One rail industry observer characterized the representatives behind this legislative power shift as "an army of dewy-eyed, steel-hearted newly-elected members of Congress [who] marched into Washington, intent on performing the unnatural act of balancing the budget and at the same time slashing taxes."[17] The House Republicans' "Contract With America," and the ideology that it represented, was the epitome of skepticism about "big government" programs like Amtrak. Championed by Speaker Newt Gingrinch, this manifesto called for "the end of government that is too big, too intrusive, and too easy with the public's money."[18] New committee and subcommittee chairs in the House were quite open to considering drastic curtailment, or privatization, of Amtrak.

Suddenly, the traditional (and costly) train services that Amtrak operated across the nation lost some of their political value in procuring legislative support, and the Claytor commitment became Amtrak's prime defense against skeptics whose criticisms of Amtrak resonated strongly with the new congressional leadership. Amtrak's ability to live within a shrinking budget on the way to achieving commercial self-sufficiency took on even greater importance.

To avoid any further credibility loss with a new Congress that he characterized as being "considerably more adverse to federal subsidies for operating and capital costs," Downs launched a further round of budget cutting to deal with Amtrak's $200 million shortfall.[19] This entailed doing away with a few of the worst-performing traditional trains, and reducing the frequency of several major long-distance routes from daily to three or four times per week. Such a cutback of both services and jobs would have been unlikely in a Democratic-controlled Congress. The Republican takeover of the House thus legitimized and spurred on some of Downs' more "radical" restructuring impulses, as well as the fare increases in 1995 and 1996 that Williams and Warren found to be a contributor to Amtrak's sharp ridership decline.[20] But while it certainly changed the way in which Amtrak did business, this shift in the balance of political power on Capitol Hill was not sufficient to achieve the skeptics' agenda of doing away with Amtrak as they knew it. The different complexion of Republican majorities in the House and Senate allowed for the ongoing contest between supporters and skeptics to be played out through the competition between the two chambers.

In the House, where skeptics predominated, the Amtrak Reform and Privatization Act of 1995 (H.R. 1788) emphasized cost cutting reforms that would reduce the expense of Amtrak's future operations by ending legislated prohibitions on contracting out work. This bill also sought to facilitate the elimination of uneconomic services by ending legislated labor protection provisions that entitled workers to up to six years of ongoing salary if they were laid off as a result of Amtrak's curtailing train operations. The House legislation also sought to replace the existing Board of Directors with an Amtrak Reform Board that would develop a business plan for commercial self-sufficiency. This plan was required to maintain only the level of route network that could support itself. An Amtrak Reform Council was also created to monitor the company's commercial progress.

The thrust of this legislation was to position Amtrak for privatization, with liquidation as a fallback position. These reforms were intended to either transform Amtrak into a profitable entity that could attract at least some private investment in the future, or to put it out of business. In the latter scenario, assets such as the Northeast Corridor could be acquired by entities that might be able to make a go of running them profitably. This bill was passed by a vote of 406 to 5. Amtrak's president publicly warned that the House legislation and its associated funding level of just $542 million (compared to the administration's request for $918.5 million) would "turn [Amtrak's] glide path to success to a slippery slope to extinction."[21]

In contrast, the Senate adhered to the earlier policy formulation from the Claytor commitment. Cost cutting and commercial reforms were coupled with proposals to significantly boost capital investment in intercity rail. For example, the Intercity Passenger Rail Trust Fund Act of 1995 (S. 1395) incorporated Amtrak's request to allocate one-half cent of federal gasoline tax revenues to an intercity rail passenger trust fund account. Had this bill become law, rail supporters' long-standing goal of obtaining a permanent source of capital funding, akin to other modes, would have been realized.

Another Senate bill, the Amtrak and Local Rail Revitalization Act of 1995 (S. 1318) sought to meet capital investment needs through the fiscal flexibility that Downs had envisioned. This legislation made intercity rail capital expenditures eligible from the mass transit account of the existing transportation trust fund, as well as authorized the issuance of tax exempt bonds to fund intercity rail capital spending.

Once again, the political standoff between skeptics and supporters of passenger rail played itself out in the 104th Congress, with none of the proposed organizational and financial reforms surviving the legislative debate over what to do about passenger trains. Senate bill 1395 never reached the Senate floor because, according to the U.S. Constitution, bills that contain revenue provisions must originate in the House, and there was no compatible legislation emerging from that chamber. On the other hand, S. 1318 was never reconciled with the reforms proposed in H.R. 1788.[22] Neither the House prescriptions for putting an end to federal government preservation of rail passenger services nor the Senate proposals to bring intercity rail "inside the tent" of federal capital transportation financing were enacted, leaving Amtrak pretty much where it had always been—in limbo.

Although not sufficient to immediately break the policy stalemate over Amtrak's fate, the congressional realignment of 1994 was enough to change the terms of debate over Amtrak's legislative framework in the 105th Congress. Legislators left the contentious issues of trust funds and fiscal flexibility behind, while returning to the Claytor commitment's promise of commercial renewal backed by public investment in rail assets. Amtrak's subsequent appropriations debate centered on three issues. First, how should commercial self-sufficiency be defined and when should it be mandated?

In 1997, the gap between operating costs and revenues remained at 17 percent, with Amtrak posting a revenue to cost ratio of 0.83 (see figure 3.3). Skeptics demanded that the same "generally accepted accounting principles" be used to gauge Amtrak as would be applied to the performance of any private sector firm. In contrast, supporters insisted that Amtrak's unique role as both a carrier and a mode of transportation demanded accounting adaptations from standard business practice. The question of when the definitive measurement of self-sufficiency should be taken was also debated. Skeptics emphasized Claytor's original commitment to end operating subsidies by 2000 while supporters argued for an extension to 2002, due to extenuating circumstances, including the shortfall of federal capital assistance which Claytor and Downs had insisted was necessary in order to achieve commercial self-sufficiency.

The second dimension of debate over how to address the Claytor commitment concerned how much should be invested in capital support for Amtrak and the form it should take. Supporters continued to argue that significant capital investment was essential to meeting Amtrak's commercial self-sufficiency target and that it should come from a permanent funding source akin to the trust funding of highway and mass transit infrastructure. Skeptics did not change their view of capital spending on Amtrak as "throwing good money after bad." They insisted that because intercity rail service was not meeting the threshold of commercial self-sufficiency, it remained illegitimate, and was thus unjustified in accessing the "mother lode" of American transportation funding through gasoline taxes. In this case, both road and transit interests echoed the skepticism that spending any amount on intercity rail that would otherwise go to their own modes represented a poor transportation policy.

Finally, the question of what, if any, consequences should be legislated in the event Amtrak failed to meet the Claytor commitment's self-sufficiency target led to contention to shape the rules of an "end game." Supporters sought to leave such considerations up to a future Congress, while skeptics argued for a privatization mandate that would liquidate Amtrak by transferring some combination of its assets and services to states and other operators.

The Amtrak Reform and Accountability Act of 1997 (ARAA) and Section 977 of the Taxpayer Relief Act of 1997 (TRA) were the product of these contentious deliberations. Both in themselves, and in their relationship to one another, they represented compromise based upon institutional innovation. Their authors found a way to advance the policy preferences of both supporters and skeptics, up to a point. What moved the legislative effort to redefine Amtrak's administrative and financial framework beyond the political deadlock that had stymied efforts in 1995 was the creation of a mutually acceptable linkage between organizational reform and infrastructure investment.

While the ARAA appeared similar to the reorganization and reform arrangements that had been proposed in 1995, the TRA's authorization of up to $2.323 billion in intercity rail capital investment was the breakthrough that allowed a significant commitment to renewing rail passenger equipment and infrastructure without breaching the formidable defenses of other modes' transportation trust funds. Section 977 of the TRA authorized Amtrak to claim a refundable credit on taxes paid by its predecessor railroads up to a maximum of $2.323 billion. The six states that (at the time) lacked Amtrak services were each eligible to claim one percent of this "rebate" for other transportation spending, leaving $2.2 billion for Amtrak. In one sense, it was a classic tax "gimmick" that enabled funding intercity rail capital investment in a way that left the modal and jurisdictional boundaries of the transportation trust funds unchallenged. In return for cashing in this newly created entitlement to these taxes, rail passenger supporters accepted many of the commercial and organizational challenges that skeptics had long demanded and that are in the ARAA.

While continuing to defer the ultimate reconciliation of these conflicting visions, the act established a timetable in law for that day of reckoning. A deadline was set in the long-running standoff regarding where America's passenger trains were headed. The ARAA authorized funding Amtrak's operating losses through 2002, with declining amounts each year. After 2002, ARAA made clear that Amtrak was expected to function without operational assistance from the federal government. Statutory provisions for labor protection payments (which had guaranteed laid-off Amtrak employees up to six years' pay) were repealed and replaced with a process of negotiation and arbitration over any severance arrangements to be made in the event of subsequent workforce contraction.[23] Legislative prohibitions on contracting out work were also repealed, with the restrictions transferred into existing labor contracts that would be up for renegotiation in 1999. Amtrak's Board of Directors was also reconstituted, with the provision for new bylaws and selection of directors (including a suggestion of employee representation) once the corporation achieved commercial self-sufficiency in 2002.

The ARAA also created a new policy actor to participate in the passenger train's transition to commercial self-sufficiency. The Amtrak Reform Council (ARC) was created to monitor and evaluate Amtrak's commercial performance. ARC was to alert Congress if the progress toward self-sufficiency was judged insufficient to end operating subsidies after 2002, and to initiate a sunset process if Amtrak did fall short of its target. This organizational embodiment of a "devil's advocate" was also charged with making recommendations to the corporation on achieving greater operating efficiency and revenue enhancement throughout the transition period. The council was specifically directed to monitor the implementation of work-rule changes, and to document resulting productivity enhancements.

And in the event that Amtrak was not operationally self-sufficient in 2002, the council was directed to immediately notify the president and Congress, and to produce a plan within ninety days that would identify a "restructured and rationalized national intercity rail passenger system."[24] At the same time, Amtrak was directed to work in parallel and "develop and submit to the Congress an action plan for the complete liquidation of Amtrak, after having the plan reviewed by the Inspector General of the Department of Transportation and the General Accounting Office for accuracy and reasonableness."[25] Under these circumstances, the act provides ninety days for Congress to adopt the restructuring plan proposed by the Amtrak Reform Council (or an amended version). If no such plan were adopted, the ARAA calls for a "liquidation disapproval resolution" to be introduced in the Senate that would give Congress the opportunity to accept or reject Amtrak's proposal for liquidation.

Although quite different from their predecessors in ideological orientation, the legislators responsible for enacting the ARAA and TRA did exhibit one common characteristic—they were incapable of exercising self-restraint from micromanaging America's passenger railroad. Like the liberal congressmen and senators who once had no qualms about directing what Amtrak must do to develop its services (e.g., run certain trains along certain routes through certain congressional districts), contemporary conservative legislators were determined to specify what Amtrak must do to reduce its subsidies (e.g., renegotiate new labor contracts, contract out, restructure its board and downsize its operations if performance fell short of breaking even in 2002). The direction of rail passenger legislation had changed, but the intent to keep Amtrak on a short policy leash—much shorter than any other intercity carrier—remained the same. Nonetheless, the ARAA and TRA did set the stage for a potential resolution of the long-standing impasse over what to do about passenger train policy. Since its passage, Amtrak has struggled mightily to pursue the mandate of self-sufficiency. While the jury is still out on the commercial outcomes, the process of running Amtrak like a for-profit business was kicked into high gear with passage of the ARAA and TRA. Since 1997, the corporation's managerial dynamism has easily approached, if not exceeded, that found in competing airline and bus carriers.

5.4. How Amtrak's CEO Became the First Casualty of the Struggle for Self-Sufficiency

Beginning almost immediately following the passage of the Amtrak Reform and Accountability Act, the corporation's temper, and tempo, changed dramatically. The legislative conflict over how far and how fast to go in "ending Amtrak as we know it" (to borrow a phrase used to characterize the contemporary replacement of America's principal welfare program, Aid to Families with Dependent Children) had created considerable tension among Amtrak's supporters. In particular, organized labor and its supporters split with management on how far to go in changing work rules and pay rates to advance the corporation's commercial prospects.

Shortly after the reauthorization legislation passed, Amtrak's Board of Directors announced the resignation of Tom Downs. The leader who had gone the furthest, to date, in reinventing public enterprise passenger railroading appeared to have proceeded at his own peril, and had been judged to have gone too far. According to Frank Wilner, an expert on both Amtrak and rail labor, Downs became a victim of the political crossfire between supporters and skeptics who had battled over the terms of Amtrak's future in 1997.[26] Facing contract negotiations with Amtrak's unionized workforce, Downs insisted upon major concessions on wages and productivity, justifying these by Amtrak's near bankruptcy and reduced political support in Congress. He sought to uncouple Amtrak's negotiations from rail labor's traditional approach to bargaining with all railroads for an across-the-board settlement. Downs strategized that such a settlement would be based on the (profitable) freight railroads' ability to pay, and would leave Amtrak with an even worse cost-to-revenue ratio.

When industry-wide negotiations bogged down, the Clinton administration appointed a Presidential Emergency Board, a mediation panel provided for in the Railway Labor Act. It offered nonbinding recommendations for a wage increase of 3.5 percent retroactive to 1995, a further 3.5 percent increase retroactive to 1997, and another 3.5 percent increase in 1999.[27] Amtrak claimed that such increases would bankrupt the company and proposed increases of 50 percent of the consumer price index.[28] Wilner suggests that Downs's resistance to a settlement was a determined effort to maintain credibility with at least some moderate skeptics in Congress, on whom Amtrak's legislative future was seen to depend.

Given the intensity of the debate over Amtrak's future and the close split among legislators, especially in the House of Representatives, over different approaches to ending Amtrak's dependence on federal subsidies, Downs resisted settling on a contract that opponents would use as "proof" that the corporation was in an economically hopeless situation. Downs likely reasoned that doing otherwise could doom Amtrak's chances to secure a workable reauthorization bill. He may have also hoped that this resulting legislation would strengthen Amtrak's hand in negotiating further labor productivity.

But when unions threatened strike action that would shut down America's intercity passenger trains, Amtrak's Board of Directors—consisting of Clinton administration appointees who were both rail supporters and, allegedly, pro-labor—took over the negotiations directly. Agreement was reached, and a new contract was signed that adopted the same wage rates as the freight railroads, but made them contingent on obtaining adequate appropriations from Congress.

Downs had been overruled by his Board of Directors in seeking to break away from "business as usual" labor relations. Amtrak estimated that this settlement added $144 million to its operating costs in 1999, and accounted for $260 million in total wage increases, signing bonuses, and retroactive payments. Some $116 million of these increases were paid out in 2000.[29]

Yet despite its accommodation of union demands, this generous settlement did not derail Amtrak's legislative reauthorization. The fact that a union-satisfying contract could also be accepted, or at least overlooked, by a Republican-dominated Congress must have discredited the Amtrak president's hard-line bargaining strategy. The ARAA was signed into law on November 13, 1997, and Tom Downs resigned as Amtrak CEO less than a month later, on December 10. While he was praised by the Amtrak Board's vice-chair and the secretary of transportation, the inescapable conclusion is that Downs felt compelled to leave his job.

The ability of Amtrak's unions to triumph in a labor dispute, to the point of apparently ousting the company's president, has focused the succeeding management team on growing Amtrak's revenues, more than on shrinking its costs. Revisiting the productivity gap between the rail workforce and that of other passenger carriers has been deferred, but the question of whether Amtrak could attain commercial self-sufficiency without significant reductions in labor costs remains.

5.5. Amtrak's Post-ARAA Blueprint for Commercial Success

Under George Warrington, Amtrak's current CEO, the corporation has rolled out a Network Growth Strategy that promises to end operating subsidies by 2002. Approved by Amtrak's Board on October 19, 1998, the plan "incorporates Amtrak's business vision to provide a market-based national system sustained by increasing passenger revenues and successful commercial ventures."[30] This strategy was built upon five key performance goals.

First, Fiscal Year (FY) 2002 gross revenues were targeted to grow by $789 million over FY 1998. This would represent a 34 percent jump over four years. Some of these revenues would come from diversification into new business ventures and joint ventures, ranging from enhanced travel and tourism activities to equipment leasing, mechanical services provision to other carriers, real estate development, telecommunications, advertising, and parking.

Second, FY 2002 ridership was projected to increase by 4.4 million over FY 1998, a 21 percent increase. Third, $180 million in "net incremental revenues" were forecast to be generated from Acela high-speed rail service in the Northeast. Amtrak stated that "the high speed rail program serves as a model for how a market-based, consumer-oriented service can produce revenues to improve the financial health of the corporation as a whole."

Fourth, Amtrak's express operations were targeted for exponential growth, with the "budget result" (i.e., contribution to bottom line) rising from $4 million in FY 1999 to $25 million in 2002. Amtrak notes that it now controls less than 1 percent of the $247-billion-a-year goods handling market, concluding that even modest gains could make a significant difference in the financial health of perennially unprofitable long-distance trains.

Building such express revenues would revive a traditional revenue stream that had contributed significant sums to intercity passenger trains' performance under private operation. But it would also raise commercial tensions with the freight carriers over which Amtrak operates, which now move such shipments in partnership with delivery and trucking companies like UPS and J.B. Hunt.

Finally, "annual operating performance" was supposed to improve by $426 million in FY 2002. This meant that the gap between cash expenses (e.g., wages, fuel, supplies, etc.) and revenues would be closed and Amtrak would be able to pass at least one variant of its commercial self-sufficiency litmus test. Both skeptics and supporters would admit that this is a bold plan indeed.

The engine pulling Amtrak's ambitious growth strategy along is a "market-based network analysis" that aims to: "Identify and characterize the existing and potential intercity travel market; Identify and develop additional commercial opportunities; Define a model for intercity passenger rail that works in the marketplace and balance . . . stakeholder interests." A key theme of the business plan is to partner with state governments to replicate the investments, and commercial potential, of its Northeast Corridor. This Corridor development program was supposed to be modeled upon, and spurred by, the achievement and attention that Acela Express trains would bring to the Northeast. The delay in their arrival has not boosted this component of Amtrak's plan to the degree that was originally forecast. Business plan references to cost containment identify "expense management" of items such as fuel purchases, other procurement, food and beverage services, and fare collection processes. Amtrak's business plan projects a 16.3 percent increase in costs over the four years between FY 99 and FY 2002, compared to a 34 percent increase in revenues.

On February 28, 2000, the Network Growth Strategy was affirmed at the White House, following a meeting of President Clinton with Amtrak's Board. Expansion plans were announced that called for adding 7 percent to Amtrak's total service, with new or augmented operations on eleven routes in twenty-one states. Amtrak's emphasis upon ridership and revenue growth has occurred at a most opportune time, with energy prices climbing and with air and road infrastructure choked with peak traffic levels from a buoyant economy. Yet progress to date, in both implementation of the business plan and in achievement of commercial results, has been slower than the ambitious growth and revenue targets.

Although the jury remains out on where Amtrak's commercial performance will take it by the end of 2002, there is no shortage of concern over whether the corporation can attain its ambitious ridership and revenue targets. And, not surprisingly, there is also no shortage of disagreement over what would constitute the benchmark of commercial success. Early in 2000, the Amtrak Reform Council issued its first report, which was contested from both within and outside the organization on the question of defining commercial self-sufficiency. Later in the year, both the Department of Transportation's Inspector General and the General Accounting Office issued warnings about Amtrak's prospects of ending its dependence on operating subsidies by 2003. Each of these assessments of Amtrak's latest struggle to renew itself illustrates a different facet of the ongoing constraints posed by America's rail passenger policy shortcomings.

5.6. The Amtrak Reform Council Enters the Fray

The Amtrak Reform Council (ARC) was legally created on December 2, 1997, along with the ARAA, but did not hold its first meeting until May 1998. Like the corporation it was created to monitor, ARC quickly became embroiled in controversy. While supporters and skeptics could agree that Amtrak was in ill health commercially speaking, their understanding of what the ARC was supposed to do about this malady differed considerably. To some, the ARC would play the role of Dr. Kevorkian and assist a terminally unprofitable enterprise to die with dignity through privatization or liquidation. Others saw the ARC more like Dr. Christiaan Barnard, performing a daring transplant of sound business practices into an ailing corporate body that could not survive much longer on its own. And more than a few supporters in the rail policy community expected the ARC to perform cosmetic surgery on Amtrak, by lifting and tucking some of the sagging performance that disfigured its books in ways that would quickly make the corporation appear more attractive with as little discomfort as possible.

The council's first annual report, entitled *A Preliminary Assessment of Amtrak*, was released on January 24, 2000. The front cover carried a large disclaimer stating: "This year's report does not reach any conclusions or make recommendations about Amtrak's long-term future. It provides a picture of the Amtrak organization as it exists today, it presents our perspective on Amtrak's performance to this juncture, and it raises questions and issues that the council believes should be addressed in its future efforts and, ultimately, by the Congress."[31]

This "perspective on Amtrak's performance" drew harsh criticism from the corporation, from its advocates, and even from within the council. Three of eleven council members refused to endorse the report. Clarence Monin, the council's labor representative, filed a seven page dissenting report that was supported by the Department of Transportation.

The Monin dissent accused the council of adopting an "aggressive anti-Amtrak and pro-privatization agenda" yielding a report that was "replete with statements which are misleading, inaccurate and unsubstantiated and [represent] the culmination of the very fiscal irresponsibility that it claims to address."[32] This dissent concluded that "instead of offering sensible proposals and working to secure a strong future for Amtrak and its workers, it conveys unnecessary pessimism about Amtrak's future, and sets the stage for the undermining and ultimate dismantling of our national railroad passenger carrier."[33] Federal Railroad Administrator Jolene Molitoris added, "As the representative of [DOT] Secretary Slater on the Council, I cannot support the report's transmittal to Congress." Molitoris went on to object that since "this Administration initiated the goal of Amtrak operating self-sufficiency and participated fully throughout the legislative process that led to inclusion of this goal in the ARAA,"[34] she was in a unique position to interpret the legislative intent of this measure, and that the council had gotten it wrong.

While the ARC has been challenged over many of the points it has raised about Amtrak's financial and managerial practices, one particular issue raised by its first report serves to epitomize the perennial divide between rail passenger supporters and skeptics, who are both represented on the council's board. The most contentious issue facing the ARC concerns the appropriate standard by which to measure Amtrak's commercial bottom line. This debate over whether Amtrak should be treated like a private business or a public enterprise is nothing new to passenger rail policy deliberations. The Reform Council's first report did not resolve the debate, but it did offer a clear expression of the various interpretations of the accounting standards that should govern the assessment of Amtrak's commercial self-sufficiency.

In its report, the ARC endorsed the position held by most rail policy skeptics that Amtrak was intended to perform as a for-profit business, and thus should be judged by the "generally accepted accounting principles" (GAAP) that financial analysts would apply to any private corporation. The council claimed that it was required to adopt GAAP criteria by statute, quoting the ARAA's direction that in making evaluations and recommendations, "the Council shall consider all relevant performance factors, including . . . appropriate methods for the adoption of uniform cost and accounting procedures throughout the Amtrak system, based on generally accepted accounting principles." It went on to state that "the Council believes that the accounting standard specifically referred to in the Council's statutory mandate, GAAP, is, both logically and under current law, the method it must use to measure Amtrak's financial performance."[35]

The report acknowledged Amtrak's position that while it does prepare its audited financial statements in accordance with GAAP, both "federal legislation and historical practice in place in FY 1997 result in an operational self-sufficiency test that is based solely on the need for federal cash for operating purposes."[36] The council estimated that taking account of depreciation and

The Japanese Shinkansen showed that a mix of new technology and market-focused service could make the passenger train an economic success story. A westbound Hikari (super-express train) at Himeji on the New Tokaido line, pictured here in 1981. (Photograph courtesy of Henry Posner III.)

The French *Train à Grande Vitesse* (TGV) was the first rail passenger renewal project that succeeded in bringing air and automobile travelers back to the rails. The train on the right is a first-generation TGV at Lyon's Perrache train station. To the left, a traditional electric locomotive illustrates the difference in size and aerodynamic design that modern technology brought to French passenger railroading. (Photograph courtesy of Karl Zimmerman.)

Germany's InterCity Express (ICE) is another contributor to Europe's rail passenger renewal success. The ICE train from Hamburg, at left, has just pulled into Frankfurt's main train station in June 2001. Passengers can make a cross-platform transfer to a regional express train that will stop at smaller towns skipped by the ICE. (Author's collection.)

As in Japan, success with an initial high-speed train generated political support for public investment in modern passenger trains. The French government supported expanding the TGV into a national network, with its hub underneath Charles de Gaulle International Airport, just outside Paris. Here, a second-generation TGV calls at the CDG Airport station, detraining passengers just below the main terminal building. Air-rail travelers can walk to their connecting flights, at a distance comparable to transfers between aircraft. (Photograph courtesy of Ross Capon.)

Another rail passenger success story derived from the TGV is the Eurostar train, which connects London with Paris and Brussels using the Channel Tunnel. Here a Eurostar is shown at London's Waterloo International station (*above*), and again about to leave the Gare du Nord in Paris (*below*). (Photographs courtesy of Karl Zimmerman.)

Part of Europe's rail passenger renewal has involved connecting airports to intercity rail networks. Frankfurt's airport boasts a new intercity train station, an addition to its existing station for trains to the city center. Here, passengers alight from a train that originated in Hamburg to connect with flights around the world. (Author's collection.)

America's railroads faced increasingly desperate financial circumstances as a result of the passenger train's decline. The bankrupt Penn Central Railroad was carrying only a handful of passengers on this one-car train bound for New York City during the winter of 1970–1971. (Photograph courtesy of Karl Zimmerman.)

In January of 1970, the Baltimore & Ohio Railroad's train #8, The Shenandoah, was down to just one locomotive and one dome coach, shown here at Pittsburgh, Pennsylvania. (Photograph courtesy of Henry Posner III.)

(*Left*) During the 1970s, many small and mid-sized American cities lost rail passenger access. A typical aftermath of the cutbacks appears in this scene at the Erie-Lackawanna Railroad's Binghampton, New York, station in 1973. The waiting room remained open three years after the last train serving this city had been abandoned. (Photograph courtesy of Karl Zimmerman.)

(*Below*) Canada's passenger trains did not face the competitive onslaught from subsidized air and auto travel modes as early, or as intensively, as their American counterparts. In 1964, the Canadian National Railways and the Canadian Pacific Railway were still cooperating in running passenger trains without a subsidy, illustrated by The International en route through Canadian Pacific's Westmount Station in suburban Montreal. In the background is a dome car from the Canadian Pacific's transcontinental fleet. (Photograph courtesy of Ross Capon.)

The Metroliner was America's most successful effort to date in reinventing the passenger train. Racing through Princeton Junction, New Jersey, in March 1973, this six-car Metroliner was typical of the profitable service that Amtrak inherited from the Pennsylvania Railroad. (Photograph courtesy of Henry Posner III.)

A less successful effort to renew North American passenger trains was the jet turbine-powered TurboTrain running between New York and Boston, which Amtrak inherited from the Penn Central Railroad. Pictured here at New Haven, Connecticut, in October 1974, Amtrak would soon withdraw the TurboTrain from service. (Photograph courtesy of Henry Posner III.)

Amtrak's early days were plagued by worn-out and obsolete equipment. Typical of these "bad old days," was Amtrak's Kansas City–New York National Limited, shown here arriving into Pittsburgh nine hours and forty-five minutes late during the summer of 1972. Note that the Penn Central has loaned a freight engine to pull this train after Amtrak's own locomotives failed while en route. (Photograph courtesy of Henry Posner III.)

One of Amtrak's earliest equipment purchases was this French-built Turboliner train, which was used in the mid 1970s for short distance services between Chicago and a number of midwestern cities. The Turboliner pictured here is en route from Chicago to Milwaukee in July 1979. (Photograph courtesy of Karl Zimmerman.)

Amtrak has counted upon the political support generated by its national network to survive the budgetary attacks by opponents in Congress and most presidential administrations over the years. This support is exemplified by the enthusiastic turnout for passenger train inaugurations, as seen in this welcoming of the Sunset Limited to Pascagoula, Mississippi in March of 1993. (Photograph courtesy of Karl Zimmerman.)

VIA Rail Canada did better than Amtrak at keeping up older equipment and maintaining consistently high service standards, but these came at a growing cost during the 1980s. The Canadian government responded to VIA's cost increases by periodically pruning the route network, canceling trains such as the original Canadian, which ran through Banff, Alberta, as pictured here in January 1989. (Photograph courtesy of Karl Zimmerman.)

In recent years, privately owned luxury trains have shown that niche markets such as "land cruising" can be profitable. The American Orient Express, pictured here at the Grand Canyon in October 1997, voyages across the United States and Canada, re-creating a golden era of passenger railroading for those who can afford such a trip down memory lane. (Photograph courtesy of Karl Zimmerman.)

Another successful private train is the Rocky Mountaineer, which acquired and then improved upon a cruise train in the Canadian Rockies that VIA had launched before its radical downsizing in 1989. The Rocky Mountaineer now offers the only way to travel one of North America's most scenic rail routes between Banff, Lake Louise, and Vancouver. (Photograph courtesy of Karl Zimmerman.)

3·27·01

The political energies expended in Congressional trench warfare over Amtrak's fate have often attracted the attention of pundits and cartoonists. Tom Toles has consistently parodied politicians who decry Amtrak's commercial performance while simultaneously expressing concern about energy, the environment, and the limitations of other transportation modes. This cartoon appeared in March 2001, when skeptics were gearing up for another effort to attack Amtrak's government subsidy. (TOLES © The Buffalo News. Reprinted with permission of UNIVERSAL PRESS SYNDICATE. All rights reserved.)

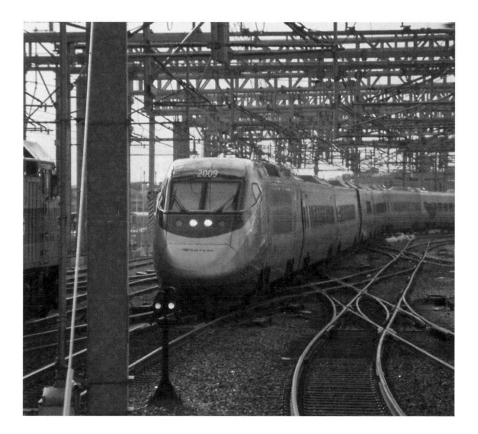

More than a generation after the TurboTrain experiment, a modern passenger train has finally arrived in Boston, Massachusetts. Pictured here is Amtrak's Acela Express, arriving at Boston's South Station on January 18, 2001. The Acela Express may accelerate the renewal of passenger trains in North America, if it reminds people of the link between supportive public policy, modern technology, innovative management techniques, and trains' profitability. (Photograph courtesy of Karl Zimmerman.)

(*Left*) Amtrak's southbound Acela Regional locomotive pauses at Metropark Station in New Jersey on August 5, 2001. (Author's collection.)

(*Below*) Amtrak's northbound Acela Express meets a southbound Acela Regional Train at Metropark Station in New Jersey on August 5, 2001. (Author's collection.)

treating the cost of "progressive maintenance" (basically the cost of regular maintenance and upgrading of its rolling stock being charged to a capital, rather than operating, budget) would add $567 million to the operating costs Amtrak would have to cover from revenues to be judged commercially self-sufficient by FY 2003.[37]

Amtrak criticized the council's analysis—quite vigorously—in an unsigned commentary and less acutely in a letter from the chair of Amtrak's Board to the chair of the Reform Council, both included in the report. The unsigned commentary resembles a legal brief in its rebuttal of the ARC's reported claims and interpretations, and its identification of adverse consequences arising from the council's actions. The commentary begins by accusing the Reform Council of a "fundamental misunderstanding about basic financial concepts related to Amtrak's business."[38] It goes on to claim that "the ARC and its counsel fundamentally confuse a statutory requirement regarding the 'adoption of uniform cost and accounting procedures' based on GAAP . . . with the requirement that Amtrak operate 'without federal operating grant funds appropriated for its benefit' beginning in Fiscal Year 2003."[39] The commentary identifies serious consequences from the council's alleged errors, insisting that "it is the Council's mandate to evaluate, not adversely influence, Amtrak's ability to achieve operating self-sufficiency." The commentary concludes that "the ARC has intentionally overlooked twenty-eight years of historical context for Amtrak, formulated conclusions that will hurt Amtrak's ability to achieve operating self-sufficiency, and most disturbingly, included in the report errors that assure that Amtrak will be disadvantaged in the financial markets."[40]

The letter from Amtrak's chair, then-Governor Tommy Thompson (R-Wis.), to the Reform Council's chair, Mr. Gil Carmichael, adopts a more conciliatory tone by emphasizing ongoing discussion and exchange of ideas regarding how to enhance Amtrak's business performance. Yet the letter does raise concerns about the public expressions of skepticism coming from Reform Council members, stating, "some people in the finance community have expressed concern about groups who claim to be 'aligned' with the ARC who have stated that the Council is proceeding down a path toward privatization." Gov. Thompson went on to state that "a few members of the Council have been quoted in the newspaper in ways that have been harmful to us. While I realize that you cannot control what members of the Council say publicly, I do believe that these comments are not in the best interest of our respective organizations."[41]

Its first annual report suggests that the ARC will resist endorsing the "financial facelift" approach to a commercial makeover that Amtrak and its supporters have been pursuing since 1997. Instead, the ARC sees its mission as assessing the prospects of more radical commercial surgery at Amtrak as a possible alternative to heading toward corporate euthanasia in 2003. The ARC's second annual report, released March 19, 2001, confirms the council's inclination to pursue fundamental change in the way Amtrak is organized and financed.[42] This report began by making a point that has been central to the analysis presented in this book, that "Amtrak, as it was created in the Rail Passenger Service Act of 1970, and as it exists today, is—through no fault of its Board or its management or its employees—inherently flawed."[43] ARC avoided blaming Amtrak's management, its board, or its employees by determining that "the barrier [to effective performance needed to attain the goals of the ARAA] is a flawed institutional structure that hampers effective planning and sound financial management, making it difficult for Amtrak to provide the efficient, reliable service that customers deserve."[44]

ARC has gone on to propose radical surgery on America's rail passenger enterprise that would disentangle the functions of a commercial carrier, an infrastructure owner and operator, and a rail passenger regulator and policy body into three distinct organizations. The carrier would be responsible for train operations and all related commercial activity such as mail and express. The infrastructure agency would take title to the Northeast Corridor as well as potential future rail passenger corridors whose infrastructure would be developed with federal, and perhaps state, funding. And the regulatory and policy agency would apply a unified, and unifying, administrative capacity to the oversight and policy analysis responsibilities that are currently distributed among Amtrak, the Federal Railroad Administration, the Department of Transportation's Inspector General, and other special purpose bodies like the ARC itself. Five options were presented that envisioned greater or lesser roles for private participation and more or less involvement by state governments in this new triumvirate of rail passenger related entities.

These options can be seen as "trial balloons" in ARC's potential preparation of a reorganization plan if Amtrak failed to meet its self-sufficiency target. While reactions to these proposals will accumulate during the course of 2001, and doubtless influence ARC's future work, the first shots taken at all five trial balloons were fired by Amtrak. Writing on behalf of Amtrak's Board of Directors, President George Warrington told ARC Chair Gil Carmichael: "We are disappointed by the policy options presented. All of the council's five options would create a new federal bureaucracy to manage the passenger rail system—an idea that runs against the trend of recent history and the will of Congress. These policy options would increase the costs and complexity of managing the system without any gains in commercial viability and without addressing the underlying policy questions."⁴⁵

Warrington expressed concern that "the ARC's current philosophical approach would add layers of governmental bureaucracy and associated tax-payer costs that complicate and delay, rather than resolve, Amtrak's dilemma." This debate over how far to go in reorganizing Amtrak is just beginning to warm up. Its outcome would at least partly depend on whether the ARC ever winds up submitting a formal restructuring plan to Congress. The other government watchdogs that have been assigned a role in overseeing Amtrak's commercial transition are sounding their own notes of caution about the prospects of achieving self-sufficiency by 2002, making the odds of a formal ARC restructuring being tabled in Congress more than a long shot.

5.7. Government Watchdogs Voice Their Concerns and Amtrak Quietly Acknowledges Them

The General Accounting Office (GAO), the U.S. government's nonpartisan and independent financial assessment agency, presented testimony to the Senate's Commerce, Science and Transportation Committee on September 26, 2000, ominously entitled "Decisions on the Future of Intercity Passenger Rail Are Approaching." Typical of this agency's disposition to confront problems (and problematic policy) head on, the GAO's report warned Congress and the rail policy community as a whole that Amtrak's commercial renewal effort risked falling short because of policy issues that government had left unresolved.

While accepting Amtrak supporters' definition of appropriate accounting categories and methods, the GAO concluded that the corporation still faced a considerable challenge, stating: "To become operationally self-sufficient by 2002—that is to reduce its budget gap to no more than the amount of excess Railroad Retirement Tax Act payments—Amtrak will have to reduce its budget gap by an additional $287 million over what it was in fiscal year 1999. This is nearly four times the reduction that Amtrak made in the last 5 years."⁴⁶

Amtrak's chances of meeting this target were judged to be at risk because of both cost and revenue problems. While Amtrak had "spent money to make money, it has realized very little benefit for the expenditures it has made." A key problem is that "Amtrak's labor costs have increased since 1995 about 10 percent above the rate of inflation."⁴⁷ Amtrak's ambitious business development forecasts are not keeping pace with the legislated timetable for self-sufficiency. "Nearly three-quarters ($1.4 billion) of the net financial benefits that Amtrak expects to achieve from 2000 through 2004 have either not yet been identified or are based on activities that Amtrak has not yet fully implemented. Amtrak officials told us they are in the process of defining specific actions associated with these initiatives but agreed they had not yet been fully defined."[48]

The report also validated Amtrak's claim that considerable capital needs existed beyond those that would be funded through the $2.2 billion provided by the TRA noting, "Amtrak's identified capital investments will exceed levels of federal capital funds by nearly $2 billion over the 2001 through 2004 period."[49] The GAO pointed out that if Amtrak succeeds commercially, even more federal funding would be needed to meet the capital and "excess" railroad retirement costs which would both rise with a growing intercity rail passenger system. While no estimate was made of railroad retirement increases, estimates of new capital range upwards of $9 billion in the medium term.[50] The GAO also pointed out that if Amtrak failed to meet the self-sufficiency target, both the liquidation plan it would draw up and the ARC's restructuring plan would present Congress with proposals in which "the nation's intercity passenger rail service could have a considerably different look."[51]

For all these reasons, the GAO concluded that Congress could not assume that Amtrak's own commercial initiatives, coupled with the legislative and financial reforms passed in 1997, would be likely to achieve operating self-sufficiency for intercity passenger trains without further policymaking. The GAO suggested that "it is not too early to begin considering a long-term vision for Amtrak and intercity passenger rail and how this vision should be structured." In other words, the GAO reminded Congress that the policy stalemate defining Amtrak's economic and political struggles since 1971 was far from over, continued to create a drag on the corporation's commercial prospects, and could not be expected to resolve itself.

The Department of Transportation's inspector general (DOT-IG) has also voiced concern over Amtrak's likely financial position in 2002. In another legislated overview of Amtrak's performance, entitled "2000 Assessment of Amtrak's Performance and Financial Requirements," the DOT-IG depicts an organization that is placing its operational integrity at risk in a gamble to build new ridership and revenues. Like the GAO, the DOT-IG accepted the less stringent accounting definition of commercial self-sufficiency that rail passenger supporters have advocated, noting "Amtrak's attainment of self-sufficiency, however, does not rest on the size of its operating loss . . . [because] the true indicator of operating self-sufficiency is Amtrak's cash loss."[52]

DOT-IG found that Amtrak's ridership and revenues had been growing strongly since 1996, with 1999 revenues 21 percent above those in 1995 and the highest in the corporation's history. But Amtrak's costs increased by 6.9 percent in 1999, with rising expenditure on labor, depreciation, and fuel. More ominously, Amtrak's operating loss was $16 million greater than planned for the first nine months of 2000 and its cash loss (the *de minimus* measure of operating self-sufficiency) was $22 million worse than planned. DOT-IG noted how new contracts had boosted labor costs by $248 million above and beyond the cost-of-living increases that were built into contracts. The report emphasized that "in order to hold down future cost growth, it is imperative that Amtrak negotiate even more aggressive productivity increases."[53]

When the DOT-IG reviewed Amtrak's 2000–2004 Strategic Business Plan, it identified $1.44 billion in net results that could not be supported by current assumptions and/or projections. If nothing were done to address these shortcomings, DOT-IG predicted that Amtrak's unfunded cash loss, the amount between results and the politically accepted commercial self-sufficiency target, would amount to $359 million in 2002 and $351 million in 2003. If corrective actions were not taken, DOT-IG saw the liquidation and restructure provisions of ARAA coming into play in 2002.

To avoid this outcome, DOT-IG counseled taking prompt and effective action to fill three major financial "holes" in Amtrak's business plan between 2000 and 2004. These centered on significant, but as yet undefined, needs for (1) cost reduction, (2) attainment of the ambitious passenger revenue growth results associated with the introduction of Acela high-speed train service in the Northeast, and (3) augmentation of the pace of developing mail and express business. A total of $737 million in undefined management actions to trim expenses represented the largest of these three holes in Amtrak's business plan. Nearly all of these actions fell into the category of expense reductions. Basically, these actions would involve further cutting costs to close the gap between all of Amtrak's previously identified cost control opportunities and the remaining federal operating subsidies that had to be eliminated. The DOT-IG suggested that, given Amtrak's high labor costs, filling this large hole would demand revisiting the economic relationship between Amtrak and its workforce.

While Amtrak had identified $59 million in expense reductions to close its budget gap in 2000, the 2001–2003 budget years would require reductions of $180 million each, three times the level of cost savings to date. The NEC and Intercity Business Units were identified as the corporate components that would have to produce the bulk of these new expense reductions. The report stated that if plans to achieve these major expense reductions were not well developed in the 2001 business plan, "we have strong doubts about Amtrak's ability to achieve commercial self-sufficiency in 2003."[54]

On the income side of the ledger, $304 million in passenger revenues was judged at risk of not materializing during the life of the business plan. While the DOT-IG judged Amtrak's revenue problems to be "less troublesome" than its expense problem, the projected revenue growth arising from the launch of Acela was deemed too optimistic. Part of the DOT-IG's caution arose from the uncertainty of when the Acela train would attain a full operational schedule. The longer the delay in launching a full service frequency, the later that Acela's revenue impacts would be felt.

But whenever the Acela attained a full service level in the Northeast, Amtrak's estimates of new ridership on the premium fare Acela Express were judged to be over-optimistic by 15 percent.[55] In other words, DOT-IG questioned whether as much of the Northeast Corridor's ridership growth would gravitate to the most expensive, and profitable, train services as Amtrak had predicted. The report estimated that less expensive (and profitable) Acela Regional trains would gain 2.5 percent more of this new business than Amtrak had forecast, translating into a 17 percent lower estimate of Acela Express ticket revenues. Projected revenue of $179 million from mail and express was also judged to be doubtful due to the slower than projected growth of this business. While DOT-IG agreed with Amtrak's projected outcome for mail and express business volumes and revenues by 2004, it judged that "Amtrak's projections between 2000 and 2002 are overly ambitious, given its historical rate of growth in these businesses."[56] Amtrak's projections were based on, among other things, obtaining permission from the freight railroads to extend the length of its trains beyond a current thirty-car limit to enable more mail and express business. The report noted that its mail and express "projections are somewhat more conservative than Amtrak's because Amtrak has historically projected growth rates that are higher than it has been able to realize."[57] The DOT-IG did endorse Amtrak's market based network analysis (MBNA) as an improvement in the corporation's analytical ability to optimize both services and their positive contribution to the company's bottom line. While pointing out opportunities for further refinement, the DOT-IG concurred that the MBNA would enable Amtrak to make the most of its network growth strategy.

Like GAO, the DOT-IG voiced concern at Amtrak's capital needs, both in terms of amounts and priorities, stating, "With a limited amount of capital funding balanced against a mandate to achieve commercial self-sufficiency, Amtrak's goal of investing sufficiently to preserve the physical integrity of the system is often at odds with making the kinds of investments necessary to improve ridership and revenues."[58] Overall, the report highlighted how the conflict between trying to achieve commercial self-sufficiency by whatever means necessary, and the responsibility of reinvesting in maintaining a safe and reliable rail passenger operation was being played out in Amtrak's capital budgeting, noting: "Amtrak's capital approval process favors projects that carry high-return-on-investment potential. Although these investments fall outside the scope of what Amtrak needs, minimally, to continue operations through 2003, Amtrak believes that without such investments, it will not be able to generate sufficient revenues to survive beyond 2002 when it must, by law, operate without Federal operating assistance. We agree that these projects are important to Amtrak's financial growth, but do not believe they should be funded at the expense of the minimum investments necessary to maintain safe, reliable operation of the railroad."[59] Deferring capital investment in maintaining a state-of-good-repair was judged to be already taking a toll, in terms of reduced reliability on the Northeast Corridor, the very region where Amtrak was counting on ridership and revenue growth to boost its bottom line.

The DOT-IG therefore recommended that Amtrak reprogram its capital expenditures from the Taxpayer Relief Act to meet minimum needs before investing in new revenue-enhancing projects. The DOT-IG also recommended that Amtrak prepare a long-term capital plan that would document the full costs needed to support both a well-maintained and growing rail passenger network in the United States. While Amtrak has embarked upon developing such a long-range capital plan, one current reality appears little changed from the past. Amtrak does not have enough capital resources to both meet its minimum maintenance needs and grow its business to achieve commercial self-sufficiency in 2003. As a result, the pressure on management to defer maintenance until after this "milestone" is achieved is overwhelming. This apparent hope that future federal capital investment would be forthcoming after commercial self-sufficiency is realized is reflected in Amtrak's latest corporate planning.

Amtrak's strategic business plan for FY 2001–2005 acknowledges these government watchdogs' warnings by making an impassioned plea for federal intervention to dramatically increase capital spending on intercity passenger trains. While still identifying commercial achievements that will arise from both growth in revenues and partnerships with other entities, this plan emphasizes a huge infusion of federal funds as being key to maintaining the viability of America's intercity passenger rail service. Less than two years before its legislatively mandated commercial self-sufficiency, Amtrak has extended the boldness of its internal reinvention efforts to a call for massive government investment in the rail passenger mode. Amtrak's plan proposes devoting 2.5% of U.S. federal transportation spending, approximately $1.5 billion per year, over twenty years to intercity passenger rail capital investment.[60] Over the first five years, $973 million annually would go to renewing existing rail passenger operations. Afterward, yearly expenditures on renewal and growth would balance out at $750 million.

While it emphasizes capital investment, Amtrak's latest business plan also addresses operating results and goals. Here the news is less positive than before. Amtrak defers the attainment of commercial self-sufficiency from 2002 to 2003, citing a number of adverse business factors.[61] The late deployment of Acela Express trains in the Northeast Corridor is acknowledged to have cost Amtrak over $150 million in projected revenue for 2000. Mail and Express revenue is also growing more slowly than projected, just as the DOT-IG had predicted. But while cutting $36 million from the bottom-line contribution that Mail and Express is projected make in 2001, Amtrak's estimate of $181 million in total revenue remains ahead of the DOT-IG's projection, which is just over $150 million for 2001. A new expense management strategy is proposed, and Amtrak states that it has reduced the amount of undefined management cost containment actions from $759 million to $125 million. The plan links capital needs and operating challenges by stating, somewhat ominously, that "If Amtrak's federal capital grant does not at least meet the authorized level in FY02, Amtrak will be required to restructure the scope of its capital intensive business."[62]

In 2001, Amtrak also issued a more complete disclosure of its financial position in conjunction with a $111 million bond issue to fund a state-of-the-art electrical sub-station at New Richmond, Pennsylvania. In a bond prospectus released by the Pennsylvania Economic Development Financing Authority, Amtrak acknowledged that it "has not achieved certain goals set forth in its [past] Business Plans" and that if the company was "unable to achieve one or more goals set forth in the Fiscal Year 2001 Business Plan . . . its ability to achieve and sustain operational self-sufficiency may be adversely affected."[63] Chief among the missed goals was the delayed introduction of Acela Express, which was expected to reduce Amtrak's "budget result" by $119 million in 2001. Northeast Corridor ticket revenue would be reduced by $83 million, but Amtrak also acknowledged that it was experiencing difficulty in collecting "liquidated damages" from the Acela Express manufacturer for late delivery of these trains. This financial disclosure statement also stated that if any depreciation of assets were included in operating expenses, as the ARC had proposed, then Amtrak would not be able to meet the commercial self-sufficiency test in 2003.[64] The disclosure repeated and slightly expanded upon a key point of the business plan, stating, "if the amount of the federal capital appropriation does not at least equal $955 million for Fiscal Year 2002, Amtrak will be required to restructure the scope of its business."[65]

Taken together, the ARC's, GAO's, and DOT-IG's recent assessments of Amtrak's performance and prospects at the height of its efforts to meet the challenge laid down by the ARAA reveal a policy landscape filled with familiar constraints on commercial renewal. Amtrak's most recent financial analysis echoes these concerns and makes it clear that self-sufficiency still depends on political decisions about how to measure and allocate public support for passenger trains. Making these decisions raises age-old questions. What criteria should be applied to measuring the success of America's rail passenger performance? How should the costs of restructuring passenger train operations be distributed (i.e., between rail labor versus taxpayers, or among different regions of the United States)? And what more needs to be said and done to enable the passenger train to take up a legitimate place in the nation's transportation system? Amtrak's reinvention from within has not resolved the political differences on these issues, and appears unlikely to do so.

Since 1998, Amtrak has struggled to meet a formidable challenge—developing an increasingly sophisticated and ambitious repertoire of business tools to help grow revenues and ridership in the search for commercial self-sufficiency before 2003. These efforts aim to satisfy the requirements of the Amtrak Reform and Accountability Act, which codified the Claytor commitment into a "litmus test" for subsequent political legitimacy. Although supporters and skeptics are little closer to being united on the place of passenger trains in America's twenty-first-century transportation system, they now share a common focus on the commercial renewal efforts that Amtrak is pursuing with increasing vigor.

During this time of high-stakes repositioning of America's public passenger train operator, we are likely to see the beginning, not the end, of serious policy deliberations over what America's objectives and goals for intercity passenger rail should be in the twenty-first century. Somewhat obscured by Amtrak's current initiatives and innovations is the fact that difficult policy choices await whatever outcome emerges in 2002. There is little question that Amtrak's success, or failure, in becoming commercially self-sufficient by 2003 will be a major influence on the coming round of policy debate. As we have seen, this market test has always been used by rail passenger skeptics for relegating Amtrak to the margins of American transportation policy.

Thus, if Amtrak were to pass its market test, one should not underestimate the impact this would have on legitimating both the company, and the rail mode in general, as a fully functional component of America's transportation system. Whether or not Amtrak succeeds, the new efforts that emerge to close the gap between its current commercial performance, projected improvements, and the additional achievements that both GAO and DOT now claim are needed to eliminate an unfunded cash loss by 2003 will impact the terms of the subsequent rail passenger policy debate. Without being able to predict that outcome, in part because the struggle to move the finish line for attaining self-sufficiency will certainly intensify, it is worth considering four sources of change that might boost Amtrak's performance in the homestretch of this race, and what these might contribute to the subsequent debate over where to go with rail passenger policy beyond 2002.

5.8. Four Sources of Potential Success in Amtrak's Renewal Effort

In considering these further boosts to Amtrak's performance, one must recognize that both economic and political factors will play important roles in either enabling, or constraining, whatever might emerge to close Amtrak's commercial gap in the homestretch to self-sufficiency. It is also important to realize that, over the years, Amtrak's prospects have often been greatly influenced by external factors beyond the control of any business plan or management initiative. Looked at this way, it appears that the most significant boosts to Amtrak's attaining commercial self-sufficiency could arise from any combination of restructured labor relations, new partnerships with state governments, continued energy price increases, and public recognition of the value of a sustainable transportation system. The first two outcomes represent economic and political initiatives that Amtrak is, or will be, actively pursuing. The latter two issues represent larger economic and political events that could significantly influence Amtrak's prospects. Each of these "change drivers" deserves some attention.

When it comes to improving its own economic fortunes, all indicators suggest that Amtrak's biggest opportunity emerges from cost reduction in general, and labor savings in particular. Labor costs are a big, and growing, part of Amtrak's budget. Since 1971, Amtrak's employees have done rather well in moderating the pressures for reduced costs and higher productivity that have impacted America's transportation workforce as a whole. At one extreme, many workers at Eastern Airlines and Pan American Airways, both of which appeared much more commercially robust than Amtrak in 1971, have seen their companies go under and their jobs vanish. Dozens of new air carriers have come and gone since airline deregulation began in 1979. And in the bus industry, many employees of Continental Trailways lost their jobs following the carrier's acquisition by Greyhound in 1987.[66] Greyhound workers were not immune from competition despite winning the battle against Trailways, with their employer going into receivership in June 1990, in the midst of a long and bitter strike by drivers. Before that strike, Greyhound employed 8,000 drivers, but by the time a new contract was finally signed in 1993, just 3,300 drivers were working for that carrier.[67]

Workers at established air and bus carriers have also seen the erosion of wages and working conditions achieved under collective agreements negotiated prior to deregulation. Two-tier wage structures, which pay new employees a fraction of their more senior colleagues' wage scale, have become a common way of implementing this transition to lower real wages and higher productivity. When such arrangements were not negotiated "voluntarily," some carriers took more extreme actions to break with past practices. Continental Airlines went into bankruptcy in 1983. During the ensuing reorganization, long-established contracts were scrapped and unions had to negotiate from a "clean slate."

Across the board, America's transportation workers make a greater contribution to their companies' bottom line, through a combination of lower wages and higher productivity, than was the case prior to deregulation and the ensuing intense competition. Amtrak's workforce may not feel especially privileged, but when compared to the workers at competing carriers they appear well off. These include wholly or partially non-unionized, start-up air carriers, like Legend or Jet Blue, whose low fares compete directly with Amtrak's corridor services and independent truckers who haul much of the express that Amtrak seeks to bring aboard its long distance trains.

Amtrak's most recent contract proves that its unions can still hold out for and win further gains, even though these might widen the gap between Amtrak's labor costs and those of its competitors. But since that conflict, and the resulting leadership change, Amtrak's new CEO has presided over innovations in labor relations that could facilitate a new relationship between Amtrak and its workforce. By introducing incentives that seek to align workers' objectives with the corporate mission of commercial success and emphasizing customer-focused training, George Warrington has opened a door to more fundamental change in the traditional, adversarial, bargaining relationship between Amtrak and its workforce.

Overcoming a century of economic conflict, at times yielding open warfare, between railroads and their workers will not be easy and would require some considerable ingenuity. But innovations toward that end are at least conceivable within Amtrak's ongoing efforts to empower its workers. These would likely have to expand into new models of cooperative workplace governance, and even more ambitious incentive plans to share the gains of commercial self-sufficiency. While this prospect might seem far-fetched, one should not discount the possibility for a new labor paradigm. If UPS and United Airlines can bridge the long-standing gulf between labor and management in large and well established carriers, then it is not impossible for Amtrak to do so.

If Amtrak and its workforce succeeded in launching a new relationship that could be shown to have helped close the gap to commercial self-sufficiency by 2003, then organized labor would share in both the credibility and legitimacy gains of the passenger train's triumph. Instead of being challenged by skeptics as self-interested parties, labor representatives could participate in the coming development of rail passenger policy as key enablers of commercial renewal. For its part, an Amtrak that demonstrated both effective management and a commitment to success among its workforce would be likely to attain greater recognition in American transportation policy.

Another source of momentum in Amtrak's approach to self-sufficiency could arise from the intergovernmental partnerships that are now being pursued. Just as labor relations hold the key to unlocking some of Amtrak's most immediate economic gains, so does a closer relationship with state governments promise the greatest chance of immediately increasing political support for the passenger train's playing a more important role in American transportation. During thirty years of "inside the beltway" political battles over every aspect of its future, Amtrak and its supporters have done all that they can to advance the passenger train's fortunes through the action of national government. What has remained largely untapped is the deep reservoir of political engagement by states in national transportation programs, as evidenced by the extensive transfers from federal trust funds to expenditures on state highways, mass transit, and airports.

Amtrak's network growth strategy targets state governments as major partners in the development of rail passenger expansion in the Pacific Northwest, the Midwest, and the Southeast. This builds upon, and would likely further deepen, the existing state partnerships for major rail passenger renewal efforts in California, New York, Michigan, and Illinois. A recent example of such efforts is the "California Passenger Rail System 20-Year Improvement Plan," produced by Amtrak West in partnership with state and regional governments.[68] This report calls for a $10.1 billion investment program that would yield a 300 percent growth in intercity rail ridership by expanding service, adding equipment, and upgrading infrastructure over the coming two decades. Should implementing such plans become the norm, and should other state governments rise to the occasion and commit significant matching funds for infrastructure improvement, a "critical mass" of state support for intercity passenger rail could help tip the balance toward commercial self-sufficiency.

While the new revenues from state-sponsored passenger trains would be unlikely to eliminate Amtrak's cash loss in themselves, the political value of both wider and deeper state financial commitment in the passenger train's future would be considerable. If Amtrak were to pass its market test with a critical mass of state engagement, then states would be encouraged to share in the credit for that achievement. And as a result, they would also be likely to play a more active role in the subsequent policy deliberations, raising the opportunity to "federalize" future rail passenger policy to adopt the funding and administrative partnerships that have proven so successful for other modes. And if Amtrak were to fall short of commercial self-sufficiency by 2003, the participation of state governments in projects that could be jeopardized by subsequent restructuring or liquidation could facilitate some sort of dispensation from, or adjustment of, the terms for this market test as set out by the ARAA.

Not all of Amtrak's economic opportunities can be created by its management, workforce, or business partners. Indeed, some of the bigger boosts to Amtrak's commercial success could come from events largely beyond its control. Among the economic circumstances that shape Amtrak's performance, the cost of energy (oil, in particular) makes the largest difference in ridership and revenues. Rising oil prices have traditionally been very good news for Amtrak because they translate into higher pump prices for gasoline and kerosene (jet fuel). Price shocks at the gas pumps and in air fares gave Amtrak much-needed boosts in 1973, and again in 1979, times when skeptics were gaining ground in their efforts to cut Amtrak back. Thus, whenever the price of oil tops $30 per barrel, the higher its price climbs, the more that the inherent energy efficiency of trains will contribute to enhancing Amtrak's bottom line. Travelers on "low fare" airlines are quite price sensitive, and Amtrak's services in the Southeast, Midwest, and California, in particular, could gain new riders from a modal shift produced by fewer bargain basement airfares. And in the Northeast, Acela's debut would be further strengthened by a rise in already high airfares between Boston, New York, and Washington.

There is good reason to suppose that higher oil prices are more than a short-term aberration. A number of respected energy researchers, along with the International Energy Agency, have concluded that the world is approaching the end of its "cheap oil" supply. Their analyses are summarized in the *Sustainable Transportation Monitor #2*, which was among the first transportation research sources to publicize this trend break.[69] Demand for conventional oil is outstripping supply, fueling the price climb that began in February 1999. While untapped conventional oil reserves can be brought into production, much of this forthcoming supply will be derived from areas where accessibility and environmental risk management will boost production costs. Nonconventional oil sources (e.g., tar sands, shale oil) will be even more expensive to refine, with production costs that increase even more steeply than conventional oil, due to the environmental and energy costs of large scale extraction. Over time, the cost of producing unconventional oil will add significantly to prices.

Recent spikes in the price of other energy sources, most notably natural gas, along with the electric utility crisis in California, have served to place energy policy high on the public policy agenda.[70] In response to this turmoil, the Bush administration has identified creating a national energy policy as a priority for the United States. While a White House spokesman has said that "the President sees an imbalance between energy supply and demand, which is best met by boosting supply," the environmental and economic costs of pursuing a supply-side approach to energy policy are bound to be challenged by advocates of conservation and greater energy efficiency.[71] Such national debates on energy policy, which have not occurred in the United States since the early 1980s, could provide rail passenger advocates with another opportunity to advance their position.

In the medium term, these significant and fundamental changes in the economics of energy are likely to enhance a long-discounted technological attribute of passenger trains, their ability to provide high-speed intercity transportation using electric traction (which can be powered by any energy source feeding a power grid). As the only intercity mode capable of adopting "off the shelf" electric traction technology, passenger trains offer one of the few alternatives to oil as a transportation energy source. Not only can they provide intercity mobility using less energy, trains can also deliver that mobility from a wide array of energy sources such as wind and hydroelectric power.

The faster and further that oil prices rise, the higher that energy policy will rise on the U.S. government's agenda. If Amtrak were to attain commercial self-sufficiency on the crest of a wave of riders and revenue that materialized because cars and planes got priced out of some intercity travelers' budgets, passenger trains would be very well positioned in the ensuing debate over future policy options. Americans would be more likely to acknowledge, and act upon, the passenger train's value when its energy efficiency appears to translate directly into an attractive intercity mobility alternative to higher priced competitors.

Another larger issue that Americans might come to face sooner, rather than later, is the external cost generated by current energy- and land-intensive means of mobility. Aircraft and automobiles are only "affordable" when many of their environmental and social impacts are not factored into the price of a ticket, or a tank of gas. Congestion on highways and in and around busy airports is just one component of this unpriced cost, but traffic-choked highways and airports may already be playing a role in some of Amtrak's recent ridership growth. Amtrak management appears to be emphasizing the train's capacity for delivering "quality time" in motion, as opposed to the stressful and unpredictable time spent at airports or on the highways surrounding many major metropolitan areas. Given the emergence of new technologies that enhance the capacity for work, shopping, and leisure-related communication and the constraints of fully utilizing these technologies while driving or flying, Amtrak could position the passenger train way ahead of its competitors in providing passengers with the fullest range of information-age amenities.

Should Amtrak succeed in developing its credibility as an antidote for congestion, even if only in certain places like the Northeast, the train's reputation for adding value to both users and communities could be enhanced at a time when Americans begin looking at more of the costs generated by air and highway travel. Climate change and "smart growth" are two policy challenges that Americans appear open to considering these days. Climate change, also known as "global warming," is a policy problem that is increasingly recognized by the American population.

Krosnick and Visser report that polling conducted by the Ohio State University Survey Research Unit in the autumn of 1997 and the winter of 1998 revealed that "large majorities of the country believed in the existence of global warming and believed that it would have undesirable consequences."[72] They also concluded that "people wanted governments, businesses, and ordinary people to do quite a bit to combat global warming but believed that very little was being done." A 1999 telephone survey conducted by the Mellman Group for the National Environmental Trust asked 1,000 adult Americans, "How important is it for the United States to take action now to reduce its emissions of gases like carbon dioxide that cause global warming. . . ?"[73] Support was quite strong, with 58 percent rating such action very important and 26 percent rating it somewhat important. Only 6 percent felt that action was very unimportant and 5 percent felt it was somewhat unimportant, with 6 percent unsure. In the distribution of public opinion, this survey found that "majorities of women (52 percent), voters under 50 (54 percent), and those living in the Northeast (61 percent) and West (52 percent) agree that speaking out on global warming is the action of a forward-thinking candidate."[74]

The collapse of negotiations on implementing the United Nation's Framework Convention on Climate Change, also known as the "Kyoto Protocol," in November 2000, followed by the arrival of George W. Bush in the White House would appear to leave public opinion and elite leadership out of sync on climate change policy. But recent reports suggest that the Bush administration may seek to promote its own policy alternative to addressing global warming that embraces market mechanisms, such as emissions trading. The environmental equivalent of a "Nixon to China move" is being urged upon the president by some in America's business community who see the sinking of the Kyoto Protocol as creating an opportunity to assert American influence.[75] Such market mechanisms could stimulate investment in zero- or low-emission rail passenger services, both in the United States and abroad.

Public support for smart growth approaches to transportation planning and development is also apparent. Mondale cites a 1999 survey conducted by the University of Minnesota Center for Survey Research which found that 85 percent of respondents in the Minneapolis–St. Paul metropolitan area agreed with the idea that neighborhoods should be walkable and transit oriented. More than 47 percent of these respondents chose adding rail and bus transit as their preferred solution to dealing with traffic congestion, as opposed to 18 percent who preferred building more roads.[76] These findings were echoed by a national survey on growth and land development conducted by Belden, Russonello & Stewart Research and Communications in September 2000. Of this representative sample of 1,007 Americans age eighteen or older, 47 percent identified public transport (including rail) as the solution for reducing traffic in their states, compared to 21 percent who chose road building.[77]

Any serious effort to address such problems would have to include transportation policy, and any transportation policy that seeks to reduce greenhouse gas emissions and sprawling development would be likely to assign a higher value to the passenger train's technical and socioeconomic attributes than it does to those of other modes. For the most part, Amtrak's struggle has only attracted limited attention and support from America's "Greens," perhaps because they have not recognized the train's potential for contributing to sustainable development in their own back yard. Bringing sustainable transportation advocates into the rail policy community in time for the debates over future options could be timely.

5.9. Financial Reckoning Will Inevitably Trigger Policy Reckoning

As Amtrak's day of reckoning approaches, the specific contribution that new initiatives and modes of participation will make to both the bottom line and the dynamism of the rail passenger policy community will become more apparent. What will also become obvious is that the ARAA has established a legislative framework that is much more explicit, although still open to interpretation, regarding what to do in the event of policy failure (e.g., Amtrak's inability to eliminate its unfunded cash loss by 2003) than it is about dealing with policy success. But even these clearer directives on addressing Amtrak's failure will trigger intensive policy deliberations and debate.

The ARAA sets out the procedures for policy development, should Amtrak fail to meet its target. But it would be naive to assume that the rail passenger policy community could focus on an "orderly" restructuring of the nation's sole intercity rail carrier, let alone consider its liquidation, without a full-blown, "knock down–drag out" policy debate over the core issues that have divided passenger train supporters and skeptics for the better part of half a century. And should Amtrak succeed in eliminating its unfunded cash loss in 2002, all indications point to the need for new policies to sustain its success as a viable enterprise. The DOT-IG has questioned the future reliability and possible safety of rail passenger operations as a result of Amtrak's current emphasis on revenue-enhancing capital investment to the neglect of minimum maintenance needs. Furthermore, the railroad retirement contributions now funded by Congress could be increased by any reduction of Amtrak's workforce, one option in meeting the aggressive expense reduction urged by the GAO and DOT-IG.

Under any scenario, policy options for the future of America's rail passenger operations appear likely to return to the forefront of government's agenda in 2002–2003. What transpires in the home stretch of Amtrak's effort to eliminate its dependence upon federal operating subsidies will undoubtedly affect the way in which such a debate begins, but where that debate winds up is another matter. The same questions that have bedeviled prior efforts to deal with America's passenger train problem are certain to be on the agenda. These include designing an appropriate means of sponsoring rail passenger infrastructure and establishing an appropriate level of financing for that commitment. They also include finding an effective intergovernmental relationship between Washington, states, and local governments that can deal with rail passenger opportunities akin to roads, transit, and aviation modes.

In sum, no matter what Amtrak accomplishes between now and its day of reckoning, the passenger train's future will demand choosing among policy options that have either deadlocked elected officials or otherwise deterred them from acting to create a workable policy framework that could support widespread renewal. The concluding chapter provides a guide to some of the principal policy options that supporters and skeptics will return to face, in the hope that some of the circumstances considered above will enable a new departure from their long-standing impasse.

Chapter 6

Setting Up the New Model Railroad in North America

Bringing Passenger Trains into a Transportation Policy for the Twenty-First Century

Transportation analysts in general, and rail passenger specialists in particular, have not posted a track record of predicting the future that should inspire much confidence. For at least half a century, visions about travelers taking to the skies in personal flying machines,[1] or coupling their vehicles together to form "personal rapid transit,"[2] have been presented as being just around the corner. Those futurists whose prognostications made it into the popular media assured people that by the twenty-first century, steel wheels on steel rails would give way to ultra-high-speed vehicles floating along thanks to magnetic levitation[3] or giant turbines that would produce immense cushions of air.[4] But in North America, at any rate, the greatest air flow associated with passenger trains has been generated by political debates over how, or even if, technology and service patterns originating in the nineteenth century should be kept going to offer communities as diverse as Seattle and Wolf Point, Montana, or Calgary and Moose Jaw, Saskatchewan, the option of travel by rail.

This discussion looks to the future, but it avoids the temptations and pitfalls arising from forecasting based upon what technology could enable, or how tomorrow's travel demands might evolve. Instead of following these notoriously unreliable guides to charting the passenger train's future, this concluding chapter directs its effort to assessing the intervening, and in many ways determining, stage of new policy options that could tip the balance between the passenger train's nineteenth- and twenty-first-century attributes. Unlike the ultramodern visions that emerge from futurists, these options for 2003 and beyond will build upon very familiar issues concerning the railroad's relationship to government, to the customers and communities it serves, and to other transport modes.

Whatever commercial accomplishments that Amtrak and VIA Rail achieve in the next few years, their long-run success will depend upon policy changes that can only come from going back to the drawing board of how passenger railroading should be organized. In both Canada and the United States, passenger trains will have made it into the twenty-first century, in spite of, rather than because of, effective public policy. Government initiatives to revisit, and overcome, the political impasse that has blocked development of a workable rail passenger policy represent the most important opportunity for achieving the passenger train's potential. The attention to policy constraints arising from rail passenger renewal efforts on both sides of the border will set the stage for a significant opportunity to resolve the stalemate that has bedeviled these efforts over the past three decades.

If Amtrak attains (or is declared to have attained) self-sufficiency, that accomplishment will serve to underscore the need for policy reforms that can translate such a singular achievement into ongoing viability. And if Amtrak falls short, the narrowing gap between its enhanced commercial performance and the threshold of economic viability would highlight the constraints that existing policy places in the way of attaining that legitimacy. So too with VIA's more modest performance enhancements. Even these limited investments in upgrading Canada's passenger trains offer the promise of generating some form of payoff in VIA's bottom line. In other words, whatever the actual performance that Amtrak and VIA post over the next few years, attention will be focused on interpreting these results as an indicator of the passenger train's long-term prospects in North America. And in confronting the outcomes of current renewal initiatives, it will be impossible for all but the most ardent dissenters in the rail policy community to deny that existing policy constraints limit passenger rail's performance. As a result, the contribution that improved rail passenger policy could make to twenty-first-century mobility will once again be up for consideration. And in the course of the subsequent policy debates, the North American passenger train's future will certainly be open for improvement.

6.1. Three Domains of Decline
That Future Policy Must Target

This chapter presents a framework that can, hopefully, guide such deliberations to a more productive outcome than the false starts and futile compromises that have been the norm in North America's rail passenger policy over the past thirty years. Before weighing the policy options which could empower a truly successful renewal, it is worth highlighting the three major failings that future rail passenger policy will need to address.

First, both Amtrak and VIA are *institutionally excluded* from the key policy structures and practices that underpin effective commercial performance of North American transportation. Publicly organized administration, planning, regulation, and finance combine to support and sustain the air and road networks that enable carriers to earn money and individuals to get where they are going by using these modes. Amtrak and VIA must make do with piecemeal administrative and financial arrangements that leave them dependent upon the "kindness of strangers." These benefactors include railroads selling access to their infrastructure at prices below its opportunity cost and political champions in Congress or cabinet who cajole their colleagues into supporting annual appropriations from the public purse. The motivation behind both forms of support can be more or less altruistic, shifting along with the debate regarding whether passenger trains should continue to be wards of the state. No airline or bus carrier doing business in this policy framework would perform any better than Amtrak or VIA has done over the years.

The biggest constraint on improvement is the necessity of action beyond the rail policy community occurring *in parallel with* the innovation from within that has recently emerged. One reason why Amtrak and VIA have been left to make good with half-measures (or less) compared to the administrative and financial arrangements that support the development of air and road transport is that access to these opportunities was intentionally denied. American transportation trust funds at both the national and state levels had legal, and in some cases constitutional, restrictions that prohibit expenditure on passenger rail. And the Canadian constitutional assignment of national railway policy to Ottawa's jurisdiction was interpreted by provinces as excluding them from any involvement in, or responsibility for, the future of interprovincial passenger trains. Rail's formal institutional exclusion from the policy mainstream of American and Canadian transportation will have to be revisited.

But in order for this kind of change to occur, some of the informal political rules now acting as barriers to harmonizing the policy frameworks that isolate rail from other modes will need to be overcome. Government and industry leaders in air and road transportation must move beyond their adversarial attitudes and approaches to dealing with the rail mode in general, and passenger trains, in particular. Such détente requires more than just the acquiescence of airlines and bus companies, however. The rail industry itself would have to contribute to such a "meeting of minds" by finding a way to step away from the stream of criticism it has produced regarding unequal treatment due to road, and to a lesser extent, air infrastructure subsidies over the previous century. Clearly, overcoming such endemic ill will among policy community participants from rail, air, and road modes will be no simple task.

The second shortcoming that must be addressed is that Amtrak and VIA Rail remain *organizationally encumbered* by their structure as large public enterprises that must serve many diverse markets on a continental scale. From labor relations to procurement to new business development, the way that these firms do business is often at odds with their competitors. The way that privately owned airlines and bus companies, let alone the auto industry, conduct their affairs remains fundamentally different than the methods of Amtrak and VIA, even following their recent efforts at marketization.

The biggest difference between the private and public carriers is that, even when they are competing in the same travel market, the former operate with virtually no constraints on their managerial discretion. Routes, services, and workforce can be changed almost at will in the air and bus business, while rail management is still bound by public interest service criteria. Future policy will have to create more room for passenger rail management to pursue business strategies that benefit from the kind of flexible operations and fluctuating workforce that airlines and bus carriers currently enjoy. This flexibility would boost the fortunes of both Amtrak and VIA, as well as creating opportunities for other rail carriers to cultivate market niches.

The third dimension of failure that must be addressed by future policy is that North American passenger trains have become *industrial orphans* during the course of their public guardianship by Amtrak and VIA. The rich network of technical skills and design capacities in passenger rail that once spread across North America's railroads, locomotive builders, rolling stock manufacturers, train signaling, and communications suppliers is now just a shadow of its former self. Along with the erosion of these skills and manufacturing capabilities has come a decline in the employment, tax base, and nationwide presence of passenger rail suppliers. The extent to which aerospace and automotive design, development, and manufacturing spread across North America, extending almost as far as the reach of these mobility modes, highlights the industrial atrophy surrounding passenger trains.

While a number of assembly plants remain in business to put together European- or Japanese-designed rail passenger equipment, only Canada's Bombardier remains in the business of designing and constructing intercity passenger trains "from the ground up." The manufacturing industry is somewhat more dynamic when passenger train equipment and technology that can be shared with freight operations are taken into account. Rail passenger infrastructure engineering skills are similarly limited, since the freight railroads now hosting most intercity passenger trains lack both the incentive and the capacity to upgrade their tracks to the level that high-speed operations require. All in all, the critical mass of engineers and designers who could meet the technical needs of a twenty-first century passenger train renewal does not now exist on this continent. Something must be done to ensure that this industrial capacity is up to the needs and opportunities that would emerge during an era of genuine rail passenger renewal.

6.2. Identifying the Best Bets for Policy Innovation

With these challenges in mind, it is possible to identify the essential choices that policy makers would confront in trying to do better. Although there is no "magic policy formula" that can guarantee success in passenger railroading, some policy options do appear more promising than others. The analysis that follows highlights those "best bets" based upon three principles.

First, it will identify promising solutions by drawing upon *actual and concrete policy initiatives* that have enabled significant achievements in rail passenger renewal outside North America. Such options will be preferred over policy proposals that are based upon abstract and universal propositions about travel behavior and transportation technology, which turn out to be increasingly dubious upon closer examination. Put simply, success stories drawn from global experience in renewing passenger trains' capacity since the 1960s are a good place to begin looking for policy solutions.

Second, it will distill the *essential values and approaches to organizing government's role in mobility* from the American and Canadian transportation policies that have contributed to the advance of modes other than passenger rail. Emulating the other modes' "best policy practices" is a valid strategy for two reasons. First, it recognizes that the passenger train's competitors are supported by a policy framework that, while far from perfect, has enabled them to both thrive commercially and to deliver mobility benefits that American and Canadian society value highly. And second, borrowing from other modes' policy values and approaches can help to facilitate their eventual acceptance of passenger trains as a legitimate counterpart, and even a partner, in North America's intermodal transportation network.

Finally, this analysis will identify *existing policy constraints and obstacles* that have limited Amtrak and VIA Rail's capacity for providing effective and efficient intercity passenger rail operations. There is no shortage of evidence regarding the damaging effects of policy constraints on attempts to innovate in North American passenger railroading. Any policy redesign effort should seek to dispense with this baggage as soon as possible.

6.3. Two Dimensions of Policy Redesign

Among the many options for organizing and delivering mobility that decision makers can choose from, two key parameters differentiate the institutional characteristics that connect specific choices into the larger framework of American and Canadian governance. These two parameters form the foundation on which this assessment of rail passenger policy options will be developed.

The key political parameter that orients public problem solving in transportation, as in other policy domains, is the appropriate location for government's authority. Both Canada and the United States are structured as political federations, meaning that different levels of government take responsibility for doing (or not doing) things on behalf of the citizenry. National, subnational (i.e., provincial or state), and, in some cases, local and regional governments each exercise jurisdiction over certain policy responsibilities based upon a constitutional division of powers. In practice, few contemporary policy problems fall into the "watertight compartments" that constitutional architects once specified for a national or subnational government's jurisdiction. But even when activities needed to formulate, implement, and finance a policy or program cross these jurisdictional boundaries, one level of government will take the lead in articulating the goals and acceptable, or even preferred, outcomes.

In transportation, both Americans and Canadians locate particular policy responsibilities in different levels of government. From infrastructure finance, to business, environmental, and safety regulation, to the direct provision of certain transportation services, provinces or states will handle certain activities and national governments will take on others. These divisions of governmental labor distinguish not only American and Canadian approaches to transportation policy from one another, but can also set one particular mode's policy framework apart from another.

For example, American highway policy was initiated by a few state road departments developing administrative and technical procedures and state governments introducing the gasoline excise tax as a means to fund infrastructure development. But it was not long before Congress created a complementary federal highway aid program and set up the Bureau of Public Roads to plan and coordinate a national road infrastructure program.[5] Over time, an integrated partnership between national and state governments emerged where Washington establishes the strategic plan and terms of financing while the states co-fund, build, and maintain the resulting infrastructure. The terms and conditions that were developed to allow both levels of government to exercise their responsibilities cooperatively has enabled the states to implement a highway system that is national in its scope and uniform in its design standard.

U.S. civil aviation got off the ground under federal policy leadership in administration, planning, and operating subsidies, but it was not long before states, and municipal governments, created their own administrative and financial arrangements to complement federal aid programs. These local initiatives were usually aimed at developing airport infrastructure. As has been noted previously, America's intercity rail policy lacks the kind of symbiosis that has enabled one level of government's initiative to be complemented by the effective and coordinated support from another.

In Canada, federalism has exhibited a less cooperative pattern in the transport domain, with the federal government taking responsibility for rail and then aviation while the provinces focus their policy efforts on roads and highways. Despite the ongoing exchange of administrative and technical information between Ottawa and the provinces, policy linkages between national and subnational transportation responsibilities have not progressed nearly as far as in the U.S. As a result, there are vast provincial disparities in the goals, the capacity, and the financing of subnational transportation responsibilities, leaving Canada with ten provincial road networks, rather than a single, national one.[6] In contrast, policy responsibilities for the air mode fall largely within the jurisdiction of national governments in both America and Canada. Subnational governments' involvement in air transportation has been limited to a subordinate role in airport development and past provincial forays into air carrier ownership. Today, aviation policy objectives are nationally oriented in both countries.

For the purposes of differentiating among rail passenger policy choices, it is useful to distinguish between those that would involve a national government's leadership and those that might rely upon provincial or state leadership. The terms by which both national and subnational governments might both be involved in rail passenger policy are also worth considering. The more explicit this division of labor in governing intercity transportation can be made *in advance of* launching new policy, the more likely it will be to succeed.

The key economic parameter that matters in delineating public policy options is whether the activity in question is a function to be carried out either primarily in the private sector (i.e., market based) or the public sector (i.e., government based). In today's world, few if any economic activities are purely private or purely public in character. Yet their identification with either one of these spheres makes a significant difference in the expectations regarding their organization, financing, and accountability. The majority of North America's transportation policy is made with the presumption that mobility will be provided by a private operator, ranging from the individual owner of a motor vehicle to a for-profit airline, bus company, or trucking firm. The largest exception to this is urban public transport which is almost entirely publicly owned and operated. In most cases, the infrastructure over which private vehicles operate is publicly owned, maintained, and financed. The key exception is the rail mode, where private operators own, maintain, and pay taxes on their infrastructure.

Rail passenger policy, as it now stands, must contend with a unique reversal of public and private involvement, compared to other transport modes. Publicly owned carriers Amtrak and VIA, each an anomaly among the many carriers doing business in the private sector, operate most of their trains over privately owned infrastructure, again in contrast to other modes. In assessing future rail passenger policy options, one needs to consider the value of harmonizing the passenger train's anomalies with the other modes.

Within the framework that is organized around the national versus subnational and public versus private choices that decision makers will confront, "packages" of policy goals and instruments can be grouped in terms of effectiveness. In other words, future policy choices about the appropriate role of the state and private enterprise, and about the role of different levels of government, could enable replacing today's jumble of incompatible or conflicting goals and instruments with more workable arrangements.

Answering the key questions which have to date been avoided or left unresolved in policy deliberations can enable the articulation of goals that future rail passenger policy might embrace. Revisiting the goals for passenger train policy can help to align these policy options more closely with the expectations of what policies applied to other modes will produce. Such reassessment should contemplate each of the questions which are noted below and should seek answers from the experience of what other modes do for (and to) the North American economy, environment, and society. Finding the right place in the transportation policy framework for rail will be helped by identifying what passenger trains can do better, cheaper, and more sustainably than other modes.

Is the mobility provided by intercity passenger trains to be treated as an end in itself, or should it sometimes be considered as a means to other economic and social ends? Should rail passenger policy focus exclusively, or even primarily, on carriers and customers, or should the needs and opportunities for workers and suppliers of rail passenger skills and technologies be included? Should the passenger train's "bottom line" be measured in commercial profit, or should other criteria be added to recognize external benefits, such as reduced congestion, energy use, and environmental impacts, that might arise from meeting mobility needs through this particular mode? Should passenger trains be designed to function as a "universal" mode—providing service that can fulfill a wide range of intercity mobility needs across North America in the way that automobiles, and to a lesser extent aviation, do? Or should rail be refocused on specific market niches for intercity travel?

When these questions are addressed, a clearer picture of the goals that rail passenger policy can pursue will become evident. Neither advocates nor enemies of the passenger train will likely appreciate all of the findings that inform the goals for a new policy. But unlike the current stalemate, competing claims regarding what rail can or cannot do for intercity passenger mobility could actually be tested out over time. Goals could thus be modified based upon the evaluation of ongoing change.

Numerous policy instruments will need to be considered for their potential contribution to implementing a new rail passenger policy. These will include:

- Financial instruments that both tax and spend on the rail mode.
- Incentives to stimulate research and commercialization of advanced rail passenger technology.
- The form and structure of any future operating subsidies.
- Arrangements for joint action by different levels of government relating to the rail mode in general, and passenger trains in particular.
- Arrangements for public-private partnerships, including "contracting out" some kinds of work that rail organizations used to perform and "contracting in" other kinds of work relating to intercity mobility that is now performed by organizations other than railroads.

- The design and enforcement of regulatory mechanisms dealing with safety and environmental and consumer protection.
- Insulating carriers from "political" pressures, either to provide uneconomic service without appropriate compensation or to meet a higher standard of scrutiny and oversight of their commercial activities than other businesses.
- Improving the "rules of engagement" for labor relations that can enhance both productivity and employees' standard of living.

Before delving into the details of particularly promising policy options, it is worth identifying how the many combinations and permutations of goals and instruments are likely to align based upon the two key parameters identified previously. Figure 6.1 builds on an earlier assessment of the reorganization options Amtrak faced in 1997.[7] It presents four out of five possible policy "packages" that could emerge from deliberations and debates that broke out of the thirty-year stalemate over what to do about passenger trains. These scenarios could emerge in either American or Canadian rail passenger reinvention efforts, albeit with somewhat different specifics. A fifth grouping of policy goals and instruments falls outside this matrix. It is the liquidation option that was written into the ARAA and thus could be applied specifically to Amtrak. The liquidation option is indeed "out of the box" and will be discussed following the other options.

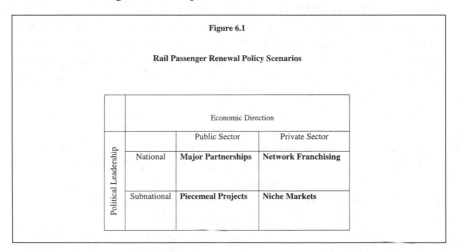

Figure 6.1

Rail Passenger Renewal Policy Scenarios

		Economic Direction	
		Public Sector	Private Sector
Political Leadership	National	**Major Partnerships**	**Network Franchising**
	Subnational	**Piecemeal Projects**	**Niche Markets**

This matrix, and the ensuing policy scenarios, recognize that fundamental organizational choices about the role of government and of the market must be made in order to create particular policy options that improve upon

Amtrak's and VIA Rail's current performance. These scenarios should not be viewed as mutually exclusive, but rather as categories of what becomes possible when the competing economic and political approaches to passenger train renewal reach an accommodation over any particular combination of these values. When that occurs, a window of opportunity for policy innovation will open.

For example, if a decision was made to create a new rail passenger policy that supported the mode's economic direction by for-profit carriers, then either of the scenarios appearing under the "Private Sector" column would begin to unfold, depending on what level of government was leading this policy reform. But neither of these scenarios mean that government's role in passenger railroading would disappear. Rather, the policy initiatives emerging from the choice to reintroduce private direction to rail passenger operations would enlarge the private sector's role in designing, delivering, and financing passenger train services but continue (and, in certain cases, expand) industry's relationship with government—just as private airlines and trucking firms work with government. Similarly, the "Subnational" row of political leadership does not mean that Ottawa or Washington would cede all policy responsibilities. Instead, it suggests that most of the initiative for new policy options would be forthcoming from provincial or state governments. Each scenario offers opportunities for closing the gap between the status quo and some form of more effective rail passenger service, but they differ in both the scope of such service and on who would shoulder the costs, and reap the rewards, of a transition from current policy.

6.4. Major Partnerships: National Leadership and Public Sector Direction

The "Major Partnerships" policy scenario would focus on overhauling the public enterprise mandate for renewing passenger trains by expanding Amtrak's and VIA Rail's capacity to forge significant new partnerships that enhance the passenger train's competitive position. Such measures would go well beyond existing initiatives in contracting out certain services (e.g., food service or equipment maintenance), or in seeking to cultivate revenue streams from ancillary services (e.g., mail and express, real estate, or commuter rail operations). This scenario would pursue a new form of joint venture in North American passenger railroading, one that enables key organizations to literally "buy into" opportunities created by public investment in renewed passenger trains. It would differ from the partnerships forged by today's public enterprises because once the stalemate over government's role in passenger railroading was resolved, private partners would stand to gain substantially more than they do today. New investments would boost the opportunity for significant rewards from partnerships with newly legitimated, and capitalized, public passenger carriers. Drawing from the three principles that were set out above for weighing rail passenger policy options, it is evident that the most valuable new partnerships would be those built upon significant rail infrastructure redevelopment and expansion.

Global experience suggests that the single most effective formula for renewing passenger trains centers on the introduction of state-of-the-art, purpose-built (or rebuilt) infrastructure that enables speed, frequency, and reliability that can out-perform autos and even aircraft in moving travelers between major cites. Whereas renewal of an entire railroad's performance can emanate from such a successful core upgrading, there is little evidence to suggest that even a multitude of smaller improvements can yield a comparable transformation. Indeed, the alternative renewal strategy based upon incremental upgrading can provide grist for the skeptics' efforts to denigrate rail's potential by contrasting the immediate and visible costs of such a strategy against the diffuse and contingent benefits that it has provided to date.

A recent attack on California's intercity rail passenger upgrading program, the most ambitious incremental renewal strategy to be implemented in North America during the 1990s, offers evidence of how the incremental renewal strategy can be used against itself. One such critical assessment was highlighted by Transportation California, an association supported by highway contractors and other beneficiaries of the state government's transportation spending.[8] That association announced that an investigation by Norm King, director of the San Bernardino County Transportation Commission, had revealed an "amazing decline in intercity rail performance," in which $2 billion invested in intercity rail during the 1990s had "produced an increase of only 1,100 new intercity round trips per day."[9] King went on to calculate a $1.8 million capital cost per additional daily rider, which subsequently required a $25,000 annual operating subsidy for each new rider. He attributed these results to a philosophical divide "between those who support rail (at any cost) and those who oppose rail (at any cost)," which had undermined the state's "ability to distinguish a good rail investment from a bad one."[10]

North American experience is replete with many other efforts at incremental improvement that have been advanced as a more or less conscious alternative to serious infrastructure renewal, with little or no success. Amtrak and VIA Rail have, from time to time, introduced new locomotives and trains, upgraded stations, and cultivated the warmth and kindness of their employ-ees. These efforts have produced a quality travel experience that is often genu-inely superior to the customer care offered by airlines, or European and Japanese railroads for that matter. But shiny trains, inviting stations, and friendly employees can only go so far in bringing travelers back to the rails, and this has not proven to be far enough to date. If the train does not offer faster, cheaper, and technologically superior travel opportunities compared with autos or planes, there is little evidence that the public will beat a path to Amtrak's or VIA's operations.

Such results point to the conclusion that incremental improvements in intercity rail do little to enable significant policy transformation of the sort that would drive a "Major Partnerships" scenario. Conversely, the "big bang" created by high-speed rail's success has enabled passenger railroads to turn the corner from being organizations that appear out of place in the modern world to becoming acclaimed contributors to a twenty-first-century trans-portation system. One reason for this is that modern infrastructure requires up-to-date, or at least updated, administrative and financial arrangements that put rail on a par with other modes.

In North America, the air and road competition that "cleaned the pas-senger train's clock" as a postwar travel option did so, in no small measure, by relying upon a better institutional mousetrap for providing their infrastruc-ture. Autos and planes benefit to no end from modern institutional arrange-ments that synchronize privately operated mobility with public administration and finance of air and road infrastructure. This public-private partnership is so successful that most travelers (and taxpayers) do not pause to think about the essential public contributions that enable "private" driving and flying. And when the very significant taxes collected and expended on air and road transportation are brought to the public's attention, most citizens pronounce themselves quite satisfied with the use of the money.

Finding the right partnership(s) is obviously a key to success in this policy scenario. The most obvious place to begin looking for such a match is with the potential partner that has both the most to offer, and also the most to gain, from casting its lot in with Amtrak or VIA. North America's freight railroad industry—private owners of the infrastructure that most passenger trains now use, tracks that could either be upgraded or augmented to enable high-speed service—offers that promise. The possibility of cultivating such a relationship was not overlooked by the architects of today's public enterprises.

Recall that America's freight railroads were provided with the option of acquiring stock in Amtrak in return for their start-up contribution to the fledgling passenger operator. Four railroads actually did obtain stock, and three took up seats on Amtrak's Board of Directors during its early years. But Amtrak turned out to have little to offer these shareholders, or indeed any other partners that were interested in making money. If anything, the policy framework that has governed Amtrak's relationship with its railroad hosts has served to frustrate any partnership potential over the years. Amtrak has the right to operate trains at avoidable cost over freight rail infrastructure. Even when it makes incentive payments for on-time operation, Amtrak does not contribute significantly to a freight railroad's bottom line. Yet passenger operations do expose freight carriers to liability when accidents occur and also take up valuable track capacity that could be used by more profitable freight trains.

VIA Rail was also initially structured as a joint venture between government and Canada's two major freight carriers, but the potential for real partnership was undermined by many of the same sorts of problems. No wonder that the rail industry has been lukewarm, at best, about the prospects for passenger operations in North America.

Under a Major Partnership scenario, federal policy leadership would be focused on creating a new opportunity for freight railroads to take a stake in passenger rail's renewal. A major partnership needs a fiscal centerpiece, some analog to the trust funds that have become the public input into airline, automotive, and truck transportation. Such a centerpiece could be created in a new policy linkage between the taxes that both freight and passenger railroads generate and the need for modernized and expanded rail infrastructure across the nation. In this partnership, Amtrak or VIA could take on the role of trustee for the public investment in rail infrastructure while itself becoming restructured along the lines of a joint venture between railroads and government.

Just as the rail passenger problem turned out to be a harbinger of competitive disadvantages that the rail freight industry would have to eventually confront, the infrastructure limitations that currently plague passenger train development will eventually catch up with freight trains, where they have not done so already. Both rail freight and passenger service require upgraded infrastructure. The extensive rationalization (i.e., downsizing) of rail infrastructure that accompanied deregulation, especially in the United States, helped freight railroads to regain their profitability. But this pruning of the fixed plant has proved to be much easier than growing the infrastructure's capacity back to accommodate new business.

And while investors have responded favorably to railroads' return from the brink of bankruptcy in the early 1980s, there has been little enthusiasm for injecting the massive sums that would be needed to add significant track capacity. Investors have proven quite averse to anteing up their cash against Uncle Sam's investment in competing road and air infrastructure. Despite reasonable returns in recent years, freight railroads do not find themselves in a position to fully fund their infrastructure needs any more. In their heyday, it was possible to charge premium prices based upon a quasi-monopoly for their transportation services. These surpluses that could once pay for the opulence of a Grand Central Terminal or its attendant four-track main line between New York and Chicago are no more. Today's freight transport market is simply too competitive to squeeze the kind of premium that would be required for large scale infrastructure development, especially when rail's competitors have no need to fund such infrastructure investments.

Under the twin pressures of traffic growth and the higher expectations by shippers for quick and timely delivery to meet tight logistics needs (e.g., "just in time" supply chain management), American railroads are now beginning to recognize that what traditionally was understood to be their greatest asset, the "crown jewels" of private infrastructure, is in fact a competitive liability. They have begun to search out, and even act upon, opportunities to modernize their infrastructure in partnership with the public sector.

Perhaps the most tangible example of this new thinking is the Alameda Corridor Project, a $2.4 billion expenditure on twenty miles of new trackage from the ports of Los Angeles and Long Beach through the heart of Los Angeles to the Union Pacific and Burlington Northern–Santa Fe Railroads' yards in the city's east.[11] This infrastructure is being built and financed by the Alameda Corridor Transportation Authority, a special-purpose public entity which has issued revenue bonds that will be paid off by $1.2 billion in railroad user fees over thirty years. These funds are augmented by grants of $400 million from the U.S. Department of Transportation, $394 million from the Ports of Long Beach and Los Angeles, $347 million by the Los Angeles County Metropolitan Transportation Authority, and $154 million from other state and federal funding sources.

The passenger train component of this project is quite small, consisting of a $44 million bypass for Amtrak and regional commuter trains over the freight corridor. Yet small as this may be, there is nonetheless a precedent for mixing public and private funds to develop rail infrastructure that will benefit both freight and passenger operations. In addition to its physical and financial achievements, the Alameda Corridor Project reflects the kind of extraordinary organizational effort that is currently required to address critical rail investment needs. Enhancing rail access to the world's third-largest port complex required a "custom tailored" policy institution that could accommodate all of the political and economic organizations having a stake in this initiative. Organizing this took the better part of a decade, meaning that the construction of policy to enable this project has taken roughly twice as long as the physical construction phase will require. Despite these organizational demands, some railroads are pursuing public-private partnerships for even larger infrastructure projects.

The Norfolk Southern (NS) Railroad has proposed that the state of Virginia share in the $900 million cost of adding a second track to its line paralleling Interstate 81, where up to 40 percent of traffic consists of heavy trucks. Norfolk Southern claims that this investment would be the most productive way to increase highway capacity, by shifting long-haul freight off the road and onto the newly expanded tracks. Norfolk Southern's senior general counsel, Wiley Mitchel Jr., told reporters, "That is just as fair and should be just as much [an] acceptable policy to invest money in a right-of-way for a railroad as it is to invest money in a right-of-way for trucks."[12] Canadian National's diffident response to the NS initiative suggests that the rail policy community is not yet united behind such a concept. CNR's spokesman commented that: "If you get into a situation where you are accepting public funds for freight infrastructure, it allows other parties to have a say in your core business. Obviously, we are opposed to that."[13]

But the idea of public investment in rail infrastructure does appear to have a growing appeal among industry leaders. Some railroads are even going as far as to justify the benefits of such investment in terms of improved quality of life. John Snow, CEO of CSX Corporation, signaled his openness to the idea of public funding for upgrading both freight and passenger rail infrastructure during a speech at Virginia Commonwealth University on November 9, 2000.[14] He identified U.S. budget surpluses and public frustration with congested highways and airports as reasons for considering the public finance of rail infrastructure "in a new light."

One of the boldest signals that the rail industry is ready to retreat from its traditional opposition to public support for infrastructure came in a keynote speech given by Robert Krebs, CEO of the Burlington Northern–Santa Fe Railroad, at the Transportation Research Board's 2001 annual meeting. Krebs stated that while government intervention "goes against my Republican instincts," the time had come to consider "some form of public financing assistance for railroad rights-of-way projects that provide public benefits, like highway congestion mitigation, air quality improvements, or public safety enhancements."[15] Krebs indicated that his conversion from opposition to government support for transportation infrastructure followed the recognition that such a policy strategy had led railroads to a dead end, noting that: "I'm not advocating higher fuel taxes for trucks or barges—we've fought that battle for too long. . . . Railroads have been fighting—and losing—the 'competitive equity' battle as long as I can remember."[16]

In order to capitalize upon this newly emerging enthusiasm for public infrastructure investment in the rail sector, a new institutional vehicle is needed. That design will have to enable government money, such as newly dedicated tax revenues, to be invested in infrastructure that is not part of the public domain in the way that airports and highways clearly are. Amtrak presents such a vehicle. It already owns key rail infrastructure in the Northeast and a limited amount of track in the Midwest where freight and passenger trains coexist.

What might a public investment program in rail infrastructure that involved Amtrak look like? The Taxpayer Relief Act of 1997's precedent offers a good place to begin such consideration. This legislation allocated $2.2 billion to Amtrak's infrastructure needs, ostensibly equivalent to tax revenues that private railroads had paid prior to 1971. If Congress could explore the distant past and discover tax revenues that merited a "rebate" to meet Amtrak's current capital needs, then earmarking future tax revenues in support of both freight and passenger rail infrastructure should also be possible.

Perhaps the tax revenue most analogous to funds currently earmarked for other modes' infrastructure spending is the rail industry's 4.3-cent-per-gallon tax on diesel fuel that was instituted in 1990 for the purpose of deficit reduction. According to the Association of American Railroads (AAR), this tax has raised $1.7 billion since being enacted, with $170 million being collected in 1999. This tax is authorized through 2002, meaning that it would come up for renewal close to the time that Amtrak's future was fairly high on the policy agenda.[17] To date, the major railroads, through the AAR, have been pressing for a repeal of the tax, citing the current budget surplus and high fuel costs.[18] When railroads pursue such a direct benefit, they are opposed both by those who see red when private industries get a "tax break" and those who are in direct competition for the movement of freight. Railroads could certainly improve their odds of getting some of these resources by making common cause with passenger rail advocates and supporting the investment of their taxes in infrastructure improvement that would benefit a public passenger carrier.

Unless a further "rebate" of past tax payments could be agreed upon in Congress, $170 million a year in annual collections would represent just a down payment on the price tag for modern passenger train infrastructure, let alone addressing the rail mode's capital needs as a whole. Given the unique ownership status of private rail infrastructure, a case could also be made for

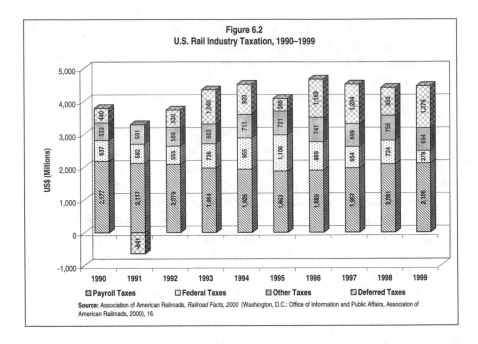

Figure 6.2
U.S. Rail Industry Taxation, 1990–1999

Source: Association of American Railroads, *Railroad Facts, 2000* (Washington, D.C.: Office of Information and Public Affairs, Associaton of American Railroads, 2000), 16.

earmarking some of the industry's corporate tax revenues for capital investment, along the lines established by the Taxpayer Relief Act. Figure 6.2 shows that the U.S. rail industry's collective tax bill has ranged from $3.8 billion to $4.5 billion between 1990 and 1999.[19] Amtrak passengers could also contribute by beginning to pay an excise tax on their tickets, something that existed before Amtrak's creation but was abolished before the launch of public enterprise. Constructing an acceptable fiscal formula would certainly be contentious, necessitating clear agreement on both a national investment plan and a stewardship arrangement.

Like the other transportation trust funds, a national plan for rail infrastructure investment would have to be developed as an integral part of the new funding arrangement. The Federal Railroad Administration would most likely have to develop such a plan, using as a core the high-speed rail corridors that were "designated" under the Intermodal Surface Transportation and Efficiency Act of 1991 (ISTEA) and the Transportation Equity Act for the 21st Century (TEA-21) legislation. While these designated corridors would form the principal foci for rail passenger investment, complementary investment priorities for rail freight remain to be identified.

Amtrak's role as trustee of these infrastructure investments could be critical to enabling public support for private industry. Opposition to simply investing public funds directly into privately-owned infrastructure would be intense, and quite legitimate. But instead of the political struggle that would certainly accompany an effort to "nationalize" any railroad's infrastructure prior to public investment, Amtrak could instead take specific responsibility for the improved infrastructure segment. In some cases, this might be clear title to the equivalent of an infrastructure "condominium" (e.g., a new track adjoining one or more privately owned tracks on a right-of-way still owned by the railroad). But in other cases, Amtrak's stake in the upgraded infrastructure might take the form of co-ownership with attendant entitlement to specific slots for passenger operation.

Railroads would, in turn, need a way to invest in Amtrak once again. The combined potential for making money from a commercially renewed passenger business along with having a seat on the board of an organization integral to public investment in rail infrastructure should be an attractive proposition. Over time, Amtrak might evolve into a true joint venture among America's railroads—sharing passenger and infrastructure development responsibilities among them in ways that create opportunities beyond the reach of any one company.

Freight railroads are not the only possible partners for Amtrak's infrastructure development. Energy companies, especially those specializing in the transmission of electricity or natural gas, might also find it attractive to share the development of rights-of-way between major metropolitan areas. And in certain areas of the United States, such as the Northeast Corridor, the Chicago hub, and southern California, regional commuter rail operators might also find it worthwhile to form significant and enduring partnerships with Amtrak that enable shared infrastructure development. Such joint ventures could be facilitated by broadening the eligibility of federal transit funding to include intercity rail infrastructure, when joint development and use by Amtrak and commuter railroads are involved.

VIA's most promising partners are also to be found in Canada's two major freight railroads, Canadian National and Canadian Pacific. Their needs for infrastructure investment differ from U.S. counterparts, in part because some of Canada's fastest growing trade volumes are now north-south, while the bulk of the country's rail infrastructure still runs east-west. But both CNR and CPR have regularly identified taxation issues as one of the top policy constraints on their competitiveness with other modes. Figure 6.3 depicts the Canadian railroad industry's tax bills for fuel, property assessments, and other excises which ranged from Can$591 million to Can$412 million between 1990 and 1999.[20]

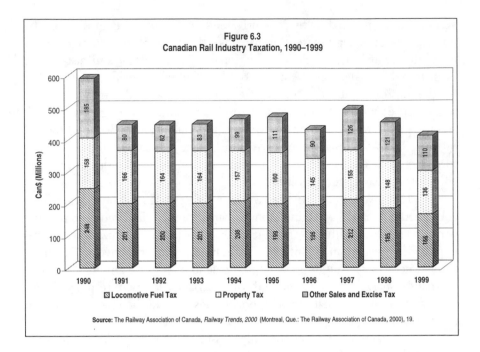

Figure 6.3
Canadian Rail Industry Taxation, 1990–1999

Source: The Railway Association of Canada, *Railway Trends, 2000* (Montreal, Que.: The Railway Association of Canada, 2000), 19.

Canada lacks the fiscal earmarking which characterizes U.S. transportation finance. Thus, there is more flexibility to develop new links between these taxes paid by railroads and the upgrading needs for both freight and passenger rail infrastructure. The federal government has fostered the creation of non-profit organizations to support air traffic control infrastructure (NAV-Canada), airport infrastructure—through the creation of local airport authorities—and port infrastructure. An excise tax on train tickets, akin to the airport and air navigation fees that are now collected as part of every airline ticket in Canada, could be an effective part of this new fiscal mix.

A recent operational innovation that might offer scope for joint ventures that include passenger railroading is the "coproduction" arrangement worked out between CNR and CPR, whereby both railroads share operation over a given infrastructure to optimize its efficiency. In Canada, the two railroads share operations in the 155-mile-long Fraser River Canyon of British Columbia, allowing all trains to run one direction over each company's track infrastructure.[21] Operations have also been consolidated over terminal trackage around Edmonton, Winnipeg, Toronto, and Ottawa. Most recently, such coordination extended to a cross-border tradeoff where CNR provided access to fourteen CPR trains per week on its Toronto to Chicago line in return for access to CPR's tracks connecting Quebec with the New York City area.[22] Further expanding such coproduction arrangements to include public passenger operations could help justify public infrastructure investment. While the means behind Canada's reorganization of rail infrastructure finance will certainly differ from those of the United States, the objective will be similar— to create mutual advantages in, and opportunities from, a new linkage between infrastructure investment supporting both freight and passenger rail.

6.5. Piecemeal Projects: Subnational Leadership and Public Sector Direction

Government leadership in rail passenger policy innovation would not necessarily emerge at the national level, however. Subnational policy initiatives have changed the course of North American transportation, such as the gasoline excise tax in 1919 and its subsequent earmarking for road infrastructure by American states, or the launch of regional public transit operations like the Government of Ontario (GO) Transit Corporation in 1967. If the political stalemate over government's role in passenger railroading continues to impede policy change in national capitals, it is quite plausible that one or more states or provinces will experiment with a particularly promising project. There are two variants of such a "Piecemeal Projects" scenario.

In the optimistic version, a new project is embraced as a way to do better than existing services provided by Amtrak and VIA. Such pursuit of success would be most likely to start where a major travel market falls within a single subnational government's jurisdiction. Its prospects would be enhanced where existing air and road infrastructure is at, or over, capacity and where environmental and community opposition to further expansion of airports and highways is strong. But a rail passenger project could also emerge where rail manufacturing jobs and other economic spin-offs can be identified and highly valued.

California and Florida have both contemplated new passenger rail operations to meet growing travel demand in key intrastate markets (e.g., Bay Area–Southern California or Miami–Orlando–Tampa) and continue to weigh the options for "going it alone" on advanced passenger train services in one way or another. Among states that have not yet gotten far along in a major rail passenger renewal project, Virginia might be considered the most promising developer. That state's recently announced plans to fund CSX track upgrading stand to reap huge mobility benefits, at incremental capital cost, by extending more of the Northeast Corridor's high-speed trains between Washington, D.C., and the state capital in Richmond.

The provinces of Quebec, and to a lesser extent, Ontario, are home to Bombardier's rail passenger manufacturing enterprise. They would thus gain around the highest payoff from the "supply side" benefits of passenger train renewal in those two provinces. Both provinces have previously explored high-speed passenger train development, although such an initiative would require joint action by two governments that are often at odds in order to serve major travel markets (e.g., Montreal–Toronto). In Canada's west, Alberta contains a single travel market between Calgary and Edmonton with a distance that is perfectly suited to fast trains. The economic development spin-offs of a new rail passenger link could be judged quite promising, if the project enabled these two cities to better integrate their economic and political activities into a single "critical mass."

The pessimistic variant of this scenario could be triggered by a deterioration or curtailment in the intercity rail services now run by Amtrak or VIA. Should either company fall far short of its performance targets, or should skeptics ever win the day in national political debates, some services would likely be cut back. Provinces and states might be left to fend for themselves, and thus be spurred into action in providing alternative operation and support of certain intercity train services.

In either variant, policy adjustments will be essential for a province or state to lead change. Moving to implement a major rail renewal initiative, such as introducing high-speed rail service, would require inventing an ambitious new set of policies, while a sudden need to substitute for Amtrak's or VIA's conventional rail passenger services would demand a quick adoption of less far-reaching measures. In either case, financing is not the only policy challenge that would call for innovation, but without a bold move to pay for whatever passenger train needs are identified, other policy adaptations would not count for much. French and German experience with transferring planning and financing responsibilities for local and regional passenger trains to subnational governments may offer some lessons to North Americans searching for models to implement a Piecemeal Projects scenario. But these European initiatives occurred as part of a larger, nationally led, rail renewal effort, and are also influenced by open access to rail infrastructure.

When it comes to states launching renewal, there is clear evidence of what will not work from efforts to date. A referendum on a new or increased tax for passenger rail, as was rejected in Ohio, offers little promise as the way to kick off the renewal effort. Public leadership implies that governments must make significant commitments to rail passenger renewal projects, as is routinely done with other transportation modes, rather than putting such options to a public vote where the cost is clear and immediate, but the benefits remain abstract and long term. A less problematic variant of this public outreach for financing passenger rail renewal can be found in California's periodic referenda on transportation investment bonds, which have raised over $2 billion for rail and public transit investments, of which roughly half has gone to intercity rail.[23] But while these bonds have funded incremental improvements in California's intercity passenger train service to date, the amounts involved fall well short of what would be required to pay for a high-speed train project. Bonds could, at most, pay for a portion of launching a major rail passenger renewal initiative.

Filling in for sudden gaps in Amtrak or VIA services would likely be met through annual appropriations, at least initially. Several states have built operating subsidies for "enhanced" Amtrak services into their budget over the years, although no such precedent exists in Canada. Making the leap beyond annual appropriations, the question of whether to fill in for Amtrak's or VIA's service or to launch a major high-speed rail project, will challenge subnational governments to embrace fiscal innovations that differ primarily in scope from the approach sketched out under the Major Partnerships scenario. Like their national counterparts, provinces and states that are serious about facilitating successful rail passenger renewal would need to explore options for earmarking some of the contribution that railroads already make to their treasury. This would be analogous to the state transportation trust funds that earmark gasoline taxes for (mostly) road building, discussed below.

Once again, freight and commuter railroads would make valid and valuable partners in the ensuing infrastructure (re)development initiative. Another policy question to be addressed would be the nature of the intercity passenger carrier and its relationship to both partners and subnational government. The organization responsible for delivering intercity passenger services within a provincial- or state-led rail renewal initiative could take many forms, which could be situated on a continuum from Amtrak and VIA filling this role at one end to wholly new public or private carriers running passenger services at the other. We can review the outlines of what these options might look like, in turn.

States already contract with Amtrak to "top up" the existing national network with additional services that are focused on meeting regional intercity mobility. While such state-supported trains were often run as "second class" operations within the national system, with slower schedules than were to be found on either the long-haul trains or in the Northeast Corridor, Amtrak has recently made state partnerships a high priority in its network growth strategy. The corporation now proposes to leverage some of its very scarce capital resources to nurturing such partnerships. If Amtrak can execute its business plan successfully, such attention and incentives might well tempt states to stick with Amtrak as their preferred carrier in a major rail initiative. In Canada, there is no precedent for provinces partnering with VIA to support regional services, making such an option less likely. But there is nothing to prevent such a partnership on a specific project.

But if Amtrak cannot deliver on its incentives for state partnership, or if either Amtrak or VIA fell into a commercial crisis and were forced to cut back service, then the prospect of a province or state seeking an alternative intercity carrier to fill in the gaps becomes more likely. Short of looking to a brand new carrier, provinces and states might work with rail passenger operators already under their jurisdiction, such as commuter carriers, to implement new intercity services. They might also work with freight railroads, several of which have (re)created passenger departments to deal with Amtrak, VIA, and new opportunities for passenger operation.

Subnational policy leadership could also create the opportunity for an entirely new carrier to enter the intercity passenger train business. Such an organization could be "custom tailored" to meet the organizational and financial needs of a particular project much more closely than Amtrak or VIA, especially if they remain embroiled in national political stalemates about the passenger train's future. Even an existing commuter or freight operator would have organizational baggage that might make it less attractive to a state or province contemplating truly innovative financing and organization of a passenger project. The possibility of introducing an established air or bus carrier into a major subnational initiative also exists.

Depending upon the jurisdiction, railroads' fuel taxes, property taxes, and other taxes would come into play as possible sources of subnational support for a rail renewal project. In Canada, and in some U.S. jurisdictions, there would be room to blend these funds with the "user fees" generated from gasoline taxes to create a genuine transportation development fund that could support projects in all modes, and even multimodal projects. But in some U.S. states, where constitutional amendments prohibit expenditure of gas tax revenues on anything other than road infrastructure, whatever fiscal policy initiative that was introduced for rail would have to be implemented in parallel with existing transportation programs.

The Piecemeal Projects scenario could not be expected to deliver a coherent and coordinated vision of twenty-first-century rail passenger potential in North America. These projects would come to fruition through either the pressure of a decline in the national carrier's ability to maintain existing service levels or the critical mass of local or regional support to do better. But, as in the case of subnational policy innovation in providing for motor vehicle mobility needs in the early twentieth century, at least some of the innovations developed to launch an isolated rail passenger renewal could later diffuse to other jurisdictions, and eventually become embodied in a future national transportation policy.

6.6. Network Franchising: National Leadership and Private Sector Direction

Should national governments in either Canada or the United States become so inclined, public enterprise passenger railroading could be eclipsed by privately run rail passenger operations. But in order to maintain both service continuity and a national network, governments would have to entice private operators into this venture. Public finance would thus remain a key policy instrument in implementing any of the various forms of privatization. Should the decision be made that a short-term upswing in operating subsidies was justified by the prospects for long-term improvement in private passenger trains' commercial effectiveness, then one or more private carriers could be found to take on this role. Governments in Ottawa or Washington would have to develop contracts specifying their minimum expectations from private operators, as well as identifying the terms by which public resources would be made available to deliver those standards.

Such an exercise in moving intercity passenger railroading back to the private sector's management would require as much, if not more, political initiative as either of the policy choices associated with scenarios featuring public sector economic direction. Not only would government have to ante up considerable resources in a transition to market-led passenger operations, but the political debate surrounding rail's place in twenty-first-century passenger transportation would still have to be waged. This scenario of returning leadership in passenger railroading to private enterprise on a national scale is labeled "Network Franchising" to capture the reality that nothing resembling a national network could emerge without some very careful planning and execution.

Evidence from the British experience with franchising strongly suggests that a government contemplating franchising must be prepared to spend more in the short to medium term on this approach to delivering a national network of passenger trains than it currently costs to operate Amtrak or VIA Rail. Significant one-time costs would be incurred to pay the consultants, lawyers, and investment bankers who would act as intermediaries in franchising and privatization. Additional costs would arise from "cleaning up" Amtrak's or VIA's balance sheets by taking on some combination of debt, severance, and pension obligations arising from current laws and contracts. Finally, significant operating subsidies would have to be incorporated into the franchise agreement(s) with private carriers. Although the operating subsidies might be expected to decline over time, capital investments in terminals, tracks, and other infrastructure could be expected to rise along with more intensive passenger operations, just as they have in the United Kingdom.

Like other paths away from the status quo, the specifics of a privately oriented rail passenger policy would depend upon the objectives. Private enterprise can deliver many policy outcomes and, like public enterprise, it will attain greatest effectiveness when the preferred results are clearly defined and aligned with the required resources. Although the "invisible hand" is often invoked as a theoretical organizing principle that would guide a market-led provision of passenger train service, the reality is that the transition from present arrangements would require political decisions regarding a framework for that market to operate within.

Short of liquidation, to be discussed below, the path toward such a Network Franchising scenario is no easier politically than any of the other scenarios. There is no easy way for government to extricate itself from public passenger railroading without addressing the contentious issues that challenge any policy initiative in this domain. Assuming that the long-term benefits of private operation were judged worth paying for, what might the policy arrangements that would facilitate a privately operated national rail passenger system in Canada or the United States look like?

Network Franchising options are likely to come down to a policy decision about money—that is, how much (or little) the train traveler is eventually expected to pay, and how much the taxpayer will kick in. If the policy expectation is that tomorrow's train traveler will have to pay all, or almost all, of her own way, then there will not be many passenger trains operating in North America as long as taxpayers continue to support sizeable investments in air and road mobility. But even under such circumstances, there would be some future for passenger trains.

In travel markets with congested highways and airports, such as the Northeastern United States, some trains like Acela Express could charge enough to cover their operating costs, although not their full infrastructure costs. States, freight railroads, or other organizations would have to take over Amtrak's physical plant and extend access to the private intercity carrier(s) on avoidable cost terms. In California, similar arrangements could emerge with access to freight railroads' infrastructure.

A recreational, rather than transportation, market niche could be filled by "rail cruise"-type trains, with luxurious services and prices to match. Privately owned, and privately held, carriers such as the American Orient Express and the Rocky Mountaineer already exist. They have been operating separately from Amtrak and VIA for more than five years with no direct public subsidies. These carriers offer convincing evidence of the potential for long-distance train travel to evolve along the same lines that transpired in ocean shipping. Since jet aircraft began flying between continents in 1958, maritime transportation has largely restructured itself to serve a growing recreational travel market.

Maritime passenger carriers continue to do business, and many earn profits. But even private rail cruise operations would require some explicit policy recognition in order to survive a transition from Amtrak's and VIA's current operations. For even though they make money, they do share some terminals, maintenance facilities, and access to freight rail infrastructure with today's public carriers. Some new arrangements would have to be made that left these operators with access to facilities and infrastructure.

If expectations are that train travelers would eventually pay a roughly equivalent share of their travel costs as people who fly or drive (i.e., less than the full cost) and that additional short term transition costs are acceptable, then Network Franchising might yield a reasonably developed national system under private management. Franchise arrangements would have to be designed with enough short-term operating subsidies to ensure that private carriers came forward to take on the operation of many short and medium distance trains. Long-distance routes could also be franchised with very basic year-round service to be supplemented, and partly supported, by the fees that private rail cruise operators would contribute to hook their equipment onto these trains at certain times of the year. This model is already operative in Alaska, where the Alaska Railroad, a state owned carrier, has been pulling luxury equipment operated by Holland America–Westours and Princess Railtours behind its regularly scheduled passenger train between Anchorage and Fairbanks since 1987.

As implied by the preceding discussion, the Network Franchising scenario will require an organizational midwife. Between the time that a decision would be taken to bring private carriers back into operating a rail passenger network and the transfer of operating responsibilities to a private carrier, some public organization would have to take on a considerable amount of planning and administrative, legal, and financial work.

In the United States, the ARAA charges the Amtrak Reform Council with developing a "post-Amtrak" operating scenario in the event that Amtrak does not meet its commercial self-sufficiency target. The law is silent on subsequent implementation of that plan. Depending on whether the council embarks on this planning effort and, if so, how its results are received, Congress could seek to extend the council's mandate to include the legal and administrative responsibilities of the franchising process. But if the council's efforts continue to generate controversy and conflict, the Department of Transportation and the Federal Railroad Administration could also take on the role of implementing rail passenger privatization.

America's previous example of railroad privatization, the sale of Conrail in 1987, illustrates that even the sale of a profit-making public enterprise was far from easy. Both the Reagan administration's enthusiasm for free enterprise, and the fact that Secretary of Transportation Elizabeth Dole happened to be married to Senate Majority Leader Robert Dole, were not sufficient to keep the sale of Conrail from becoming caught in a political crossfire. The administration's preferred strategy, selling Conrail in its entirety to the Norfolk Southern (NS), was opposed by much of the investment banking community, led by Morgan Stanley. When Transportation Secretary Dole claimed that she "had to think of the public interest," she implied that a $1.2 billion cash offer that NS made in 1995 carried less risk than floating Conrail's shares through an initial public offering.[24] But during the course of intense political skirmishing, in which Conrail's senior management, Morgan Stanley, shippers, communities, and other interests all took to the halls of Congress, the Department of Transportation was forced to drop its preferred privatization strategy and pursue an initial public offering, which wound up netting the government $1.88 billion.[25] Conrail's privatization suggests that whatever administrative organization is to be charged with rail passenger franchising, conflicts are likely to spill over into Congress. Furthermore, whatever network plan is produced will likely serve as the starting point for political wheeling and dealing that could likely yield a very different outcome than the official proposal.

In Canada, the federal Ministry of Transport would be the most likely organization to preside over a rail passenger franchising process. The Ministry has quite a track record in reorganizing Canada's airport, air navigation, and port management activities, which it transferred to non-profit port and airport authorities, and to NAV-Canada. In these cases, "white papers" outlining the administrative and financial principles that would govern such a transfer were developed in advance.[26] The Ministry also studied rail passenger franchising during 1999. Without any white paper setting forth the objectives and assessment criteria for this exercise, one can only assume that the significant short-term costs of a Network Franchising scenario influenced the decision to direct capital grants to a public enterprise (VIA Rail) over the coming five years. But government's capital investment plan does include a demonstration project for franchising, which could "test the waters" for more significant steps in this direction in the future.

Network Franchising's potential for success would depend upon the terms by which infrastructure access is provided. Such terms could be expected to differ considerably between the Northeast, where access to, along with operational control over, Amtrak's crown-jewel Northeast Corridor infrastructure would come along with the franchise, and the rest of the country, where freight railroads would continue to own and operate the rail infrastructure.

In the Northeast, prospective carriers could be expected to eagerly compete for the passenger franchise, especially if it came with operating rights for freight or commuter trains in the corridor. Northeast freight and commuter operations could make this region's passenger franchise profitable, if the corridor's infrastructure was kept up by government and user fees were collected from operators along the same lines as air and road carriers.

Elsewhere, freight railroads would play a key role in franchising arrangements, the specifics depending on their degree of enthusiasm. Freight railroads could become enthusiastic bidders to take on passenger rail franchises directly, in effect returning to the model of subsidized operations that were the norm in Canada prior to VIA Rail's creation. But the incentives for such a reengagement would have to be considerable—surpassing the opportunity costs of both new freight business and a new role in supplying passenger franchisees with infrastructure.

Freight railroads could also hedge their bets and become involved in Network Franchising by supplying access to the new carriers that would provide the actual interface with passengers. This could be done on a simple fee-for-service basis as is typical of the rail access arrangements of most, but not all, of the luxury rail cruises now operating. Or, freight railroads could partner with new carriers, a trend that is already established in their joining forces with organizations (e.g., third party logistics providers) to develop new markets (e.g., intermodal container traffic) based upon meeting new types of customer needs.

Freight railroads could also be unenthusiastic, or even unwilling, franchise participants if access provisions were legislated into the transfer arrangements. While some sort of access "safety net" might be necessary, the goodwill of infrastructure owners cannot be compelled. Amtrak's and VIA's histories both suggest that an adversarial relationship between carrier and infrastructure owner is a sure recipe for poor operational performance and schedule reliability.

Once the dust was to settle after such a transformation, and private carriers began operating passenger trains on a large scale, where would a Network Franchising scenario lead? There are almost certain to be "growing pains" associated with such a transition. These are unlikely to be as extreme as the recent operational and financial chaos of Great Britain's private rail franchises. Still, any slippage in safety or service standards would certainly trigger protests and calls for government intervention.

As with road and air transport, government's role in intercity rail travel would not disappear, but it would shift into something resembling a silent partner with the private carriers. Sponsorship of some infrastructure, oversight for safety and service standards, along with long-run intermodal planning would remain public sector activities, while private carriers would gain increasing operational and commercial autonomy. Over time, the private policy actors (e.g., carriers) that become operators are likely also to become effective advocates for policies that allocate public resources to their mode. Airlines, trucking carriers, and bus companies demonstrate how legitimacy in the marketplace can be leveraged to advantage in transportation policy, in ways that even a profit-making public enterprise like Conrail had difficulty getting away with.

If it posts promising results, Network Franchising might bring some skeptics around to supporting intercity rail investment. This would facilitate developing a rail passenger renewal along lines that parallel government's support for other modes. Where private carriers have taken on North American intercity train operations in the rail-cruise segment of the travel market, ridership, revenue, and profit trends have generally been positive. But these are small niches in a very large and diverse market. There is, thus, much uncertainty surrounding a nationwide Network Franchising scenario.

6.7. Niche Markets: Subnational Leadership and Private-Sector Direction

While moving the bulk of a national network of passenger trains from public enterprise to private operation represents a pretty tall order, passing on only the most promising operations would be less difficult. In such a "Niche Markets" scenario, governments would cease treating passenger rail as a national responsibility, with the expectation that trains would contribute to meeting national mobility needs. Instead, some states or provinces would fill in the policy gap to attain the benefits of quite specific passenger train projects and services, without any pretense that these could, or should, add up to a coherent whole.

The most promising market niche for passenger train service in North America remains the Northeast Corridor. Here, population, geography, and air and road infrastructure constraints combine with the North American anomaly of publicly owned rail infrastructure to offer a unique opportunity for a potentially profitable rail passenger service under private operation. Should Washington divest itself of the Northeast Corridor, assuming that the states along its route were prepared to take responsibility for that rail infrastructure by organizing an interstate compact or commission to manage it, then a private carrier could be found to operate intercity passenger trains.

The next most promising market niche for passenger train service that conforms to political boundaries could be found in the states of California or Florida. These states have already acquired rail infrastructure for regional and commuter passenger operations and could build upon such a base to supervise franchisees operating intercity passenger trains along these, and other, tracks. California, and to a lesser extent Florida, also have in place a rail passenger oversight capacity through their support of Amtrak's incrementally upgraded services.

In Canada, provincial governments could take on the role of organizational midwife for enticing private carriers to embark upon intraprovincial passenger operations. The most promising such travel markets would be in Ontario, and between Calgary and Edmonton. An initiative between Vancouver, Seattle, and Portland might also be possible if British Columbia could find a way to work with the states of Oregon and Washington. But none of these prospects is particularly promising, unless subnational governments place some serious incentives on the table.

Unless policy changes were made that enabled states to spend transportation trust funds more flexibly (e.g., by redirecting federal gasoline and aviation and airport tax revenues into intercity rail spending), the amount of resources available to support the transition and initial operations of new carriers would be quite limited. Consequently, the service levels would be modest indeed. On the whole, states and provinces are not particularly flush with revenue, unlike national governments that are currently awash in budget surpluses, so that the market niches for passenger trains spun off to private operation under subnational governments' initiative would indeed be quite small.

6.8. Looking at Liquidation

Another policy initiative that could be played out either independently, or in combination with one of the above scenarios, would be the liquidation of some or all of the assets at Amtrak or VIA Rail. Skeptics in American and Canadian government have certainly contemplated ways of winding down their respective public passenger carriers in such a fashion. There are several ways that the assets and liabilities of these entities could be laid to rest.

These enterprises could be directed to plan for an orderly wrap up of their operations. This approach is found in the Amtrak Reform and Accountability Act, which calls upon the corporation to draw up its own liquidation plan in case it does not attain commercial self-sufficiency by 2003. VIA could be the subject of a liquidation plan prepared by the Transport Minister, as there is no precedent for a Crown Corporation being directed to put itself out of business in Canada.[27]

Another option would be to turn authority in liquidating rail passenger assets over to the courts. American railroad policy has regularly relied upon the courts to manage, or at least supervise, railroad liquidation and reorganization. Canadian courts have been involved in commercial restructuring of airlines and bus companies. Going to the courts would be one way for government to "pass the buck" following a decision to amputate passenger trains from national transportation policy, but it could also be pursued to facilitate a transfer of assets to private carriers while salvaging the government's investment in rail passenger equipment and infrastructure.

In the United States, any form of liquidation would have a high probability of precipitating a legal epidemic of claims and counterclaims surrounding Amtrak's various obligations. Washington, state governments, Amtrak, various creditors (including some major foreign lenders), labor unions, and other stakeholders would likely become embroiled in legal disputes over responsibility for loans, labor protection payments, and other obligations that Amtrak has taken on over the years. VIA Rail is less entangled with third parties through loans and other obligations, meaning that a liquidation of its assets would be less likely to trigger protracted legal conflict.

While introducing bankruptcy and other legal proceedings into the process of restructuring passenger trains would make the judiciary a major new participant in developing rail passenger policy, it would also make it virtually impossible, particularly in the United States, to achieve the quick and clean break with past policy that rail passenger skeptics have aspired to for so long. Thus the very finality that makes liquidation appear attractive to skeptics would likely degenerate into protracted legal wrangling that adds time, uncertainty, and costs to this ostensibly clean break with public enterprise passenger railroading. To the extent that it could play a useful role in rail passenger renewal, an extent that is sure to be hotly debated, liquidation would be most effective not as an end in itself, but as a complementary means to policy goals that have been reconciled and legitimated through political deliberations. Should it be pursued as an alternative to those deliberations, liquidation is likely to cause more problems than it resolves.

6.9. Taking the Next Steps

The above scenarios, along with much of the rest of this book, have hopefully served to illustrate that there is indeed a choice between all or nothing in contemporary North American passenger train policy. Recent history suggests that neither the supporters of a rail passenger renaissance, nor the skeptics who see ongoing operations as throwing good money after bad, will carry the day in turning their positions into definitive American or Canadian transportation policy. Thirty years of political stalemate only emphasize the futility of boiling rail passenger policy options down to a choice between "Save the Trains" or "Cut the Subsidies." Indeed, serious efforts to identify, evaluate, and—above all—implement more workable policy alternatives are both necessary and possible.

From time to time, necessity and opportunity coincide to create policy windows where what is needed also becomes possible, and what is possible actually becomes accomplished by public officials who are confronted by competing issues and interests. The years 2002 and 2003 appear to present such a window of policy opportunity for Amtrak. In VIA Rail's case such a window is less certain, but one is likely to open around 2004 or 2005. At these times, the public carriers' efforts to do better commercially and the financial measures that governments have put in place to tide them through such renewal will have run their course. And then what? In a transportation sector where deregulation has opened up widespread competition from air and road carriers, and even precipitated a commercial renaissance of sorts among rail freight carriers, the sheer magnitude of innovation and commercial success will prompt rail policy community participants to think, "What comes next?"

If this examination has added anything to that deliberation, it will be to encourage policy participants to revisit the "hard" questions about how private enterprise ought to relate to government support for passenger travel, and how national and subnational governments ought to pursue their transportation responsibilities in tandem. These issues have regularly been sidestepped as governments and policy communities tried to come up with "quick fixes" for the economic decline of traditional railroad passenger service. These questions are certainly difficult, but they are not impossible to resolve. And should energy and environmental concerns rise on the policy agenda, the opportunity to do better at rail passenger policy will be seen to have even greater value than simply addressing the commercial shortcomings of two public passenger carriers.

Reenvisioning the future of North American intercity passenger rail services and reengineering the institutions that can deliver that future will require revisiting the national/subnational and public/private dimensions of what makes for successful transportation policy in Canada and the United States. When the policy community of governments and private firms engaged in shaping the future of North America's passenger trains begins to resemble those involved in air or road transportation, then the political legitimacy and economic opportunities for the entire rail mode will align to enable change for the better. Such a vision, and the degree of change that it implies from business as usual in surface transportation policy, may sound too challenging to those inured to the trench warfare that has characterized the pursuit of preservationist policy by Amtrak and VIA Rail.

Yet those who find such a future unrealistic, or are concerned about the formidable obstacles that appear to block the emergence of such a vision, should reconsider what the preceding chapters have documented about the last thirty years. The results of relegating the passenger train to a contested public guardianship at the fringe of the transportation policy communities in Canada and the United States speak for themselves. In both nations, the closing decades of the twentieth century must unfortunately be counted as a time of missed opportunities in intercity passenger railroading. The best use that can now be made of the considerable investments of American and Canadian governments, not to mention the efforts of so many dedicated staff who got Amtrak and VIA through some difficult days, is to learn the lessons of what did not work and apply this knowledge to doing better in the future.

Even the most superlative entrepreneurs would fail at renewing the passenger train under the transportation policies that remain in place on this continent today. Changing policy is essential to really improving what passenger trains could offer travelers, taxpayers, and business partners in Canada and the United States. Such a new departure for North America's passenger trains is long overdue.

Afterword

North America's transportation policies were on the front line when hijacked airliners slammed into the World Trade Center and the Pentagon on September 11, 2001. In less than an hour, the boundary between civilian and military dimensions of transportation had been breached, with aircraft across Canada and the United States grounded *en masse* due to concerns over further suicidal attacks from the air. When these planes took off again, it was into the skies of a changed world where new modes of "normal" activity are still far from being established. What does appear likely is that new transportation priorities will either supplement, or substitute for, the existing policy objectives that left Americans vulnerable to mass murder by such a commonplace way of travel.

Before September 11, most policy experts and decision-makers had regarded civil aviation, and transportation more generally, as a mature industry needing little in the way of direction from government. Aircraft were seen to be no different economically than "buses with wings," a phrase that had regularly been trotted out to describe the airline industry's competitive dynamics during the 1990s. In this paradigm, transportation security was mostly equated with preventing accidents, something that could be assured through a discrete set of safety regulations and oversight by government inspectors while the rest of transportation policy was inspired by market forces. Competition among private carriers was presumed to maximize the efficiency by which goods and people could circulate on the world's most mobile continent.

It is now apparent that key elements of that transportation policy paradigm were sorely lacking and that these shortcomings exposed North Americans to significant risks. Just as it is now obvious that buses could not have been transformed into the weapons of mass terror that hijacked aircraft became, it is also clear that market forces could not be expected to yield adequate protection against such a threat. The profit motive and cost minimization were simply not up to the challenge of securing America's skies from a takeover by suicidal terrorists. The results unleashed a wave of distrust and fear among the traveling public that has yet to run its course.

What changes in transportation policy will emerge as Canada and the United States take a close look at how to defend effectively against the risks that became apparent on September 11? While it is too soon to predict the specifics of these changes, it is safe to bet that the emerging policies will create more room for government leadership in planning and managing all means of mobility. Private carriers will certainly continue to play an important role in "delivering the goods," as well as the people, to North American destinations. But they will likely do so in a policy framework that leaves much less of the direct and indirect outcomes from freight and passenger transportation to chance. While markets can provide innovation and efficiency, governments will be pressed to offer more in the way of guarantees against catastrophic outcomes, both for those aboard ships, planes, trains, and automobiles as well as those along their routes.

How far governments go in taking on new civilian transportation responsibilities will be most influenced by two factors. The first impetus to changing policy will arise from short-term efforts to combat terrorism at home and abroad. Given the unprecedented damage inflicted by several dozen hijackers and their accomplices, who may have spent as little as $200,000 to mount their devastating attacks,[1] policy-makers will certainly revise their tolerance for risk in civilian transportation downward. The key question is how far the measures taken against terrorist networks and states that harbor them will drive risk reduction efforts in North American transportation.

Early indications are that the United States, at least, is prepared to go a long way in taking diplomatic, financial, intelligence, and military actions in executing its war on terrorism. The further Canada and the United States go with their campaign against global terrorism, the closer to "zero tolerance" that security goals in civilian transportation policies are likely to move, and the more that these changes would be influenced by strategies emanating from law enforcement, intelligence, and military agencies. Such calculations would tend to weigh the collective benefits of transportation security higher than the economic costs they would impose on carriers or users.

An example of how this logic would play out can be seen in how the reopening of Washington's Reagan-National Airport differed from that of other U.S. airports, both in timing and outcome. The Department of Transportation's Federal Aviation Administration was called upon to certify airport security following the terrorist attack, and cleared all facilities within a week in an attempt to get the nation's air travel operations back to "business as usual." Due to Reagan-National's proximity to the Pentagon, White House, and U.S. Capitol, the National Security Agency and the Secret Service were called upon to certify this airport's security before operations resumed. These agencies gave no priority to economic considerations, took over three weeks to certify Reagan-National's seciurity, and initially proposed reconfiguring flight operations in a way that would have cut the airport's capacity by up to 65 percent as the preferred option for assuring appropriate safety against terrorist attack.[2] When Reagan-National did reopen on October 4, every flight had an armed undercover sky marshal aboard and passengers were required to remain belted into their seats for one-half hour prior to landing on inbound flights and one-half hour following takeoff on departures.[3]

If such an approach to risk management were to become the new policy norm in other areas of transportation, it would significantly shift the balance toward security at the cost of economic efficiency. The commercial strategies of many air and surface carriers would have to be radically revised to ensure economic survival under such circumstances. Indeed, all but the most perfunctory policy initiatives to enhance transportation security can be expected to trigger new commercial strategies by carriers.

The second impetus to changing transportation policy will come from differences in travel behavior. The immediate drop in all forms of travel will likely be transitory, but mobility patterns that emerge in the months following September 11 could well influence the adaptation of transportation policies as some modes gain business while others lose it.

It does not take great imagination to see Americans, in particular, retreating from all forms of travel that require sharing personal space with strangers, into the perceived security of their most familiar transport means, the automobile. Nor is it clairvoyant to predict a significant drop in air travel that will last beyond the immediate uncertainty and concerns about terrorist threats.

Air travel is likely to be depressed in the medium and possibly the long term, either by further acts of terrorism (even those occurring beyond North America) or by the effects of enhanced security. Will business travelers switch to surface transportation if they have to spend two hours going through appropriate security screening for a forty-five-minute flight? And will budget travelers be able to afford the price of the enhanced inspections and counterterrorism measures that will be introduced, if such costs are passed on to users? Without vast new subsidies to pay for the direct and indirect costs of such security, it is hard to imagine that the demand for air travel will not be affected. Both flying and driving could also be influenced by changes to the price and availability of imported oil that might arise from a protracted and aggressive military campaign against terrorists and the as yet unknown nations that are targeted as their allies. ·

Rail and intercity bus travel spiked upward immediately after September 11, as people who had never set foot on either mode sought alternatives to grounded and severely disrupted flights. For the five days following the attacks, Amtrak's ridership was up 17 percent to around 80,000 daily passengers.[4] The transformation of Reagan-National Airport into a "maximum security" facility and the increased check-in deadlines for all flights will provide an especially valuable boost to Amtrak's new *Acela Express*, whose competitive position against airline "shuttles" between Washington, New York, and Boston is certainly strengthened. Commercial projections that once looked optimistic will likely become more realistic for Amtrak's flagship operation. In a sudden reversal of prior ambivalence about the train's future, many are taking a new look at Amtrak in light of its ability to move travelers when airlines were incapacitated.

The evidence for an effective alternative to air travel for trips under 600 miles is already resonating strongly with news media in the Northeast. On September 24, the *Washington Post* editorialized that "increased Amtrak use has underscored what its supporters have said all along—that train service remains an essential part of the country's transportation system."[5] The *New York Times'* editorial writers, often skeptical regarding Amtrak's effectiveness, appeared to see things in a new light on September 25, writing, "Stranded travelers made a fortuitous discovery when the airlines shut down after the terrorist attacks: The country still has an intercity rail system."[6] Judged by these reactions, the balance of public opinion appears to be tipping away from skepticism and toward support of passenger trains' contribution to American mobility.

Media and public officials in the South, Midwest, and West—where travelers have little or no back-up to planes for high-speed travel—have also begun to call for more attention to passenger trains. Editorials in Milwaukee and Spokane typify this demand for broadening the scope of aviation alternatives beyond the Northeast. Both within the rail policy community and beyond, the skeptics' frame of reference that depicted rail passenger development as a wasteful extravagance and emphasized Amtrak's shortcomings as justification for avoiding rail investments will certainly be diminishing, and could even be undermined, in the aftermath of September 11's attacks.

The looming battle over Amtrak's re-authorization in 2002 is likely to unfold very differently than anyone would have imagined before September 11. With $15 billion in domestic airline subsidies passed into law with massive bipartisan support,[7] Amtrak's life or death struggle to attain "commercial self-sufficiency" looks less dire than it once did. Amtrak president George Warrington wasted little time in calling for abandonment of that litmus test, stating that the self-sufficiency requirement is "inappropriate, impractical, and irrational in the context of recent events and public expectations."[8] In debating whether to drop commercial self-sufficiency as the benchmark for deciding upon government's support of Amtrak, skeptics will be very hard pressed to make the case that market forces should be allowed to rule.

Where, then, should North American passenger rail policy be heading in this time of changing realities about transportation and homeland security? Elsewhere, Joseph Szyliowicz and I have argued for taking a systemic approach to enhanced security in North American transportation, and offered some unconventional thinking about the role of passenger trains. We wrote that in new policies extending beyond immediate reinforcement of civil aviation's integrity and financial viability, "The goal should not simply be to safeguard one part of North America's transportation capacity, but rather to develop a more robust, integrated network that can provide redundancy and multiply the available mobility options."[9] Modern passenger trains belong in such a vision for many reasons. These days, high-speed rail—the key that unlocked passenger trains' renewal in Europe and Japan—has a new appeal in light of anxiety about a vulnerable air transport network. Trains have a proven ability to both substitute for air travel in corridors of up to 600 miles and to feed travelers onto longer flights at hubs in Paris, Frankfurt, and Zurich, among others. The absence of such travel options in most parts of North America, and its costs, are now increasingly obvious.

Should skepticism about Amtrak and VIA continue to recede, while people discover that trains can be improved by plans and proposals that have, to date, been stymied by the policy stalemate chronicled in this book, then the odds of developing a new policy framework will change for the better. While the nature of change in rail passenger policy remains to be determined, the chances for such a new departure look more likely amid the unprecedented upheavals following September 11's tragic terrorist attacks.

Notes

1. Public Policy: The Key to Rail Passenger Renewal

1. T.C. Keefer, *Philosophy of Railroads* (Toronto: Univ. of Toronto Press, 1972).

2. For an excellent social history of railroad transportation, see Nicholas Faith, *The World the Railways Made* (London: Pimlico, 1990).

3. Gregory Lee Thompson, *The Passenger Train in the Motor Age: California's Rail and Bus Industries, 1910–1941* (Columbus, Ohio: Ohio State Univ. Press, 1993), 10.

4. In addition to Thompson's detailed assessment of California, see John F. Stover, *The Life and Decline of the American Railroad* (New York: Oxford Univ. Press, 1970). For an interpretation of how the political backlash against railroad excesses became the principal cause of that industry's decline, see Albro Martin, *Enterprise Denied: Origins of the Decline of American Railroads, 1897–1917* (New York: Columbia Univ. Press, 1971).

5. For a good overview, see William D. Coleman and Grace Skogstad, *Policy Communities and Public Policy in Canada: A Structural Approach* (Mississauga, Ont.: Copp Clark Pitman, 1990).

6. Paul Pierson has elaborated upon the idea of the "feedback loop," by which policy creates political action on the part of individuals and organizations in "When Effect Becomes Cause: Policy Feedback and Political Change," *World Politics* 45, no. 4 (July 1993): 595–628.

7. NIMBY stands for "Not In My BackYard" and denotes those who oppose any form of development that would impact their local area.

8. For more details about how institutional durability has differentiated American and French transportation policy, see Anthony Perl, "Financing Transport Infrastructure: The Effects of Institutional Durability in French and American Policymaking," *Governance* 4, no. 4 (October 1991): 365–402.

9. For the evidence of an explicit conspiracy to replace rail transit with buses, see Glenn Yago, *The Decline of Transit: Urban Transportation in German and U.S. Cities, 1900–1970* (Cambridge, U.K.: Cambridge Univ. Press, 1984); and David Gurin, "Trolley Transit in New York," *Bulletin of the National Railway Historical Society* 42, no. 1–2 (1977). For an argument that even these conspiracy theories are overblown see Sy Adler, "The Transformation of the Pacific Electric Railway: Bradford Snell, Roger

Rabbit, and the Politics of Transportation in Los Angeles," *Urban Affairs Quarterly* 27, no. 1 (September 1991): 51–86.

10. Ryohei Kakumoto, "Sensible Politics and Transport Theories?—Japan's National Railways in the 20th Century," *Japan Railway & Transport Review* 22 (December 1999): 27.

11. Kiyohiko Yoshitake, *An Introduction to Public Enterprise in Japan* (London: Sage Publications, 1973), 58.

12. H. Strobel and A. Straszak, "Subsystems Analysis," in *The Shinkansen Program: Transportation, Railway, Environmental, Regional, and National Development Issues*, ed. A. Straszak (Laxenburg, Austria: International Institute for Applied Systems Analysis, 1981), 82.

13. M. Nishida, "Development of Advanced High-Speed Trains in Japan," in *International Symposium on Traffic and Transportation Technologies, IVA '79, June 18–20, 1979* (Hamburg, Germany: Bundesministerium für Forschung und Technologie, 1979), 26–27.

14. M. Nishida, "History of the Shinkansen," in *The Shinkansen High-Speed Rail Network of Japan: Proceedings of an IIASA Conference, June 27–30, 1977*, eds. A. Straszak and R. Tuch (Toronto: Pergamon Press, 1977), 11–20.

15. H. Knop and A. Straszak, "The Shinkansen and National Development Issues," in *The Shinkansen Program: Transportation, Railway, Environmental, Regional, and National Development Issues*, ed. A. Straszak (Laxenburg, Austria: International Institute for Applied Systems Analysis, 1981), 425.

16. Bill Hosakawa, *Old Man Thunder: Father of the Bullet Train* (Denver, Colo.: Sogo Way, 1997), 174.

17. Hosakawa, *Old Man Thunder*, 178.

18. Strobel and Straszak, "Subsystems Analysis," 81.

19. Kakumoto, "Sensible Politics and Transport Theories?," 27–28.

20. Hosokawa, *Old Man Thunder*, 178.

21. "Japan is Building Speedy Rail Line," *New York Times*, 26 April 1959, 20. Conversion to 2000 amount made using consumer price index data available at Robert C. Sahr (Oregon State University), *Consumer Price Index (CPI) Conversion Factors to Convert to (estimated) Dollars of the Year 2000*, 2000. http://www.orst.edu/dept/pol_sci/fac/sahr/cv00.pdf (17 March 2001).

22. Hosokawa, *Old Man Thunder*, 200.

23. "Japanese Build a Super-Railroad," *Business Week*, 1 December 1962, 89.

24. "Japan's Fast Train—How It's Working Out," *U.S. News & World Report*, 25 January 1965, 70.

25. Hosokawa, *Old Man Thunder*, 176.

26. Strobel and Straszak, "Subsystems Analysis," 80–81.

27. T. Yorino, "Environmental Problems and the Shinkansen," in *The Shinkansen High-Speed Rail Network of Japan: Proceedings of an IIASA Conference, June 27–30, 1977*, eds. A. Straszak and R. Tuch (Toronto: Pergamon Press, 1977), 157.

28. The *New York Times* reported that Japan Airlines' seat occupancy on the Tokyo–Osaka route dropped below 50 percent during the Shinkansen's first year of

operation. See Emerson Chapin, "Japan's Airlines Step Up Service," *New York Times*, 14 March 1965, sec. S, 21.

29. "New Japan Train Cuts Air Travel," *New York Times*, 28 February 1965, sec. S, 18.

30. Details of the financial arrangements surrounding the nationalization of French railroads can be found in Joseph Jones, *The Politics of Transport in Twentieth Century France* (Kingston, Ont.: McGill-Queen's Univ. Press, 1984).

31. For an overview of the policy dynamics of public enterprise in France's energy sector, see Harvey B. Feigenbaum, *The Politics of Public Enterprise: Oil and the French State* (Princeton: Princeton Univ. Press, 1985).

32. Groupe de travail du comité interministériel des enterprises publiques, *Rapport sur les Entreprises Publiques* (Paris: La Documentation Française, 1967).

33. Jack Hayward, *The State and the Market Economy: Industrial Patriotism and Economic Intervention in France* (New York: New York Univ. Press, 1986), 229.

34. Details about SNCF's "intellectual conversion" into a more market-oriented public enterprise can be found in M. Fourniau and G. Ribeill, "La grande vitesse sur rail en France et en R.F.A.," *La grande technologie entre l'État et le marché*, eds. E. Brenac, D. Finon, and P. Muller (Grenoble: CERAT, 1991).

35. Institut National de la Statistique et des Études Économiques—Ile-De-France, *Ile-de-France à la page, Mensuel*, no. 171 (Juillet 1999): 4.

36. Institut National de la Statistique et des Études Économiques—Rhône Alpes, *La Lettre*, no. 63 (Juillet 1999): 1.

37. Jacques Pavaux, *Rail/Air Complementarity in Europe: The Impact of High-Speed Train Services* (Paris: Institute of Air Transport, 1991).

38. For a comparison of the French and German approaches to linking technology to passenger train revitalization, see James A. Dunn Jr. and Anthony Perl, "Policy Networks and Industrial Revitalization: High Speed Rail Initiatives in France and Germany," *Journal of Public Policy* 14, no. 3 (July 1994): 311–43.

39. François Plassard, "France," in *Report of the Hundred and Fifth Round Table on Transport Economics held in Paris on 7th–8th November 1996 on the following topic: Infrastructure Induced Mobility* (Paris: European Conference of Ministers of Transport, 1998), 122.

40. Judith Patterson and Anthony Perl, "The TGV Effect: A Potential Opportunity for Reconciling Sustainability with Aviation," *World Transport Policy & Practice* 5, no. 1 (1999): 39–45.

41. While both Nice and Toulouse do have trains to and from Paris that are operated by TGV equipment, these operate over conventional track for much of their journeys, with trip times of five hours or more.

42. Plassard, "France," 126.

43. For an exploration of the infrastructure innovation that enabled the TGV's connectivity with air travel, see Anthony Perl, "Redesigning an Airport for International Competitiveness: The Politics of Administrative Innovation at CDG," *Journal of Air Transport Management* 4, no. 4 (October 1998): 189–99.

44. Anthony Perl and James A. Dunn Jr., "Globalization and the Diffusion of

High-Speed Ground Transportation Systems: Obstacles, Opportunities, and Entrepreneurs," in *Rail International: 3rd World Congress on High-Speed Rail Proceedings* (Brussels: International Railway Congress Association, 1998), 211–15.

45. France began to decentralize its administrative system by transferring a growing list of responsibilities (including some in transportation) to regional and local governments in 1982, but this was after the initial TGV had been implemented.

46. Ferdinand Protzman, "Germany Rolls Out Its Fast Train," *New York Times*, 30 May 1991, sec. D, 1.

47. HSB, *Studie über ein Schnellverkehrssystem: Systemanalyse und Ergebnisse* (Munich: HSB Studiengesellschaft, 1971).

48. Michael M. Atkinson and William D. Coleman, "Strong States and Weak States: Sectoral Policy Networks in Advanced Capitalist Economies," *British Journal of Political Science* 19, no. 1 (1989), 55.

49. Michael Marray, "German Greens Go Off the Rails," *European*, 18 May 1998, 24.

50. "Wirtschaftswoche: Look From Within (Im eigenen Lande prüfen)," *El Mundo* (Santa Cruz), 5 November 1998.

51. "Not Enough Passengers for Transrapid (Dem Transrapid fehlen Fahrgäste)," *Die Welt* (Berlin), 13 July 1999.

52. "Germany to Build Transrapid Train, Even if Costs Exceed 6.1 bln dm—Minister," *AFX Europe*, 16 June 1999.

53. Tony Paterson, "Rumbling Grows on Fast Track to Berlin," *European*, 7 November 1996, 4.

54. "Deutsche Bahn Head Defends Transrapid (Bahn-Chef verteidigt Transrapid)," *Die Welt* (Berlin), 3 July 1999.

55. "Regional Governments Keen to Save Transrapid (Lander Wollen Transrapid retten)," *Die Welt* (Berlin), 7 December 1999.

56. "German Govt 'Determined' to Build Single-Track Transrapid Train," *AFX Europe*, 16 September 1999.

57. "Struck Backs Transrapid Plan (Struck stutzt Transrapid Plan)," *Die Welt* (Berlin), 20 September 1999.

58. "DaimlerChrysler's Adtranz Chief Says Transrapid Project has No Future," *AFX Europe*, 12 October 1999.

59. "Transrapid Consortium Seeks Compensation (Transrapid-Konsortium will Schadenersatz)," *Die Welt* (Berlin), 28 January 2000.

2. Building on Achievement: A "New Model Railroad" for the Twenty-First Century

1. In the six figures that follow, Japanese data were obtained from Fumitoshi Mizutani, "An Assessment of the Japan Railway Companies Since Privatization: Performance, Local Rail Service and Debts," *Transport Reviews* 19, no. 2 (1999): 119. European data were obtained from European Commission Directorate-General for Energy and Transport, *EU Transport in Figures: Statistical Pocket Book 2000* (Brussels:

European Commission Directorate-General for Energy and Transport, 2000), 81. American data were obtained from U.S. Department of Transportation, Bureau of Transportation Statistics, *National Transportation Statistics, 1999* (Washington, D.C.: Bureau of Transportation Statistics, 1999), 46–47. United States data excludes buses as no figures were available for 1970 and 1980. Also, U.S. "Commuter and Transit" for 1970 excludes transit figures, as data was not available for that year. Japanese "Private Railway Co's" figures were determined by subtracting Japanese (National) Railway passenger-miles from total Japanese railway passenger-miles. All European Union and Japanese passenger-kilometers were converted to passenger-miles in order to produce comparable data. Passenger-mile data for each mode were then divided by the population of each country during the years 1970, 1980, and 1990. All passenger-miles were rounded off to the nearest single unit.

2. James A. Dunn Jr. and Anthony Perl, "Toward a 'New Model Railway' for the 21st Century: Lessons From Five Countries," *Transportation Quarterly* 55, no. 2 (spring 2001): 43–57.

3. For information about European transportation deregulation and how the resulting competition influenced rail renewal, see D.M. van de Velde, *Changing Trains: Railway Reform and the Role of Competition: The Experience of Six Countries* (Brookfield, Vt.: Ashgate, 1999). For information on Japanese airline deregulation, see Joan M. Feldman, "Testing Reform in a Mass Market," *Air Transport World* 32, Issue 7, July 1995, 24–32.

4. For details and analysis of EU Directive 91/440 see Christopher Knill and Dirk Lehmkuhl, "An Alternative Route of European Integration: The Community's Railway Policy," *West European Politics* 23, no. 1 (January 2000), 65–88.

5. Information on the recent history and financing of Réseau Ferré de France is drawn from that company's English language web site. See Réseau Ferré de France, *RFF: French Railway Network Owner and Manager*, 2001. http://www.rff.fr/e34n34uk/fproforg.htm (26 February 2001).

6. Réseau Ferré de France, *Réseau Ferré de France's Ranking*, 2001. http://www.rff.fr/e34n34uk/popaaa.htm (26 February 2001).

7. Réseau Ferré de France, *The Reform of Reform: Statement by the Minister of Facilities, Transport and Housing*, n.d. http://www.rff.fr/e34n34uk/popref.htm (26 February 2001).

8. Réseau Ferré de France, *The Main Lines of the 2001 Investment Budget*, 2001. http://www.rff.fr/e34n34uk/fprofpol.htm (26 February 2001).

9. David Owen, "A Fine Way to Run a Railway—and Turn a Profit," *Financial Times*, 8 January 2001, 12.

10. Réseau Ferré de France, *Investment Policy: The New Investment Financing Rules*, 2001. http://www.rff.fr/e34n34uk/fprofpol.htm (26 February 2001).

11. Uta Harnischfeger, "German Rail Chief Spurns the British Way: But Plans for the Privatisation of Deutsche Bahn have Run into a Hail of Criticism," *Financial Times*, 1 November 2000, 2.

12. Deregulierungskommission, *Marköffnung und Wettbewerb* (Bonn: Bundeswirtschaftsministerium, 1990).

13. Gerhard Lehmbruch, "The Institutional Framework of German Regulation," in *The Politics of German Regulation*, ed. Kenneth Dyson (Aldershot: Dartmouth Publishing, 1992), 45–46.

14. Frank-Matthias Ludwig, "German Railways Face a Decade of Reform," *Railway Gazette International*, July 1993, 479–80; German Information Service, "Railroad Reform Approved: East, West Railways to Merge and Be Privatized," *The Week in Germany*, 10 December 1993, 5.

15. P.H. Bowers, "Railway Reform in Germany," *Journal of Transport Economics and Policy* 30, no. 1 (January 1996): 96.

16. Steve Bennett, "Franz Heads Both DB Passenger Units," *International Railway Journal*, September 2000, 22.

17. Quoted in David Briginshaw, "DB's Two Biggest Rail Projects Suffer Setbacks," *International Railway Journal*, September 2000, 36.

18. Ralph Atkins, "Chief of Deutsche Bahn is Dismissed," *Financial Times*, 15 September 1999, 3.

19. Ibid.

20. "Light at the End of the Tunnel," *Economist*, 10 February 2001, 66.

21. Jorn Paterak and Haig Simonian, "Scale of German Rail Losses Revealed," *Financial Times*, 6 November 2000, 15.

22. "DB Suffers Financial Setback," *International Railway Journal*, June 2000, 2.

23. Haig Simonian, "Germany to Use Phone Windfall to Help Rail," *Financial Times*, 22 September 2000, 2.

24. "German Rail Fails to Come Out of the Red," *International Railway Journal*, December 2000, 4.

25. Harvey Feigenbaum, Jeffrey Henig, and Chris Hamnett, *Shrinking the State: The Political Underpinnings of Privatization* (Cambridge, U.K.: Cambridge Univ. Press, 1998), 72.

26. Andrew Pendleton and Jonathon Winterton, introduction to *Public Enterprise in Transition: Industrial Relations in State and Privatized Corporations*, eds. Andrew Pendleton and Jonathon Winterton (London: Routledge, 1993), 12.

27. For a detailed account of British Rail's commercial reorganization and privatization of ancilliary enterprises, see Terence R. Gourvish, "British Rail's 'Business-Led' Organization, 1977–1990: Government-Industry Relations in Britain's Public Sector," *Business History Review* 64, no. 1 (spring 1990): 109–49.

28. International Union of Railways, *Chronological Railway Statistics 1970–1997* (Paris: UIC, 1999), tables B 51 and B 73.

29. "The Rail Billionaires," *Economist*, 3 July 1999, 57.

30. Historical and technical details regarding British Rail's HST can be found at Lexcie Corporation, *Lexcie's Guide to BR TOPS Locomotive & Multiple Units*, 19 February 1999. http://www.lexcie.zetnet.co.uk/tops-2-pic.htm (18 March 2001).

31. Information about the APT-E can be found at Lexcie Corporation, *The Advanced Passenger Train: Its Evolution*, n.d. http://www.lexcie.zetnet.co.uk/apt2.htm (17 March 2001); and Oliver Keating (High Speed Trains), *The Advanced Passenger Train*, n.d. http://www.o-keating.com/hsr/apt.htm (17 March 2001). Further information

about British high-speed rail programs can be found in Roger Barnett, "British Rail's Intercity 125 and 225," *Built Environment* 19, no. 3–4 (1999): 163–82. See also "High-Speed Train Sets New Record," *Times* (London), 11 August 1975, 2; and B.G. Sephton, "High Speed Train Prototype Proves Its Worth," *Railway Gazette International*, February 1975, 58–63.

32. Information about the APT-P can be found at Railway Age Intercity APT, *APT-P Preservation Update*, January 27, 2001. http://www.therailwayage.co.uk/apt/index.htm (08 March 2001); and Keating, *The Advanced Passenger Train*. See also Michael Baily, "British Rail Unveils Its 150 mph Train," *Times* (London), 8 June 1978, 4; "Maiden Run for Train of Future," *Times* (London), 7 December 1981, 2; Tom Kizzia, "Britain's Trouble-Plagued APT Gets Ready for New Tests," *Railway Age*, 10 May 1982, 19; "British Rail's New Train Tops 100 mph (Later It Limped Home)," *Times* (London), 8 December 1981, 24; and "Advanced Passenger Train Catches Cold," *Times* (London), 10 December 1981, 3.

33. Gourvish, "British Rail's 'Business-Led' Organization," 137.

34. Quoted at Railway Age Intercity APT, *New Intercity Trains*, 9 December 2000. http://www.therailwayage.co.uk/apt/ (8 March 2001).

35. John Preston, "The Franchising and Re-franchising of Passenger Rail Services in Britain" (paper no. 01–2425 presented at the eightieth annual meeting of the Transportation Research Board, Washington, D.C., 7-11 January 2001).

36. José A. Gómez-Ibáñez, "Splitting the Ties: The Privatization of British Rail," *Access: Research at the University of California Transportation Center* 14 (spring 1999): 23.

37. D.M. van de Velde, introduction to *Changing Trains: Railway Reform and the Role of Competition* (Brookfield, Vt.: Ashgate, 1999), 1.

38. Andrze Krause, "Please Unbotch the Railways," *New Statesman*, 11 December 2000, 5.

39. "The Rail Billionaires," 60.

40. Keith Harper, "Rail Passenger Complaints Rise by 154% in Two Years," *The Guardian Weekly*, 19 August 1999, 10.

41. "The Rail Billionaires," 60.

42. Details about Railtrack's maintenance schedule at Hatfield are taken from Edwin Unsworth, "U.K. Rail Safety Questioned," *Business Insurance*, 23 October 2000, 59–60.

43. "How Not to Run a Railway," *Economist*, 23 November 2000, 65–66.

44. "What Comes After Hell," *Economist*, 16 December 2000, 59–60. The 40 percent decline in passengers was reported by Sarah Lyall, "Railways' Frightful State is the Talk of Britain," *New York Times*, 10 December 2000, sec. L, 3.

45. "Gross Mismanagement: Rail Chaos is Damaging the Economy as Well as the Public," *Times* (London), 2 December 2000, 29.

46. "What Comes After Hell," 59–60.

47. Stuart Nagel has coined this term to describe the policy process equivalent of a "positive sum" economic gain, whereby all participants can simultaneously come out ahead of their best initial expectations. See Stuart S. Nagel, *The Policy Process and Super-Optimum Solutions* (Commack, N.Y.: Nova Science Publishers, 1994).

3. Sidetrack: How North American Rail Passenger Renewal Got Delayed by the Stalemate Over Public Enterprise Legitimacy

1. Federal funding to Amtrak is divided into four categories: "Operating," "Capital," "Overall" and "Taxpayer Relief Act" (TRA). These amounts can be found in Amtrak, *Annual Report, 1999* (Washington, D.C.: National Railroad Passenger Corporation, 1999); and Frank N. Wilner, *The Amtrak Story* (Omaha, Nebr.: Simmons-Boardman, 1994), 89. Capital funding includes Northeast Corridor Improvement Project payments to Amtrak, which were detailed in Federal Railroad Administration, *Privatization of Intercity Rail Passenger Service in the United States* (Washington, D.C.: Federal Railroad Administration, 1998), Appendix A. According to Amtrak's annual report of 1999, Taxpayer Relief Act funds amounted to $1.2 billion in both 1998 and 1999. Of these funds, approximately $1.3 billion had been spent as of June 1999. For details, see Phyllis F. Scheinberg, *Intercity Passenger Rail: Increasing Amtrak's Accountability for Its Taxpayer Relief Act Funds*, Report no. GAO/T-RCED-00–116 (Washington, D.C.: U.S. General Accounting Office, 2000); and Phyllis F. Scheinberg, *Intercity Passenger Rail: Amtrak Faces Challenges in Improving Its Financial Condition*, Report no. GAO/T-RCED-00–30 (Washington, D.C.: U.S. General Accounting Office, 2000). "Overall Funding" in 1999 is distinguished from "Capital" and "Operating" funding due to changed accounting procedures, in which the federal government's appropriation was lumped into a single sum, designated as qualified capital expenditures. See Note 5 in Amtrak, *Annual Report*, 1999, 32. In figure 3.1, TQ stands for a "Transition Quarter" which Amtrak adopted to bring its fiscal year into alignment with the government's fiscal year.

2. The Government of Canada did not make any capital grants to VIA for the years 1998 and 1999. Instead, an Asset Renewal Fund was created enabling VIA to apply the proceeds from the sale or lease of certain assets, as well as the savings from the rationalization of maintenance, to meet capital and restructuring costs. This Asset Renewal Fund generated $16.5 million in 1998 and $33.5 million in 1999, but as these were internally generated funds, they are not counted as net additions to VIA's government funding. For further information on VIA's current accounting procedures, see VIA Rail Canada, *Annual Report, 1999* (Montreal, Que.: VIA Rail Canada, 1999). "Network Restructuring Recovery" pertains to government payments commencing in 1990 that offset significant costs arising from the reductions in VIA service. Federal payments under this program supported payouts under labor agreements, writing down the value of surplus assets, and other costs incurred, such as lease cancellation penalties. For more information, see VIA Rail Canada, *Annual Report, 1991* (Montreal, Que.: VIA Rail Canada), 16.

3. George W. Hilton, *The Transportation Act of 1958: A Decade of Experience* (Bloomington, Ind.: Indianapolis Univ. Press, 1969).

4. Ibid., 37.

5. Ibid., 38.

6. Interstate Commerce Commission, *Railroad Passenger Train Deficit: Docket #31954* (Washington, DC: Interstate Commerce Commission, 1958), 30.

7. Ibid., 69.

8. R. Kent Weaver, *The Politics of Industrial Change: Railway Policy in North America* (Washington, D.C.: Brookings Institution, 1985), 41.

9. Theodore Lowi, "American Business, Public Policy, Case-Studies, and Political Theory," *World Politics* 16, no. 4 (July 1964): 677–715. Paul Pierson, "When Effect Becomes Cause: Policy Feedback and Political Change," *World Politics* 45, no. 4 (July 1993): 595–628.

10. James Q. Wilson, ed., *The Politics of Regulation* (New York: Basic Books, 1980).

11. David B. Truman, *The Governmental Process: Political Interests and Public Opinion* (New York: Alfred A. Knopf, 1951), 519.

12. Interstate Commerce Commission, *ICC Examiner Foresees End of Passenger Service by 1970* (Washington, D.C.: Interstate Commerce Commission, 1958), 72.

13. Anthony Perl, "Public Enterprise as an Expression of Sovereignty: Reconsidering the Origins of Canadian National Railways," *Canadian Journal of Political Science* 27, no. 1 (1994): 23–52.

14. Perl, Anthony, "Superbureaucrats and Superhighways: An Institutional Explanation for Variation in American and Canadian Highway Policies," (paper presented at the annual meeting of the American Political Science Association, Chicago, Ill., September 1992).

15. House of Commons, Standing Committee on Transport and Communications, *Minutes of Proceedings and Evidence*, no. 2, 3 March 1966, 68–134.

16. House of Commons, Standing Committee on Transport and Communications, *Minutes of Proceedings and Evidence*, no. 22, 5 July 1966, 1578–1655.

17. Ibid.

18. William A. Niskanen, *Bureaucracy and Representative Government* (Chicago, Ill.: Aldine, 1971).

19. James Q. Wilson, *Bureaucracy: What Government Agencies Do and Why They Do It* (New York: Basic Books, 1989).

20. Board of Transport Commissioners for Canada, *Judgements, Orders, Regulations and Rulings*, vol. 56 (Ottawa, Ont.: The Queen's Printer, 1966), 55.

21. Canada, *Royal Commission on Transportation*, vol. 1 (Ottawa, Ont.: Queen's Printer, 1961), 18.

22. Canadian Transport Commission, Research Branch, *An Analysis of Railway Transport Committee Decisions, 1967–1980*, Report no. 1982/06E (Ottawa, Ont.: Canadian Transport Commission, 1981), 8.

23. Canadian Transport Commission, Rail Transport Committee, *Reasons for Order No. R-6313* (Ottawa, Ont.: Canadian Transport Commission, 1970), 403.

24. Anthony Perl, "Getting What You Pay For: The Politics of Public Investment in Amtrak and VIA Rail Canada," in *Selected Proceedings of the Sixth World Conference on Transport Research*, vol. 3 (Lyon, France: Chirat, 1993), 1583.

25. Charles E. Lindblom, "Still Muddling, Not Yet Through," *Public Administration Review* 39, no. 6 (November/December 1979): 519.

26. John F. Stover, *The Life and Decline of the American Railroad* (New York, N.Y.: Oxford Univ. Press, 1970), 236–37.

27. Donald M. Itzkoff, *Off the Track: The Decline of the Intercity Passenger Train in the United States* (Westport, Conn.: Greenwood Press, 1985), 99.

28. Ralph C. Deans, "Railroad Nationalization," *Editorial Research Reports* 4, no. 27 (1973): 460.

29. Joseph R. Daughen and Peter Binzen, *The Wreck of the Penn Central* (Boston, Mass.: Little, Brown and Company, 1971), 255.

30. Robert E. Bedingfield, "Cautions on U.S. Rail Role: Calls Take-Over a Threat, but at 'Prohibitive' Cost," *New York Times*, 9 March 1971, 47.

31. Federal Railroad Administration, *Privatization of Intercity Rail Passenger Service in the United States* (Washington, D.C.: Federal Railroad Administration, 1998).

32. Senate Committee on Commerce, *Rail Passenger Service Act of 1970: Report to Accompany S. 3706*, 91st Cong., 2d sess., 1970, S. Rept. 91–765, 89.

33. Lloyd Musolf, *Uncle Sam's Private, Profitseeking Corporations* (Lexington, Mass.: Lexington Books, 1983), 50.

34. Senate Committee on Commerce, Subcommittee on Surface Transportation, *Passenger Train Service Legislation, Hearings on S. 674, et al.*, 91st Cong., 1st sess., 1969, 18.

35. George W. Hilton, *Amtrak: The National Railroad Passenger Corporation* (Washington, D.C.: The American Enterprise Institute for Public Policy Studies, 1980), 15.

36. Interestingly, and perhaps ironically, CPR and CNR now hold the common stock in Amtrak that was taken out by the Milwaukee Road and the Grand Trunk Western, which were (or became) subsidiaries of these Canadian carriers. As a result, Canada's private railroads now own 8 percent of Amtrak's common shares, while having no stake whatsoever in VIA Rail. The Amtrak Reform and Accountability Act stipulates that these common shares are scheduled to be repurchased at "fair market value" in 2003, once Amtrak attains self-sufficiency. Amtrak has proposed buying back these shares, which were issued with a par value of US$10 for $0.03 each, but the shareholders rejected this offer.

37. William D. Grampp, "'Railpax' Key: Avoiding the ICC," *Wall Street Journal*, 25 March 1971, 8.

38. Tom Wicker, "A Railroad Euthanasia Plan?," *New York Times*, 25 March 1971, 39.

39. Christopher Lydon, "2 Courts Uphold Amtrak System; Service is Begun," *New York Times*, 1 May 1971, 34.

40. Christopher Lydon, "Trains in Amtrak, Although Still Scarce, Have Become Clean and More Punctual," *New York Times*, 17 October 1971, 74.

41. Wilner, *The Amtrak Story*, 57.

42. Weaver, *The Politics of Industrial Change*, 87.

43. Weaver, *The Politics of Industrial Change*, 95.

44. David Nice, "Passenger Rail Service: Decline and Resurgence," *Transportation Quarterly* 50, no. 4 (1996): 99.

45. Anthony Haswell, "Amtrak—A Critical Appraisal From the Viewpoint of the Consumer," in *Proceedings—Thirteenth Annual Meeting Transportation Research Forum*, vol. 13, no. 1 (Oxford, Ind.: The Richard B. Cross Company, 1972), 114.

46. George W. Hilton, *Amtrak: The National Railroad Passenger Corporation,* (Washington: D.C.: American Enterprise Institute for Public Policy Research, 1980), 62–67.

47. Jean Love, Wendell Cox, and Stephen Moore, *Amtrak at Twenty-Five: End of the Line for Taxpayer Subsidies,* Cato Policy Analysis no. 266 (Washington, D.C.: Cato Institute, 1996).

48. Senate Committee on Appropriations, Subcommittee on Transportation, *Department of Transportation and Related Agencies Appropriations for Fiscal Year 1999: Hearings on H.R. 4328/S. 2307,* testimony of Robert W. Poole, Jr., The Reason Foundation, 105th Cong., 2nd sess., 1998.

49. The operating ratios presented here build upon both the data and methodology found in Wilner, *The Amtrak Story,* 89. In calculating expenses, Wilner excluded the following cost categories from his calculation of operating expenses: depreciation; mandatory payments (i.e. railroad retirement); post-retirement health benefits; taxes; and congressionally imposed labor-protection payments. Wilner's methodology was extended beyond 1994 by excluding the following expense categories found in Amtrak's annual report: employee related expenses; depreciation; and excess railroad retirement taxes equivalent to the revenue amount provided for under the heading "Federal grants." In calculating Amtrak's revenues, federal grant payments in all years, and Taxpayer Relief Act funds which were listed in "Revenues" during 1998 and 1999 have been excluded. Amtrak uses an alternative methodology to arrive at its operating ratio figures. For more details, see Amtrak, *Annual Report, 1999,* 19, 42. Data for revenues and expenses prior to 1994 were provided by Amtrak's Office of Government and Public Affairs. See Wilner, *The Amtrak Story,* endnote 6. Data from 1994 onward was obtained from Amtrak's *Annual Reports.*

50. These figures were obtained from Federal Transit Administration, *National Transit Database: Data Tables for 1999,* n.d. http://www.ntdprogram.com/NTD/ NTDData.nsf/1999+TOC?OpenView&Count=50 (11 March 2001), tables 1, 11. Total operating revenues (excluding federal, state and local government funding) were divided by total operating expenses.

51. Love, Cox, and Moore, *Amtrak at Twenty-Five.*

52. Stephen Moore, *Amtrak Subsidies: This Is No Way to Run a Railroad,* May 22, 1997. http://www.cato.org/dailys/5–22–97.html (15 Feb. 2001).

53. Senate Committee on Appropriations, Subcommittee on Transportation, *Department of Transportation and Related Agencies Appropriations for Fiscal Year 1999: Hearings on H.R. 4328/S. 2307,* testimony of Robert W. Poole Jr., 105th Cong., 2d sess., 1998.

54. Stephen B. Goddard, *Getting There: The Epic Struggle between Road and Rail in the American Century* (New York, N.Y.: Basic Books, 1994), 195–96.

55. Peter Lyon, *To Hell in a Day Coach: An Exasperated Look at American Railroads* (Philadelphia, Pa.: J.B. Lippincott Co., 1968), 226.

56. Joseph Vranich, *Supertrains: Solutions to America's Transportation Gridlock* (New York: St. Martin's Press, 1991), 327–28.

57. United States Conference of Mayors, *Statement of Timothy M. Kaine on behalf*

of the United States Conference of Mayors before the Committee on Commerce, Science, and Transportation on Amtrak Oversight, September 26, 2000. http://www.usmayors.org/uscm/news/press_releases/documents/amtraktestimony.pdf (15 February 2000).

58. House Committee on Transportation and Infrastructure, Subcommittee on Railroads, *High Speed Rail Programs,* testimony of William C. Nevel, High-Speed Ground Transportation Association, 105th Cong., 2d sess., 1997.

59. National Association of Railroad Passengers, Letter from Assistant Director Scott Leonard to Senator Frank Lautenberg, August 23, 1999. Mimeo.

60. The Amtrak Reform and Accountability Act of 1997, discussed in Chapter 5, repealed the statutory basis of labor protection payments, which continue under a somewhat reduced formula that was arrived at through binding arbitration in October of 1999.

61. House Committee on Transportation and Infrastructure, Subcommittee on Railroads, *Amtrak's Current Situation: Hearings on H.R. 88—046CC,* statement of Gregory E. Lawler, Executive Director, Safe Transit and Rail Transportation, 104th Cong., 1st sess., 1996.

62. Anthony Perl and James A. Dunn Jr., "Reinventing Amtrak: The Politics of Survival," *Journal of Policy Analysis and Management* 16, no. 4 (fall 1997): 598–614.

63. Some U.S. railroads are quite active politically. See *Bloomberg News* (David Ward, Bill McQuillen, and Rip Watson), "Union Pacific Brings Train and Money to Convention," August 03, 2000. http://quote.bloomberg.com/newsarchive/?sidenav=front (17 March 2001) for information about Union Pacific Railroad's political activity and Frank N. Wilner, "Washington: Up Close and Ugly," *Traffic World,* 16 October 2000, 12–14, for a comparison of how railroads stacked up against other transportation firms in contributing to the U.S. elections in 2000.

64. Anthony Perl, "Financing Transport Infrastructure: The Effects of Institutional Durability in French and American Policymaking," *Governance* 4, no. 4 (October 1991): 365–402.

65. Canadian Transport Commission, Economic and Social Analysis Branch, *An Historical Review of Direct Transport Subsidies in Canada,* Report no. ESAB 75–8 (Ottawa, Ont.: Canadian Transport Commission, 1975), 31.

66. Ibid., 31–32.

67. J. Lukasiewicz, "Public Policy and Technology: Passenger Rail in Canada as an Issue of Modernization," *Canadian Public Policy* 5, no. 4 (autumn 1979): 520.

68. The Ontario Northland Railway was initiated by the province of Ontario in 1902, and the British Columbia Railway became a public enterprise in 1918. Both have operated passenger trains independently of CN, CPR, and then VIA Rail, and continue to do so today.

69. Adil Cubukgil and Richard M. Soberman, "Costs of Rail Passenger Service in Canada: An Examination of Institutional Problems," in *Proceedings—Twenty-Fifth Annual Meeting: Transportation Research Forum,* vol. 25, no. 4 (Phillipsburg, N.J.: Harmony Press, 1984), 69.

70. Mark Bunting, *Changing Trains: A Commercially Sustainable Railway Passenger Policy for Canada* (Kingston, Ont.: P.M. Bunting & Associates, 1998), 2.

71. Transport Canada, *Directive for the Guidance of the Canadian Transport Commission on Rail Passenger Services, January 29, 1976* (Ottawa, Ont.: Transport Canada, 1976).

72. Transport Canada, *Paper on a Canadian Rail Passenger Program, January 29, 1976* (Ottawa, Ont.: Transport Canada, 1976), 5.

73. Ibid., 6.

74. Ibid., 7–8.

75. Ibid., 8.

76. Michael Jackson, ed., introduction to *Proceedings of the First National Rail Passenger Conference, October 29–31, 1976* (Regina, Sask.: University of Regina, 1977), 6.

77. Canadian National Railways, *Annual Report* (Montreal, Que.: Canadian National Railways, 1976), 13.

78. A.R. Campbell, "Mr. A.R. Campbell," in *Proceedings of the First National Rail Passenger Conference, October 29–31, 1976,* ed. Michael Jackson (Regina, Sask.: University of Regina, 1977), 39.

79. Transport Canada, Railway Transportation Directorate, *Evaluation of Legislative Alternatives for VIA Rail Canada (VIA), Part One, Legislative Strategy for VIA Rail Canada,* first draft (Ottawa, Ont.: Transport Canada, 1978), 8.

80. Ibid., 9.

81. A.R. Campbell, "A Submission to the Canadial Transport Commission Regarding Rationalization of Maritime Rail Passenger Services" (Ottawa, Ont: Canadian Transport Commission, June 2, 1977), 4.

82. Lukasiewicz, "Public Policy and Technology," 524.

83. Transport Canada, *Evaluation of Legislative Alternatives,* 5.

84. Ibid., 10.

85. Otto Lang, "Address by the Honourable Otto Lang," in *Proceedings of the First National Rail Passenger Conference, October 29–31, 1976,* ed. Michael Jackson (Regina, Sask.: University of Regina, 1977), 18.

86. Transport Canada, *Evaluation of Legislative Alternatives,* 32–33.

87. VIA Rail Canada, *Five Year Plan and 1978 Budget* (Montreal, Que.: VIA Rail Canada, 1977), 3.

88. Ibid., 4.

89. Cubukgil and Soberman, "Costs of Rail Passenger Service in Canada," 13.

90. Task Force on Rail Passenger Service, *Report of the Task Force on Rail Passenger Service: The Last Straw* (Ottawa, Ont.: Task Force on Rail Passenger Service, 1981), 29.

91. Ibid., 15.

92. Ibid., 16.

93. Richard Soberman, "High Speed Trains for Canada: Technological Excellence, Groundless Conviction, or Bureaucratic Obsession?," in *Essays in Canadian Surface Transportation,* ed. Filip Palda (Vancouver, B.C.: The Fraser Institute, 1995), 98.

94. VIA Rail Canada, *Summary of the 1985–89 Corporate Plan; Summary of the 1985 Capital Budget* (Montreal, Que.: VIA Rail Canada, 1985), 1.

95. James A. Dunn Jr. and Anthony Perl, "Policy Networks and Industrial Revitalization: High Speed Rail Initiatives in France and Germany," *Journal of Public Policy* 14, no. 3 (July 1994): 311–43.

96. VIA Rail Canada, *The Acquisition of Rail Passenger Trains for Transport Canada and VIA Rail Canada Inc.: Lessons Learned* (Montreal, Que.: VIA Rail Canada, 1979), 4.

97. Ibid., 14.

98. Ata M. Kahn, *VIA Rail Canada: An Analysis of VIA's Potential in Fulfilling Rail Passenger Policy Objectives—Working Paper* (Ottawa, Ont.: Science Council of Canada, 1980), 24.

99. Canada, Senate Standing Committee on Transport and Communications, no. 11, Appendix "TC-11-A," 29 May 1984, 11A:3.

100. VIA Rail Canada, *The Acquisition of Rail Passenger Trains,* 2.

101. Thomas Wade Herren Jr., "Northeast Corridor High Speed Rail Passenger Service" (Master's thesis, University of Rhode Island, 1969), 19.

102. VIA Rail Canada, *The Renaissance of Passenger Rail: Brief to the Standing Committee on Transport and Communications, Senate of Canada, for its Enquiry into the National Rail Passenger Service Provided to Canadians by VIA Rail Canada Inc., Presented by Pierre A.H. Franche, President and Chief Executive Officer, VIA Rail Canada* (Montreal, Que.: VIA Rail, 1984), 7.

103. Transport Canada, Economic Analysis Directorate, *Rail Passenger Improvements In the Quebec City–Windsor Corridor* (Ottawa, Ont.: Transport Canada, 1984), 1–2.

104. Khan, *VIA Rail Canada,* 36.

105. Jerome T. Bentley, *Issues in Subsidization with Attention to the Subsidization of Passenger Rail Service* (Ottawa, Ont.: Economic Council of Canada, 1985), 123.

106. House of Commons, Standing Committee on Transport, *Minutes of Proceedings and Evidence of the Standing Committee on Transport,* no. 38, 21 May 1987, 38:32–38:33.

107. House of Commons, "Bill C-97: An Act Respecting Rail Passenger Transportation," 24 February 1986, *House of Commons Bills,* no. C81–C106 (1984–1986) (Ottawa, Ont.: Minister of Supply and Services, 1986), 22903–5–22903–6.

108. VIA Rail Canada, *Summary of the 1986–1990 Corporate Plan; Summary of the Revised 1985 Operating Budget; Summary of the Revised 1985 Capital Budget; Summary of the 1986 Operating Budget; Summary of the 1986 Capital Budget* (Montreal, Que.: VIA Rail Canada, 1986).

109. Ibid., 5.

110. VIA Rail Canada, *Summary of the 1988–1992 Corporate Plan; Summary of the 1988 Operating Budget; Summary of the 1988 Capital Budget* (Montreal, Que.: VIA Rail Canada, 1988), 1.

111. Ibid., 4.

112. Peter Howell, "VIA's Budget Cut as President Fired," *Toronto Star,* 4 May 1989, sec. A, 1.

113. Peter Howell, "De Belleval: 'I Gave it My Best Shot,'" *Toronto Star,* 4 May 1989, sec. A, 17.

114. Marc Clark, "VIA's Rocky Future: An Executive Resigns to Protest Cutbacks," *Maclean's,* 15 May 1989, 17.

115. Kevin Dougherty, "Hint of Route Sell-Offs: VIA Rail Gets New Chief," *Financial Post,* 4 May 1989, 1.

116. The operating ratio in this study was calculated using the methodology VIA Rail currently uses to determine its "cash operating ratio." Data are drawn from VIA Rail's Annual Reports. Two types of revenue are accounted for: "Passenger" and "Other." These are divided by the following expense categories: customer services; equipment maintenance; marketing and sales; support services; general and administrative; amortization; and income and federal large corporation taxes. "Amortization of properties" as well as the "losses (gains) on write-off, retirement and disposal of properties" listed in the Statement of Cash Flows, are subsequently subtracted from these expense categories. This method of calculating expenses was used beginning in 1988, when the amortization of properties and losses (gains) on properties was first recorded. Prior to 1988, amortization was excluded from the expense category of VIA's operating ratio. This exclusion is roughly comparable to the subtraction of "amortization of properties" and "losses (gains) on properties" from VIA's more recent expenses. VIA Rail's 1993 Annual Report explicitly recognized the difficulty in comparing expense data from the 1980s with those of the 1990s, stating: "The key financial indicators and operating statistics summarize the performance of VIA. Data for years prior to 1990 is [*sic*] not comparable due to the network restructuring that took place at the beginning of 1990." See VIA Rail Canada, *Annual Report, 1993* (Montreal, Que.: VIA Rail Canada, 1993), 1. Also excluded from VIA's operating expenses were the substantial network restructuring and reorganization charges that commenced in October 1989.

117. Information about VIA Rail's restructuring during the 1990s was obtained from VIA Rail Canada, "VIA Rail Canada Inc.: The Funding Challenge," Mimeo, and Michael Gushue, "Presentation to EuroRail Congress '99," 26–28 January 1999, Hotel Lutétia Paris, Montreal, Que.: Via Rail Canada, 1999. Mimeo.

118. Canada, House of Commons, Standing Committee on Transport, *The Renaissance of Passenger Rail in Canada: Report of the Standing Committee on Transport* (Ottawa, Ont.: Public Works and Government Services Canada–Publishing, 1998), 13.

119. Details regarding VIA's expenditure of these funds can be found in *VIA's Investment Strategy* available at http://www.viarail.ca/en.fram.renaissance.html (26 May 2001).

4. False Starts with High Speed: State and Provincial Efforts to Leapfrog Amtrak's and VIA's Perennial Problems

1. Anthony Perl and James A. Dunn Jr., "Building the Political Infrastructure for High Speed Rail in North America," *Transportation Quarterly* 50, no. 1 (winter 1996): 5–22.

2. Rohit T. Aggarwala, "The States, New Modes, and Federal Transportation Policy: Lessons From History for High-Speed Rail," *Transportation Quarterly* 52, no. 3 (summer 1998): 53–67.

3. Paul A. Sabatier, "Policy Change Over a Decade or More," in *Policy Change and Learning: An Advocacy Coalition Approach*, eds. Paul A. Sabatier and Hank C. Jenkins-Smith (Boulder, Colo.: Westview Press, 1993), 13–39.

4. For another temporal perspective on how transportation issues get addressed, see James A. Dunn Jr., *Driving Forces: The Automobile, Its Enemies, and the Politics of Mobility* (Washington, D.C.: Brookings Institution, 1998), 19–22.

5. Claiborne Pell, *Megalopolis Unbound: The Supercity and the Transportation of Tomorrow* (New York: Praeger, 1966), 34–35.

6. Ibid., 15.

7. Ibid.

8. Ibid., 142.

9. This is a term that James A. Dunn Jr. and I have coined to capture the combination of revamped technology and technique that is introduced to overcome both the technical "retardation" that Pell identified, and also its organizational counterpart. The concept is developed more fully in chapter 2.

10. Calculation made using consumer price index conversion factor available at Robert C. Sahr (Oregon State University), *Consumer Price Index (CPI) Conversion Factors to Convert to (estimated) Dollars of the Year 2000*, 2000. http://www.orst.edu/dept/pol_sci/fac/sahr/cv00.pdf (17 March 2001).

11. Comptroller General of the United States, *Report to the Congress: Administration of Metroliner and Turbo-Train Projects*, Report B-164497(5) (Washington, D.C.: Comptroller General of the United States, 1971), 14.

12. "Shuttle Flights Hearten Eastern: 6,147 Took No-Frill Trips in First Week, Line Says," *New York Times*, 10 May 1961, 90.

13. Joseph R. Daughen and Peter Binzen, *The Wreck of the Penn Central* (Boston, Mass.: Little, Brown and Company, 1971), 46–47.

14. Donald M. Itzkoff, *Off the Track: Intercity Passenger Train in the United States*. (Westport, Conn.: Greenwood Press, 1985), 90.

15. Daughen and Binzen, *The Wreck of the Penn Central*, 136.

16. Comptroller General of the United States, *Report to the Congress*, 5.

17. Dan Cupper, "20 Years of Metroliner Service: Not Ultra High Speed, But at 125 mph, Fast Enough," *Passenger Train Journal*, March 1989, 10.

18. "Gremlins Slow High-Speed Trains," *Business Week*, 3 August 1968, 104.

19. "Budd Tries to Get Out of Its Rail Cars," *Business Week*, 2 May 1970, 17.

20. James W. Diffenderfer, "Metroliner Experiences: An Engineering and Economic Review of Developments After a Year's Token Operation," (paper presented at the sixty-ninth annual convention of the American Railway Engineering Association, Chicago, Ill., 18 March 1970), 10.

21. Ibid., 11.

22. Thomas C. Southerland and William McCleery, *The Way to Go: The Coming Revival of U.S. Rail Passenger Service* (New York: Simon and Schuster, 1973), 128.

23. R. Kent Weaver, *The Politics of Industrial Change: Railway Policy in North America* (Washington, D.C.: Brookings Institution, 1985).

24. Pell, *Megalopolis Unbound*, 163.

25. Coalition of Northeastern Governors, *About CONEG*, 2000. http://www.coneg.org/about/default.htm (22 Feb. 2001).

26. CONEG High Speed Rail Task Force, *REPORT of the CONEG High Speed Rail Task Force: Volume I.* (Washington, D.C.: CONEG High Speed Rail Task Force, 1989), 1.

27. Ibid., 7.

28. Ibid., 3.

29. Ibid., 7.

30. Ibid., 25.

31. Ibid.

32. Coalition of Northeastern Governors, *The Growth of Intercity Rail*, October 1, 1997. http://www.coneg.org/programs/policies/growth.htm (22 February 2001).

33. Joseph Vranich, "The Puzzling Politics of High Speed Rail," *Railway Age*, October 1992, 51–59.

34. *Amtrak Authorization and Development Act of 1992*, Public Law 102–533, 102d Cong., 2d sess. (27 October 1992).

35. Jeffrey Krasner, "Study Warns of Problems on Rail Line," *Wall Street Journal*, 22 December 1999, sec. NE, 1, Eastern edition.

36. Details about the electrification and reconstruction of Amtrak's New Haven–Boston route can be found in U.S. Office of Inspector General, *Audit Report: Amtrak's High-Speed Rail Electrification Project*, Report no. RT-2000–020 (Washington, D.C.: Office of Inspector General, 1999). See also Anthony Perl and Tony Turrittin, "Measuring the Environmental Impacts of High Speed and Maglev in North America: What Railway Designers Need to Know," paper presented at the World Congress on Railway Research, October 19-23, 1999, Tokyo, Japan, (conference papers available on CD-ROM).

37. Daniel Machalaba, "Bombardier Group to Build Speedy Train for Amtrak," *Wall Street Journal*, 18 March 1996, sec. A, 4, Eastern edition.

38. Daniel Machalaba, "All Aboard? Amtrak's Metroliner Has Disappearing-Railroad Blues," *Wall Street Journal*, 10 March 1999, sec. B, 1, Eastern edition.

39. "Japanese Bullet Trains for Amtrak," *Railway Age*, 31 August 1981, 16.

40. National Railroad Passenger Corporation, *Emerging Corridors: Amtrak* (Washington, D.C.: National Railroad Passenger Corporation, 1981).

41. "Japanese Bullet Trains for Amtrak," *Railway Age*, 31 August 1981, 16.

42. Linda Grant and David Smollar, "'Bullet' Train Between L.A., San Diego Planned," *Los Angeles Times*, 1 April 1982, sec. A, 1.

43. See "West Coast Bullet Train Suffers a Fatal Wound," *Iron Age*, 18 January 1985, 13; and Judith Cummings, "Plan for High-Speed Train on West Coast is Scrapped," *New York Times*, 24 November 1984, sec. A, 17.

44. Frank E. Shaffer, "Newsfront: Loan, Interest Repaid," *Modern Railroads*, February 1984, 12–14.

45. Frank Malone, "The Great Train Race," *Railway Age*, January 1984, 52.

46. George C. Smith and Earl Shirley, "High-Speed Rail in California: Avoidable Controversy," *Right of Way*, October 1987, 17–21.

47. The Edmund G. "Pat" Brown Institute of Government Affairs, *High/Super Speed Rail in Southern California: Projects, Technology, Finance and Public Policy Implica-*

tions, February 10 (Los Angeles, Calif.: The Edmund G. "Pat" Brown Institute of Government Affairs, 1984), 1.

48. Leslie Berkman, "Bullet Train Data Assailed by Consultant: Riders and Revenues Vastly Overstated, Tustin Report Says," *Los Angeles Times*, 26 October 1983, sec. A, 14.

49. Robert Roberts, "High Speed, a New Rail Industry," *Modern Railroads*, August 1983, 50.

50. "Laying a U.S. Track for High-Speed Trains," *Business Week*, 25 April 1983, 49.

51. The Edmund G. "Pat" Brown Institute of Government Affairs, *High/Super Speed Rail in Southern California*, 27.

52. Tom Ichniowski, "High-Speed Rail is Jumping the Track," *Business Week*, 10 December 1984, 46.

53. Lawrence D. Gilson, "Can Entrepreneurs Save Mass Transit?: Private Transportation is a Pipe Dream," *New York Times*, 26 May 1985, sec. C, 2.

54. Smith and Shirley, "High-Speed Rail in California," 18.

55. Roberts, "High Speed, a New Rail Industry," 51.

56. David Smollar, "His Name's Bonde, and He's 007 to the Bullet Train's Promoters," *Los Angeles Times*, 12 October 1983, sec. B, 4.

57. The Edmund G. "Pat" Brown Institute of Government Affairs, *High/Super Speed Rail in Southern California*, 6.

58. Gilson, "Can Entrepreneurs Save Mass Transit?," sec. C, 2.

59. "In Transit: Why AHSRC failed," *Railway Age*, February 1985, 42.

60. Douglas John Bowen and Jessica Stern, "California Votes $3 Billion For Rail," *Railway Age*, July 1990, 86–87.

61. California High-Speed Rail Authority, *News Releases: California High-Speed Rail Authority Starts*, August 16, 2000. http://www.cahighspeedrail.org/news_release/index.cfm?PressID=15 (3 February 2001).

62. "Winners and Losers for 1999—A Good Year for the High Court, A Tough One for Big-City Mayors," *Wall Street Journal*, 29 December 1999, sec. CA, 1, Eastern edition.

63. Hugh Heclo, *Modern Social Politics in Britain and Sweden: From Relief to Income Maintenance* (New Haven, Conn.: Yale Univ. Press, 1974), 315.

64. Joseph Vranich, *Supertrains: Solutions to America's Transportation Gridlock* (New York: St. Martin's Press, 1993), 173.

65. The Ohio Rail Transportation Authority, *Ohio State Rail Plan Update 1982–83* (Columbus, Ohio: The Ohio Rail Transportation Authority, 1983), 1.

66. Bill Paul, "Ohio Looks to High Speed Passenger Trains," *Modern Railroads*, March 1981, 51.

67. The Ohio Rail Transportation Authority, *RailOhio: the Rail Plan for Ohio, 1978–79* (Columbus, Ohio: The Ohio Rail Transportation Authority, 1979), 21.

68. Ibid., 23.

69. Ohio Rail Transportation Authority, *Ohio High Speed Intercity Rail Passenger Program: Executive Summary* (Cleveland, Ohio: Dalton, Dalton, Newport, 1980), 15–16.

70. Ibid., 5.

71. Ibid., 16.

72. Paul, "Ohio Looks to High Speed Passenger Trains," 52.

73. "Newsfront: Ohio Says 'No' to High Speed Rail," *Modern Railroads*, January 1983, 14.

74. Gus Welty, "High-Speed Rail: Down to Serious Business," *Railway Age*, February 1985, 49.

75. Texas High-Speed Rail Authority, *Report to the 73rd Texas Legislature by the Texas High-Speed Rail Authority* (Austin, Tex.: Texas High-Speed Rail Authority, 1992), 3.

76. Marc H. Burns, *High Speed Rail in the Rear-View Mirror: A Final Report of the Texas High-Speed Rail Authority* (Austin, Tex.: Marc H. Burns, 1995), 16–17.

77. Sverdrup Corporation, *Texas High Speed Rail Authority: Engineering Aspects of the High-Speed Rail Franchise Applications: Advisory Report* (United States: Sverdrup Corporation, 1991), I-6, cited in Burns, *High Speed Rail in the Rear-View Mirror*, 17.

78. William C. Vantuono, "Despite Setbacks, High Speed Rail Moves Ahead," *Railway Age*, April 1994, 65.

79. Ibid.

80. Texas High-Speed Rail Authority, *Report to the 73rd Texas Legislature*, 11.

81. John Sharp, *Texas High Speed Rail Authority: Performance Review* (Texas: Comptroller of Public Accounts, 1992), 21. Emphases in original.

82. Texas High-Speed Rail Authority, *Report to the 73rd Texas Legislature*, 13.

83. These include intercity flights between Dallas–Fort Worth International Airport, Dallas–Love Field, Houston Hobby Airport, Houston Bush Intercontinental Airport, and San Antonio International Airport. Market share was calculated based upon the number of passengers carried, which was obtained from U.S. Department of Transportation, Bureau of Transportation Statistics, *Nonstop Segment T-100* and *Form 298-C* data banks.

84. Joan M. Feldman, "Seriously Successful," *Air Transport World*, 31, no. 1, January 1994, 67.

85. Holt Hackney, "Air Strike on Austin: Why Southwest Airlines is Lobbying to Derail High-Speed Rail," *Financial World*, 16 October 1990, 32.

86. "Southwest Warns Texas City Against Using Public Funds for Train System," *Aviation Week & Space Technology*, 25 November 1991, 42.

87. Kathy F. Powell, "Southwest Airlines V. High-Speed Rail: More Powerful than a Locomotive," *Journal of Air Law and Commerce* 60, no. 4 (May-June 1995): 1097.

88. Texas High-Speed Rail Authority, *Report to the 73rd Texas Legislature*, 12.

89. Helen Ng, "A High-Speed Rail Revolution in the U.S.?: Lessons from the French and Texas TGV" (Master's thesis, Massachusetts Institute of Technology, 1995), 30, cited in Burns, *High Speed Rail in the Rear-View Mirror*, 34.

90. Charles River Associates Inc., *Independent Ridership and Passenger Revenue Projections for the Texas TGV Corporation: High Speed Rail System in Texas* (Boston, Mass.: Charles River and Associates, 1993), E-21.

91. Powell, "Southwest Airlines V. High-Speed Rail," 1095.

92. Texas High-Speed Rail Authority, *Report to the 73rd Texas Legislature*, 14.

93. Burns, *High Speed Rail in the Rear-View Mirror*, 27.

94. John S. Robey, "High-Speed Rail in Texas: Its Rise and Fall," *Transportation Quarterly* 48, no. 4 (autumn 1994): 406.

95. Ibid., 411.

96. Texas High-Speed Rail Authority, *Report to the 73rd Texas Legislature*, 9.

97. Sharp, *Texas High Speed Rail Authority*, 7.

98. Ibid., 8. Emphasis added.

99. Burns, *High Speed Rail in the Rear-View Mirror*, 28.

100. John Racine, "Texas: Around the Nation," *The Bond Buyer*, 5 November 1991, 724B.

101. Robey, "High-Speed Rail in Texas," 409.

102. "Texas TGV Corp. Wins Funding Reprieve," *Railway Age*, December 1992, 18.

103. Burns, *High Speed Rail in the Rear-View Mirror*, 32–33.

104. Tara Parker-Pope, "As Funding Deadline Nears, Bullet Train Appears Dead," *Wall Street Journal*, 15 December 1993, sec. T, 4, Eastern edition.

105. "What Happened (and What Didn't Happen) in Texas," *Railway Age*, February 1994, 24.

106. Burns, *High Speed Rail in the Rear-View Mirror*, 35.

107. Robey, "High-Speed Rail in Texas."

108. Welty, "High-Speed Rail: Down to Serious Business," 44–50.

109. Claudio Dallavalle and Jack E. Heiss, "Florida's High Speed Rail Project: Building a Public-Private Partnership," in *1997 Proceedings of the American Railway Engineering Association*, vol. 98 (Washington, D.C.: American Railway Engineering Association, 1997), 353.

110. Anthony Perl, "Financing Transport Infrastructure: The Effects of Institutional Durability in French and American Policymaking," *Governance* 4, no. 4 (October 1991): 365–402.

111. Heidi Tolliver, "Tracking the (High Speed) Fox," *Mass Transit*, July-August 1996, 35.

112. "Florida DOT Awards High Speed Rail Franchise," *Railway Age*, March 1996, 33.

113. "Florida High Speed Rail Link," *Project Finance*, June 1998, 19.

114. Toby Fildes, "Florida's Track Record," *Project & Trade Finance*, June 1996, 28.

115. U.S. General Accounting Office, *Surface Infrastructure: High-Speed Rail Projects in the United States*, Report no. GAO/RCED-99-44 (Washington, D.C.: U.S. General Accounting Office, 1999), 7.

116. *Transportation Equity Act for the 21st Century/Transportation Infrastructure Finance and Innovation Act of 1998*, Public Law 105–178, 105th Cong., 2d sess. (9 June 1998).

117. U.S. General Accounting Office, *Surface Infrastructure: High-Speed Rail Projects in the United States*, Report no. GAO/RCED-99-44 (Washington, D.C.: U.S. General Accounting Office, 1999), 11.

118. "High Speed Moves Forward in Florida—Maybe," *Railway Age*, October 1996, 24.

119. Thomas Lynch, "An Analysis of the Impacts of Florida High Speed Rail," in *High Speed Rail in the U.S.: Super Trains for the Millennium*, ed., Thomas Lynch (Amsterdam: Gordon and Breach Science Publishers, 1998), 147–63.

120. David Gedney, "Florida Overland Express: A Public Private Partnership for High-Speed Rail in the USA," *Rail International*, September-October 1998, 210.

121. John D. McKinnon, "A Lack of Cash May Derail Express Train," *Wall Street Journal*, 28 January 1998, sec. F, 2, Eastern edition.

122. John D. McKinnon, "Lawmakers Accept Trip to France," *Wall Street Journal*, 10 June 1998, sec. F, 1, Eastern edition.

123. Ibid.

124. Jim Molis, "Florida Commission Urges Caution When Using Ridership Survey Results," *The Bond Buyer*, 5 August 1998, 3.

125. Mark Silva, "Concerns on Florida Bullet Train Plan Shouldn't Derail it, State Says," *Knight-Ridder/Tribune Business News*, 5 August 1998.

126. Robert Johnson, "Lawmakers May Blow Whistle on Bullet Train," *Wall Street Journal*, 11 November 1998, sec. F, 1, Eastern edition.

127. U.S. General Accounting Office, *Surface Infrastructure: High-Speed Rail Projects in the United States*, 16.

128. Ibid., 1.

129. Ibid., 2.

130. P.S. Dempsey, A.R. Goetz, and J.S. Szyliowicz, *Denver International Airport: Lessons Learned* (New York: McGraw-Hill, 1997), 1.

131. Ibid., 257–58.

132. State of Florida, *Governor Bush to Withhold State Funding for High Speed Rail Project*, January 14, 1999. http://www.state.fl.us/eog/press_releases/1999/January/1–14_highspeed_rail.html (23 February 2001).

133. William C. Vantuono, "Florida's Governor Derails FOX," *Railway Age*, February 1999, 22.

134. John D. McKinnon, "State's East Coast Could Soon Be Back On Track," *Wall Street Journal*, 17 February 1999, sec. F, 2, Eastern edition.

135. Cecil Foster, "High-Speed Train Becomes a Bandwagon," *Globe & Mail*, 20 September 1989, sec. B, 1.

136. Shawn McCarthy, "Quebec to Toronto by Rail at 320 kph? $11–Billion High-Speed Line Would Need Big Money from Governments," *Globe & Mail*, 8 May 1998, sec. A, 8.

137. Richard Mackie, "Plan for High-Speed Train Line on Track," *Globe & Mail*, 6 March 1990, sec. A, 15.

138. Foster, "High-Speed Train Becomes a Bandwagon," sec. B, 7.

139. Ontario/Québec Rapid Train Task Force, *Ontario/Québec Rapid Train Task Force Final Report* (Ottawa, Ont.: Ontario/Québec Rapid Train Task Force, 1991), 6–3.

140. Ibid.

141. Ontario/Québec Rapid Train Task Force, *Final Report*, EXECSUM 9.
142. Ibid., 6–5.
143. Ibid.
144. James Daw, "Go Slow on Fast Train, Task Force Report Says," *Toronto Star*, 6 June 1991, sec. C, 3.
145. Sheila McGovern, "Bombardier, ABB Hit Campaign Trail to Pitch High-Speed Rail Systems," *Montreal Gazette*, 7 June 1991, sec. D, 3.
146. Transport Canada, Gouvernement du Québec Ministère des Transports, and Ministry of Transportation of Ontario, *Québec–Ontario High Speed Rail Project: Final Report, August 1995* (Ottawa, Québec, and Toronto: Transport Canada, Gouvernement du Québec Ministère des Transports, and Ministry of Transportation of Ontario, 1995), 84.
147. Ibid.
148. Ibid., 86.
149. Ibid., v–vi, 88.
150. Ibid., 84.
151. Ibid., 85–86.
152. Ibid., 87. See also Bruce Campion-Smith, "Provincial Bullet Train Too Costly, Study Says," *Toronto Star*, 30 August 1995, sec. A, 13.
153. Ibid. (*Québec–Ontario High Speed Rail Project*), 86, 84.
154. Ibid., 89.
155. Julius Lukasiewicz, "Rail Service Slashed Despite $7.6 Billion in Subsidies," *Ottawa Citizen*, 3 October 1995, sec. A, 15.
156. Richard Soberman, "High Speed Trains for Canada: Technological Excellence, Groundless Conviction, or Bureaucratic Obsession?," in *Essays in Canadian Surface Transportation*, ed., Philip K. Palda (Vancouver, B.C.: The Fraser Institute, 1995), 132–33.
157. After 21 years of under-use, Montreal's Mirabel International Airport was finally closed to scheduled domestic flights. These, along with almost all international scheduled flights, relocated to Dorval airport in 1997.
158. Toronto's Terminal One accommodated international flights with 747 aircraft, and continues to receive such flights to this day.
159. No urban transit system has ever been launched using magnetically levitated vehicles.
160. Soberman, "High Speed Trains for Canada," 133.
161. Ibid., 137.
162. LYNX, *Proposed Alignment and Trainset Layout* (Montreal, Que.: Lynx Consortium, April 1998).
163. LYNX, *Summary* (Montreal, Que.: Lynx Consortium, April 1998), 4–7.
164. McCarthy, "Quebec to Toronto by Rail at 320 kph?," sec. A, 8.
165. LYNX, *Summary*.
166. Jim Brown, "High-Speed Rail System a Dream: But Collenette Cool to Spending Federal Funds On It?," (*Newfoundland*) *Telegram*, 22 October 1998, 40.
167. House Standing Committee on Transport, *The Renaissance of Passenger Rail*

in Canada: Report of the Standing Committee on Transport (Ottawa, Ont.: Public Works and Government Services Canada–Publishing, 1998), 36.

168. Ibid., 38.

169. Ibid., 39.

170. Ibid., 40.

171. McCarthy, "Quebec to Toronto by Rail at 320 kph?," sec. A, 8.

172. Douglas McArthur, "Business Travel: Speedy New U.S. Train Shows How Far VIA Is Off the Track," *Globe and Mail*, 7 July 1999, sec. C, 8.

5. Reinventing Amtrak: The Drive for Commercial Self-Sufficiency by 2003

1. Luther S. Miller, "W. Graham Claytor, Jr., Former Amtrak Chief, Dies at 82," *Railway Age*, June 1994, 22.

2. "Coming Soon: The Death of Passenger Trains?," *U.S. News & World Report*, 29 April 1985, 83.

3. House Committee on Energy and Commerce, Subcommittee on Transportation and Hazardous Materials, *Amtrak Reauthorization: Hearing Before the Subcommittee on Transportation and Hazardous Materials of the Committee on Energy and Commerce on H.R. 2364*, 101st Cong., 1st sess., 17 May 1989, 87–88.

4. Amtrak, *Annual Report* (Washington, D.C.: National Railroad Passenger Corporation, 1989), 2.

5. Senate Committee on Appropriations, Subcommittee on Transportation and Related Agencies, *Department of Transportation and Related Agencies Appropriations for Fiscal Year 1991: Hearings on H.R. 5229*, 101st Cong., 2d sess., 1990, 469.

6. House Committee on Energy and Commerce, Subcommittee on Transportation and Hazardous Materials, *Amtrak Reauthorization: Hearing Before the Subcommittee on Transportation and Hazardous Materials on H.R. 5*, 102d Cong., 2d sess., February 1992, 48.

7. Ibid., 55.

8. During Claytor's tenure, Amtrak negotiated an industry-leading contract with its locomotive engineers and conductors that switched from mileage-based pay (using a scale that was calculated when steam engines could pull a train about one hundred miles in eight hours) to hourly pay. These and similar productivity boosts allowed Amtrak to lead the world's passenger railroads in overall cost recovery during the late 1980s.

9. "Thomas M. Downs Named Amtrak President, Chairman," *Railway Age*, January 1994, 27.

10. Theodore W. Scull, "Amtrak Enters a New Era: PTJ Interviews the Railroad's New President," *Passenger Train Journal*, March 1994, 23.

11. Bureau of Transportation Statistics, *Intermodal Surface Transportation Efficiency Act of 1991*, n.d. http://www.bts.gov/ntl/DOCS/istea.html (13 March 2001).

12. Thomas M. Downs, "Preserving Passenger Railroading," *Railway Age*, June 1996, 67.

13. "Amtrak President: We Must Be 'Smaller, Faster,'" *Travel Weekly*, 14 No-

vember 1994, 60.

14. Randolph R. Resor, "Should Amtrak Survive as a National Rail System?," *Transportation Quarterly* 53, no. 1 (winter 1999): 93–94.

15. Daniel Machalaba and Daniel Pearl, "Amtrak Plans To Slash Service, Cut 5,500 Jobs—Bold Proposal Aims to Close Budget Gap, Sidetrack Efforts to End Subsidy," *Wall Street Journal*, 15 December 1994, sec. A, 3, Eastern edition.

16. House Committee on Transportation and Infrastructure, Subcommittee on Railroads, *Amtrak's Current Situation*, 104th Cong., 1st sess., 1996, 93.

17. Luther S. Miller, "Transit Rides Out a Tempest," *Railway Age*, January 1996, 43.

18. U.S. House of Representatives, *Republican Contract With America*, 27 September 1994, n.d. http://www.house.gov/house/Contract/CONTRACT.html (15 February 2001).

19. Friends of Amtrak, *Letter from Tom Downs to Craig O'Connell, 19 December 1995*, n.d. http://trainweb.com/crocon/amarchives95.html (12 December 2000).

20. Daniel G. Williams and Joseph J. Warren, "Amtrak Revenues, Fares, and Ridership in the 1990s: Trends and Passenger Revenues Forecast Errors," *Transportation Journal* 36, no. 4 (summer 1997): 8.

21. Luther S. Miller, "A Kinder, Gentler Congress? It Must be Election Time," *Railway Age*, August 1996, 18.

22. Details of the legislative maneuverings that preceded the Amtrak Reform and Accountability Act of 1997 can be found in Stephen J. Thompson, *Amtrak and the 104th Congress* (Washington, D.C.: Congressional Research Service, 1997), CRS-1–CRS-2.

23. After negotiations over nonstatutory labor protection arrangements broke down in 1998, Amtrak and its unions submitted their differences over labor protection to an arbitration panel which reduced the maximum benefit from six to five years' pay for displaced workers with more than twenty-five years of service, while eliminating labor protection benefits to workers with less than two years of service. Amtrak employees between these extremes would be eligible for payments on a sliding scale, starting at six months worth of labor protection for those having between two and three years of service, rising to a one-year eligibility for workers with between three and five years of service, and increasing by six months for every additional five years of service up to the five-year maximum. Amtrak estimates that approximately 20 percent of its workers eligible for labor protection payments have at least twenty years' worth of service. See Amtrak Reform Council, *A Council Policy Paper: A Summary of Current Legislative Provisions Prescribing the Legal and Regulatory Framework Governing the National Railroad Passenger Corporation (Amtrak)*, Washington, D.C.: Amtrak Reform Council, 2000, 23.

24. *Amtrak Reform and Accountability Act of 1997*, Public Law 105–134, 105th Cong., 1st sess. (2 December 1997), sec. 204–c.

25. Ibid.

26. Frank N. Wilner, "Guest Opinion—Railroading Amtrak's CEO," *Journal of Commerce*, 8 January 1998, 7A.

27. Stephen J. Thompson, *Amtrak: Background and Selected Public Policy Issues II*, Report no. 97–030 (Washington, D.C.: Congressional Research Service, 1997).

28. AFL Transportation Trades Department, "AFL-CIO Resolution 4–97, Mobilizing Transportation Labor to Protect Amtrak Workers, 7 October 1997," 1999. http://cgi.ttd.org/foxweb.exe/ttddview?33I (13 March 2001).

29. Phyllis F. Scheinberg, *Testimony of United States General Accounting Office: Intercity Passenger Rail: Decisions on the Future of Amtrak and Intercity Passenger Rail Are Approaching*, Report no. GAO/T-RCED-00–277 (Washington, D.C.: U.S. General Accounting Office, 2000), 6.

30. Amtrak, *Strategic Business Plan: FY1999–2002* (Washington, D.C.: National Railroad Passenger Corporation, 1998).

31. Amtrak Reform Council, *A Preliminary Assessment of Amtrak: The First Annual Report of the Amtrak Reform Council* (Washington, D.C.: Amtrak Reform Council, 2000).

32. Ibid., 52.

33. Ibid., 58.

34. Ibid., 59.

35. Ibid., 8.

36. Ibid., 9.

37. Ibid., 11.

38. Ibid., x.

39. Ibid., xiv.

40. Ibid., xvi.

41. Ibid., 50.

42. Amtrak Reform Council, *Intercity Rail Passenger Service in America: Status, Problems, and Options for Reform: The Second Annual Report of the Amtrak Reform Council* (Washington, D.C.: Amtrak Reform Council, 2001). http://www.amtrakreformcouncil.gov/second.html (21 March 2001).

43. Amtrak Reform Council, *Intercity Rail Passenger Service in America*, x.

44. Ibid., 2.

45. Trains.com, *Railroading: Letter from Amtrak President George D. Warrington to ARC Chairman Gilbert E. Carmichael*, March 16, 2001. http://www.trains.com/content/dynamic/articles/000/000/000/831orgnt.asp (21 March 2001).

46. Scheinberg, *Testimony of United States General Accounting Office*, 4.

47. Ibid., 5.

48. Ibid., 6.

49. Ibid., 9.

50. Ibid., 10.

51. Ibid., 11.

52. U.S. Department of Transportation, Inspector General, *2000 Assessment of Amtrak's Financial Performance and Requirements*, Report No. CR-2000–121 (Washington, D.C.: U.S. Department of Transportation, Office of Inspector General, 2000), 1.

53. Ibid., 6.

54. Ibid., 13.

55. Ibid., 14.

56. Ibid., 22.

57. Ibid., 23.

58. Ibid., 35.

59. Ibid., 43–44.

60. Amtrak, Building a Commercial Enterprise: FY 01–05 Financial Plan Update (Washington, D.C.: National Railroad Passenger Corporation, 2001), 44–45.

61. Ibid., 26–27.

62. Ibid., 35.

63. Pennsylvania Economic Development Financing Authority, *Prospectus: $110,795,000 Exempt Facilities Revenue Bonds (Amtrak Project), Series A of 2001*, 16 February 2001 (Harrisburg, Pa.: Pennsylvania Economic Development Financing Authority), A-18-20; A-52.

64. Ibid., A-44.

65. Ibid., A-48.

66. See Laurie McGinley and Andy Pasztor, "Greyhound Gets Clearance to Run Trailways for Now," *Wall Street Journal*, 3 July 1987, 1, Eastern edition; and Francis C. Brown III, "Greyhound Sets $80 Million Pact With Trailways—Bus Line to Acquire Routes, Assets of Competitor, Will Be Sole U.S. Carrier," *Wall Street Journal*, 22 June 1987, 1, Eastern edition.

67. Robert Tomsho and Kevin G. Salwen, "Greyhound, ATU in Talks to Shape Tentative Contract, End Labor Dispute," *Wall Street Journal*, 19 April 1993, sec. B, 10, Eastern edition.

68. Amtrak West, *California Passenger Rail System 20–Year Improvement Plan: Summary Report*, March 2001, 2001. http://www.amtrakwest.com/califuture/5yearplan.htm (19 March 2001); and Amtrak West, *California Passenger Rail System 20–Year Improvement Plan: Technical Report*, March 2001, at the same location.

69. The Centre for Sustainable Transportation, *Sustainable Transportation Monitor* 2 (February 1999). See http://www.cstctd.org/CSTadobefiles/stmonitorissue2adobe.pdf (20 March 2001).

70. Highlights of the energy crisis in California, and in other sectors that depend heavily upon natural gas can be found in Rene Sanchez, "California Crisis Has Residents Seething," *Washington Post*, 11 February 2001, sec. A, 1; Robert Gavin, "California Energy Crisis: Power Crunch Roils Other Western States—Utilities Seek Higher Rates, Companies Idle Plants; 'It's an Economy Crisis,'" *Wall Street Journal*, 24 January 2001, sec. A, 2, Eastern edition; and Susan Warren, "Price of Natural Gas Hits Boiling Point—Everyone Knows Oil Is Up, But Now Cost for Gas Has Blown Right Past It," *Wall Street Journal*, 18 December 2000, sec. A, 2, Eastern edition.

71. "Editorial: The Energy Equation," *Washington Post*, 5 February 2001, sec. A, 18.

72. Jon A. Krosnick and Penny S. Visser, *The Impact of the Fall 1997 Debate About Global Warming On American Public Opinion: Executive Summary* (Washington, D.C.: Resources For the Future, 1998).

73. B. Biagini, P. Kelley, and G. Starikoff, *Disconnect: Americans Want Action Against Global Warming, But Their Government Still Hasn't Kept Its Promises* (Washington, D.C.: National Environmental Trust, 1999), 2.

74. Ibid., 3.

75. John Carey, "Global Warming: Why Team Bush Could Generate Some Heat," *Business Week*, 12 February 2001, 47.

76. Ted Mondale, "Transportation—A Major Player in Smart Growth," *ITE Journal*, November 2000, 40.

77. Belden, Russonello & Stewart Research and Communications, *National Survey on Growth and Land Development September 2000 for Smart Growth America* (Washington, D.C.: SmartGrowth America, 2000). This report is available at: http://www.smartgrowthamerica.com/poll.pdf (19 March 2001).

6. Setting Up the New Model Railroad in North America: Bringing Passenger Trains into a Transportation Policy for the Twenty-First Century

1. Tim Beardsley, "Aeronautics: But Where are the Cupholders?," *Scientific American*, December 1999, 50.

2. Suman Bandrapalli, "My Mass Transit," *Christian Science Monitor*, November 19, 1998. http://www.csmonitor.com/durable/1998/11/19/p11s1.htm (15 March 1998).

3. James Glanz, "Maglev: Will it Ever Really Fly?," *R & D*, August 1993, 40–42.

4. Tracked Hovercraft Ltd., *A Cost Comparison of Three Tracked Air Cushion Vehicle Configurations*, Report no. FRA-RT-71–68 (Washington, D.C.: Department of Transportation, Office of High Speed Ground Transportation, 1970).

5. For a history of America's road building bureaucracy, see Bruce E. Seely, *Building the American Highway System: Engineers as Policy Makers* (Philadelphia, Pa.: Temple Univ. Press, 1987). For an analysis of the financial innovation that made it possible, see John C. Burnham, "The Gasoline Tax and the Automobile Revolution," *The Mississippi Valley Historical Review* 48, no. 3 (December 1961): 435–59.

6. Anthony Perl, "Superbureaucrats and Superhighways: An Institutional Explanation for Variation in American and Canadian Highway Policies" (paper presented at the annual meeting of the American Political Science Association, Chicago, Ill., September 1992).

7. Anthony Perl and James A. Dunn Jr., "Reinventing Amtrak: The Politics of Survival," *Journal of Policy Analysis and Management* 16, no. 4 (1997): 598–614.

8. Information about Transportation California and its membership can be found at Transportation California, *Transportation California*, 2000. http://www.transportationca.com/about_transcal/ (6 March 2001).

9. Transportation California, "All Rail is Not Created Equal: Study Shows Amazing Decline in Intercity Rail Performance," January 2001. http://www.transportationca.com/archives/all_rail.shtml (05 March 2001).

10. Ibid.

11. Information about the Alameda Corridor Project, as well as the special purpose authority that was created to finance and implement it, can be found at the web
site of the Alameda Corridor Transportation Authority, *ACTA*, 1999. http://
www.acta.org/main_menu_acta.htm (15 March 2001).

12. Daniel Machalaba, "Railroads Learn to Like Public Funding: Plans to Expand Freight Infrastructure Arise on Both Coasts," *Wall Street Journal*, 1 May 2000,
sec. A, 2, Eastern edition.

13. Ibid.

14. Chip Jones, "CEO of Richmond, VA-Based Rail Firm Urges Creation of High-
Speed Rail System," *Richmond (Va.) Times-Dispatch*, 9 November 2000, sec. B, 10.

15. Taken from Railway Age, *Late Breaking Industry News*, March 7, 2001. http://
www.railwayage.com/breaking_news_archive.html (15 March 2001).

16. Ibid.

17. Details about U.S. taxation of motor fuels can be found in Bernard Gelb
(Congressional Research Service), *Transportation Fuel Taxes Early in the 105th Congress*, March 17, 1997. http://www.cnie.org/nle/trans-5.html (15 March 2001).

18. The AAR's position on diesel fuel taxation is clearly expressed in the July 25,
2000, Congressional testimony of CEO Edward Hamberger, available at Association
of American Railroads, *Speeches: Testimony of Edward R. Hamberger, President and Chief
Executive Officer, Association of American Railroads, Before the Subcommittee on Ground
Transportation, Committee on Transportation and Infrastructure, House of Representatives
on H.R. 4746, The "Emergency Rural and Small Railroad Preservation Act*, July 25, 2000."
http://www.aar.org/pressrel.nsf/d46318ab0a4791f0852563f70053b736/
7ccd583cd7b6772e852569280057925e?OpenDocument (15 March 2001).

19. Association of American Railroads, *Railroad Facts, 2000* (Washington, D.C.:
Office of Information and Public Affairs, Association of American Railroads, 2000), 16.

20. Railway Association of Canada, *Railway Trends, 2000* (Montreal, Que.: The
Railway Association of Canada, 2000), 19.

21. "Rail Update: But Hey—No Hard Feelings," *Railway Age*, August 2000, 17.

22. "CN, CP Share Routes," *Railway Track and Structures*, September 2000, 5.

23. Douglas J. Bowen and Jessica Stern, "California Votes $3 Billion for Rail,"
Railway Age, July 1990, 86.

24. Lee Smith, "Is this Any Way to Sell a Railroad?," *Fortune*, 25 May 1987, 92.

25. C.Y. Baldwin and S. Bhattacharyya, "Choosing the Method of Sale: A Clinical
Study of Conrail," *Journal of Financial Economics* 30, no. 1 (November 1991): 73–75.

26. See Transport Canada, *National Airports Policy* (Ottawa, Ont.: Transport
Canada, 1994); and Transport Canada, *National Marine Policy* (Ottawa, Ont.: Transport Canada, 1995).

27. Once such a plan was drawn up, VIA could be mandated to manage its own
liquidation, as the Cape Breton Development Corporation is now doing in selling off
its coal mining and processing assets. See President of the Treasury Board, *Crown
Corporations and Other Corporate Interests of Canada* (Ottawa, Ont.: Minister of Public
Works and Government Services Canada, 2000), 6.

Afterword

1. See James Risen and David Johnston, "Man Sought as Possible Organizer of Attacks," *New York Times*, September 21, 2001, web edition.

2. Katherine Shaver and Spencer S. Hsu, "With Airport, Roads Closed, Travel Stalls," *Washington Post*, September 21, 2001, p. A01.

3. Josh White, "Flights into National Depart from the Normal," *Washington Post*, October 5, 2001, p. A20. See also Katherine Q. Seelye, "Shuttles from New York to Washington Return to Sky," *New York Times on the Web*, October 5, 2001, www.nytimes.com.

4. Don Phillips, "The View From the Ground—Amtrak: The Boost That Began Sept. 11 May Not Be Temporary," *Washington Post*, September 23, 2001, p. F01.

5. "Keep the Trains Running," *Washington Post*, September 24, 2001, p. A20.

6. "Trains Need Help, Too," *New York Times on the Web*, September 25, 2001, www.nytimes.com.

7. Associated Press, "Bush OK's $15B Airline Aid Package," *New York Times on the Web*, September 23, 2001, www.nytimes.com.

8. Don Phillips, "The View From the Ground—Amtrak: The Boost That Began Sept. 11 May Not Be Temporary," *Washington Post*, September 23, 2001, p. F01.

9. Anthony Perl and Joseph Szyliowicz, "High Speed Rail Is a Key Tool in Making Air Travel Safer," *Ottawa Citizen*, September 27, 2001, p. B4.

Bibliography

Adler, Sy. "The Transformation of the Pacific Electric Railway: Bradford Snell, Roger Rabbit, and the Politics of Transportation in Los Angeles." *Urban Affairs Quarterly* 27, no. 1 (September 1991): 51–86.

"Advanced Passenger Train Catches Cold." *Times* (London), 10 December 1981, 3.

AFL Transportation Trades Department. "AFL-CIO Resolution 4–97, Mobilizing Transportation Labor to Protect Amtrak Workers, 7 October 1997." 1999. HTTP://cgi.ttd.org/foxweb.exe/ttddview?33I (13 March 2001).

Aggarwala, Rohit T. "The States, New Modes, and Federal Transportation Policy: Lessons From History for High-Speed Rail." *Transportation Quarterly* 52, no. 3 (summer 1998): 53–67.

Alameda Corridor Transportation Authority. *ACTA.* 1999. http://www.acta.org/main_menu_acta.htm (15 March 2001).

Amtrak. *Annual Report, 1989.* Washington, D.C.: National Railroad Passenger Corporation, 1989.

———. *Annual Report, 1999.* Washington, D.C.: National Railroad Passenger Corporation, 1999.

———. *Strategic Business Plan: Building a Commercial Enterprise, FY01–05 Financial Plan Update.* Washington, D.C.: National Railroad Passenger Corporation, 2001.

———. *Strategic Business Plan: FY1999–2002.* Washington, D.C.: National Railroad Passenger Corporation, 1998.

Amtrak Authorization and Development Act of 1992. Public Law 102–533. 102d Cong., 2d sess., 27 October 1992.

"Amtrak President: We Must Be 'Smaller, Faster.'" *Travel Weekly,* 14 November 1994, 60.

Amtrak Reform and Accountability Act of 1997. Public Law 105–134. 105th Cong., 1st sess., 2 December 1997.

Amtrak Reform Council. *A Council Policy Paper: A Summary of Current Legislative Provisions Prescribing the Legal and Regulatory Framework Governing the National Railroad Passenger Corporation (Amtrak).* Washington, D.C.: Amtrak Reform Council, 2000.

———. *Intercity Rail Passenger Service in America: Status, Problems, and Options for*

Reform: The Second Annual Report of the Amtrak Reform Council. Washington, D.C.: Amtrak Reform Council, 2001.

————. *A Preliminary Assessment of Amtrak: The First Annual Report of the Amtrak Reform Council.* Washington, D.C.: Amtrak Reform Council, 2000.

Amtrak West. *California Passenger Rail System 20–Year Improvement Plan: Summary Report, March 2001.* 2001. http://www.amtrakwest.com/califuture/5yearplan.htm (19 March 2001).

————. *California Passenger Rail System 20–Year Improvement Plan: Technical Report.* March 2001. http://www.amtrakwest.com/califuture/5yearplan.htm (19 March 2001).

Association of American Railroads. *Railroad Facts, 2000.* Washington, D.C.: Office of Information and Public Affairs. Association of American Railroads, 2000.

————. *Speeches: Testimony of Edward R. Hamberger, President and Chief Executive Officer, Association of American Railroads, Before The Subcommittee On Ground Transportation, Committee On Transportation and Infrastructure, House of Representatives On H.R. 4746, The "Emergency Rural and Small Railroad Preservation Act."* July 25, 2000. http://www.aar.org/pressrel.nsf/d46318ab0a4791f0852563f70053b736/7ccd583cd7b6772e852569280057925e?OpenDocument (15 March 2001).

Atkins, Ralph. "Chief of Deutsche Bahn is Dismissed." *Financial Times,* 15 September 1999, 3.

Atkinson, Michael M., and William D. Coleman. "Strong States and Weak States: Sectoral Policy Networks in Advanced Capitalist Economies." *British Journal of Political Science* 19, no. 1 (1989): 47–67.

Baily, Michael. "British Rail Unveils its 150 mph Train." *Times* (London), 8 June 1978, 4.

Baldwin, C.Y., and S. Bhattacharyya. "Choosing the Method of Sale: A Clinical Study of Conrail." *Journal of Financial Economics* 30, no. 1 (November 1991): 69–98.

Bandrapalli, Suman. "My Mass Transit." *Christian Science Monitor.* November 19, 1998. http://www.csmonitor.com/durable/1998/11/19/p11s1.htm (15 March 1998).

Barnett, Roger. "British Rail's Intercity 125 and 225." *Built Environment* 19, no. 3–4 (1999): 163–82.

Beardsley, Tim. "Aeronautics: But Where are the Cupholders?" *Scientific American,* December 1999, 50.

Bedingfield, Robert E. "Cautions on U.S. Rail Role: Calls Take-Over a Threat, but at 'Prohibitive' Cost." *New York Times,* 9 March 1971, 47.

Belden, Russonello & Stewart Research and Communications. *National Survey on Growth and Land Development September 2000 for Smart Growth America.* Washington, D.C.: SmartGrowth America, 2000.

Bennett, Steve. "Franz Heads Both DB Passenger Units." *International Railway Journal,* September 2000, 21–27.

Bentley, Jerome T. *Issues in Subsidization with Attention to the Subsidization of Passenger Rail Service.* Ottawa, Ont.: Economic Council of Canada, 1985.

Berkman, Leslie. "Bullet Train Data Assailed by Consultant: Riders and Revenues

Vastly Overstated, Tustin Report Says." *Los Angeles Times*, 26 October 1983, sec. A, 14.

Biagini, B., P. Kelley, and G. Starikoff. *Disconnect: Americans Want Action Against Global Warming, But Their Government Still Hasn't Kept Its Promises*. Washington, D.C.: National Environmental Trust, 1999.

Bloomberg News (David Ward, Bill McQuillen, and Rip Watson). "Union Pacific Brings Train and Money to Convention." 3 August 2000. http://quote.bloomberg.com/newsarchive/?sidenav=front (17 March 2001)

Board of Transport Commissioners for Canada. *Judgements, Orders, Regulations and Rulings*. Vol. 56. Ottawa, Ont.: The Queen's Printer, 1966.

Bowen, Douglas John, and Jessica Stern. "California Votes $3 Billion For Rail." *Railway Age*, July 1990, 86–92.

Bowers, P.H. "Railway Reform in Germany." *Journal of Transport Economics and Policy* 30, no. 1 (January 1996): 95–102.

Briginshaw, David. "DB's Two Biggest Rail Projects Suffer Setbacks." *International Railway Journal*, September 2000, 36–40.

"British Rail's New Train Tops 100 mph (Later it Limped Home)." *Times* (London), 8 December 1981, 24.

Brown, Jim. "High-Speed Rail System a Dream: But Collenette Cool to Spending Federal Funds On It?" (*Newfoundland*) *Telegram*, 22 October 1998, 40.

Brown III, Francis C. "Greyhound Sets $80 Million Pact With Trailways—Bus Line to Acquire Routes, Assets of Competitor, Will Be Sole U.S. Carrier." *Wall Street Journal*, 22 June 1987, 1, Eastern edition.

"Budd Tries to Get Out of Its Rail Cars." *Business Week*, 2 May 1970, 16–17.

Bunting, Mark. *Changing Trains: A Commercially Sustainable Railway Passenger Policy for Canada*. Kingston, Ont.: P.M. Bunting & Associates, 1998.

Burnham, John C. "The Gasoline Tax and the Automobile Revolution." *Mississippi Valley Historical Review* 48, no. 3 (December 1961): 435–59.

Burns, Marc H. *High Speed Rail in the Rear-View Mirror: A Final Report of the Texas High-Speed Rail Authority*. Austin, Tex.: Marc H. Burns, 1995.

California High-Speed Rail Authority. *News Releases: California High-Speed Rail Authority Starts*. 16 August 2000. http://www.cahighspeedrail.org/news_release/index.cfm?PressID=15 (3 February 2001).

Campbell, A.R. "Mr. A.R. Campbell." In *Proceedings of the First National Rail Passenger Conference, October 29–31, 1976*. Edited by Michael Jackson, 39–42. Regina, Sask.: University of Regina, 1977.

———. "A Submission to the Canadian Transport Commission Regarding Rationalization of Maritime Rail Passenger Services by A.R. Campbell, General Manager, Passenger Services, CP Rail." Ottawa, Ont.: Canadian Transport Commission, 2 June 1977.

Campion-Smith, Bruce. "Provincial Bullet Train Too Costly, Study Says." *Toronto Star*, 30 August 1995, sec. A, 13.

Canada. House of Commons. "Bill C-97: An Act Respecting Rail Passenger Transportation, 24 February 1986." *House of Commons Bills*. Nos. C81–C106 (1984–1986). Ottawa, Ont.: Minister of Supply and Services, 1986.

Canada. House of Commons. Standing Committee on Transport. *Minutes of Proceedings and Evidence of the Standing Committee on Transport*, no. 38, 21 May 1987, 1–101.

Canada. House of Commons. Standing Committee on Transport and Communications. *Minutes of Proceedings and Evidence*, no. 2, 3 March 1966, 68–134.

———. *Minutes of Proceedings and Evidence*, no. 22, 5 July 1966, 1578–1655.

Canada. House of Commons. Standing Committee on Transport. *The Renaissance of Passenger Rail in Canada: Report of the Standing Committee on Transport.* Ottawa, Ont.: Public Works and Government Services Canada–Publishing, 1998.

Canada. President of the Treasury Board. *Crown Corporations and Other Corporate Interests of Canada.* Ottawa, Ont.: Minister of Public Works and Government Services Canada, 2000.

Canada. *Royal Commission on Transportation*. Vol. 1. Ottawa, Ont.: Queen's Printer, 1961.

Canada. Senate. Standing Committee on Transportation and Communications, no. 11, *Appendix TC-11-A*, 29 May, 1984.

Canada. Task Force on Rail Passenger Service. *Report of the Task Force on Rail Passenger Service: The Last Straw.* Ottawa, Ont.: Task Force on Rail Passenger Service, 1981.

Canadian National Railways. *Annual Report*. Montreal, Que.: Canadian National Railways, 1976.

Canadian Transport Commission. *CTC Annual Report.* Ottawa, Ont.: Information Canada: 1972–1976.

Canadian Transport Commission. Economic and Social Analysis Branch. *An Historical Review of Direct Transport Subsidies in Canada.* Report no. ESAB 75–8. Ottawa, Ont.: Canadian Transport Commission, 1975.

Canadian Transport Commission. Research Branch. *An Analysis of Railway Transport Committee Decisions, 1967–1980.* Report no. 1982/06E. Ottawa, Ont.: Canadian Transport Commission, 1981.

Canadian Transport Commission. Rail Transport Committee. *Reasons for Order No. R-6313.* Ottawa, Ont.: Canadian Transport Commission, 1970.

Carey, John. "Global Warming: Why Team Bush Could Generate Some Heat." *Business Week*, 12 February 2001, 47.

Centre for Sustainable Transportation, The. *Sustainable Transportation Monitor 2* (February 1999). http://www.cstctd.org/CSTadobefiles/stmonitorissue2adobe.pdf (23 May 2001).

Chapin, Emerson. "Japan's Airlines Step Up Service." *New York Times*, 14 March 1965, sec. S, 21.

Charles River Associates Inc. *Independent Ridership and Passenger Revenue Projections for the Texas TGV Corporation: High Speed Rail System in Texas.* Boston, Mass.: Charles River and Associates, 1993.

Clark, Marc. "VIA's Rocky Future: An Executive Resigns to Protest Cutbacks." *Maclean's*, 15 May 1989, 17.

"CN, CP Share Routes." *Railway Track and Structures*, September 2000, 5.

Coalition of Northeastern Governors. *About CONEG.* 2000. http://www.coneg.org/about/default.htm (22 Feb. 2001).

———. *The Growth of Intercity Rail.* October 1, 1997. http://www.coneg.org/programs/policies/growth.htm (22 February 2001).

Coleman, William D., and Grace Skogstad. *Policy Communities and Public Policy in Canada: A Structural Approach.* Mississauga, Ont.: Copp Clark Pitman, 1990.

"Coming Soon: The Death of Passenger Trains?" *U.S. News & World Report*, 29 April 1985, 83.

Comptroller General of the United States. *Report to the Congress: Administration of Metroliner and Turbo-Train Projects.* Report B-164497(5). Washington, D.C.: Comptroller General of the United States, 1971.

CONEG High Speed Rail Task Force. *REPORT of the CONEG High Speed Rail Task Force: Volume I.* Washington, D.C.: CONEG High Speed Rail Task Force, 1989.

Cubukgil, Adil, and Richard M. Soberman. "Costs of Rail Passenger Service in Canada: An Examination of Institutional Problems." In *Proceedings—Twenty-Fifth Annual Meeting: Transportation Research Forum.* Vol. 25. No. 4, 69–75. Phillipsburg, N.J.: Harmony Press, 1984, 69.

Cummings, Judith. "Plan for High-Speed Train on West Coast is Scrapped." *New York Times*, 24 November 1984, sec. A, 17.

Cupper, Dan. "20 Years of Metroliner Service: Not Ultra High Speed, But at 125 mph, Fast Enough." *Passenger Train Journal*, March 1989, 9–12.

"DaimlerChrysler's Adtranz Chief Says Transrapid Project Has No Future." *AFX Europe*, 12 October 1999.

Dallavalle, Claudio, and Jack E. Heiss. "Florida's High Speed Rail Project: Building a Public-Private Partnership." In *1997 Proceedings of the American Railway Engineering Association.* Vol. 98, 353–63. Washington, D.C.: American Railway Engineering Association, 1997.

Daughen, Joseph R., and Peter Binzen. *The Wreck of the Penn Central.* Boston, Mass.: Little, Brown and Company, 1971.

Daw, James. "Go Slow on Fast Train, Task Force Report Says." *Toronto Star*, 6 June 1991, sec. C, 3.

"DB Suffers Financial Setback." *International Railway Journal*, June 2000, 2.

Deans, Ralph C. "Railroad Nationalization." *Editorial Research Reports* 4, no. 27 (1973): 459–76.

Dempsey, P.S., A.R. Goetz, and J.S. Szyliowicz. *Denver International Airport: Lessons Learned.* New York: McGraw-Hill, 1997.

Deregulierungskommission. *Marköffnung und Wettbewerb.* Bonn: Bundeswirtschaftsministerium, 1990.

"Deutsche Bahn Head Defends Transrapid (Bahn-Chef verteidgt Transrapid)." *Die Welt* (Berlin), 3 July 1999.

Diffenderfer, James W. "Metroliner Experiences: An Engineering and Economic Review of Developments After a Year's Token Operation." Paper presented at the sixty-ninth annual convention of the American Railway Engineering Association, Chicago, Ill., 18 March 1970.

Dominion Bureau of Statistics. *Railway Transport: Operating and Traffic Statistics.* Part 4. Ottawa, Ont.: Dominion Bureau of Statistics, 1968–1970.

Dougherty, Kevin. "Hint of Route Sell-Offs: VIA Rail Gets New Chief." *The Financial Post,* 4 May 1989, 1.

Downs, Thomas M. "Preserving Passenger Railroading." *Railway Age,* June 1996, 67.

Dunn, James A. Jr., *Driving Forces: The Automobile, Its Enemies, and the Politics of Mobility.* Washington, D.C.: Brookings Institution, 1998.

Dunn, James A. Jr., and Anthony Perl, "Toward a "New Model Railway" for the 21st Century: Lessons From Five Countries." *Transportation Quarterly* 55, no.2 (spring 2001): 43–57.

"Editorial: The Energy Equation." *Washington Post,* 5 February 2001, sec. A, 18.

Edmund G. "Pat" Brown Institute of Government Affairs, The. *High/Super Speed Rail in Southern California: Projects, Technology, Finance and Public Policy Implications, February 10.* Los Angeles, Calif.: The Edmund G. "Pat" Brown Institute of Government Affairs, 1984.

European Commission Directorate-General for Energy and Transport. *EU Transport in Figures: Statistical Pocket Book 2000.* Brussels: European Commission Directorate-General for Energy and Transport, 2000.

Faith, Nicholas. *The World the Railways Made.* London: Pimlico, 1990.

Feigenbaum, Harvey B. *The Politics of Public Enterprise: Oil and the French State.* Princeton: Princeton Univ. Press, 1985.

Feigenbaum, Harvey, Jeffrey Henig, and Chris Hamnett. *Shrinking the State: The Political Underpinnings of Privatization.* Cambridge, U.K.: Cambridge Univ. Press, 1998.

Feldman, Joan M. "Seriously Successful." *Air Transport World,* January 1994, 60–67.

———. "Testing Reform in a Mass Market." *Air Transport World,* July 1995, 24–32.

Fildes, Toby. "Florida's Track Record." *Project & Trade Finance,* June 1996, 28.

"Florida DOT Awards High Speed Rail Franchise." *Railway Age,* March 1996, 32–33.

"Florida High Speed Rail Link." *Project Finance,* June 1998, 19.

Foster, Cecil. "High-Speed Train Becomes a Bandwagon." *Globe and Mail,* 20 September 1989, sec. B, 1.

Fourniau, M., and G. Ribeill. "La grande vitesse sur rail en France et en R.F.A." In *La grande technologie entre l'État et le marché.* Edited by E. Brenac, D. Finon, and P. Muller. Grenoble: CERAT, 1991.

Friends of Amtrak. *Letter from Tom Downs to Craig O'Connell, 19 December 1995.* n.d. http://trainweb.com/crocon/amarchives95.html (12 December 2000).

Gavin, Robert. "California Energy Crisis: Power Crunch Roils Other Western States— Utilities Seek Higher Rates, Companies Idle Plants; 'It's an Economy Crisis.'" *Wall Street Journal,* 24 January 2001, sec. A, 2, Eastern edition.

Gedney, David. "Florida Overland Express: A Public Private Partnership for High-Speed Rail in the USA." *Rail International,* September-October 1998, 208–10.

Gelb, Bernard (Congressional Research Service). *Transportation Fuel Taxes Early in the 105th Congress.* March 17, 1997. http://www.cnie.org/nle/trans-5.html (15 March 2001).

"German Govt 'Determined' to Build Single-Track Transrapid Train." *AFX Europe,* 16 September 1999.

German Information Service. "Railroad Reform Approved: East, West Railways to Merge and Be Privatized." *The Week in Germany,* 10 December 1993, 5.

"German Rail Fails to Come Out of the Red." *International Railway Journal,* December 2000, 4.

"Germany to Build Transrapid Train, Even if Costs Exceed 6.1 bln dm—Minister." *AFX Europe,* 16 June 1999.

Gilson, Lawrence D. "Can Entrepreneurs Save Mass Transit?: Private Transportation is a Pipe Dream." *New York Times,* 26 May 1985, sec. C, 2.

Glanz, James. "Maglev: Will it Ever Really Fly?." *R & D,* August 1993, 40–42.

Goddard, Stephen B. *Getting There: The Epic Struggle between Road and Rail in the American Century.* New York, N.Y.: Basic Books, 1994.

Gómez-Ibáñez, José A. "Splitting the Ties: The Privatization of British Rail." *Access: Research at the University of California Transportation Center* 14 (spring 1999).

Gourvish, Terence R. "British Rail's 'Business-Led' Organization, 1977–1990: Government-Industry Relations in Britain's Public Sector." *Business History Review* 64, no. 1 (spring 1990): 109–49.

Grampp, William D. "'Railpax' Key: Avoiding the ICC." *Wall Street Journal,* 25 March 1971, 8.

Grant, Linda, and David Smollar. "'Bullet' Train Between L.A., San Diego Planned." *Los Angeles Times,* 1 April 1982, sec. A, 1.

"Gremlins Slow High-Speed Trains." *Business Week,* 3 August 1968, 104–5.

"Gross Mismanagement: Rail Chaos is Damaging the Economy as Well as the Public." *Times* (London), 2 December 2000, 29.

Groupe de travail du comité interministériel des enterprises publiques. *Rapport sur les Entreprises Publiques.* Paris: La Documentation Française, 1967.

Gurin, David. "Trolley Transit in New York." *Bulletin of the National Railway Historical Society* 42, no. 1–2 (1977).

Gushue, Michael. "Presentation to EuroRail Congress '99," 26—28 January 1999, Hotel Lutétia Paris, Montreal, Que.: Via Rail Canada, 1999. Mimeo.

Hackney, Holt. "Air Strike on Austin: Why Southwest Airlines is Lobbying to Derail High-Speed Rail." *Financial World,* 16 October 1990, 32–33.

Harnischfeger, Uta. "German Rail Chief Spurns the British Way: But Plans for the Privatisation of Deutsche Bahn Have Run into a Hail of Criticism." *Financial Times,* 1 November 2000, 2.

Harper, Keith. "Rail Passenger Complaints Rise by 154% in Two Years." *Guardian Weekly,* 19 August 1999, 10.

Haswell, Anthony. "Amtrak—A Critical Appraisal From the Viewpoint of the Consumer." In *Proceedings—Thirteenth Annual Meeting Transportation Research Fo-*

rum. Vol. 13, no. 1, 113–29. Oxford, Ind.: The Richard B. Cross Company, 1972.

Hayward, Jack. *The State and the Market Economy: Industrial Patriotism and Economic Intervention in France.* New York: New York Univ. Press, 1986.

Heclo, Hugh. *Modern Social Politics in Britain and Sweden: From Relief to Income Maintenance.* New Haven, Conn.: Yale Univ. Press, 1974.

Herren, Jr., Thomas Wade. "Northeast Corridor High Speed Rail Passenger Service." Master's thesis, University of Rhode Island, 1969.

"High Speed Moves Forward in Florida—Maybe." *Railway Age,* October 1996, 24.

"High-Speed Train Sets New Record." *Times* (London), 11 August 1975, 2.

Hilton, George W. *Amtrak: The National Railroad Passenger Corporation.* Washington, D.C.: The American Enterprise Institute for Public Policy Studies, 1980.

———. *The Transportation Act of 1958: A Decade of Experience.* Bloomington, Ind.: Indianapolis Univ. Press, 1969.

Hosakawa, Bill. *Old Man Thunder: Father of the Bullet Train.* Denver, Colo.: Sogo Way, 1997.

"How Not to Run a Railway." *Economist,* 23 November 2000, 65–66.

Howell, Peter. "De Belleval: 'I Gave it My Best Shot.'" *Toronto Star,* 4 May 1989, sec. A, 17.

———. "VIA's Budget Cut as President Fired." *Toronto Star,* 4 May 1989, sec. A, 1.

HSB. *Studie über ein Schnellverkehrssystem: Systemanalyze und Ergebnisse.* Munich: HSB Studiengesellschaft, 1971.

Ichniowski, Tom. "High-Speed Rail is Jumping the Track." *Business Week,* 10 December 1984, 46.

"In Transit: Why AHSRC Failed." *Railway Age,* February 1985, 42.

Instutit National de la Statistique et des Études Économiques—Ile-De-France. *Ile-de-France à la page, Mensuel,* no. 171 (Juillet 1999).

Institut National de la Statistique et des Études Économiques—Rhône Alpes. *La Lettre,* no. 63 (Juillet 1999).

International Union of Railways (UIC). *Chronological Railway Statistics, 1970–1997.* Paris: International Union of Railways, 2000.

———. *Development of High Speed Rail Traffic in Europe.* n.d. http://www.uic.asso.fr/gv/common/trafic_gv.htm (13 March 2001).

———. *Development of High Speed Rail Traffic in Japan and Europe.* n.d. http://www.uic.asso.fr/gv/common/trafic_gv.htm (13 March 2001).

International Union of Railways (UIC). Centre de Statistique. *Rail Traffic Statistics of the UIC European Railways: January to December 1999.* 2000. http://www.uic.asso.fr/uk/stats/index.html (10 November 2001).

Itzkoff, Donald M. *Off the Track: The Decline of the Intercity Passenger Train in the United States.* Westport, Conn.: Greenwood Press, 1985.

Jackson, Michael, ed. Introduction to *Proceedings of the First National Rail Passenger Conference, October 29–31, 1976,* 3–8. Regina, Sask.: University of Regina, 1977.

"Japan is Building Speedy Rail Line." *New York Times,* 26 April 1959, 20.

"Japanese Build a Super-Railroad." *Business Week,* 1 December 1962, 88–89.

"Japanese Bullet Trains for Amtrak." *Railway Age*, 31 August 1981, 16.

"Japan's Fast Train—How It's Working Out." *U.S. News & World Report*, 25 January 1965, 69–70.

Johnson, Robert. "Lawmakers May Blow Whistle on Bullet Train." *Wall Street Journal*, 11 November 1998, sec. F, 1, Eastern edition.

Jones, Chip. "CEO of Richmond, VA-Based Rail Firm Urges Creation of High-Speed Rail System." *Richmond (Va.) Times-Dispatch*, 9 November 2000, sec. B, 10.

Jones, Joseph. *The Politics of Transport in Twentieth Century France*. Kingston, Ont.: McGill-Queen's Univ. Press, 1984.

Kahn, Ata M. *VIA Rail Canada: An Analysis of VIA's Potential in Fulfilling Rail Passenger Policy Objectives—Working Paper*. Ottawa, Ont.: Science Council of Canada, 1980.

Kakumoto, Ryohei. "Sensible Politics and Transport Theories?—Japan's National Railways in the 20th Century." *Japan Railway & Transport Review* 22 (December 1999): 23–33.

Keating, Oliver (High Speed Trains). *The Advanced Passenger Train*. n.d. http://www.o-keating.com/hsr/apt.htm (17 March 2001).

Keefer, T.C. *Philosophy of Railroads*. Toronto: Univ. of Toronto Press, 1972.

Kizzia, Tom. "Britain's Trouble-Plagued APT Gets Ready for New Tests." *Railway Age*, 10 May 1982, 19.

Knill, Christopher, and Dirk Lehmkuhl. "An Alternative Route of European Integration: The Community's Railway Policy." *West European Politics* 23, no. 1 (January 2000), 65–88.

Knop, H., and A. Straszak. "The Shinkansen and National Development Issues." In *The Shinkansen Program: Transportation, Railway, Environmental, Regional, and National Development Issues*. Edited by A. Straszak, 416–98. Laxenburg, Austria: International Institute for Applied Systems Analysis, 1981.

Knutton, Mike. "Time For a Re-Think of HS Rail Priorities?" *International Railway Journal*, July 1999, 14–16.

Krasner, Jeffrey. "Study Warns of Problems on Rail Line." *Wall Street Journal*, 22 December 1999, sec. NE, 1, Eastern edition.

Krause, Andrze. "Please Unbotch the Railways." *New Statesman*, 11 December 2000, 5.

Krosnick, Jon A., and Penny S. Visser. *The Impact of the Fall 1997 Debate About Global Warming On American Public Opinion: Executive Summary*. Washington, D.C.: Resources For the Future, 1998.

Lang, Otto. "Address by the Honourable Otto Lang." In *Proceedings of the First National Rail Passenger Conference, October 29–31, 1976*. Edited by Michael Jackson, 14–22. Regina, Sask.: University of Regina, 1977.

"Laying a U.S. Track for High-Speed Trains." *Business Week*, 25 April 1983, 49.

Lehmbruch, Gerhard. "The Institutional Framework of German Regulation." In *The Politics of German Regulation*. Edited by Kenneth Dyson, 29–52. Aldershot: Dartmouth Publishing, 1992.

Lexcie Corporation. *The Advanced Passenger Train: Its Evolution*. n.d. http://www.lexcie.zetnet.co.uk/apt2.htm (17 March 2001).

———. *Lexcie's Guide to BR TOPS Locomotive & Multiple Units.* February 19, 1999. http://www.lexcie.zetnet.co.uk/tops-2–pic.htm (18 March 2001).

"Light at the End of the Tunnel." *Economist,* 10 February 2001, 66.

Lindblom, Charles E. "Still Muddling, Not Yet Through." *Public Administration Review* 39, no. 6 (November/December 1979): 517–26.

Love, Jean, Wendell Cox, and Stephen Moore. *Amtrak at Twenty-Five: End of the Line for Taxpayer Subsidies.* Cato Policy Analysis no. 266. Washington, D.C.: Cato Institute, 1996.

Lowi, Theodore. "American Business, Public Policy, Case-Studies, and Political Theory." *World Politics* 16, no. 4 (July 1964): 677–715.

Ludwig, Frank-Matthias. "German Railways Face a Decade of Reform." *Railway Gazette International,* July 1993, 478–80.

Lukasiewicz, Julius. "Public Policy and Technology: Passenger Rail in Canada as an Issue of Modernization." *Canadian Public Policy* 5, no. 4 (autumn 1979): 518–32.

———. "Rail Service Slashed Despite $7.6 Billion in Subsidies." *Ottawa Citizen,* 3 October 1995, sec. A, 15.

Lyall, Sarah. "Railways' Frightful State Is the Talk of Britain." *New York Times,* 10 December 2000, sec. L, 3.

Lydon, Christopher. "Trains in Amtrak, Although Still Scarce, Have Become Clean and More Punctual." *New York Times,* 17 October 1971, 74.

———. "2 Courts Uphold Amtrak System; Service is Begun." *New York Times,* 1 May 1971, 34.

Lynch, Thomas. "An Analysis of the Impacts of Florida High Speed Rail." In *High Speed Rail in the U.S.: Super Trains for the Millennium.* Edited by Thomas Lynch, 147–63. Amsterdam: Gordon and Breach Science Publishers, 1998.

LYNX. *Proposed Alignment and Trainset Layout.* Montreal, Que.: Lynx Consortium, April 1998.

———. *Summary.* Montreal, Que.: Lynx Consortium, April 1998.

Lyon, Peter. *To Hell in a Day Coach: An Exasperated Look at American Railroads.* Philadelphia, Pa.: J.B. Lippincott, 1968.

Machalaba, Daniel. "All Aboard? Amtrak's Metroliner Has Disappearing-Railroad Blues." *Wall Street Journal,* 10 March 1999, sec. B, 1, Eastern edition.

———. "Bombardier Group to Build Speedy Train for Amtrak." *Wall Street Journal,* 18 March 1996, sec. A, 4, Eastern edition.

———. "Railroads Learn to Like Public Funding: Plans to Expand Freight Infrastructure Arise on Both Coasts." *Wall Street Journal,* 1 May 2000, sec. A, 2, Eastern edition.

Machalaba, Daniel, and Daniel Pearl. "Amtrak Plans To Slash Service, Cut 5,500 Jobs—Bold Proposal Aims to Close Budget Gap, Sidetrack Efforts to End Subsidy." *Wall Street Journal,* 15 December 1994, sec. A, 3, Eastern edition.

Mackie, Richard. "Plan for High-Speed Train Line on Track." *Globe and Mail,* 6 March 1990, sec. A, 15.

"Maiden Run for Train of Future." *Times* (London), 7 December 1981, 2.

Malone, Frank. "The Great Train Race." *Railway Age*, January 1984, 46–54.

Marray, Michael. "German Greens Go Off the Rails." *European*, 18 May 1998, 24.

Martin, Albro. *Enterprise Denied: Origins of the Decline of American Railroads, 1897–1917*. New York: Columbia Univ. Press, 1971.

McArthur, Douglas. "Business Travel: Speedy New U.S. Train Shows How Far VIA is Off the Track." *Globe and Mail*, 7 July 1999, sec. C, 8.

McCarthy, Shawn. "Quebec to Toronto by Rail at 320 kph? $11–Billion High-Speed Line Would Need Big Money from Governments." *Globe and Mail*, 8 May 1998, sec. A, 8.

McGinley, Laurie, and Andy Pasztor. "Greyhound Gets Clearance to Run Trailways for Now." *Wall Street Journal*, 3 July 1987, 1, Eastern edition.

McGovern, Sheila. "Bombardier, ABB Hit Campaign Trail to Pitch High-Speed Rail Systems." *(Montreal) Gazette*, 7 June 1991, sec. D, 3.

McKinnon, John D. "A Lack of Cash May Derail Express Train." *Wall Street Journal*, 28 January 1998, sec. F, 2, Eastern edition.

———. "Lawmakers Accept Trip to France." *Wall Street Journal*, 10 June 1998, sec. F, 1, Eastern edition.

———. "State's East Coast Could Soon Be Back On Track." *Wall Street Journal*, 17 February 1999, sec. F, 2, Eastern edition.

Miller, Luther S. "A Kinder, Gentler Congress? It Must be Election Time." *Railway Age*, August 1996, 18.

———. "Transit Rides Out a Tempest." *Railway Age*, January 1996, 43–49.

———. "W. Graham Claytor, Jr., Former Amtrak Chief, Dies at 82." *Railway Age*, June 1994, 22.

Mizutani, Fumitoshi. "An Assessment of the Japan Railway Companies Since Privatization: Performance, Local Rail Service and Debts." *Transport Reviews* 19, no. 2 (1999): 117–39.

Molis, Jim. "Florida Commission Urges Caution When Using Ridership Survey Results." *The Bond Buyer*, 5 August 1998, 3.

Mondale, Ted. "Transportation-A Major Player in Smart Growth." *ITE Journal*, November 2000, 39–43.

Moore, Stephen. *Amtrak Subsidies: This Is No Way to Run a Railroad*. 22 May 1997. http://www.cato.org/dailys/5–22–97.html (15 Feb. 2001).

Musolf, Lloyd. *Uncle Sam's Private, Profitseeking Corporations*. Lexington, Mass.: Lexington Books, 1983.

Nagel, Stuart S. *The Policy Process and Super-Optimum Solutions*. Commack, N.Y.: Nova Science Publishers, 1994.

National Railroad Passenger Corporation. *Emerging Corridors: Amtrak*. Washington, D.C.: National Railroad Passenger Corporation, 1981.

"New Japan Train Cuts Air Travel." *New York Times*, 28 February 1965, sec. S, 18.

"Newsfront: Ohio Says 'No' to High Speed Rail." *Modern Railroads*, January 1983, 14.

Ng, Helen. "A High-Speed Rail Revolution in the U.S.?: Lessons from the French and Texas TGV." Master's thesis, Massachusetts Institute of Technology, 1995.

Nice, David. "Passenger Rail Service: Decline and Resurgence." *Transportation Quarterly* 50, no. 4 (1996): 95–106.

Nishida, M. "Development of Advanced High-Speed Trains in Japan." In *International Symposium on Traffic and Transportation Technologies, IVA '79, June 18–20, 1979.* Hamburg, Germany: Bundesministerium für Forschung und Technologie, 1979, 23–42.

———. "History of the Shinkansen." In *The Shinkansen High-Speed Rail Network of Japan: Proceedings of an IIASA Conference, June 27–30, 1977.* Edited by A. Straszak and R. Tuch, 11–20. Toronto: Pergamon Press, 1977.

Niskanen, William A. *Bureaucracy and Representative Government.* Chicago, Ill.: Aldine, 1971.

"Not Enough Passengers for Transrapid (Dem transrapid Fehlen Fahrgäste)." *Die Welt* (Berlin), 13 July 1999.

Ohio Rail Transportation Authority. *Ohio High Speed Intercity Rail Passenger Program: Executive Summary.* Cleveland, Ohio: Dalton, Dalton, Newport, 1980.

———. *Ohio State Rail Plan Update 1982–83.* Columbus, Ohio: The Ohio Rail Transportation Authority, 1983.

———. *RailOhio: the Rail Plan for Ohio, 1978–79.* Columbus, Ohio: The Ohio Rail Transportation Authority, 1979.

Ontario/Québec Rapid Train Task Force. *Ontario/Québec Rapid Train Task Force Final Report.* Ottawa, Ont.: Ontario/Québec Rapid Train Task Force, 1991.

Owen, David. "A Fine Way to Run a Railway—and Turn a Profit." *Financial Times,* 8 January 2001, 12.

Parker-Pope, Tara. "As Funding Deadline Nears, Bullet Train Appears Dead." *Wall Street Journal,* 15 December 1993, sec. T, 4, Eastern edition.

Paterak, Jorn, and Haig Simonian. "Scale of German Rail Losses Revealed." *Financial Times,* 6 November 2000, 15.

Paterson, Tony. "Rumbling Grows on Fast Track to Berlin." *European,* 7 November 1996, 4.

Patterson, Judith, and Anthony Perl. "The TGV Effect: A Potential Opportunity for Reconciling Sustainability with Aviation." *World Transport Policy & Practice* 5, no. 1 (1999): 39–45.

Paul, Bill. "Ohio Looks to High Speed Passenger Trains." *Modern Railroads,* March 1981, 51.

Pavaux, Jacques. *Rail/Air Complementarity in Europe: The Impact of High-Speed Train Services.* Paris: Institute of Air Transport, 1991.

Pell, Claiborne. *Megalopolis Unbound: The Supercity and the Transportation of Tomorrow.* New York: Praeger, 1966.

Pendleton, Andrew, and Jonathon Winterton. Introduction to *Public Enterprise in Transition: Industrial Relations in State and Privatized Corporations,* 1–21. London: Routledge, 1993.

Pennsylvania Economic Development Financing Authority. *Prospectus: $110,795,000 Exempt Facilities Revenue Bonds (Amtrak Project), Series A of 2001,* 16 February

2001. Harrisburg, Pa.: Pennsylvania Economic Development Financing Authority.

Perl, Anthony. "Financing Transport Infrastructure: The Effects of Institutional Durability in French and American Policymaking." *Governance* 4, no. 4 (October 1991): 365–402.

———. "Getting What You Pay For: The Politics of Public Investment in Amtrak and VIA Rail Canada." In *Selected Proceedings of the Sixth World Conference on Transport Research*. Vol. 3, 1579–1590. Lyon, France: Chirat, 1993.

———. "Public Enterprise as an Expression of Sovereignty: Reconsidering the Origins of Canadian National Railways." *Canadian Journal of Political Science* 27, no. 1 (1994): 23–52.

———. "Redesigning an Airport for International Competitiveness: The Politics of Administrative Innovation at CDG." *Journal of Air Transport Management* 4, no. 4 (October 1998): 189–99.

———. "Superbureaucrats and Superhighways: An Institutional Explanation for Variation in American and Canadian Highway Policies." Paper presented at the annual meeting of the American Political Science Association, Chicago, Ill., September 1992.

Perl, Anthony, and James A. Dunn Jr. "Building the Political Infrastructure for High Speed Rail in North America." *Transportation Quarterly* 50, no. 1 (winter 1996): 5–22.

———. "Globalization and the Diffusion of High-Speed Ground Transportation Systems: Obstacles, Opportunities, and Entrepreneurs." In *Rail International: 3rd World Congress on High-Speed Rail Proceedings*, 211–15. Brussels: International Railway Congress Association, 1998.

———. "Policy Networks and Industrial Revitalization: High Speed Rail Initiatives in France and Germany." *Journal of Public Policy* 14, no. 3 (July-December 1994): 311–43.

———. "Reinventing Amtrak: The Politics of Survival." *Journal of Policy Analysis and Management* 16, no. 4 (1997): 598–614.

Perl, Anthony, and Tony Turrittin. "Measuring the Environmental Impacts of High Speed Rail and Maglev in North America: What Railway Designers Need to Know." Paper presented at the World Congress on Railway Research, October 19–23, 1999, Tokyo, Japan. (Conference papers available on CD-ROM.)

Pierson, Paul. "When Effect Becomes Cause: Policy Feedback and Political Change." *World Politics* 45, no. 4 (July 1993): 595–628.

Plassard, François. "France." In *Report of the Hundred and Fifth Round Table on Transport Economics held in Paris on 7th–8th November 1996 on the following topic: Infrastructure Induced Mobility*, 111–42. Paris: European Conference of Ministers of Transport, 1998.

Powell, Kathy F. "Southwest Airlines v. High-Speed Rail: More Powerful than a Locomotive." *Journal of Air Law and Commerce* 60, no. 4 (May-June 1995): 1091–1138.

Preston, John. "The Franchising and Re-franchising of Passenger Rail Services in Britain." Paper no. 01–2425 presented at the Eightieth Annual Meeting of the Transportation Research Board, Washington, D.C., 7–11 January 2001.

Protzman, Ferdinand. "Germany Rolls Out Its Fast Train." *New York Times*, 30 May 1991, sec. D, 1.

Racine, John. "Texas: Around the Nation." *Bond Buyer*, 5 November 1991, 724B.

"Rail Update: But Hey—No Hard Feelings." *Railway Age*, August 2000, 17.

Railway Age. *Late Breaking Industry News*. 7 March 2001. http://www.railwayage.com/breaking_news_archive.html (15 March 2001).

Railway Age Intercity APT. *APT-P Preservation Update*. 27 January 2001. http://www.therailwayage.co.uk/apt/index.htm (8 March 2001).

———. *New Intercity Trains*. 9 December 2000. http://www.therailwayage.co.uk/apt/ (8 March 2001).

Railway Association of Canada, The. *Railway Trends, 2000*. Montreal, Que.: The Railway Association of Canada, 2000.

"Regional Governments Keen to Save Transrapid (Lander Wollen Transrapid Retten)." *Die Welt* (Berlin), 7 December 1999.

Resor, Randolph R. "Should Amtrak Survive as a National Rail System?" *Transportation Quarterly* 53, no. 1 (winter 1999): 93–107.

Réseau Ferré de France. *Investment Policy: The New Investment Financing Rules*. 2001. http://www.rff.fr/e34n34uk/fprofpol.htm (26 February 2001).

———. *The Main Lines of the 2001 Investment Budget*. 2001. http://www.rff.fr/e34n34uk/fprofpol.htm (26 February 2001).

———. *Réseau Ferré de France's Ranking*. 2001. http://www.rff.fr/e34n34uk/popaaa.htm (26 February 2001).

———. *The Reform of Reform: Statement by the Minister of Facilities, Transport and Housing*, n.d. http://www.rff.fr/e34n34uk/popref.htm (26 February 2001).

———. *RFF: French Railway Network Owner and Manager*. 2001. http://www.rff.fr/e34n34uk/fproforg.htm (26 February 2001).

Roberts, Robert. "High Speed, a New Rail Industry." *Modern Railroads*, August 1983, 46–51.

Robey, John S. "High-Speed Rail in Texas: Its Rise and Fall." *Transportation Quarterly* 48, no. 4 (autumn 1994): 403–21.

Rochet, Pierre-Louis. *Stimulating TGV Traffic-Growth: SNCF as a Case in Point*. Paper presented at High Speed Ground Transportation Association Conference, Seattle, Wash., June 1999.

Sabatier, Paul A. "Policy Change Over a Decade or More." In *Policy Change and Learning: An Advocacy Coalition Approach*. Edited by Paul A. Sabatier and Hank C. Jenkins-Smith, 13–39. Boulder, Colo.: Westview Press, 1993.

Sahr, Robert C. (Oregon State University). *Consumer Price Index (CPI) Conversion Factors to Convert to (estimated) Dollars of the Year 2000*, 2000. http://www.orst.edu/dept/pol_sci/fac/sahr/cv00.pdf (17 March 2001).

Sanchez, Rene. "California Crisis Has Residents Seething." *Washington Post*, 11 February 2001, sec. A, 1.

Scheinberg, Phyllis F. *Intercity Passenger Rail: Amtrak Faces Challenges in Improving Its Financial Condition.* Report no. GAO/T-RCED-00–30. Washington, D.C.: U.S. General Accounting Office, 2000.

———. *Intercity Passenger Rail: Increasing Amtrak's Accountability for Its Taxpayer Relief Act Funds.* Report no. GAO/T-RCED-00–116. Washington, D.C.: U.S. General Accounting Office, 2000.

———. *Testimony of United States General Accounting Office: Intercity Passenger Rail: Decisions on the Future of Amtrak and Intercity Passenger Rail Are Approaching.* Report no. GAO/T-RCED-00–277. Washington, D.C.: U.S. General Accounting Office, 2000.

Scull, Theodore W. "Amtrak Enters a New Era: PTJ Interviews the Railroad's New President." *Passenger Train Journal,* March 1994, 20–27.

Seely, Bruce E. *Building the American Highway System: Engineers as Policy Makers.* Philadelphia, Pa.: Temple Univ. Press, 1987.

Sephton, B.G. "High Speed Train Prototype Proves Its Worth." *Railway Gazette International,* February 1975, 58–63.

Shaffer, Frank E. "Newsfront: Loan, Interest Repaid." *Modern Railroads,* February 1984, 12–14.

Sharp, John. *Texas High Speed Rail Authority: Performance Review.* Texas: Comptroller of Public Accounts, 1992.

"Shuttle Flights Hearten Eastern: 6,147 Took No-Frill Trips in First Week, Line Says." *New York Times,* 10 May 1961, 90.

Silva, Mark. "Concerns on Florida Bullet Train Plan Shouldn't Derail it, State Says." *Knight-Ridder/Tribune Business News,* 5 August 1998.

Simonian, Haig. "Germany to Use Phone Windfall to Help Rail." *Financial Times,* 22 September 2000, 2.

Smith, George C., and Earl Shirley. "High-Speed Rail in California: Avoidable Controversy." *Right of Way,* October 1987, 17–21.

Smith, Lee. "Is this Any Way to Sell a Railroad?" *Fortune,* 25 May 1987, 91–98.

Smollar, David. "His Name's Bonde, and He's 007 to the Bullet Train's Promoters." *Los Angeles Times,* 12 October 1983, sec. B, 4.

Soberman, Richard. "High Speed Trains for Canada: Technological Excellence, Groundless Conviction, or Bureaucratic Obsession?" In *Essays in Canadian Surface Transportation.* Edited by Philip K. Palda. Vancouver, B.C.: The Fraser Institute, 1995. 93–140.

Southerland, Thomas C., and William McCleery. *The Way to Go: The Coming Revival of U.S. Rail Passenger Service.* New York: Simon and Schuster, 1973.

"Southwest Warns Texas City Against Using Public Funds for Train System." *Aviation Week & Space Technology,* 25 November 1991, 42.

Statistics Canada. *Railway Transport: Operating and Traffic Statistics.* Part 4. Ottawa, Ont.: Statistics Canada, 1971–1977.

State of Florida. *Governor Bush to Withhold State Funding for High Speed Rail Project.* 14 January 1999. http://www.state.fl.us/eog/press_releases/1999/January/1–14_highspeed_rail.html (23 February 2001).

Stover, John F. *The Life and Decline of the American Railroad*. New York, N.Y.: Oxford Univ. Press, 1970.

Strobel, H., and A. Straszak. "Subsystems Analysis." In *The Shinkansen Program: Transportation, Railway, Environmental, Regional, and National Development Issues*. Edited by A. Straszak, 49–146. Laxenburg, Austria: International Institute for Applied Systems Analysis, 1981.

"Struck Backs Transrapid Plan (Struck stutzt Transrapid Plan)." *Die Welt* (Berlin), 20 September 1999.

Sverdrup Corporation. *Texas High Speed Rail Authority: Engineering Aspects of the High-Speed Rail Franchise Applications: Advisory Report*. United States: Sverdrup Corporation, 1991.

Texas High-Speed Rail Authority. *Report to the 73rd Texas Legislature by the Texas High-Speed Rail Authority*. Austin, Tex.: Texas High-Speed Rail Authority, 1992.

"Texas TGV Corp. Wins Funding Reprieve." *Railway Age*, December 1992, 18.

"The Rail Billionaires." *Economist*, 3 July 1999, 57–60.

"Thomas M. Downs Named Amtrak President, Chairman." *Railway Age*, January 1994, 27.

Thompson, Gregry Lee. *The Passenger Train in the Motor Age: California's Rail and Bus Industries, 1910–1941*. Columbus, Ohio: Ohio State Univ. Press, 1993.

Thompson, Stephen J. *Amtrak and the 104th Congress*. Washington, D.C.: Congressional Research Service, 1997.

———. *Amtrak: Background and Selected Public Policy Issues II*. Report no. 97–030. Washington, D.C.: Congressional Research Service, 1997.

Tolliver, Heidi. "Tracking the (High Speed) Fox." *Mass Transit*, July-August 1996, 32–43.

Tomsho, Robert, and Kevin G. Salwen. "Greyhound, ATU in Talks to Shape Tentative Contract, End Labor Dispute." *Wall Street Journal*, 19 April 1993, sec. B, 10, Eastern edition.

Tracked Hovercraft Ltd. *A Cost Comparison of Three Tracked Air Cushion Vehicle Configurations*. Report no. FRA-RT-71–68. Washington, D.C.: Department of Transportation. Office of High Speed Ground Transportation, 1970.

Trains.com. *Railroading: Letter from Amtrak President George D. Warrington to ARC Chairman Gilbert E. Carmichael*. 16 March 2001. http://www.trains.com/content/dynamic/articles/000/000/000/831orgnt.asp (21 March 2001).

Transport Canada. *Directive for the Guidance of the Canadian Transport Commission on Rail Passenger Services, January 29, 1976*. Ottawa, Ont.: Transport Canada, 1976.

———. *National Airports Policy*. Ottawa, Ont.: Transport Canada, 1994.

———. *National Marine Policy*. Ottawa, Ont.: Transport Canada, 1995.

———. *Paper on a Canadian Rail Passenger Program, January 29, 1976*. Ottawa, Ont.: Transport Canada, 1976.

Transport Canada. Economic Analysis Directorate. *Rail Passenger Improvements In the Quebec City–Windsor Corridor*. Ottawa, Ont.: Transport Canada, 1984.

Transport Canada. Gouvernement du Québec Ministère des Transports, and Ministry of Transportation of Ontario. *Québec–Ontario High Speed Rail Project: Final Report, August 1995*. Ottawa, Québec, and Toronto: Transport Canada,

Gouvernement du Québec Ministère des Transports, and Ministry of Transportation of Ontario, 1995.

Transport Canada. Railway Transportation Directorate. *Evaluation of Legislative Alternatives for VIA Rail Canada (VIA)*. Part one. *Legislative Strategy for VIA Rail Canada*. First draft. Ottawa, Ont.: Transport Canada, 1978.

Transportation California. "All Rail is Not Created Equal: Study Shows Amazing Decline in Intercity Rail Performance." January 2001. http://www.transportationca.com/archives/all_rail.shtml (5 March 2001).

———. *Transportation California*. 2000. http://www.transportationca.com/about_transcal/ (6 March 2001).

Transportation Equity Act for the 21st Century/Transportation Infrastructure Finance and Innovation Act of 1998. Public Law 105–78. 105th Cong., 2d sess., 9 June 1998.

"Transrapid Consortium Seeks Compensation (Transrapid-Konsortium will Schadenersatz)." *Die Welt* (Berlin), 28 January 2000.

Truman, David B. *The Governmental Process: Political Interests and Public Opinion*. New York: Alfred A. Knopf, 1951.

United States Conference of Mayors. *Statement of Timothy M. Kaine on behalf of the United States Conference of Mayors before the Committee on Commerce, Science, and Transportation on Amtrak Oversight*. 26 September 2000. http://www.usmayors.org/uscm/news/press_releases/documents/amtraktestimony.pdf (15 February 2000).

Unsworth, Edwin. "U.K. Rail Safety Questioned." *Business Insurance*, 23 October 2000, 59–60.

U.S. Bureau of Transportation Statistics. *Intermodal Surface Transportation Efficiency Act of 1991*. n.d. http://www.bts.gov/ntl/DOCS/istea.html (13 March 2001).

U.S. Congress. House. Committee on Energy and Commerce. Subcommittee on Transportation and Hazardous Materials. *Amtrak Reauthorization: Hearing Before the Subcommittee on Transportation and Hazardous Materials of the Committee on Energy and Commerce on H.R. 2364*, 101st Cong., 1st sess., 17 May 1989.

———. *Amtrak Reauthorization: Hearing Before the Subcommittee on Transportation and Hazardous Materials on H.R. 5*, 102d Cong., 2d sess., February 1992.

U.S. Congress. House. Committee on Transportation and Infrastructure. Subcommittee on Railroads. *Amtrak's Current Situation*, 104th Cong., 1st sess., 1996.

———. *Amtrak's Current Situation: Hearings on H.R. 88—046CC*. Statement of Gregory E. Lawler, Executive Director, Safe Transit and Rail Transportation, 104th Cong., 1st sess., 1996.

———. *High Speed Rail Programs*. Testimony of William C. Nevel, High Speed Ground Transportation Association, 105th Cong., 2d sess., 1997.

U.S. Department of Transportation. Bureau of Transportation Statistics. *National Transportation Statistics, 1999*. Washington, D.C.: Bureau of Transportation Statistics, 1999.

U.S. Department of Transportation. Inspector General. *2000 Assessment of Amtrak's Financial Performance and Requirements*. Report no. CR-2000–121. Washington, D.C.: U.S. Department of Transportation. Office of Inspector General, 2000.

U.S. Federal Railroad Administration. *Privatization of Intercity Rail Passenger Service in the United States.* Washington, D.C.: Federal Railroad Administration, 1998.

U.S. Federal Transit Administration. *National Transit Database: Data Tables for 1999.* n.d. http://www.ntdprogram.com/NTD/NTDData.nsf/ 1999+TOC?OpenView&Count=50 (11 March 2001).

U.S. General Accounting Office. *Surface Infrastructure: High-Speed Rail Projects in the United States.* Report no. GAO/RCED-99-44. Washington, D.C.: U.S. General Accounting Office, 1999.

U.S. House of Representatives. *Republican Contract With America,* 27 September 1994. n.d. http://www.house.gov/house/Contract/CONTRACT.html (15 February 2001).

U.S. Interstate Commerce Commission. *ICC Examiner Foresees End of Passenger Service by 1970.* Washington, D.C.: Interstate Commerce Commission, 1958.

———. *Railroad Passenger Train Deficit: Docket #31954.* Washington, D.C.: Interstate Commerce Commission, 1958.

U.S. Office of Inspector General. *Audit Report: Amtrak's High-Speed Rail Electrification Project.* Report no. RT-2000–020. Washington, D.C.: Office of Inspector General, 1999.

U.S. Senate. Committee on Appropriations. Subcommittee on Transportation and Related Agencies. *Department of Transportation and Related Agencies Appropriations for Fiscal Year 1991: Hearings on H.R. 5229,* 101st Cong., 2d sess., 1990.

———. *Department of Transportation and Related Agencies Appropriations for Fiscal Year 1999: Hearings on H.R. 4328/S. 2307.* Testimony of Robert W. Poole, Jr., The Reason Foundation, 105th Cong., 2d sess., 1998.

U.S. Senate. Committee on Commerce. *Rail Passenger Service Act of 1970: Report to Accompany S. 3706,* 91st Cong., 2d sess., 1970, S. Rept. 91–765.

U.S. Senate. Committee on Commerce. Subcommittee on Surface Transportation. *Passenger Train Service Legislation, Hearings on S. 674, et al.,* 91st Cong., 1st sess., 1969.

Van de Velde, D.M. *Changing Trains: Railway Reform and the Role of Competition: The Experience of Six Countries.* Brookfield, Vt.: Ashgate, 1999.

Vantuono, William C. "Despite Setbacks, High Speed Rail Moves Ahead." *Railway Age,* April 1994, 57–66.

———. "Florida Governors Derail FOX." *Railway Age,* February 1999, 22.

VIA Rail Canada. *The Acquisition of Rail Passenger Trains for Transport Canada and VIA Rail Canada Inc.: Lessons Learned.* Montreal, Que.: VIA Rail Canada, 1979.

———. *Annual Report.* Montreal, Que.: VIA Rail Canada, 1980–1999.

———. *Five Year Plan and 1978 Budget.* Montreal, Que.: VIA Rail Canada, 1977.

———. *The Renaissance of Passenger Rail: Brief to the Standing Committee on Transport and Communications, Senate of Canada, for its enquiry into the national rail passenger service provided to Canadians by VIA Rail Canada Inc., Presented by Pierre A.H. Franche, President and Chief Executive Officer, VIA Rail Canada.* Montreal, Que.: VIA Rail, 1984.

———. *Summary of the 1985–89 Corporate Plan; Summary of the 1985 Capital Budget.* Montreal, Que.: VIA Rail Canada, 1985.

————. *Summary of the 1986–1990 Corporate Plan; Summary of the Revised 1985 Operating Budget; Summary of the Revised 1985 Capital Budget; Summary of the 1986 Operating Budget; Summary of the 1986 Capital Budget*. Montreal, Que.: VIA Rail Canada, 1986.

————. *Summary of the 1988–1992 Corporate Plan; Summary of the 1988 Operating Budget; Summary of the 1988 Capital Budget*. Montreal, Que.: VIA Rail Canada, 1988.

————. *VIA's Investment Strategy*. Montreal, Que.: VIA Rail Canada, n.d. http://www.viarail.ca/en.fram.renaissance.html (26 May 2001).

————. *VIA Rail Canada Inc.: The Funding Challenge*. Montreal, Que.: VIA Rail Canada, n.d. Mimeo.

Vranich, Joseph. "The Puzzling Politics of High Speed Rail." *Railway Age*, October 1992, 51–59.

————. *Supertrains: Solutions to America's Transportation Gridlock*. New York: St. Martin's Press, 1991.

Warren, Susan. "Price of Natural Gas Hits Boiling Point—Everyone Knows Oil Is Up, But Now Cost for Gas Has Blown Right Past It." *Wall Street Journal*, 18 December 2000, sec. A, 2, Eastern edition.

Weaver, R. Kent. *The Politics of Industrial Change: Railway Policy in North America*. Washington, D.C.: Brookings Institution, 1985.

Welty, Gus. "High-Speed Rail: Down to Serious Business." *Railway Age*, February 1985, 49.

"West Coast Bullet Train Suffers a Fatal Wound." *Iron Age*, 18 January 1985.

"What Comes After Hell." *Economist*, 16 December 2000, 59–60.

"What Happened (and What Didn't Happen) in Texas." *Railway Age*, February 1994, 24.

Wicker, Tom. "A Railroad Euthanasia Plan?" *New York Times*, 25 March 1971, 39.

Williams, Daniel G., and Joseph J. Warren. "Amtrak Revenues, Fares, and Ridership in the 1990s: Trends and Passenger Revenues Forecast Errors." *Transportation Journal* 36, no. 4 (summer 1997): 5–16.

Wilner, Frank N. *The Amtrak Story*. Omaha, Nebr.: Simmons-Boardman, 1994.

————. "Guest Opinion—Railroading Amtrak's CEO." *Journal of Commerce*, 8 January 1998, 7A.

————. "Washington: Up Close and Ugly." *Traffic World*, 16 October 2000, 12–14.

Wilson, James Q. *Bureaucracy: What Government Agencies Do and Why They Do It*. New York: Basic Books, 1989.

Wilson, James Q., ed. *The Politics of Regulation*. New York: Basic Books, 1980.

"Winners and Losers for 1999—A Good Year for the High Court, A Tough One for Big-City Mayors." *Wall Street Journal*, 29 December 1999, sec. CA, 1, Eastern edition.

"Wirtschaftswoche: Look From Within (Im eigenen lände prufen)." *El Mundo* (Santa Cruz), 5 November 1998.

Yago, Glenn. *The Decline of Transit: Urban Transportation in German and U.S. Cities, 1900–1970*. Cambridge, U.K.: Cambridge Univ. Press, 1984.

Yorino, T. "Environmental Problems and the Shinkansen." In *The Shinkansen High-Speed Rail Network of Japan: Proceedings of an IIASA Conference, June 27–30, 1977.* Edited by A. Straszak and R. Tuch, 155–70. Toronto: Pergamon Press, 1977.

Yoshitake, Kiyohiko. *An Introduction to Public Enterprise in Japan.* London: Sage Publications, 1973.

Index